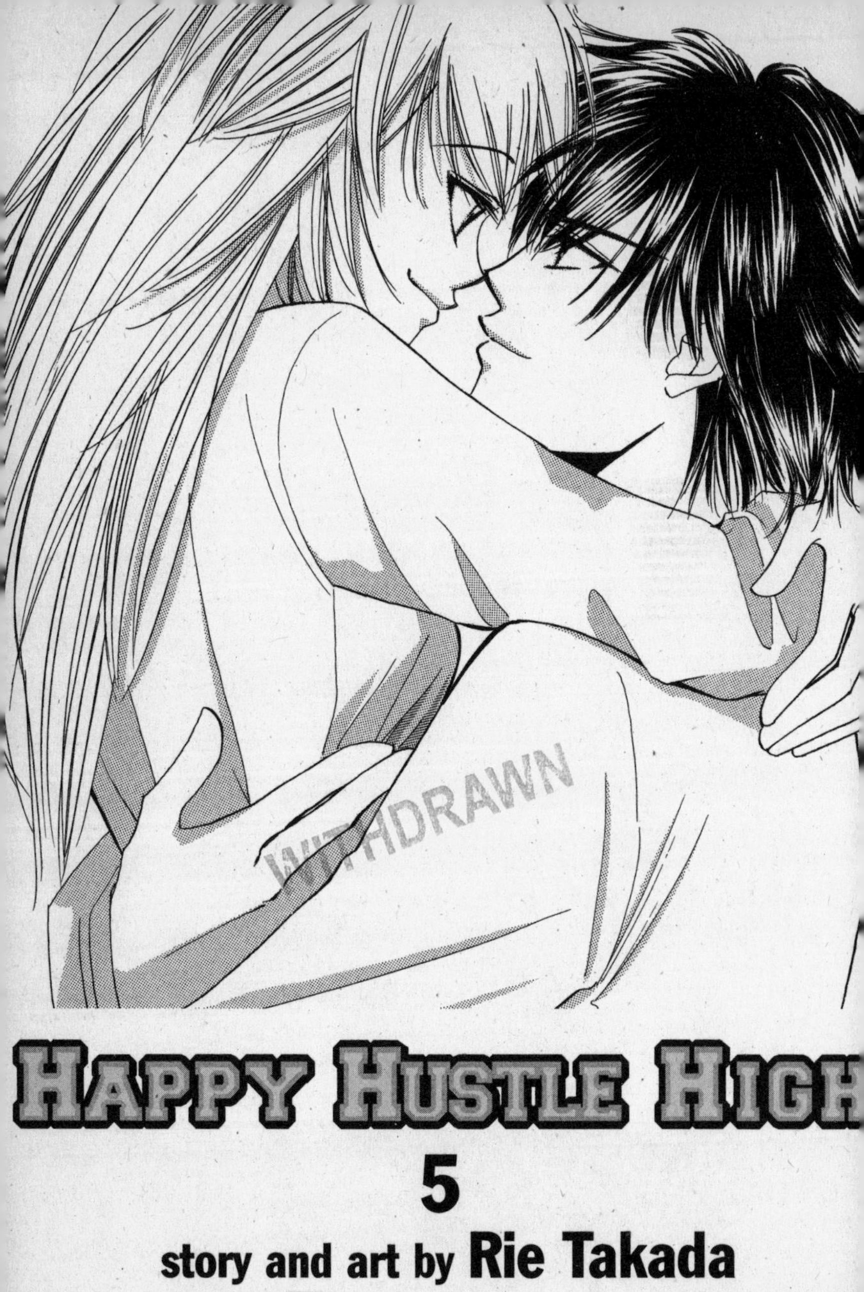

HAPPY HUSTLE HIGH

5

story and art by Rie Takada

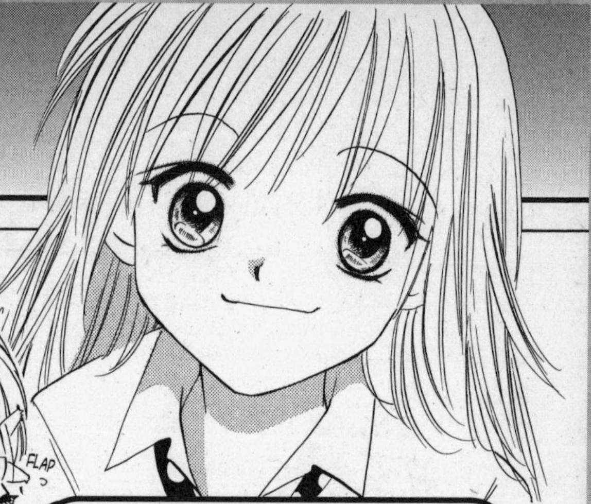

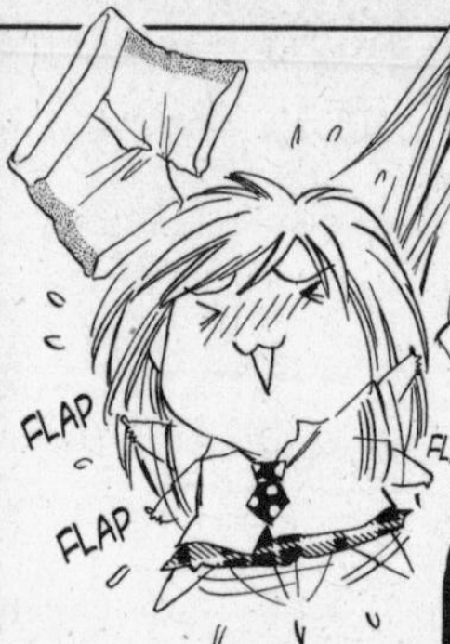
FLAP
FLAP
FLAP

• •HANABI OZORA• •

The former heroine (?) of an all-girls school. Hates injustice. Loves sports. Can fight like a guy. Her biggest problem? Wa-a-a-ay too much messy hair.

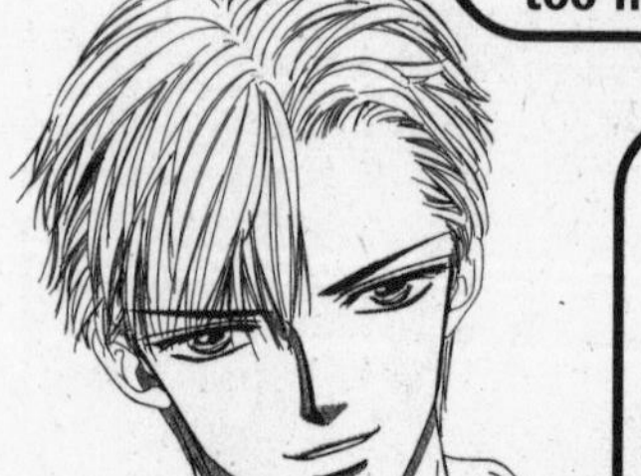

• •TAKERU SUNO• •

Hanabi's childhood pal. He's lived the past decade in Denmark. Now he's back in Japan saying he "practically raised Hanabi." He's pushy, cocky—and just as cute as Yasu.

HAPPY HUSTLE HIGH
Vol.5
CHARACTERS

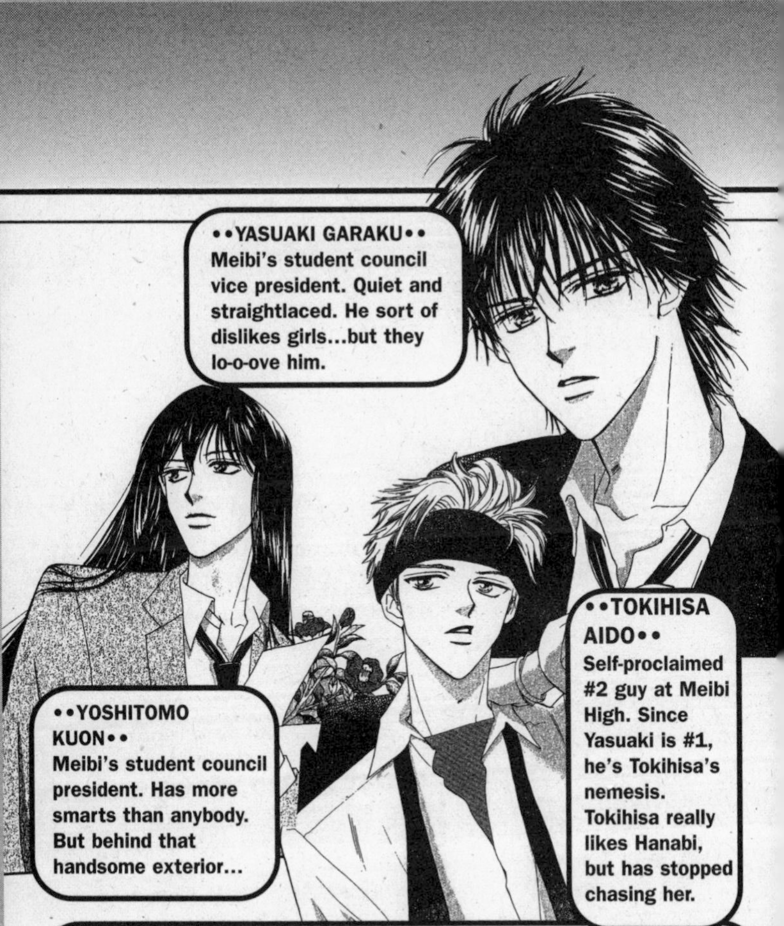
••YASUAKI GARAKU••
Meibi's student council vice president. Quiet and straightlaced. He sort of dislikes girls...but they lo-o-ove him.
••TOKIHISA AIDO••
Self-proclaimed #2 guy at Meibi High. Since Yasuaki is #1, he's Tokihisa's nemesis. Tokihisa really likes Hanabi, but has stopped chasing her.
••YOSHITOMO KUON••
Meibi's student council president. Has more smarts than anybody. But behind that handsome exterior...

•••STORY•••

An ordinary all-girls school merges with Meibi High, an elite all-boys school. Hanabi, a popular tomboy, becomes the girls' rep on a student council full of hot guys. She soon gets a reputation as one tough cookie! Hanabi even starts dating former girl-hater Yasuaki. Enter Takeru Suno, Hanabi's childhood pal. After ten years away, Take suddenly reappears—and declares war against Yasu! Hanabi starts falling for her old friend, but soon realizes Yasu is her true one-and-only. ♥ Yasuaki and Hanabi hook up again, but are they ready to enter that big scary world beyond...kissing?

HAPPY HUSTLE HIGH

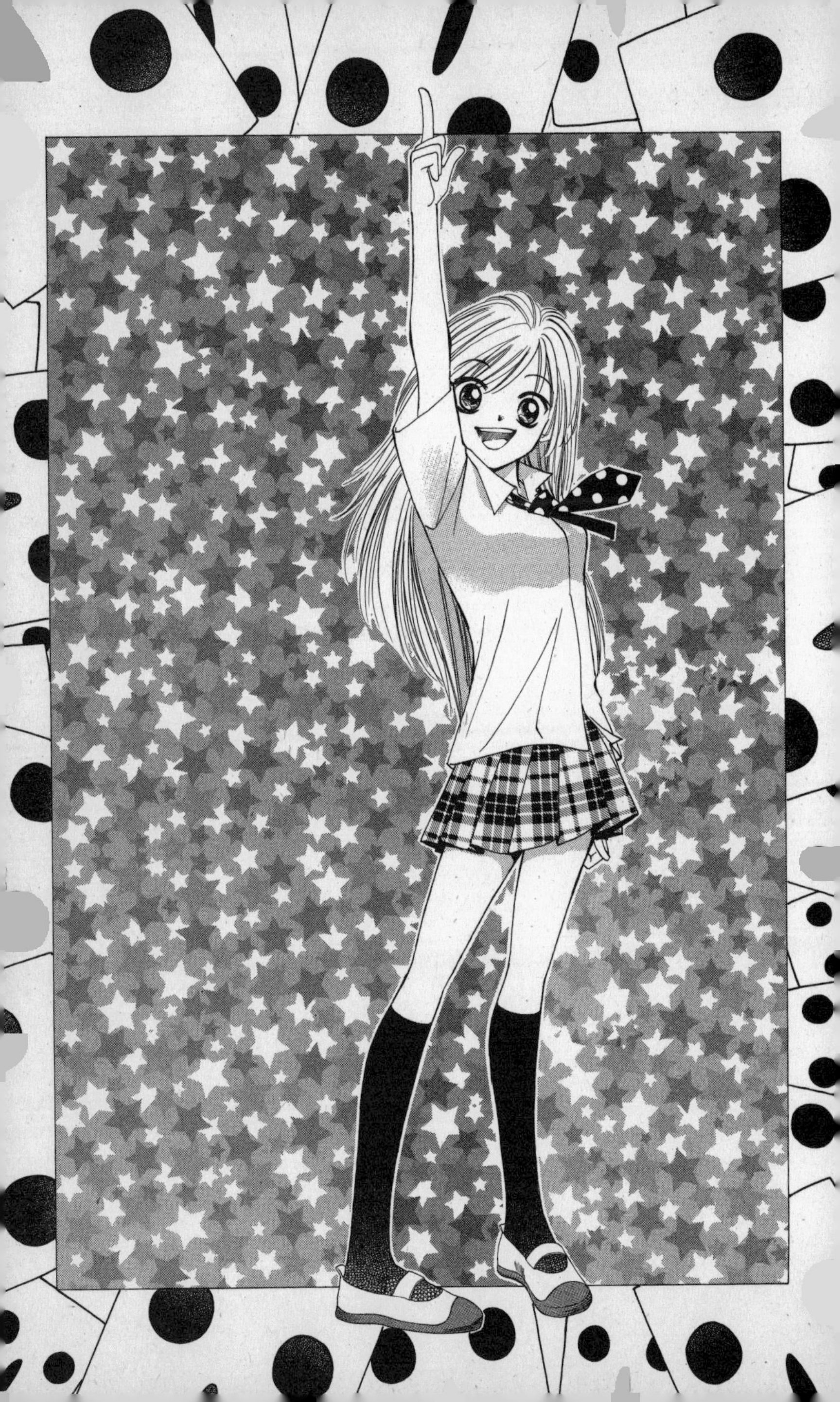

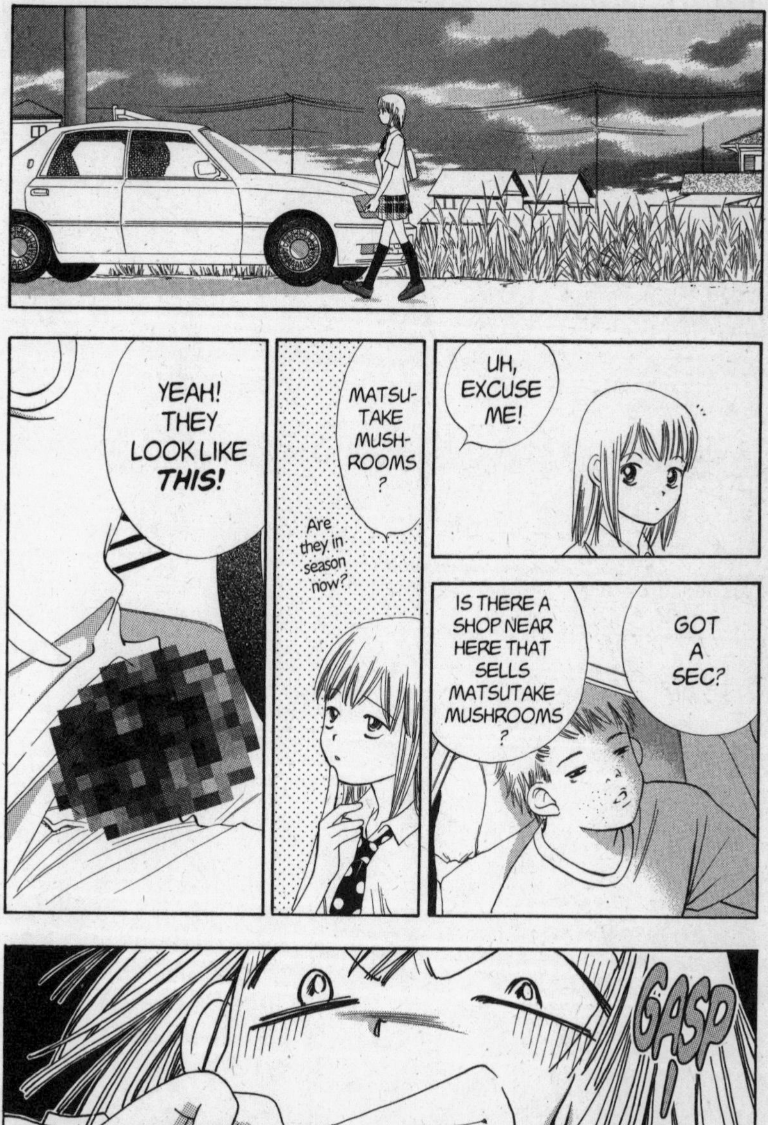

UH, EXCUSE ME!
GOT A SEC?
IS THERE A SHOP NEAR HERE THAT SELLS MATSUTAKE MUSHROOMS?
MATSU-TAKE MUSH-ROOMS?
Are they in season now?
YEAH! THEY LOOK LIKE THIS!
GASP
!!

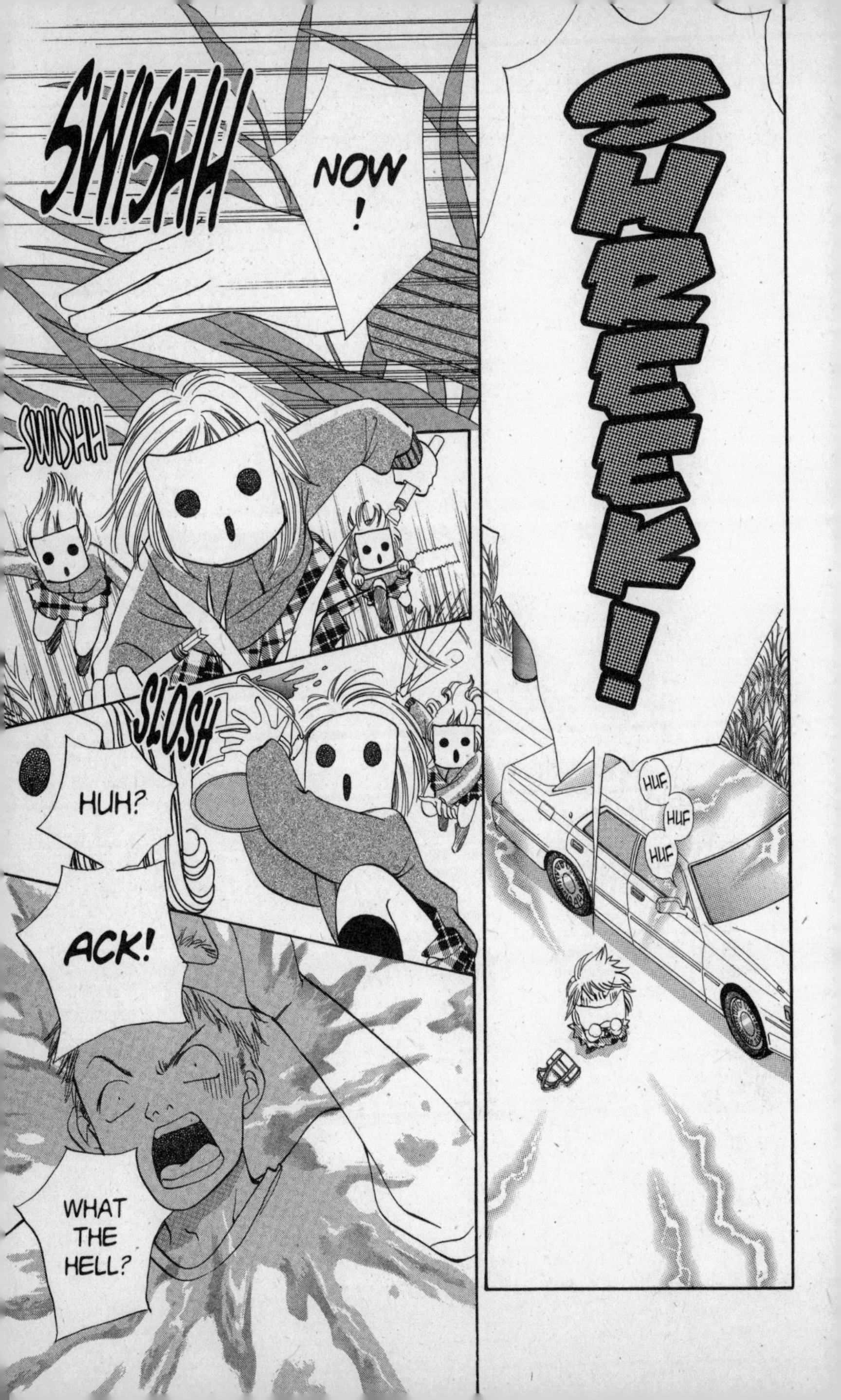
SHREEK!
HUF
HUF
HUF
SWISHH
NOW!
SWISHH
SLOSH
HUH?
ACK!
WHAT THE HELL?

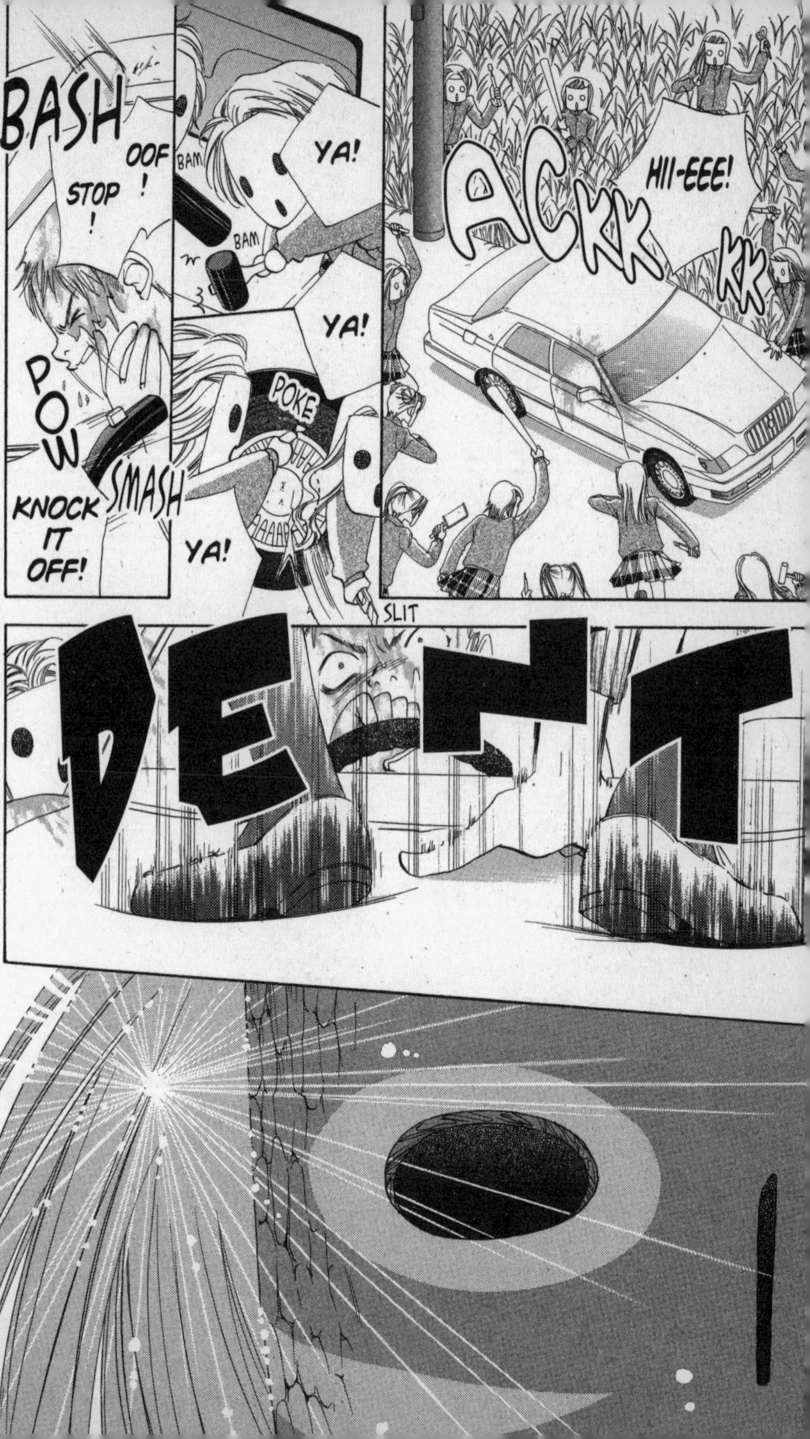
ACKK
HII-EEE!
KK
YA!
BAM
BAM
YA!
POKE
YA!
SLIT
BASH
OOF!
STOP!
POW
SMASH
KNOCK IT OFF!
DENT

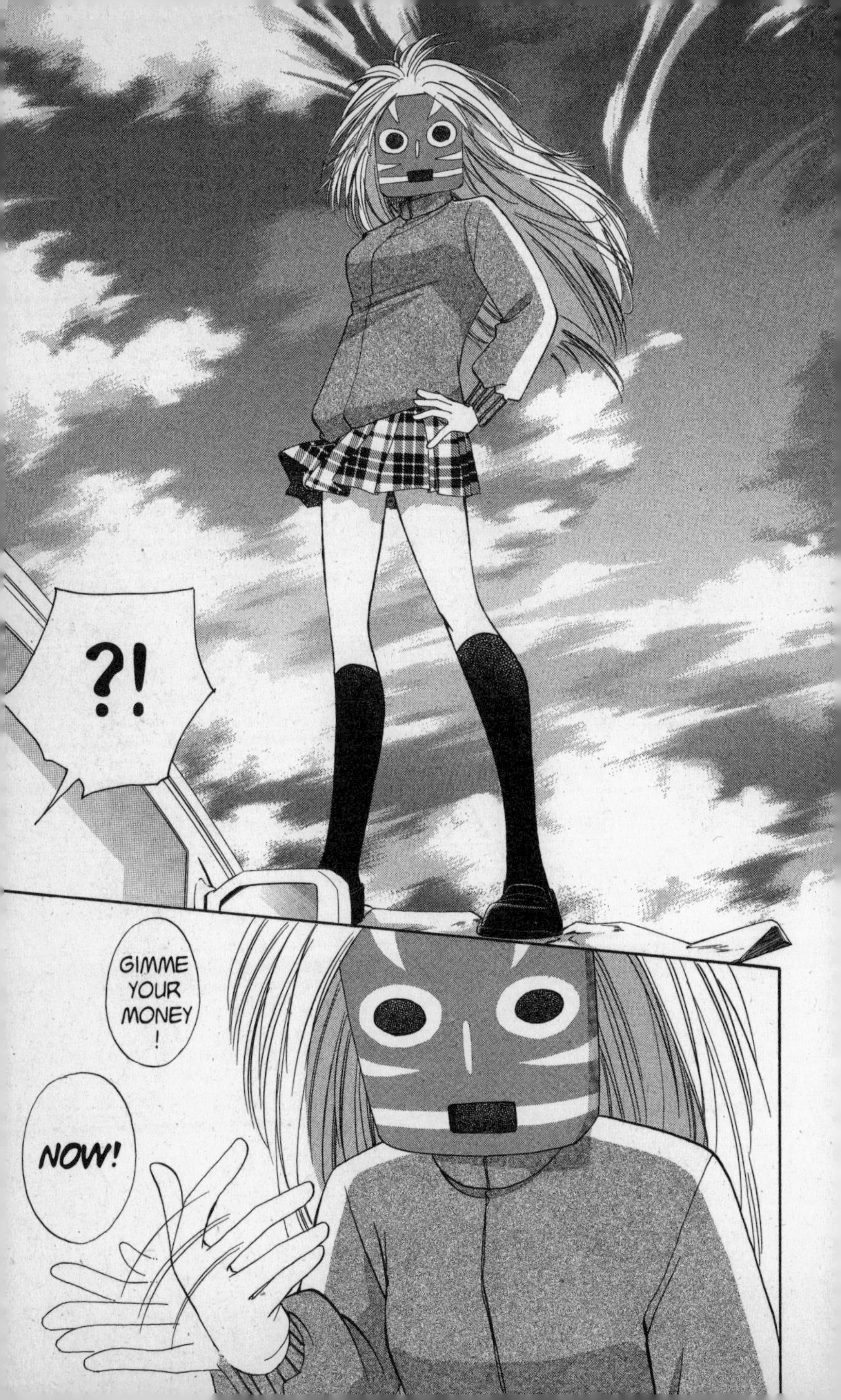
?!
GIMME YOUR MONEY!
NOW!

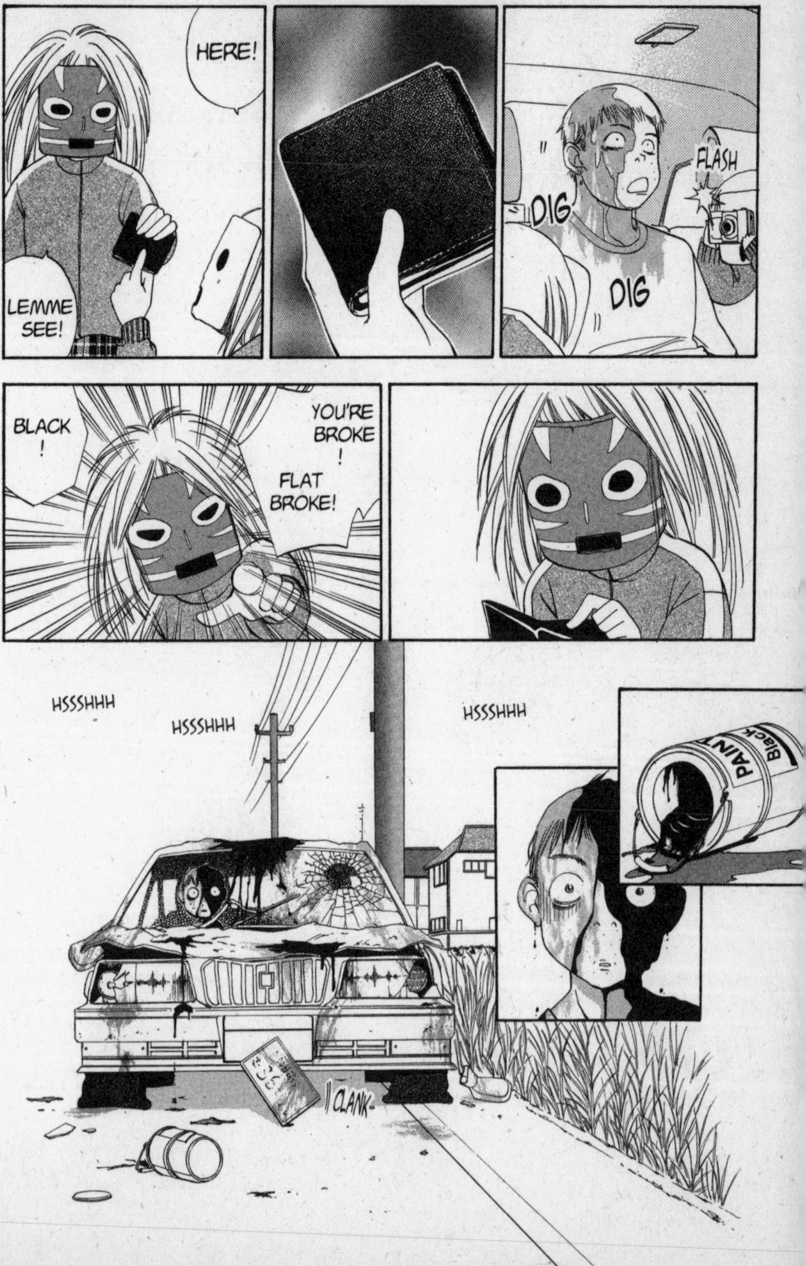

FLASH
DIG
DIG
HERE!
LEMME SEE!
YOU'RE BROKE!
BLACK!
FLAT BROKE!
PAINT Black
HSSSHHH
HSSSHHH
HSSSHHH
CLANK

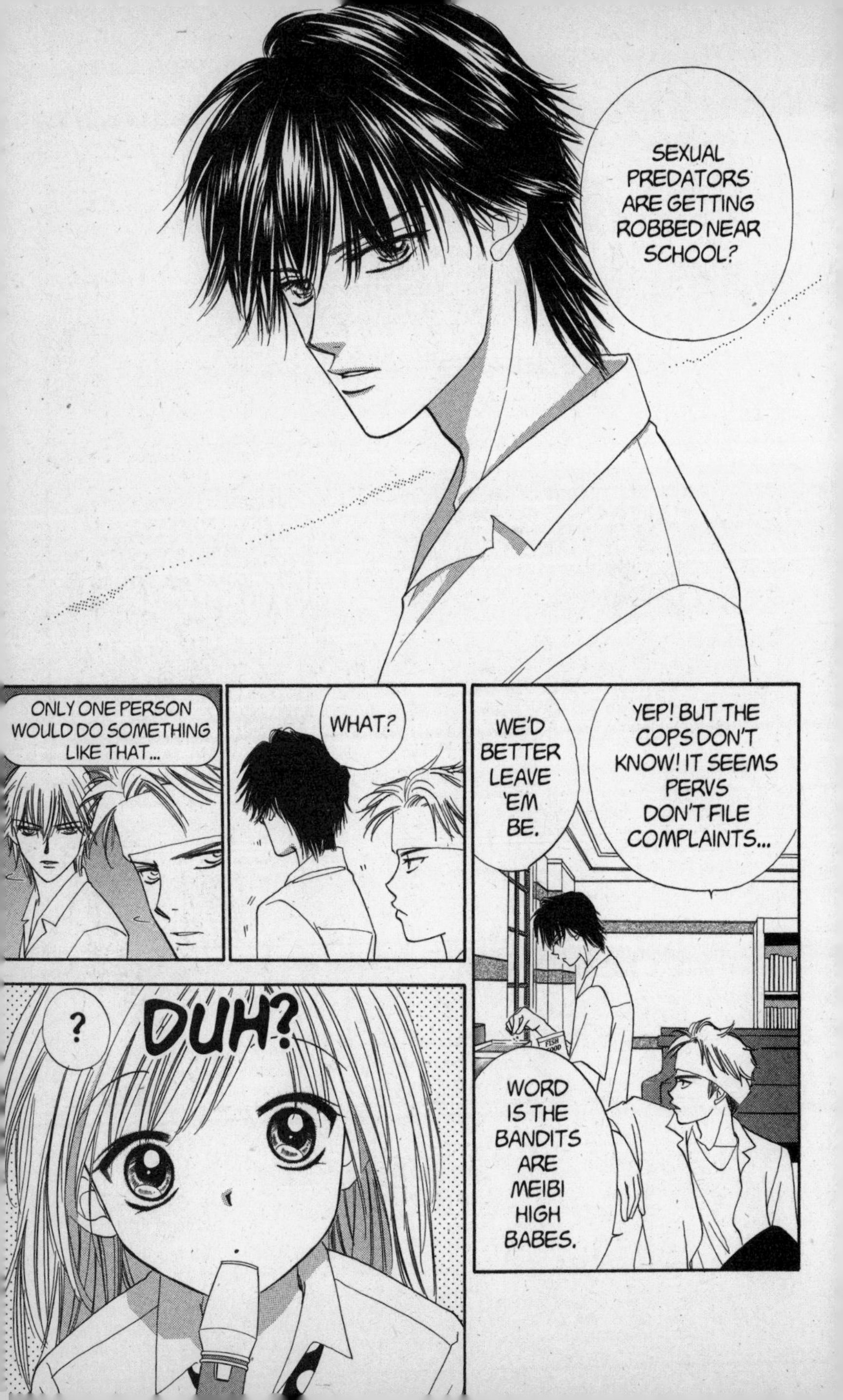

SEXUAL PREDATORS ARE GETTING ROBBED NEAR SCHOOL?
YEP! BUT THE COPS DON'T KNOW! IT SEEMS PERVS DON'T FILE COMPLAINTS...
WE'D BETTER LEAVE 'EM BE.
WORD IS THE BANDITS ARE MEIBI HIGH BABES.
WHAT?
ONLY ONE PERSON WOULD DO SOMETHING LIKE THAT...
DUH?
?

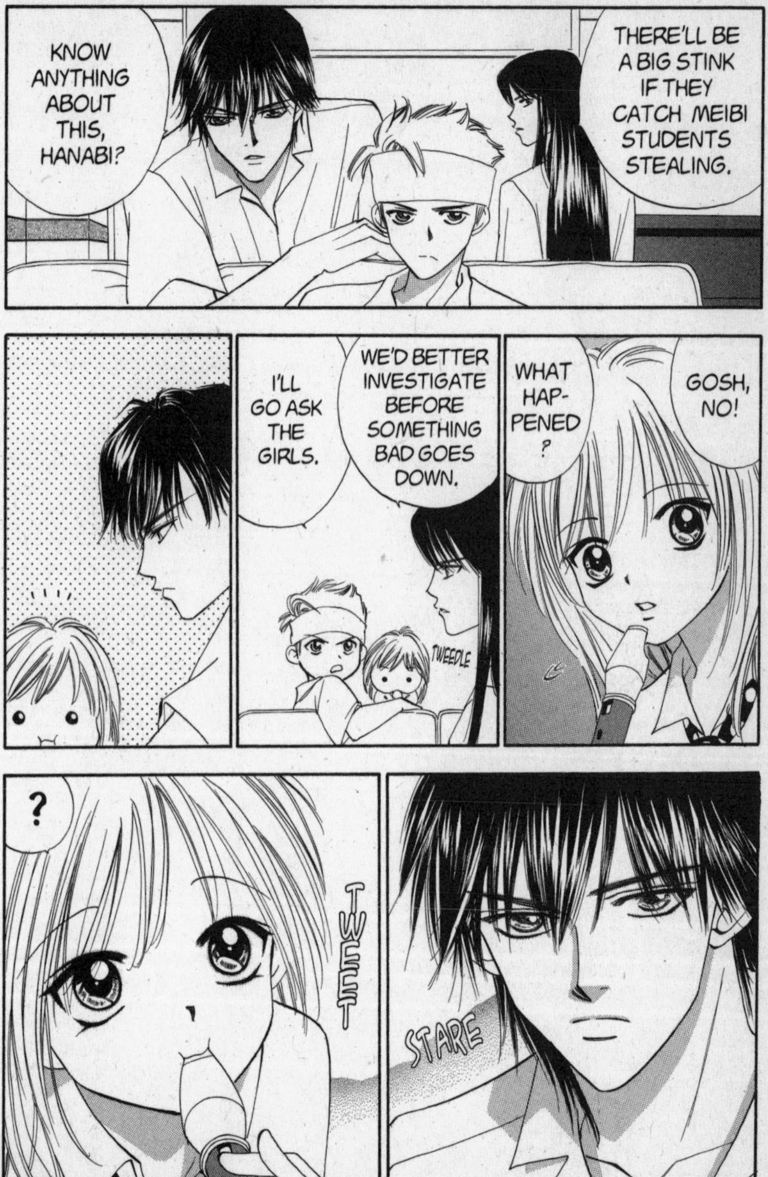
THERE'LL BE A BIG STINK IF THEY CATCH MEIBI STUDENTS STEALING.
KNOW ANYTHING ABOUT THIS, HANABI?
GOSH, NO!
WHAT HAPPENED?
WE'D BETTER INVESTIGATE BEFORE SOMETHING BAD GOES DOWN.
I'LL GO ASK THE GIRLS.
TWEEDLE
STARE
?
TWEET

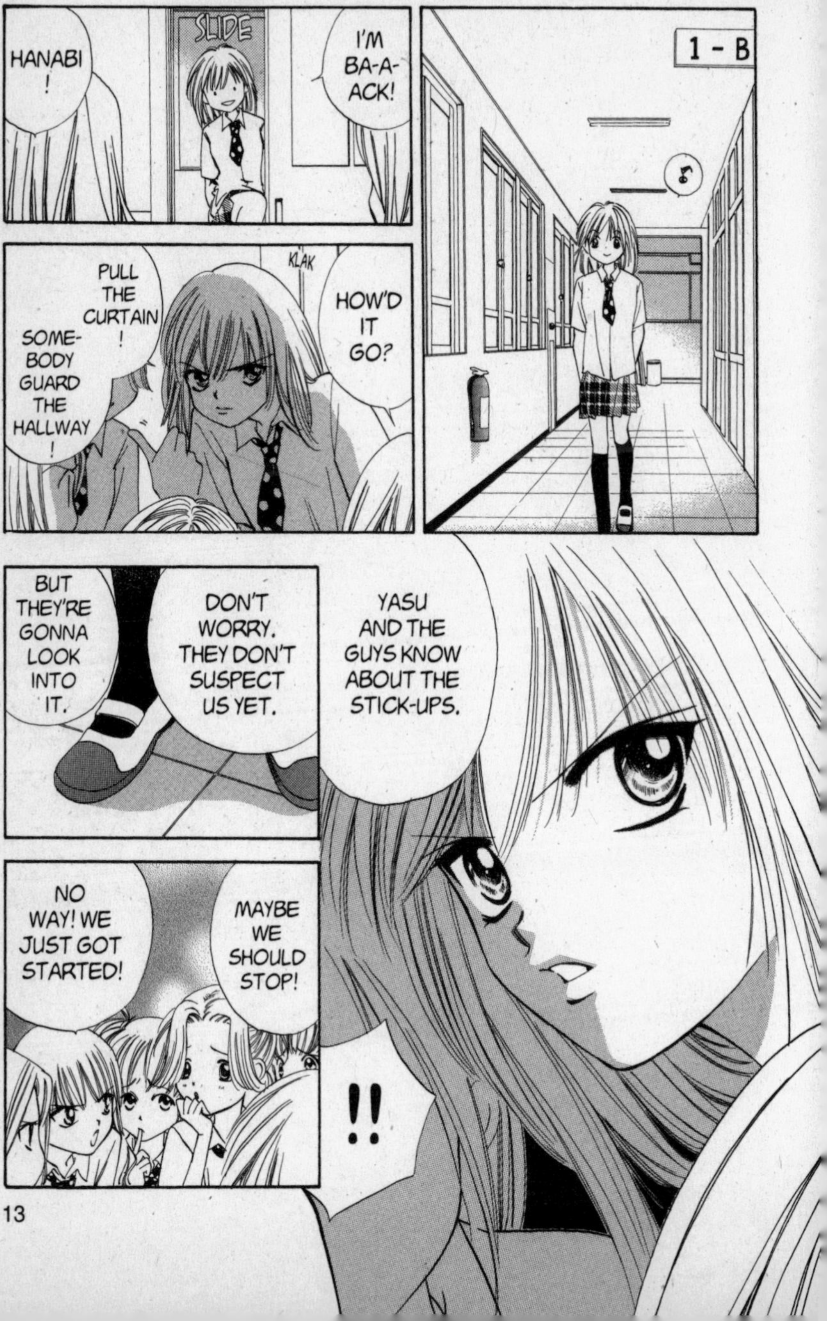
1 - B
SLIDE
I'M BA-A-ACK!
HANABI!
KLAK
HOW'D IT GO?
PULL THE CURTAIN!
SOME-BODY GUARD THE HALLWAY!
YASU AND THE GUYS KNOW ABOUT THE STICK-UPS.
DON'T WORRY. THEY DON'T SUSPECT US YET.
BUT THEY'RE GONNA LOOK INTO IT.
MAYBE WE SHOULD STOP!
NO WAY! WE JUST GOT STARTED!
!!

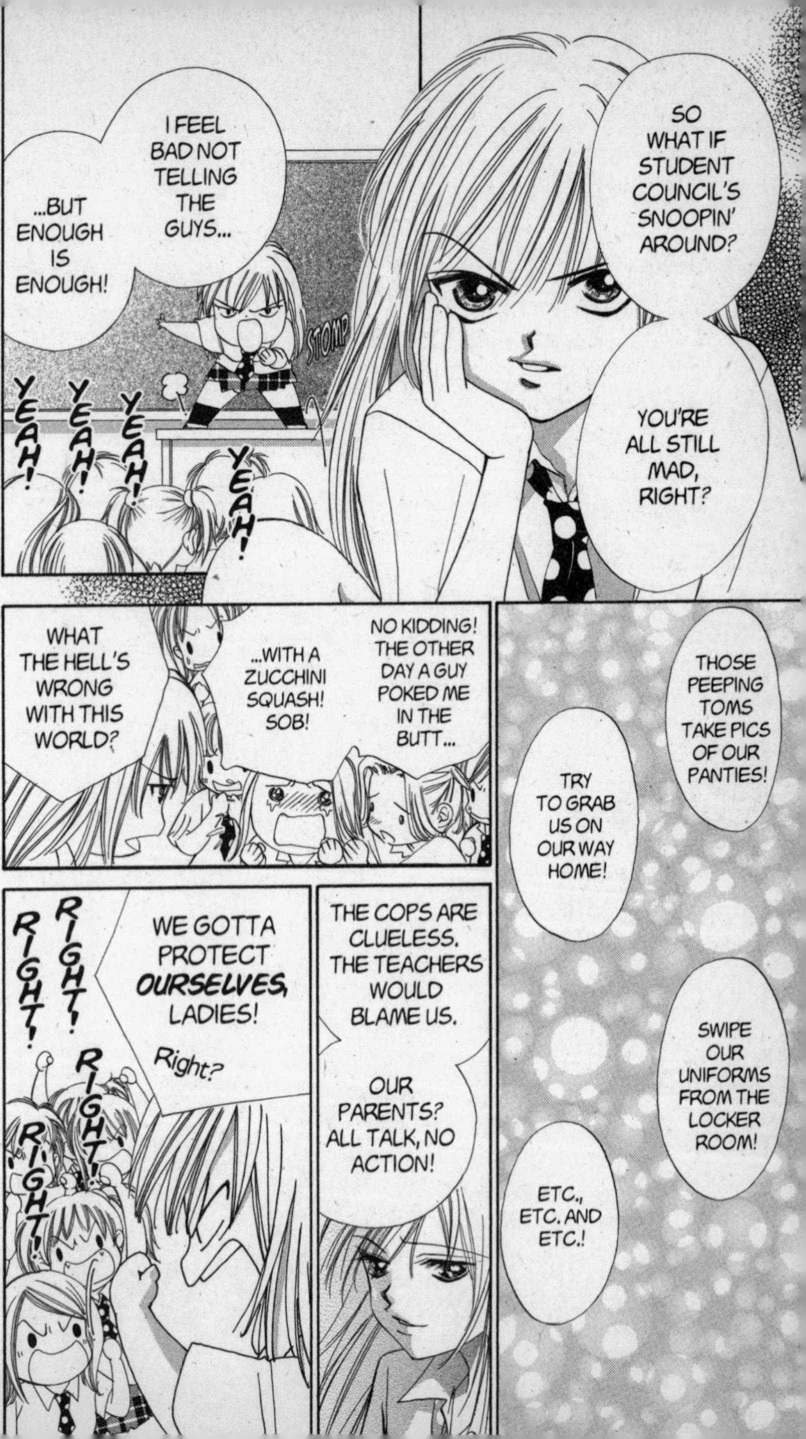
SO WHAT IF STUDENT COUNCIL'S SNOOPIN' AROUND?
YOU'RE ALL STILL MAD, RIGHT?
I FEEL BAD NOT TELLING THE GUYS...
...BUT ENOUGH IS ENOUGH!
STOMP
YEAH!
YEAH!
YEAH!
YEAH!
THOSE PEEPING TOMS TAKE PICS OF OUR PANTIES!
TRY TO GRAB US ON OUR WAY HOME!
SWIPE OUR UNIFORMS FROM THE LOCKER ROOM!
ETC., ETC. AND ETC.!
NO KIDDING! THE OTHER DAY A GUY POKED ME IN THE BUTT...
...WITH A ZUCCHINI SQUASH! SOB!
WHAT THE HELL'S WRONG WITH THIS WORLD?
THE COPS ARE CLUELESS. THE TEACHERS WOULD BLAME US.
OUR PARENTS? ALL TALK, NO ACTION!
WE GOTTA PROTECT **OURSELVES,** LADIES!
Right?
RIGHT!
RIGHT!
RIGHT!
RIGHT!

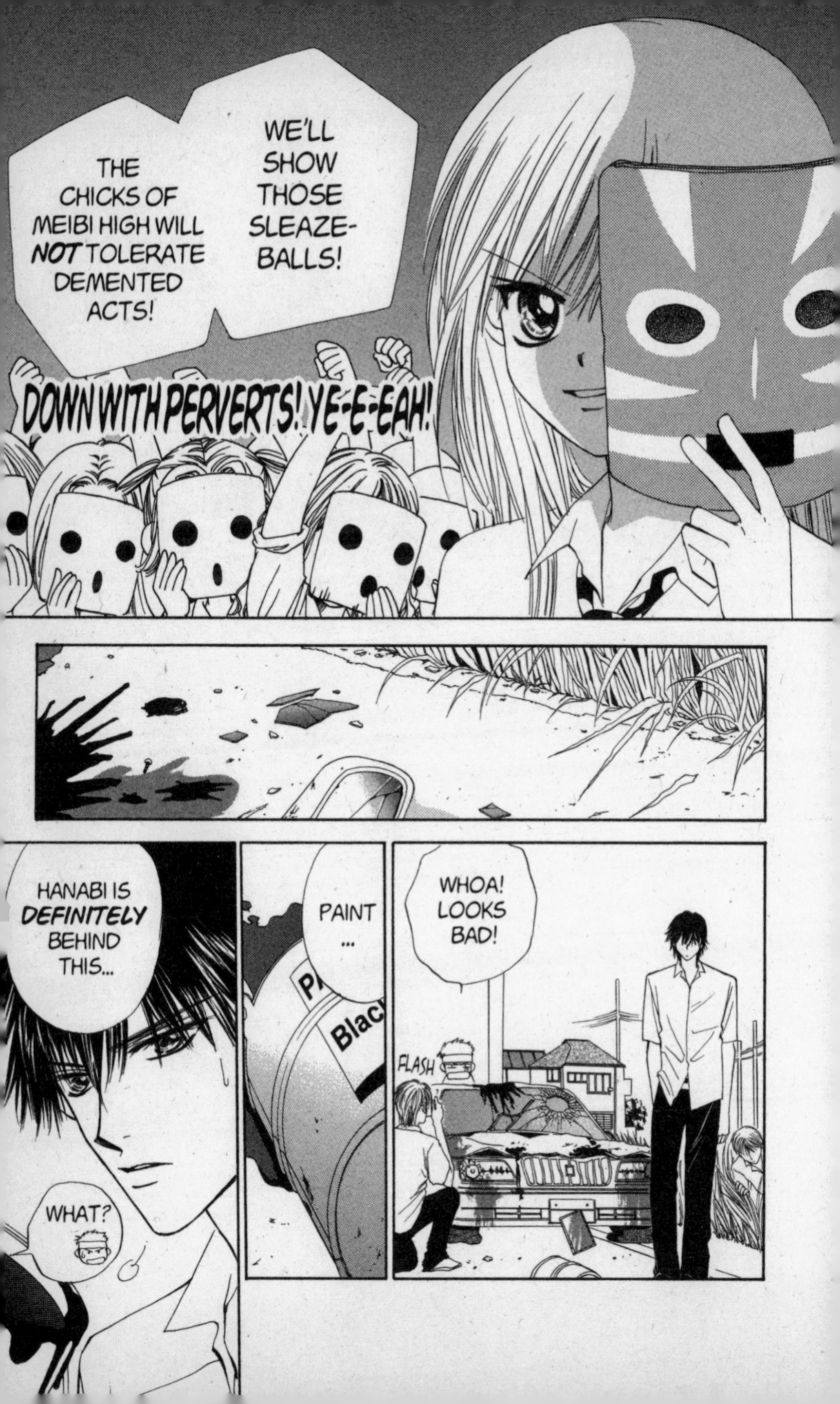
WE'LL SHOW THOSE SLEAZE-BALLS!
THE CHICKS OF MEIBI HIGH WILL NOT TOLERATE DEMENTED ACTS!
DOWN WITH PERVERTS! YE-E-EAH!
WHOA! LOOKS BAD!
FLASH
PAINT ...
HANABI IS DEFINITELY BEHIND THIS...
WHAT?

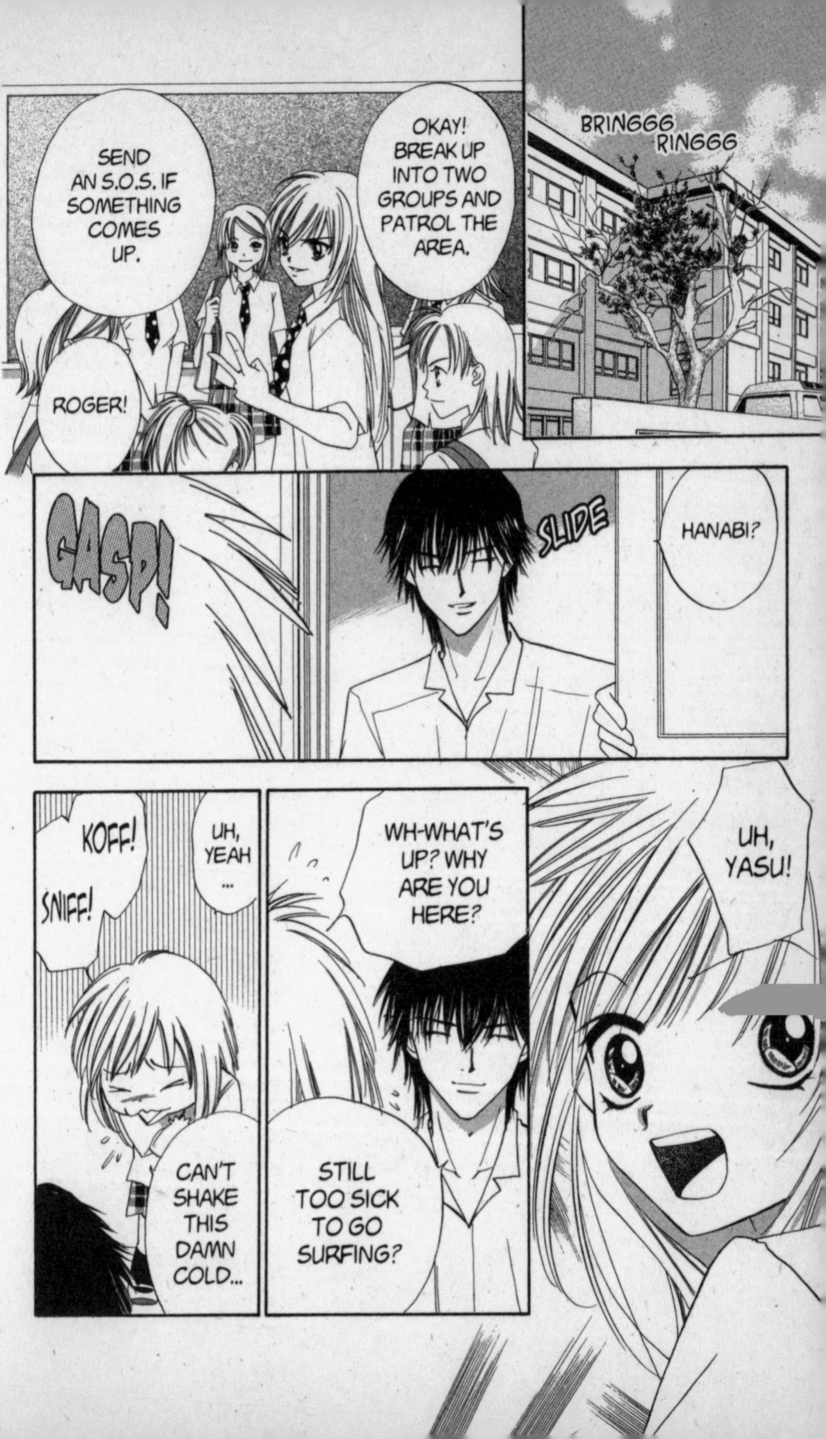
BRINGGG RINGGG
OKAY! BREAK UP INTO TWO GROUPS AND PATROL THE AREA.
SEND AN S.O.S. IF SOMETHING COMES UP.
ROGER!
HANABI?
SLIDE
GASP!
UH, YASU!
WH-WHAT'S UP? WHY ARE YOU HERE?
STILL TOO SICK TO GO SURFING?
UH, YEAH...
KOFF!
SNIFF!
CAN'T SHAKE THIS DAMN COLD...

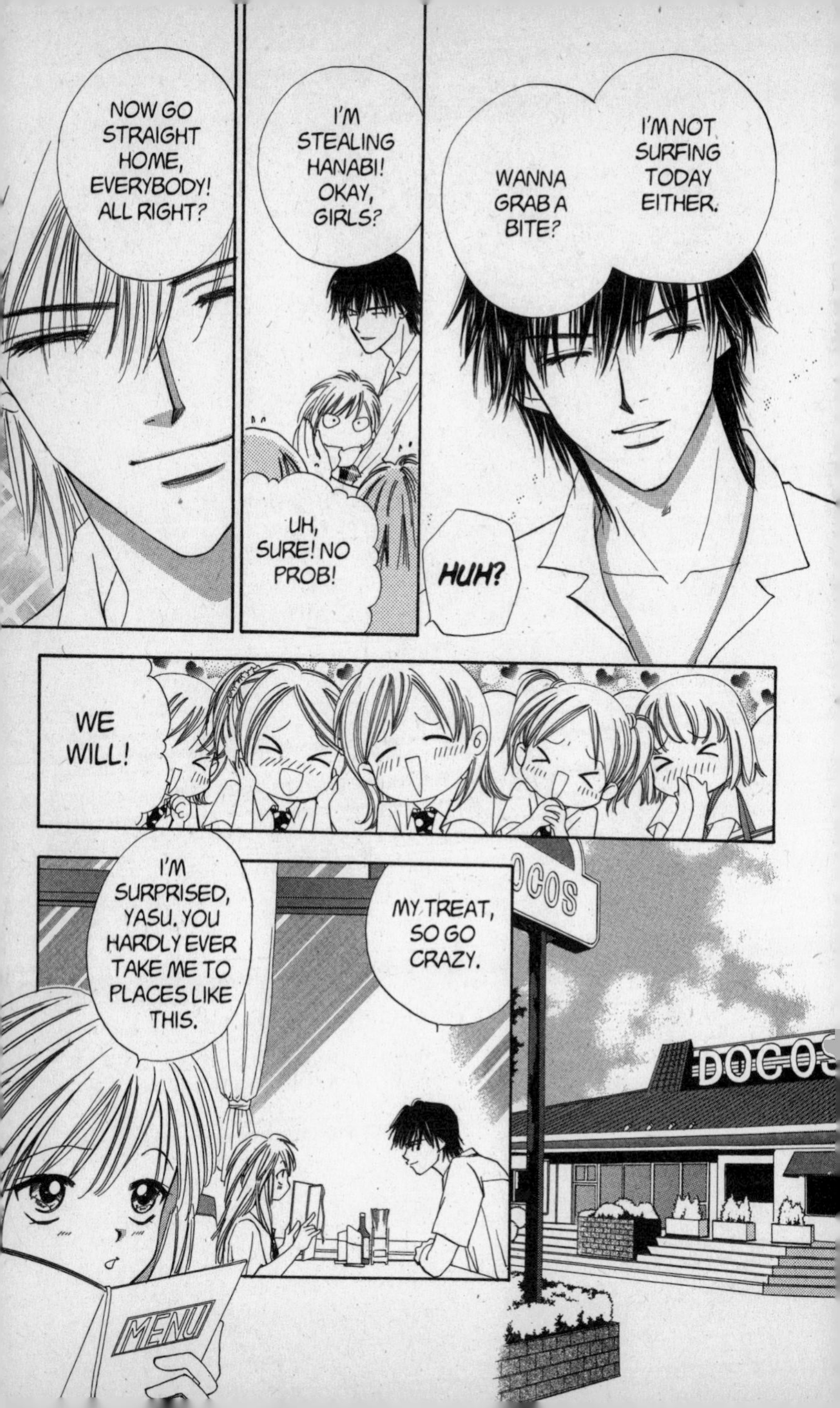
I'M NOT SURFING TODAY EITHER.
WANNA GRAB A BITE?
HUH?
I'M STEALING HANABI! OKAY, GIRLS?
UH, SURE! NO PROB!
NOW GO STRAIGHT HOME, EVERYBODY! ALL RIGHT?
WE WILL!
DOCOS
DOCOS
MY TREAT, SO GO CRAZY.
I'M SURPRISED, YASU. YOU HARDLY EVER TAKE ME TO PLACES LIKE THIS.
MENU

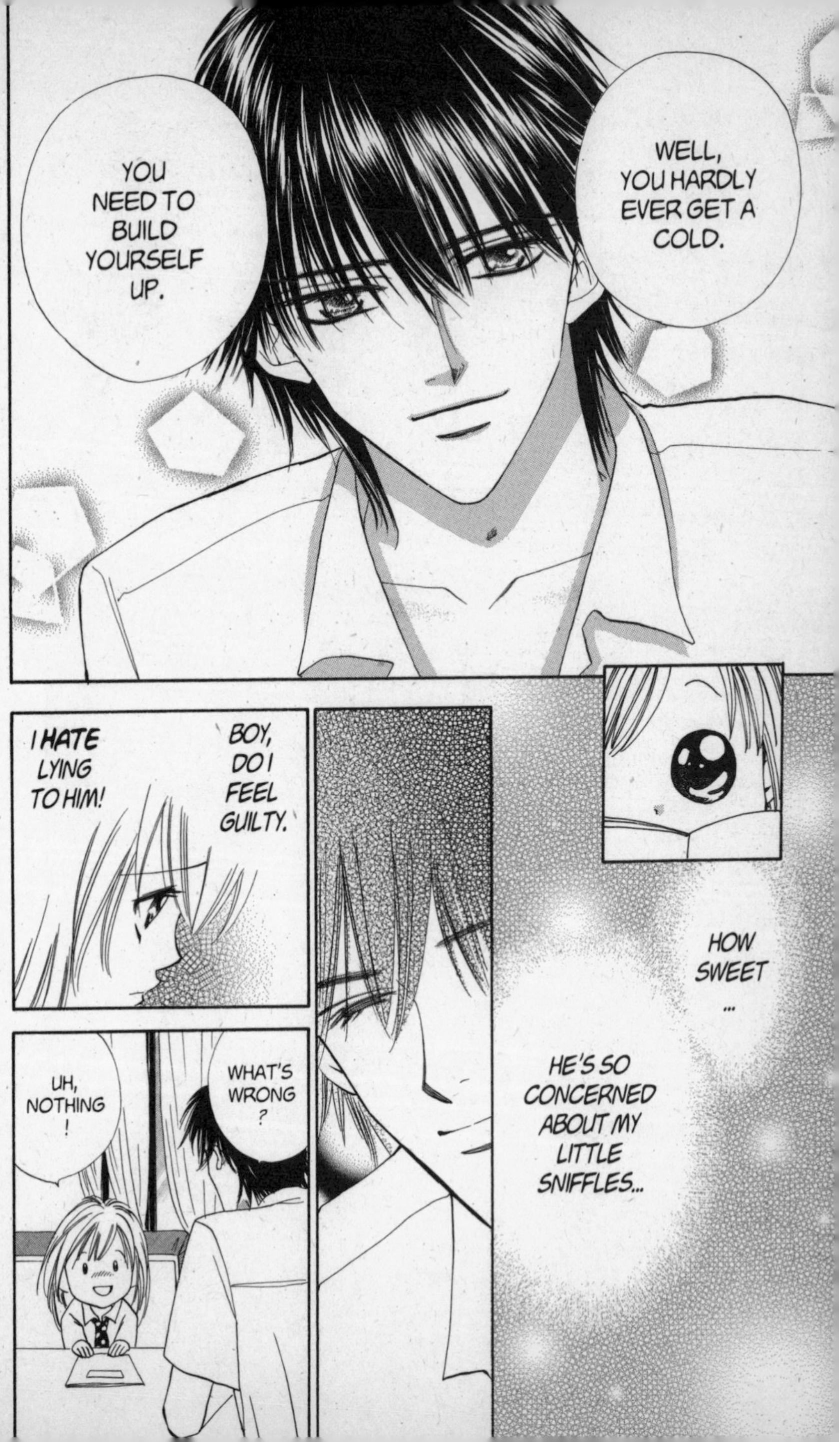
WELL, YOU HARDLY EVER GET A COLD.
YOU NEED TO BUILD YOURSELF UP.
HOW SWEET ...
HE'S SO CONCERNED ABOUT MY LITTLE SNIFFLES...
BOY, DO I FEEL GUILTY.
I HATE LYING TO HIM!
WHAT'S WRONG ?
UH, NOTHING !

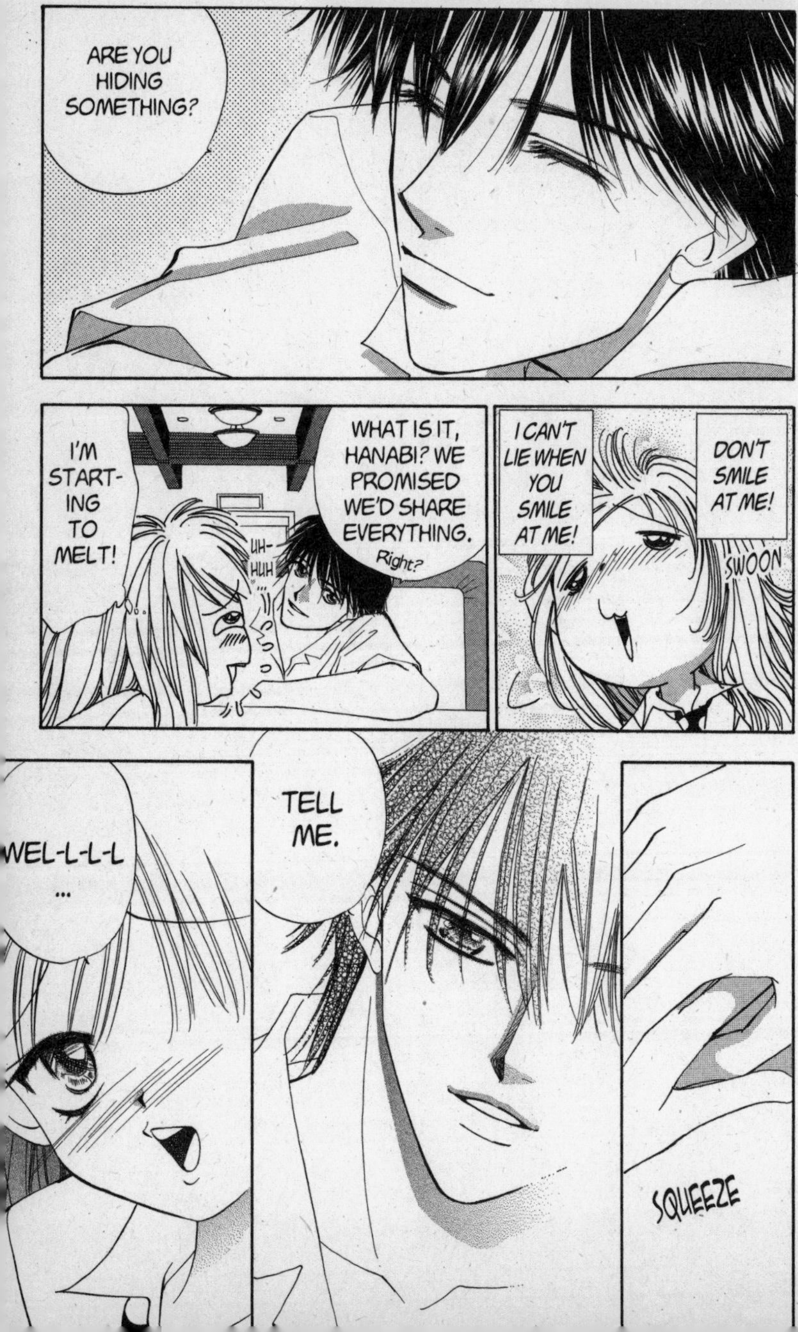
ARE YOU HIDING SOMETHING?
DON'T SMILE AT ME!
I CAN'T LIE WHEN YOU SMILE AT ME!
SWOON
WHAT IS IT, HANABI? WE PROMISED WE'D SHARE EVERYTHING. Right?
UH-HUH...
I'M STARTING TO MELT!
SQUEEZE
TELL ME.
WEL-L-L-L ...

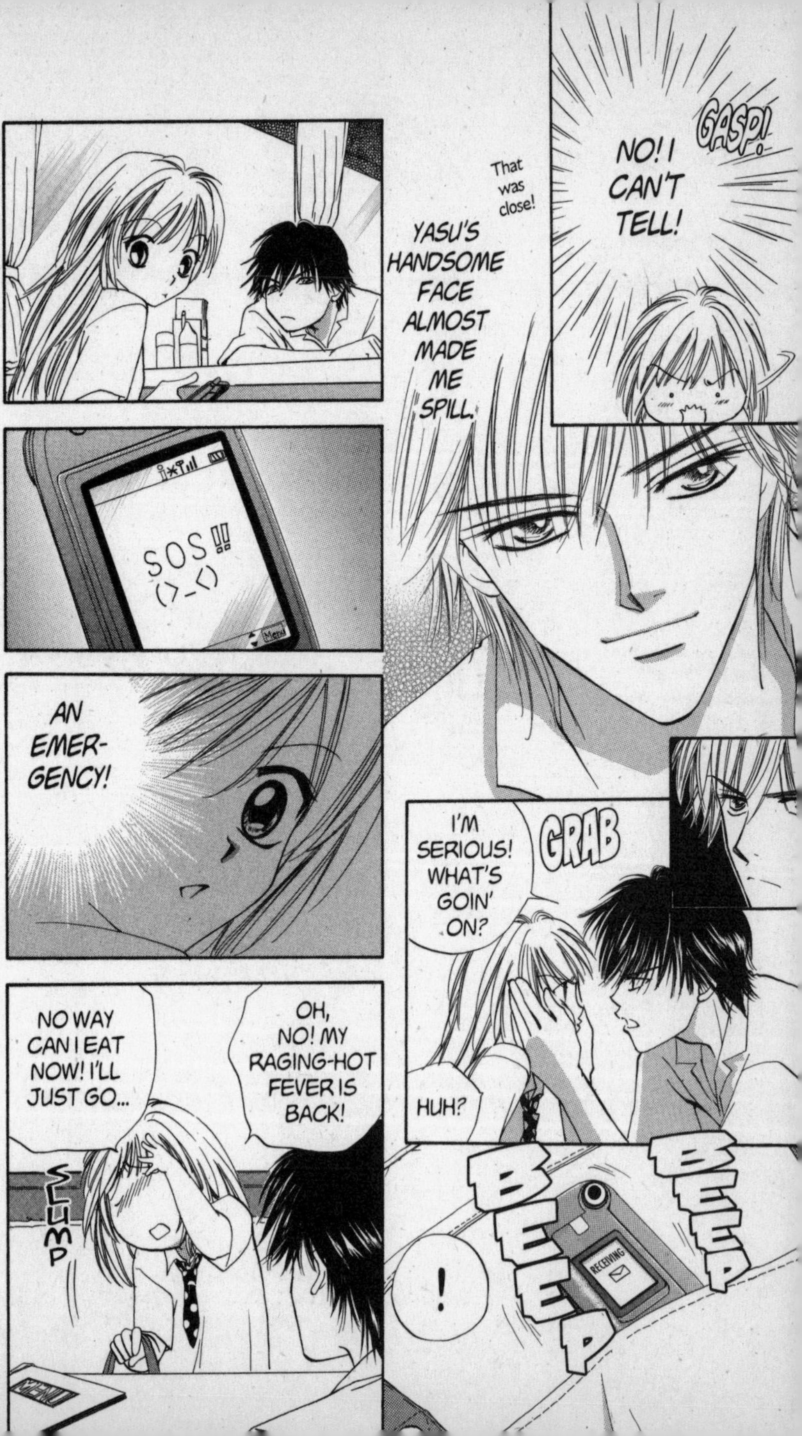
GASP!
NO! I CAN'T TELL!
That was close!
YASU'S HANDSOME FACE ALMOST MADE ME SPILL.
GRAB
I'M SERIOUS! WHAT'S GOIN' ON?
HUH?
BEEEP
BEEEP
!
RECEIVING
SOS!! (>_<)
Menu
AN EMERGENCY!
OH, NO! MY RAGING-HOT FEVER IS BACK!
NO WAY CAN I EAT NOW! I'LL JUST GO...
SLUMP
MENU

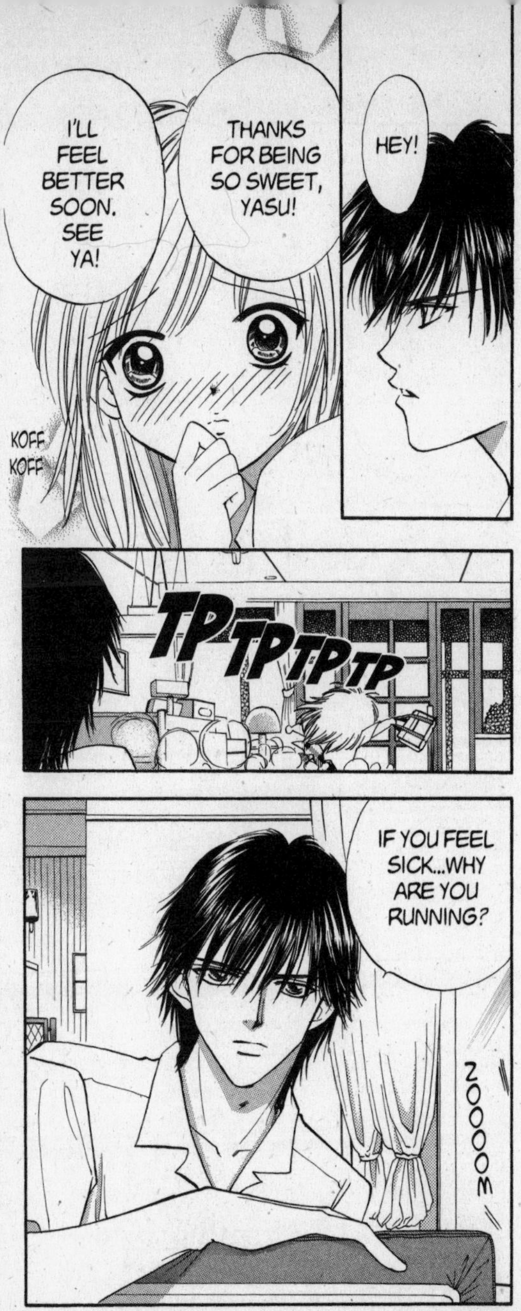
HEY!
THANKS FOR BEING SO SWEET, YASU!
I'LL FEEL BETTER SOON. SEE YA!
KOFF KOFF
TP TP TP TP TP
IF YOU FEEL SICK...WHY ARE YOU RUNNING?
ZOOOOOM

GOODBYE 2004

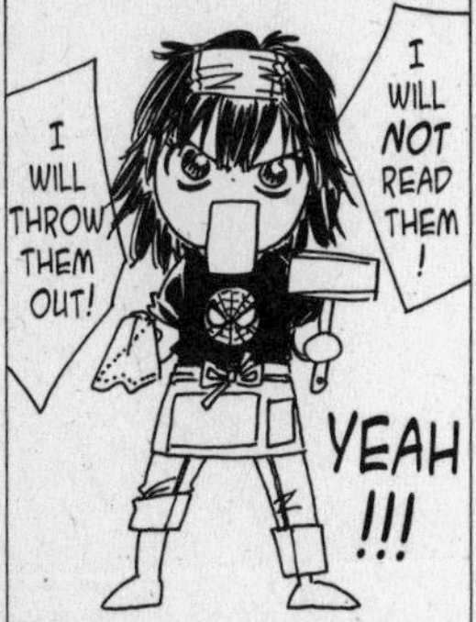
I WILL NOT READ THEM!
I WILL THROW THEM OUT!
YEAH !!!

AFTER I FINISHED H3 AT THE BEGINNING OF DECEMBER, I CLEANED MY HOUSE FROM TOP TO BOTTOM. THE HARDEST THING TO DEAL WITH WAS ALL THE PAPER! I HANG ONTO SO MUCH MANGA STUFF, THINKING I CAN USE IT LATER. AND I'M JUST AS BAD WITH HOBBY BOOKS...

I TIDIED UP FOR TWO WEEKS WITH ONE REWARD IN MIND: READING K-1 DYNAMITE, A SERIES I'VE BEEN LOOKING FORWARD TO, IN A NICE CLEAN ROOM. IT FELT SOOOO GOOD! I EVEN HAD TIME TO MAKE SPECIAL NEW YEAR'S CUISINE. SO THE END OF **2004** WAS VERY PRODUCTIVE!

K-1 WAS GOOD, TOO.

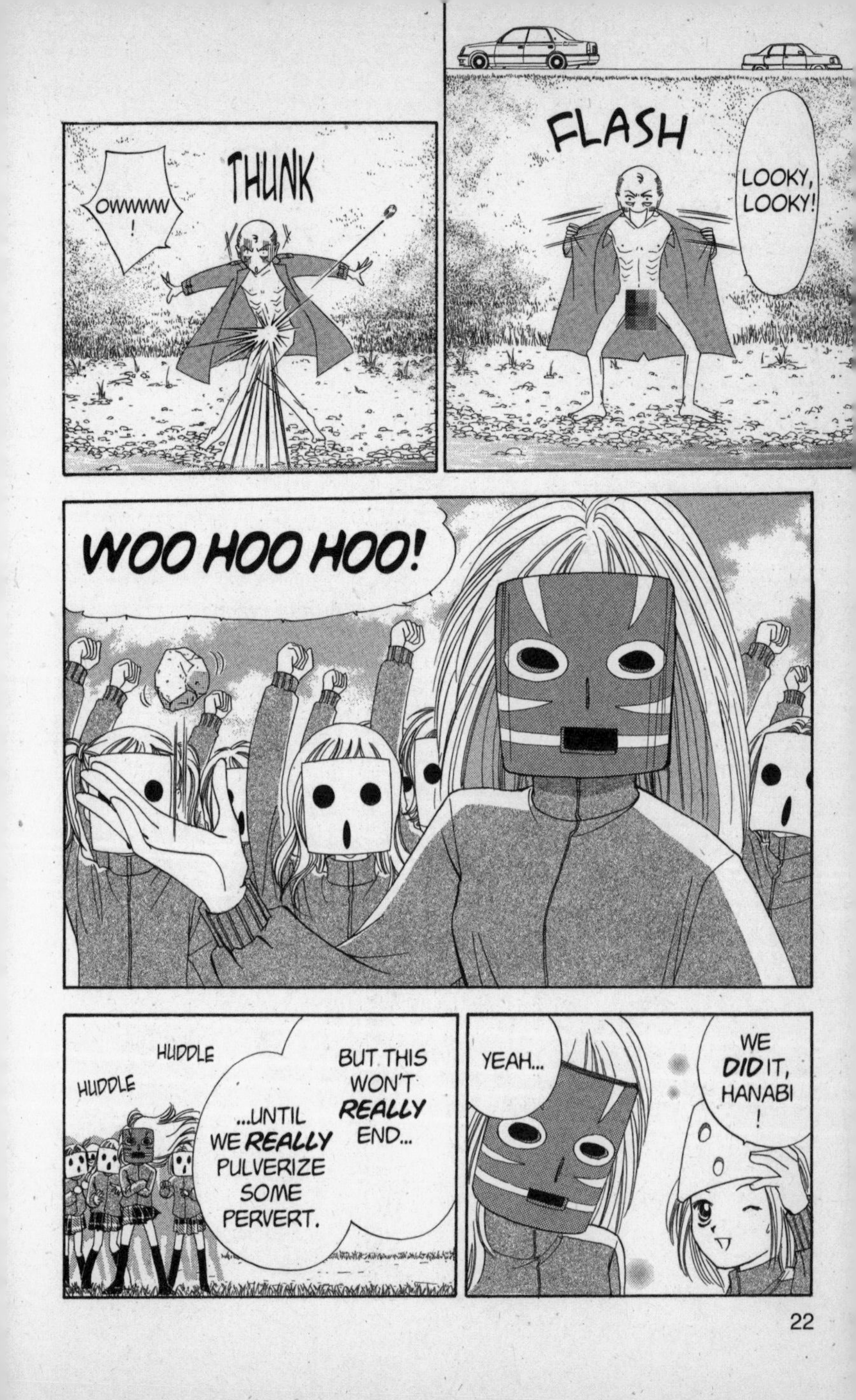
FLASH
LOOKY, LOOKY!
THUNK
OWWWW!
WOO HOO HOO!
WE DID IT, HANABI!
YEAH...
BUT THIS WON'T REALLY END...
...UNTIL WE REALLY PULVERIZE SOME PERVERT.
HUDDLE
HUDDLE

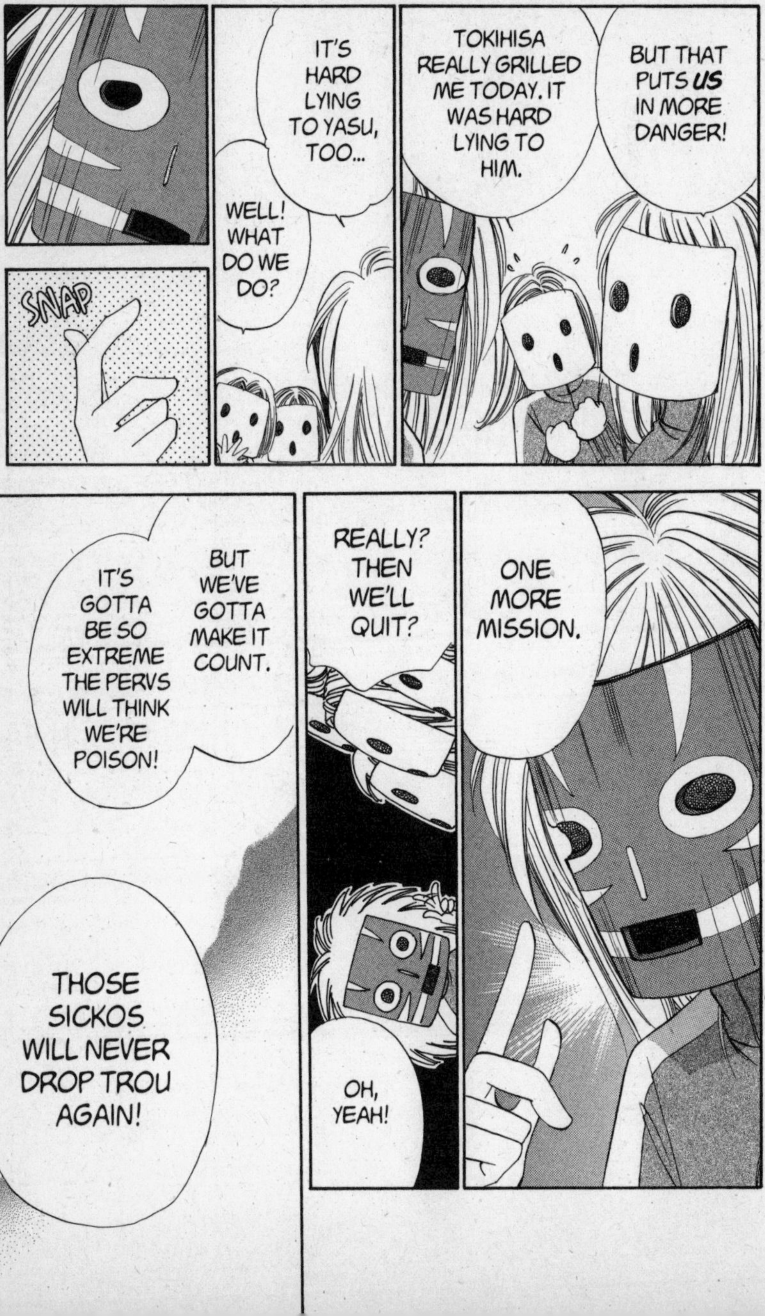
BUT THAT PUTS US IN MORE DANGER!
TOKIHISA REALLY GRILLED ME TODAY. IT WAS HARD LYING TO HIM.
IT'S HARD LYING TO YASU, TOO...
WELL! WHAT DO WE DO?
SNAP
ONE MORE MISSION.
REALLY? THEN WE'LL QUIT?
OH, YEAH!
BUT WE'VE GOTTA MAKE IT COUNT.
IT'S GOTTA BE SO EXTREME THE PERVS WILL THINK WE'RE POISON!
THOSE SICKOS WILL NEVER DROP TROU AGAIN!

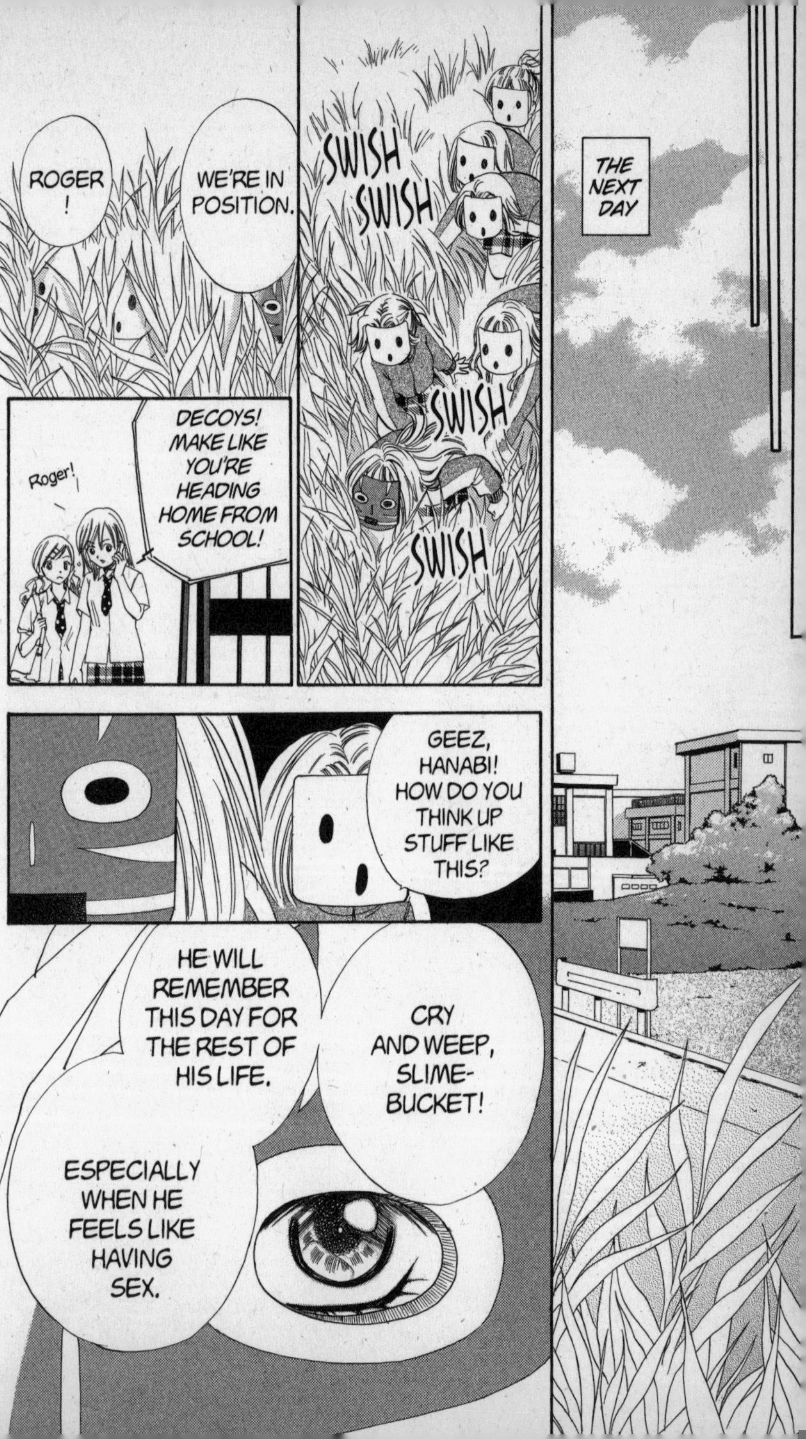
THE NEXT DAY
SWISH SWISH
SWISH
SWISH
WE'RE IN POSITION.
ROGER!
DECOYS! MAKE LIKE YOU'RE HEADING HOME FROM SCHOOL!
Roger!
GEEZ, HANABI! HOW DO YOU THINK UP STUFF LIKE THIS?
CRY AND WEEP, SLIME-BUCKET!
HE WILL REMEMBER THIS DAY FOR THE REST OF HIS LIFE.
ESPECIALLY WHEN HE FEELS LIKE HAVING SEX.

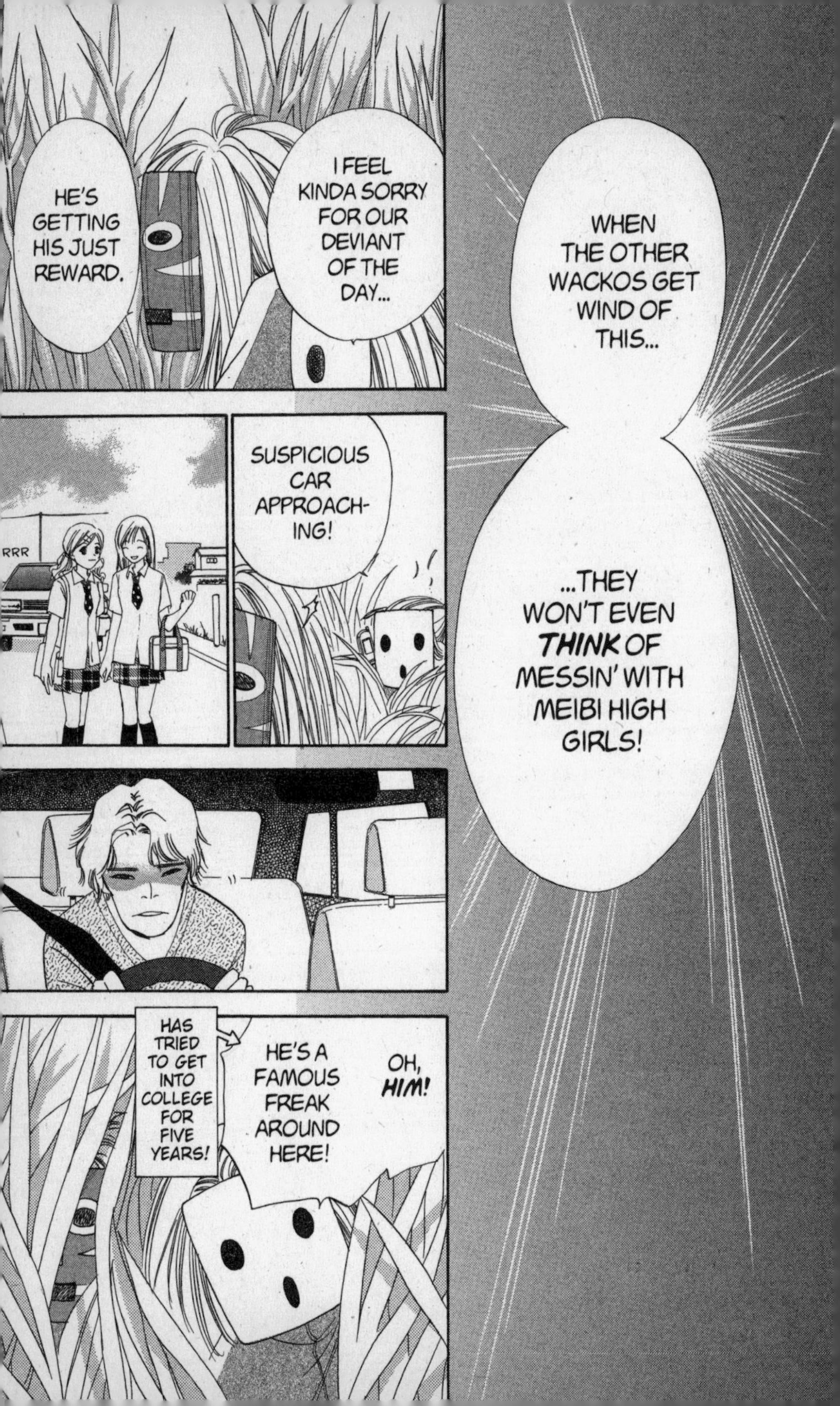
WHEN THE OTHER WACKOS GET WIND OF THIS...
...THEY WON'T EVEN *THINK* OF MESSIN' WITH MEIBI HIGH GIRLS!
I FEEL KINDA SORRY FOR OUR DEVIANT OF THE DAY...
HE'S GETTING HIS JUST REWARD.
SUSPICIOUS CAR APPROACH-ING!
RRR
OH, *HIM!*
HE'S A FAMOUS FREAK AROUND HERE!
HAS TRIED TO GET INTO COLLEGE FOR FIVE YEARS!

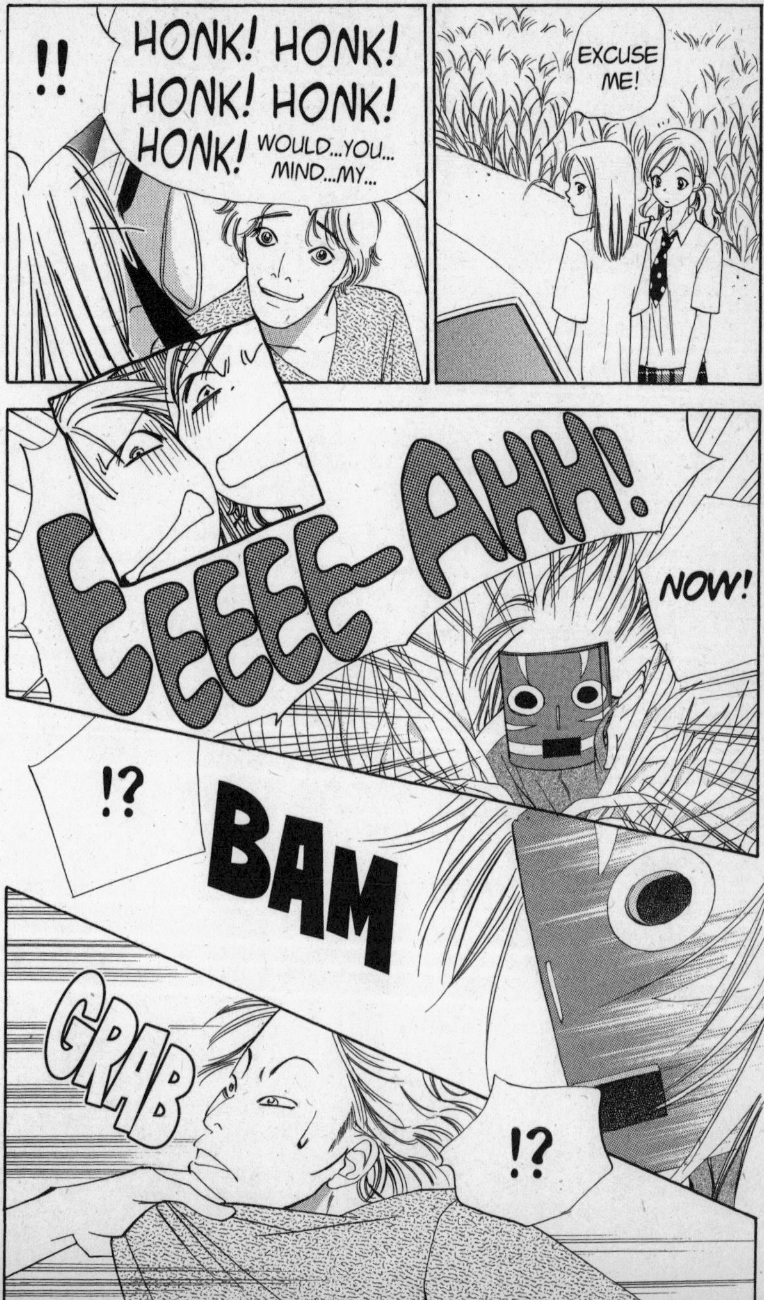
EXCUSE ME!
...
HONK! HONK! HONK! HONK! HONK! WOULD...YOU... MIND...MY...
!!
NOW!
EEEEE-AHH!
BAM
!?
!?
GRAB

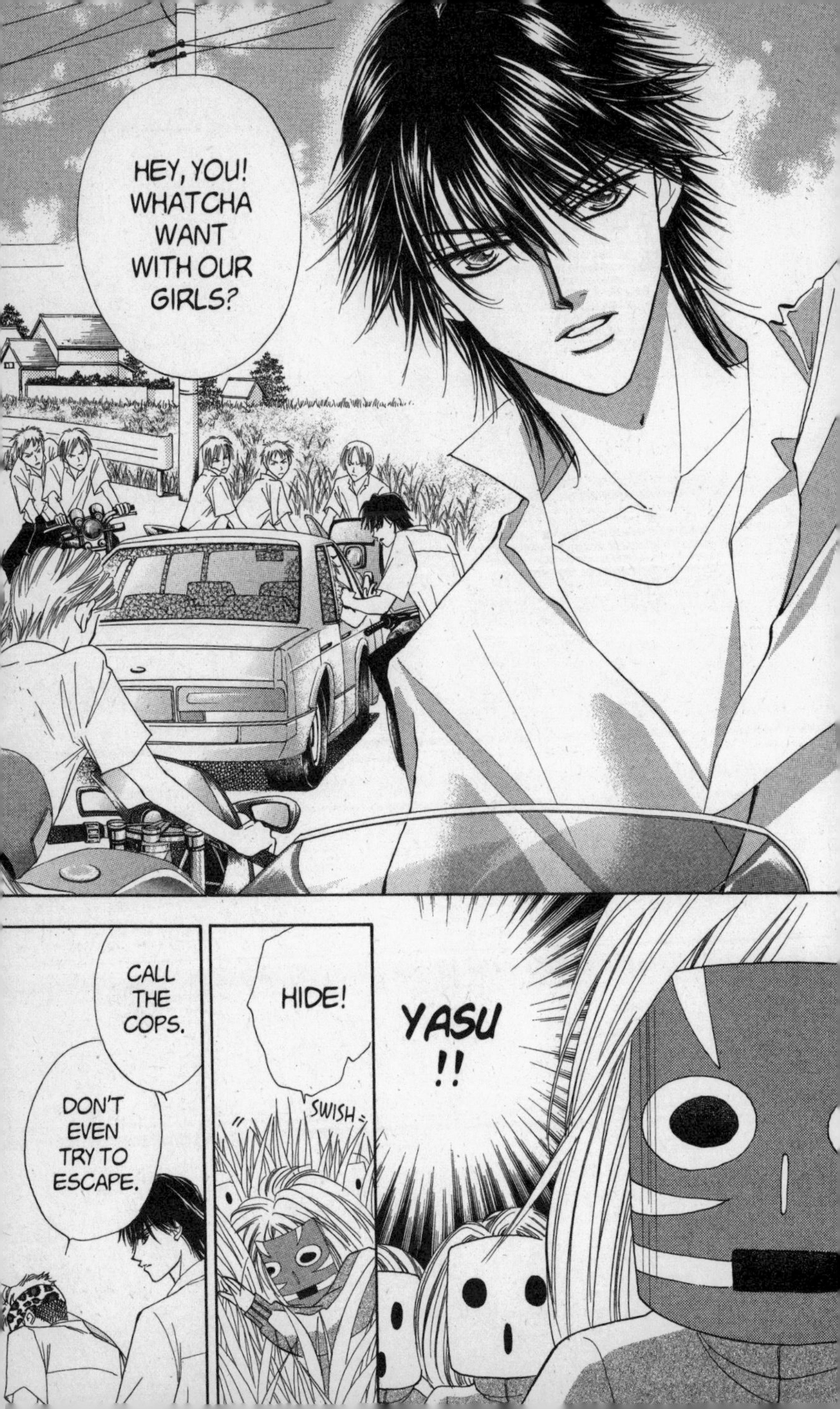
HEY, YOU! WHATCHA WANT WITH OUR GIRLS?
YASU !!
HIDE!
SWISH
CALL THE COPS.
DON'T EVEN TRY TO ESCAPE.

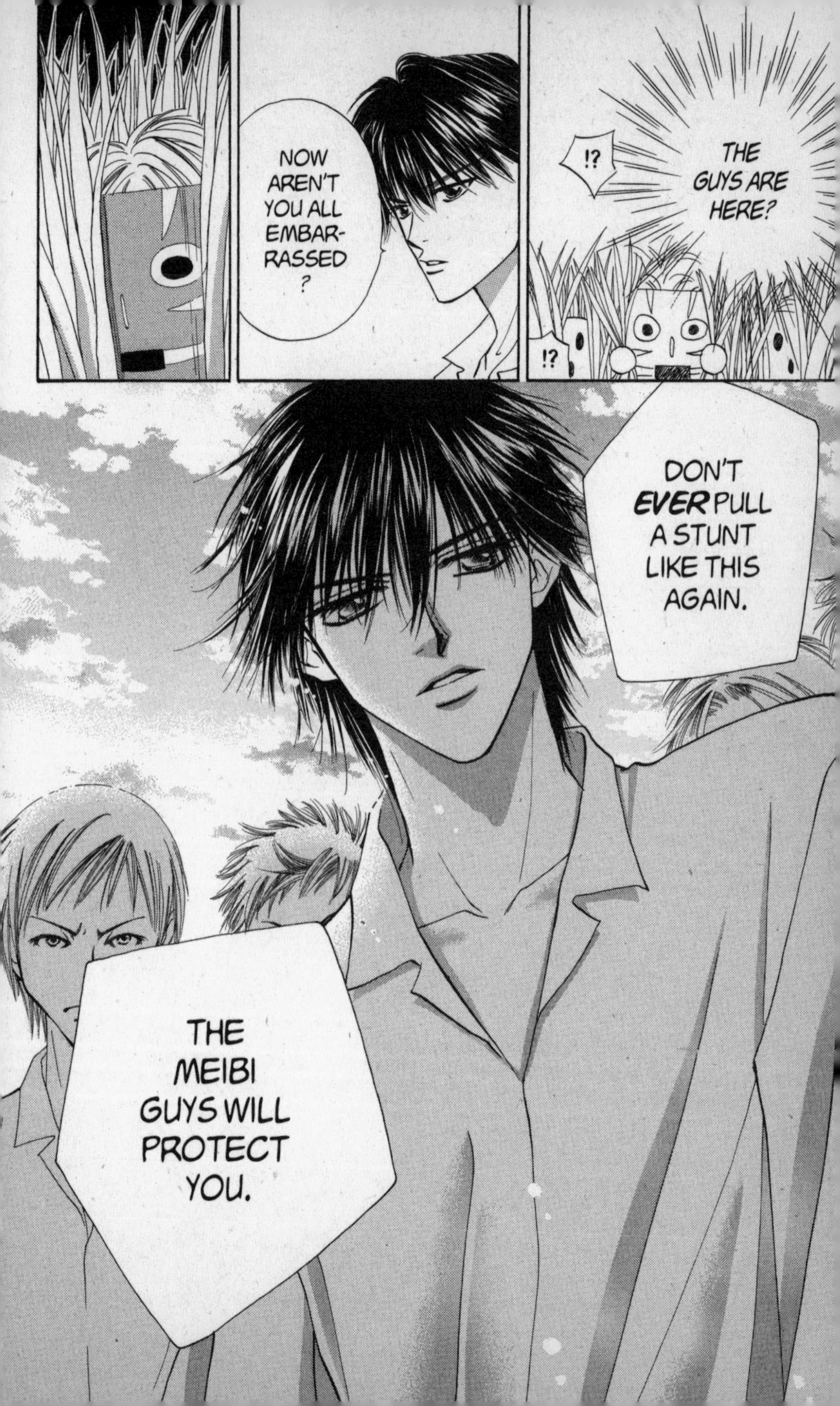
THE GUYS ARE HERE?
!?
!?
NOW AREN'T YOU ALL EMBARRASSED?
DON'T **EVER** PULL A STUNT LIKE THIS AGAIN.
THE MEIBI GUYS WILL PROTECT YOU.

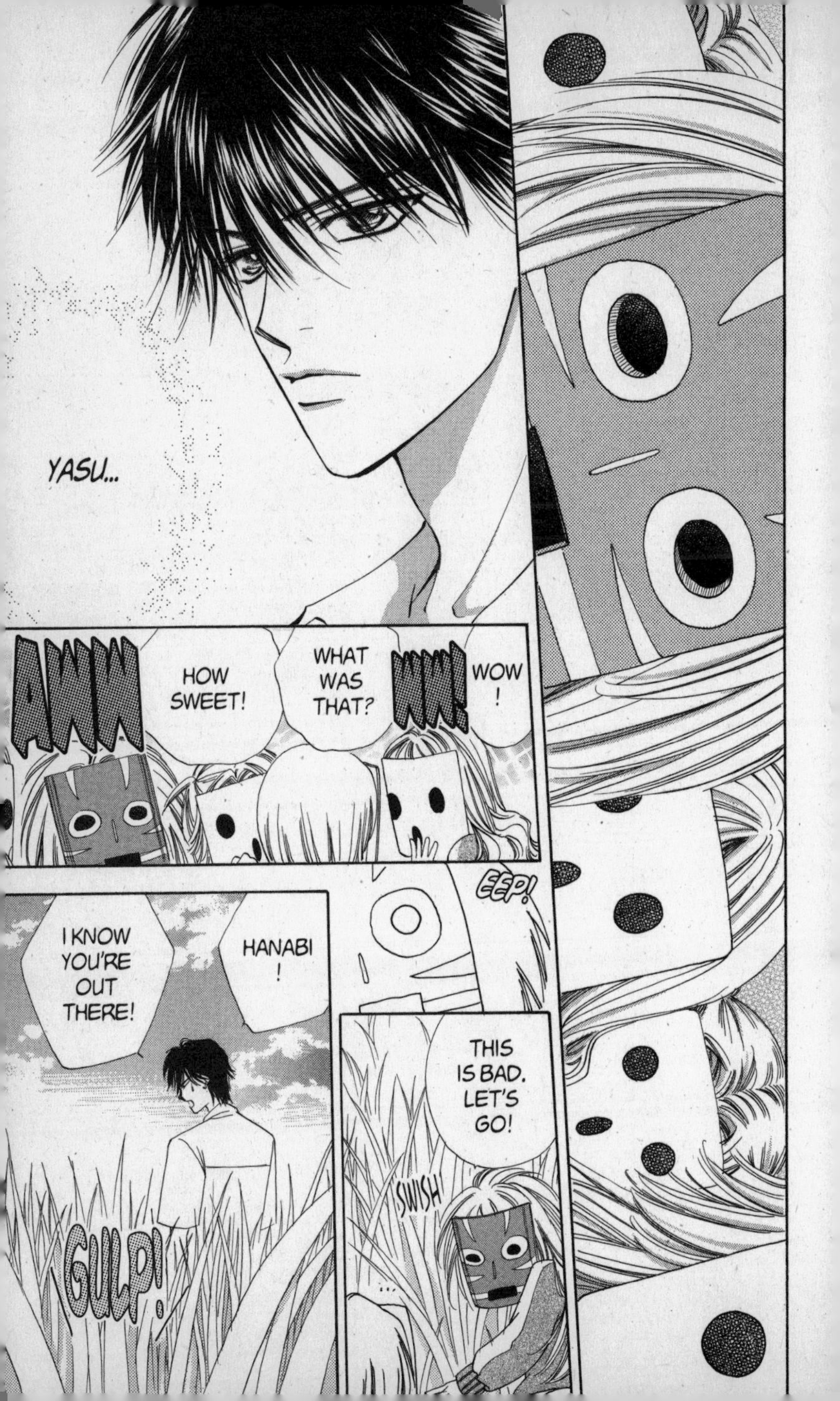
YASU...
WOW!
WW!
WHAT WAS THAT?
HOW SWEET!
AWW
EEP!
HANABI!
I KNOW YOU'RE OUT THERE!
GULP!
THIS IS BAD. LET'S GO!
SWISH
...

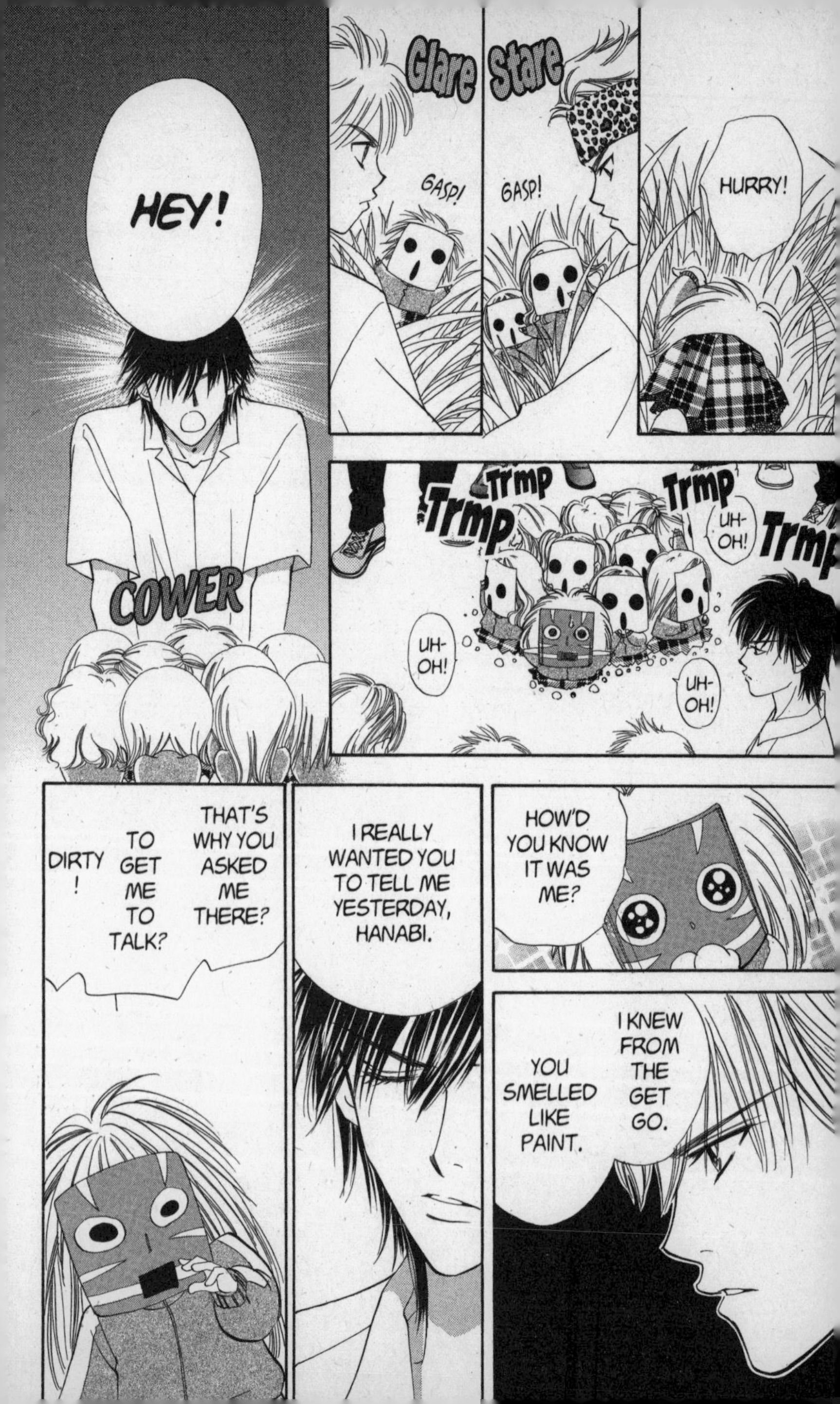
HURRY!
Stare
GASP!
Glare
GASP!
Trmp
UH-OH!
Trmp
Trmp
Trmp
UH-OH!
UH-OH!
HEY!
COWER
HOW'D YOU KNOW IT WAS ME?
I KNEW FROM THE GET GO.
YOU SMELLED LIKE PAINT.
I REALLY WANTED YOU TO TELL ME YESTERDAY, HANABI.
THAT'S WHY YOU ASKED ME THERE?
TO GET ME TO TALK?
DIRTY!

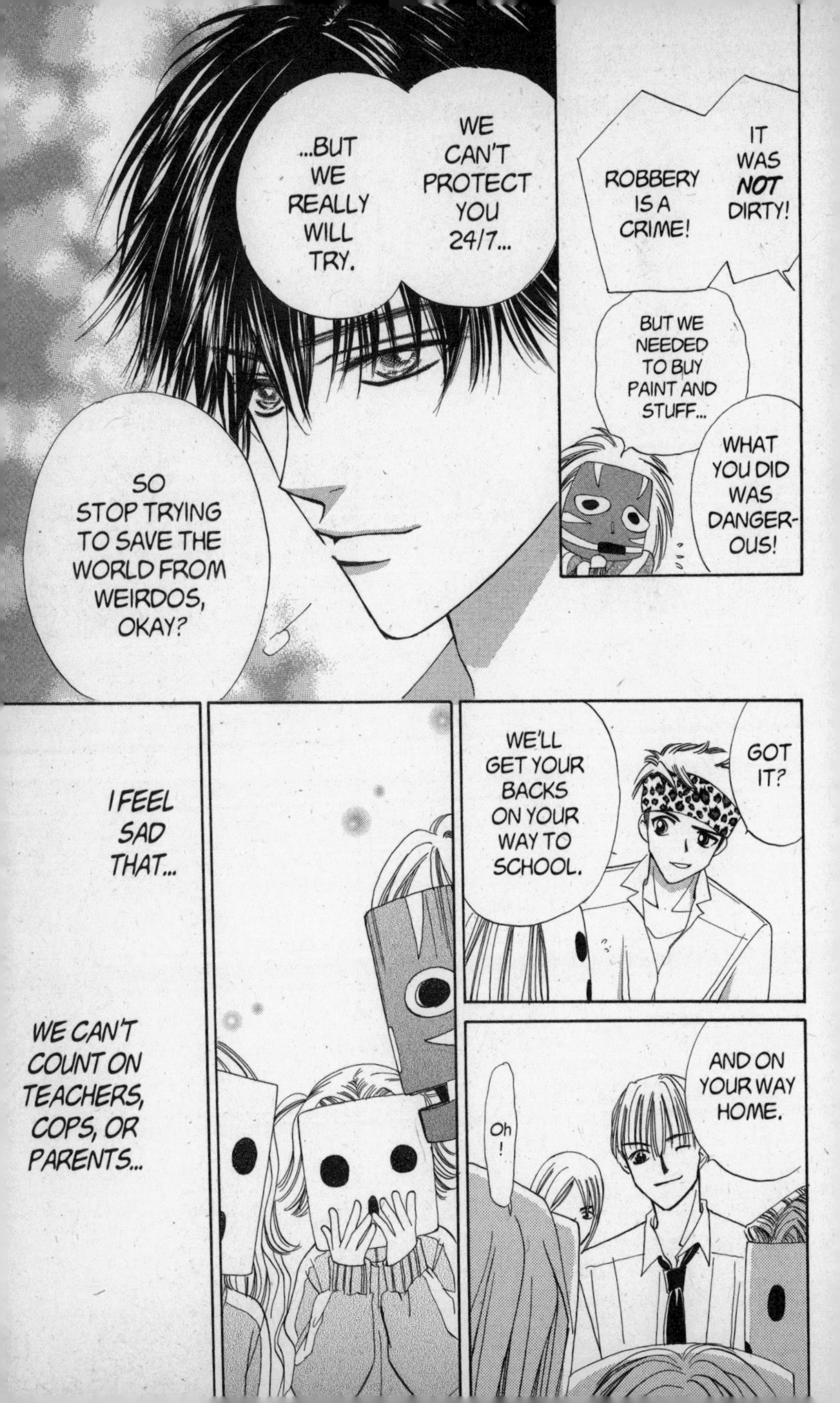
IT WAS NOT DIRTY!
ROBBERY IS A CRIME!
BUT WE NEEDED TO BUY PAINT AND STUFF...
WHAT YOU DID WAS DANGEROUS!
WE CAN'T PROTECT YOU 24/7...
...BUT WE REALLY WILL TRY.
SO STOP TRYING TO SAVE THE WORLD FROM WEIRDOS, OKAY?
GOT IT?
WE'LL GET YOUR BACKS ON YOUR WAY TO SCHOOL.
AND ON YOUR WAY HOME.
Oh!
I FEEL SAD THAT...
WE CAN'T COUNT ON TEACHERS, COPS, OR PARENTS...

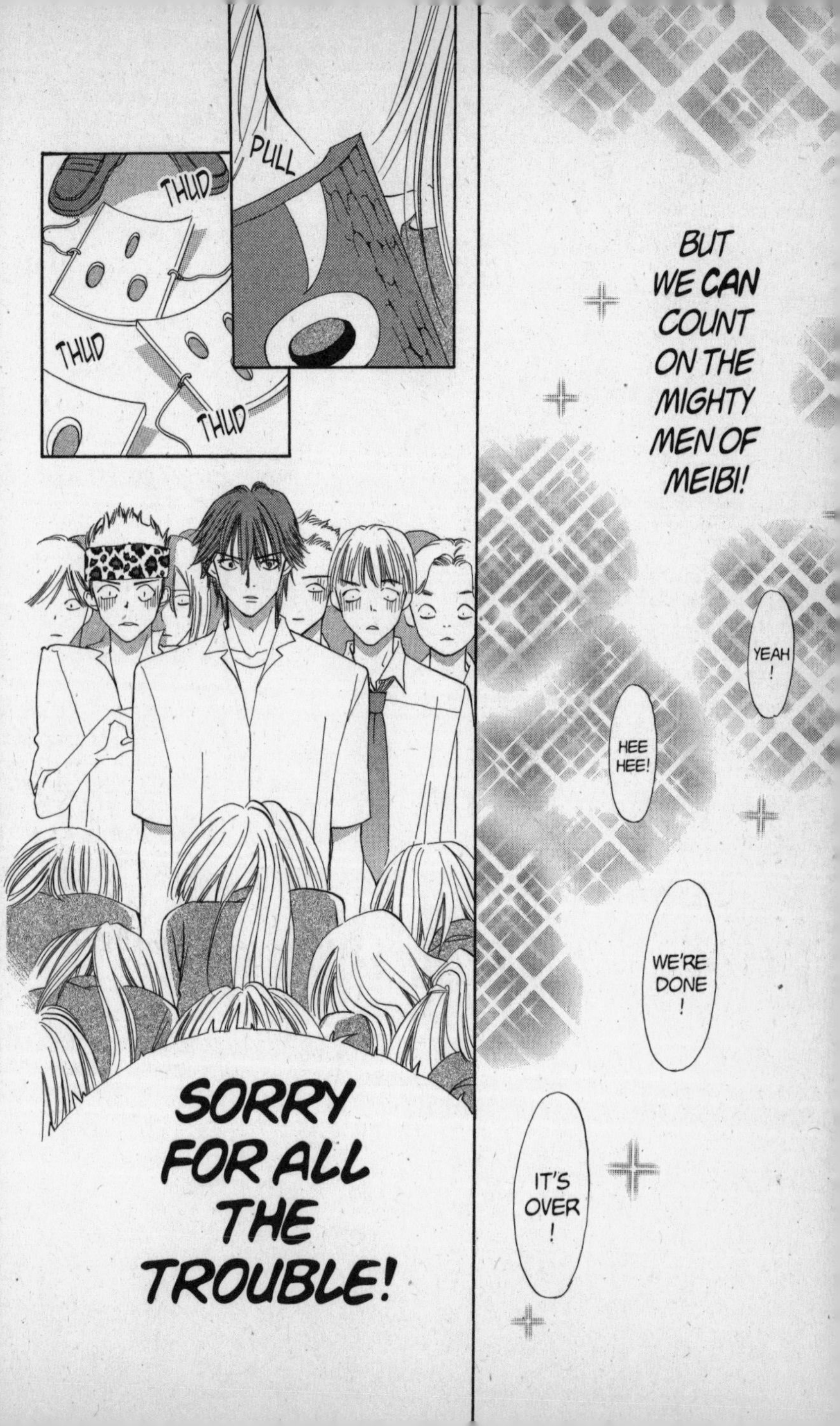
BUT WE CAN COUNT ON THE MIGHTY MEN OF MEIBI!
YEAH!
HEE HEE!
WE'RE DONE!
IT'S OVER!
PULL
THUD
THUD
THUD
SORRY FOR ALL THE TROUBLE!

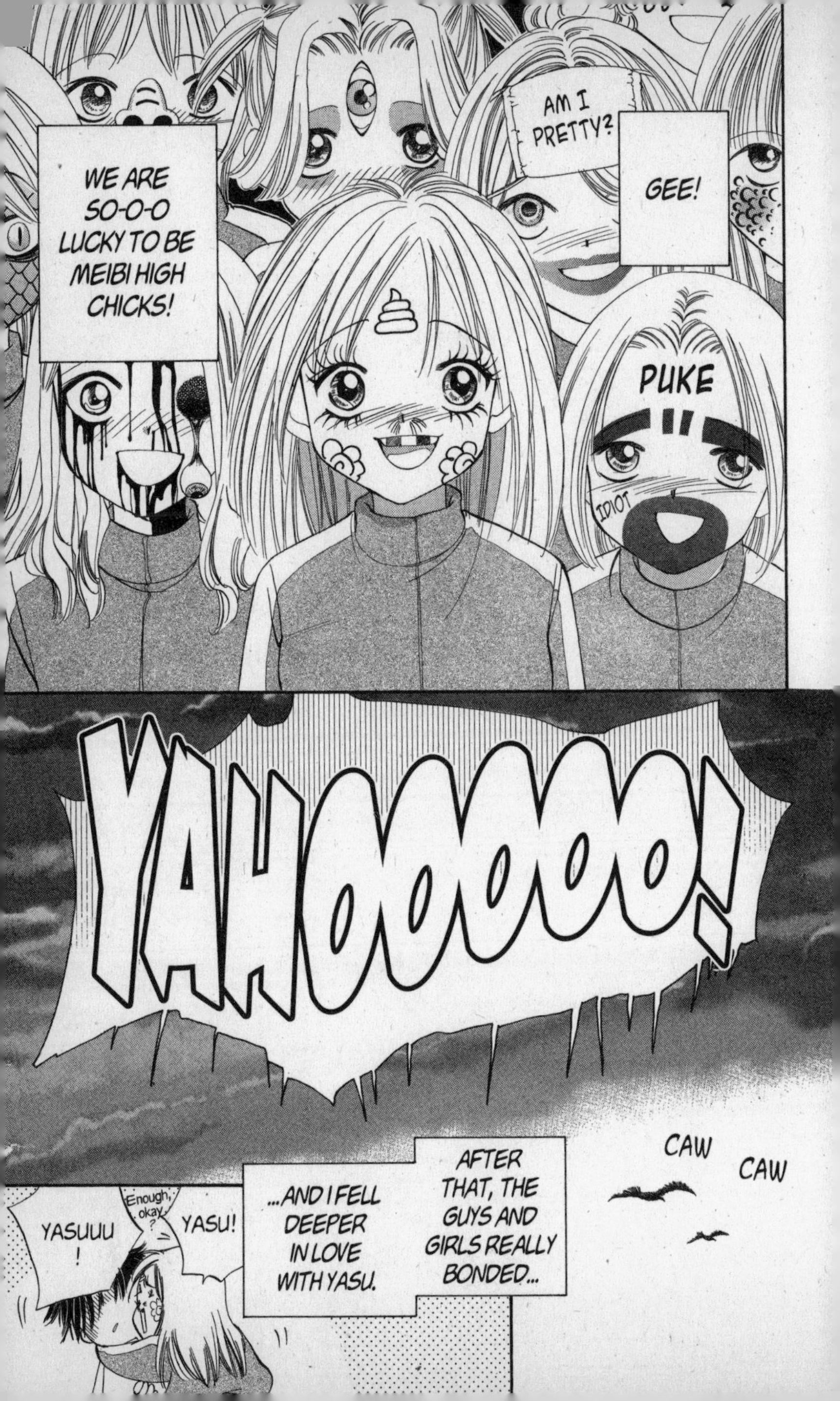
AM I PRETTY?
GEE!
PUKE
IDIOT
WE ARE SO-O-O LUCKY TO BE MEIBI HIGH CHICKS!
YAHOOOOO!
CAW
CAW
AFTER THAT, THE GUYS AND GIRLS REALLY BONDED...
...AND I FELL DEEPER IN LOVE WITH YASU.
YASU!
Enough, okay?
YASUUU!

HAPPY
HUST
HIGH

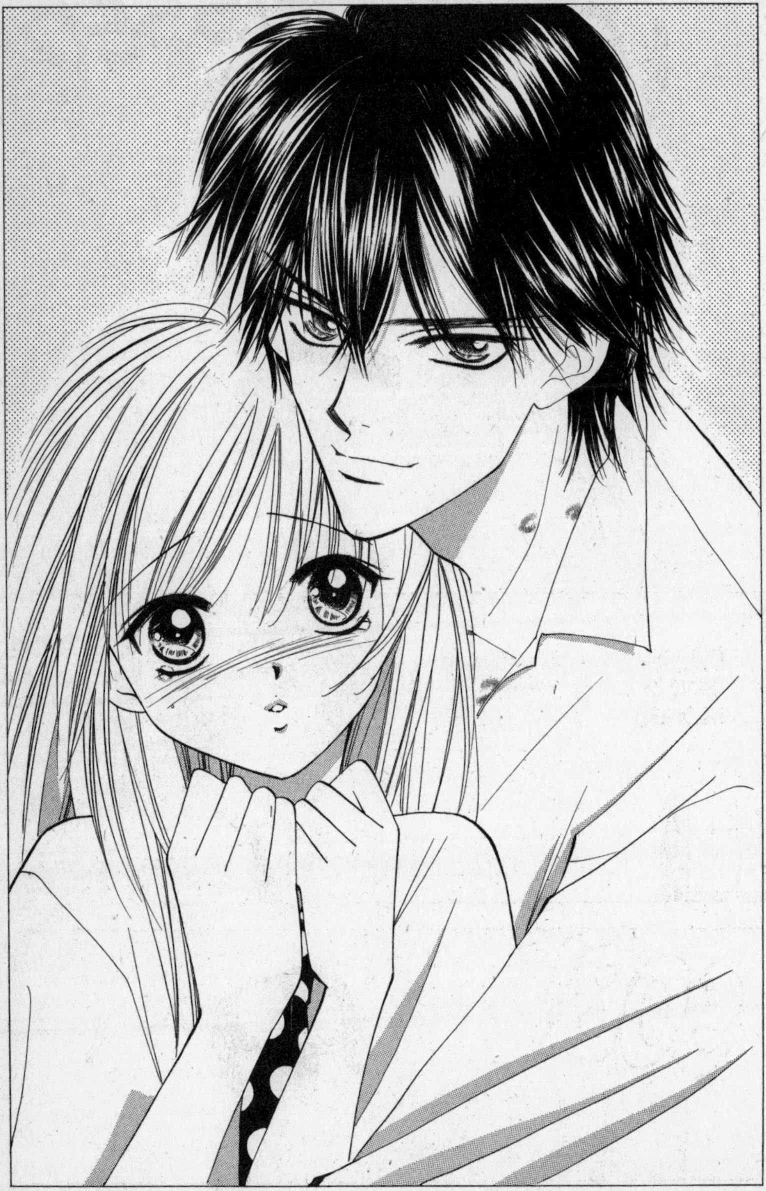

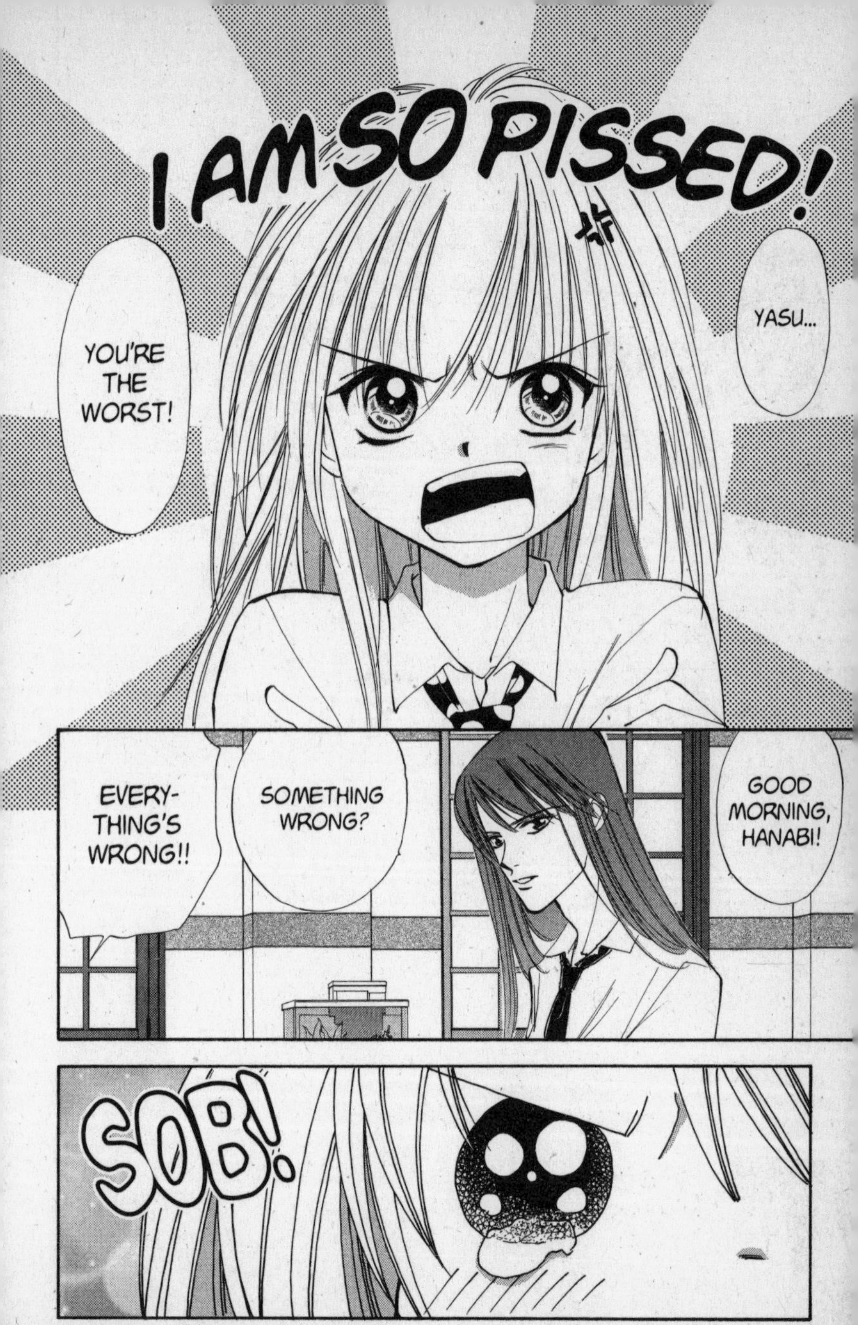
I AM SO PISSED!
YASU...
YOU'RE THE WORST!
GOOD MORNING, HANABI!
SOMETHING WRONG?
EVERY-THING'S WRONG!!
SOB!

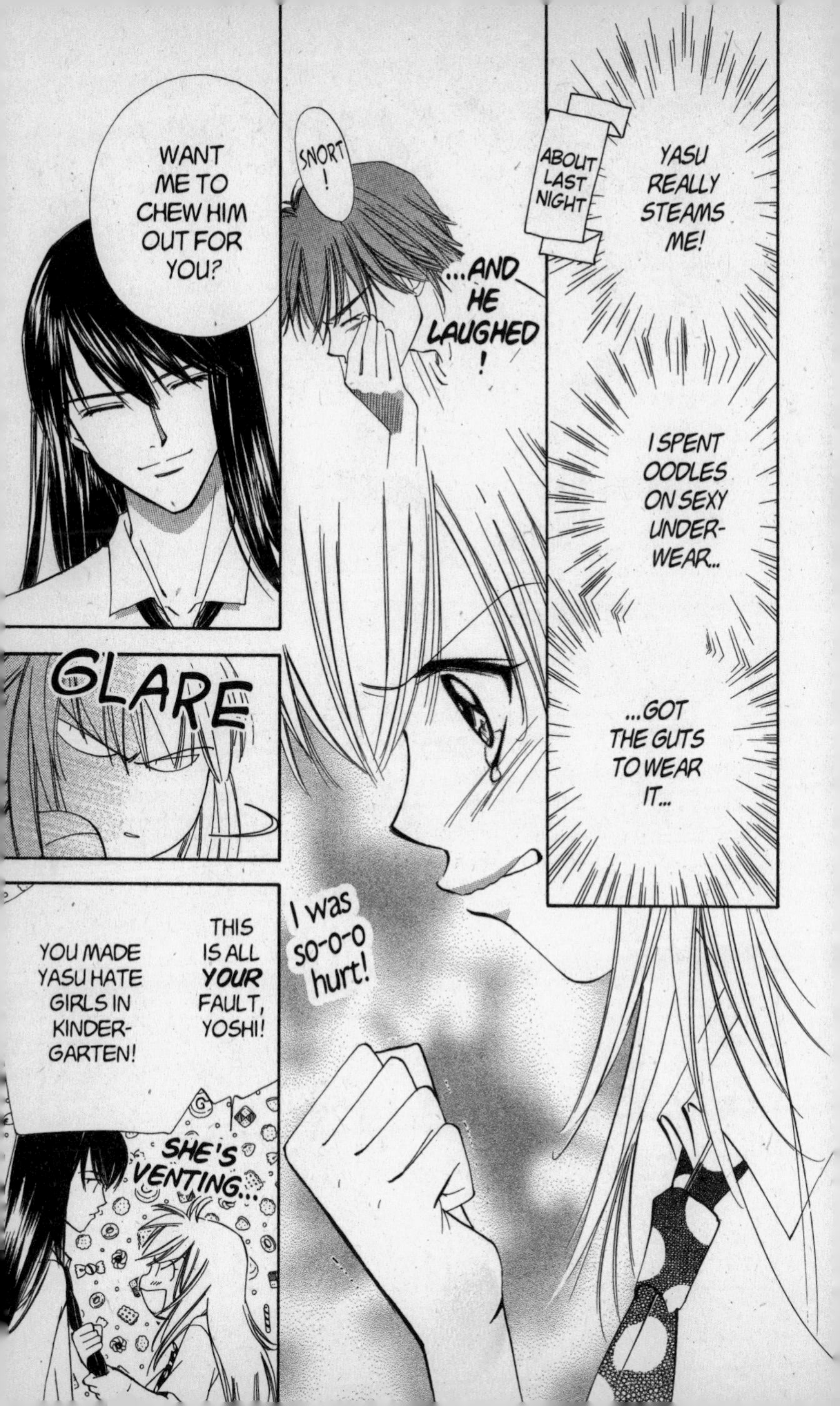

ABOUT LAST NIGHT
YASU REALLY STEAMS ME!
I SPENT OODLES ON SEXY UNDER-WEAR...
...GOT THE GUTS TO WEAR IT...
SNORT!
...AND HE LAUGHED!
I was so-o-o hurt!
WANT ME TO CHEW HIM OUT FOR YOU?
GLARE
THIS IS ALL **YOUR** FAULT, YOSHI!
YOU MADE YASU HATE GIRLS IN KINDER-GARTEN!
SHE'S VENTING...

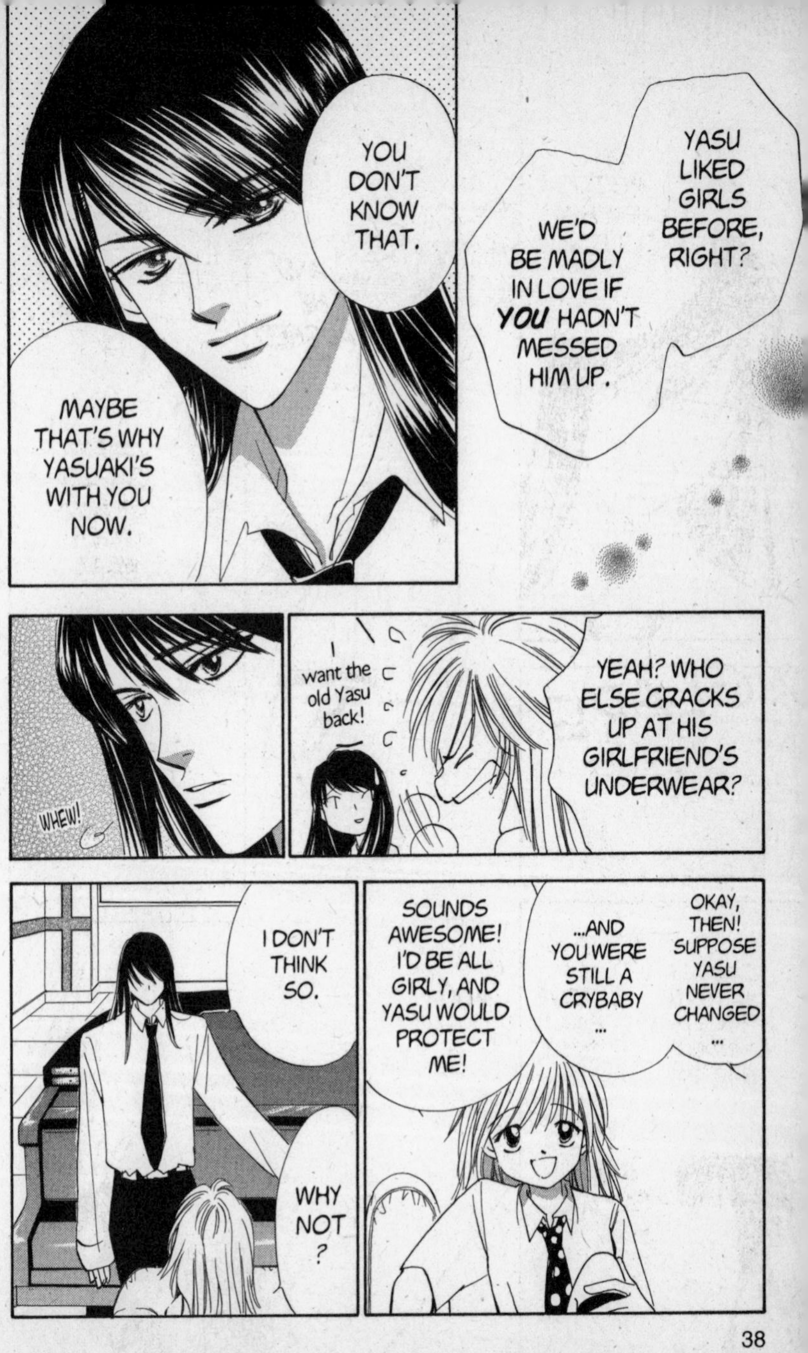
YASU LIKED GIRLS BEFORE, RIGHT?
WE'D BE MADLY IN LOVE IF *YOU* HADN'T MESSED HIM UP.
YOU DON'T KNOW THAT.
MAYBE THAT'S WHY YASUAKI'S WITH YOU NOW.
YEAH? WHO ELSE CRACKS UP AT HIS GIRLFRIEND'S UNDERWEAR?
I want the old Yasu back!
WHEW!
OKAY, THEN! SUPPOSE YASU NEVER CHANGED...
...AND YOU WERE STILL A CRYBABY...
SOUNDS AWESOME! I'D BE ALL GIRLY, AND YASU WOULD PROTECT ME!
I DON'T THINK SO.
WHY NOT?

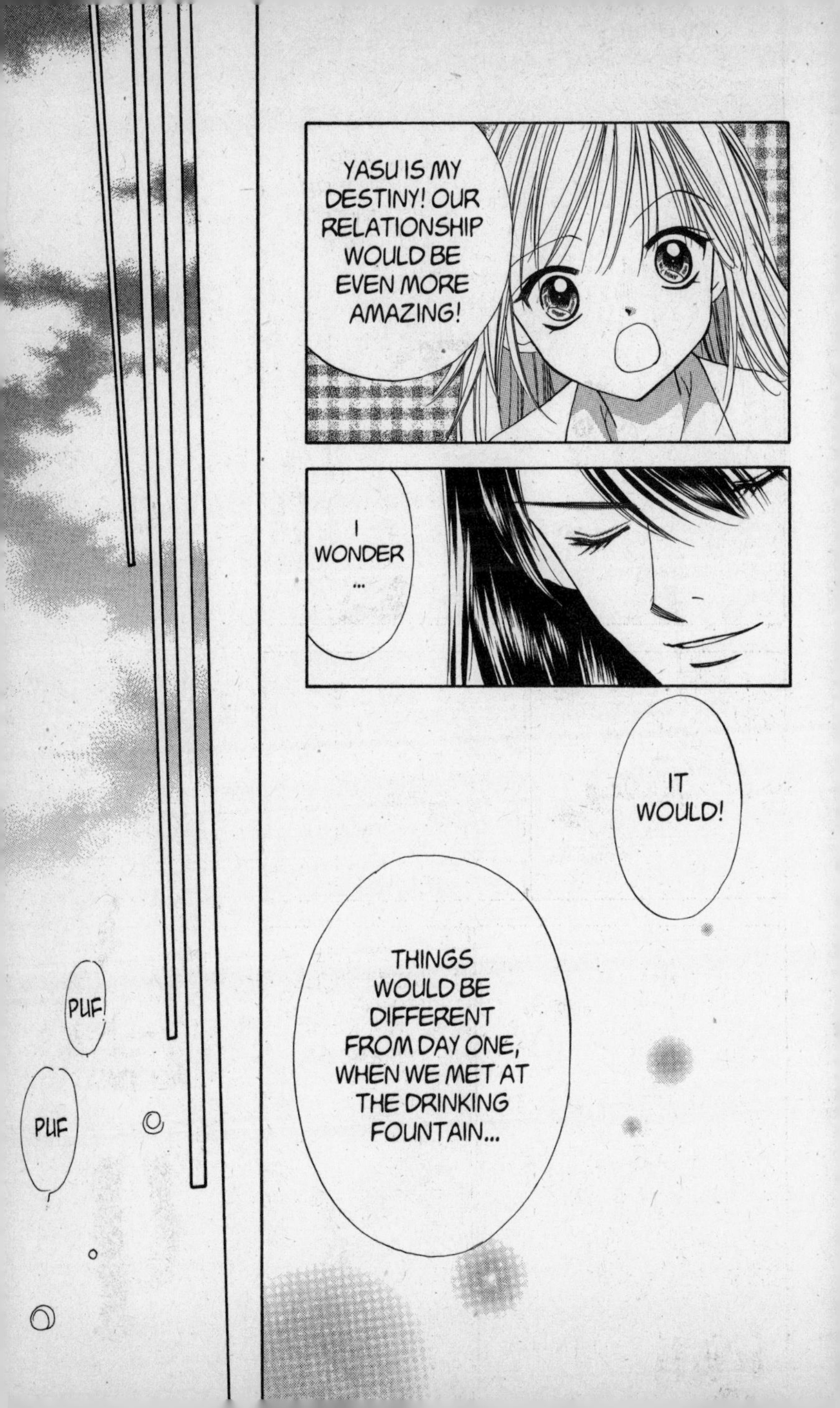
YASU IS MY DESTINY! OUR RELATIONSHIP WOULD BE EVEN MORE AMAZING!
I WONDER ...
IT WOULD!
THINGS WOULD BE DIFFERENT FROM DAY ONE, WHEN WE MET AT THE DRINKING FOUNTAIN...
PUF
PUF

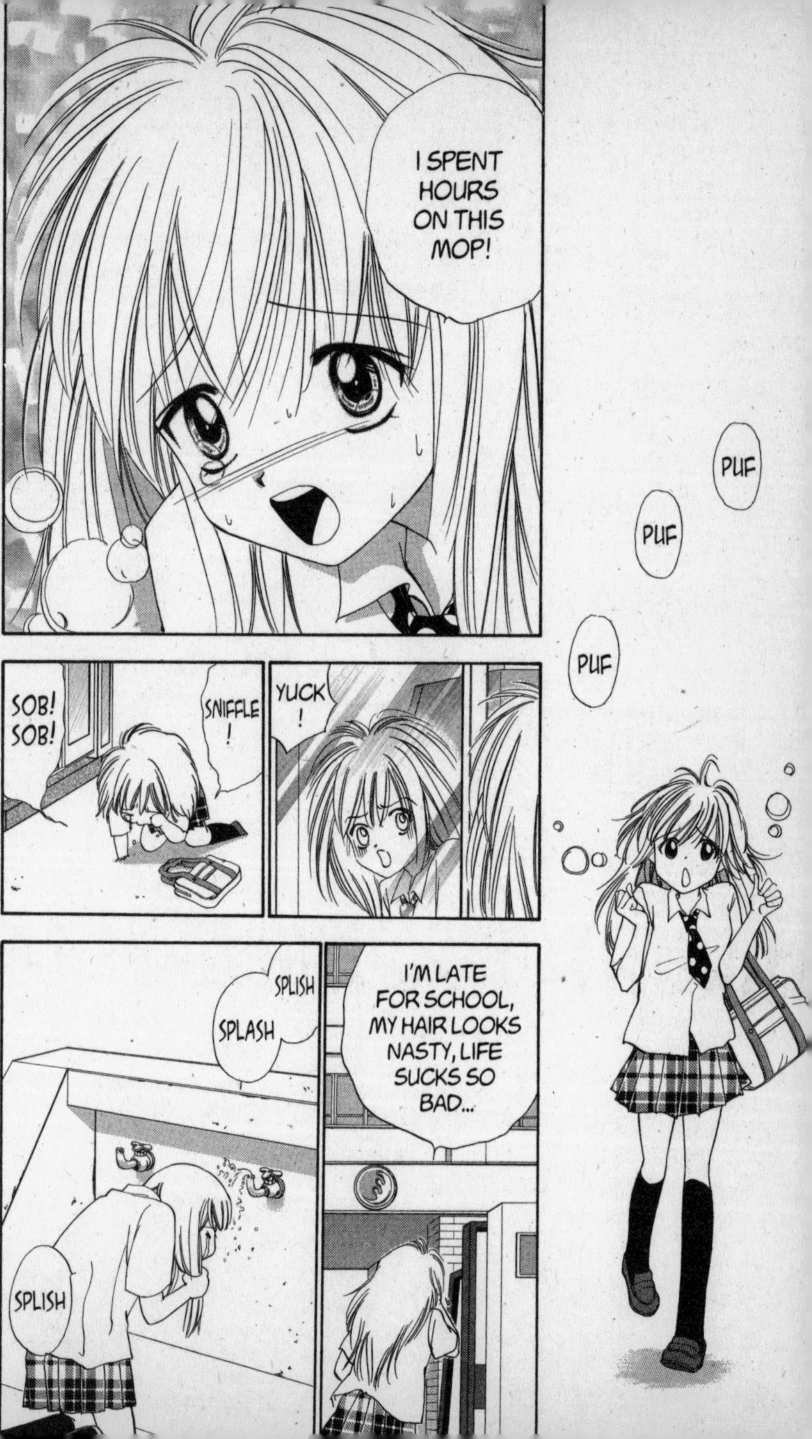
PUF
PUF
PUF
I SPENT HOURS ON THIS MOP!
YUCK!
SNIFFLE!
SOB! SOB!
I'M LATE FOR SCHOOL, MY HAIR LOOKS NASTY, LIFE SUCKS SO BAD...
SPLISH
SPLASH
SPLISH

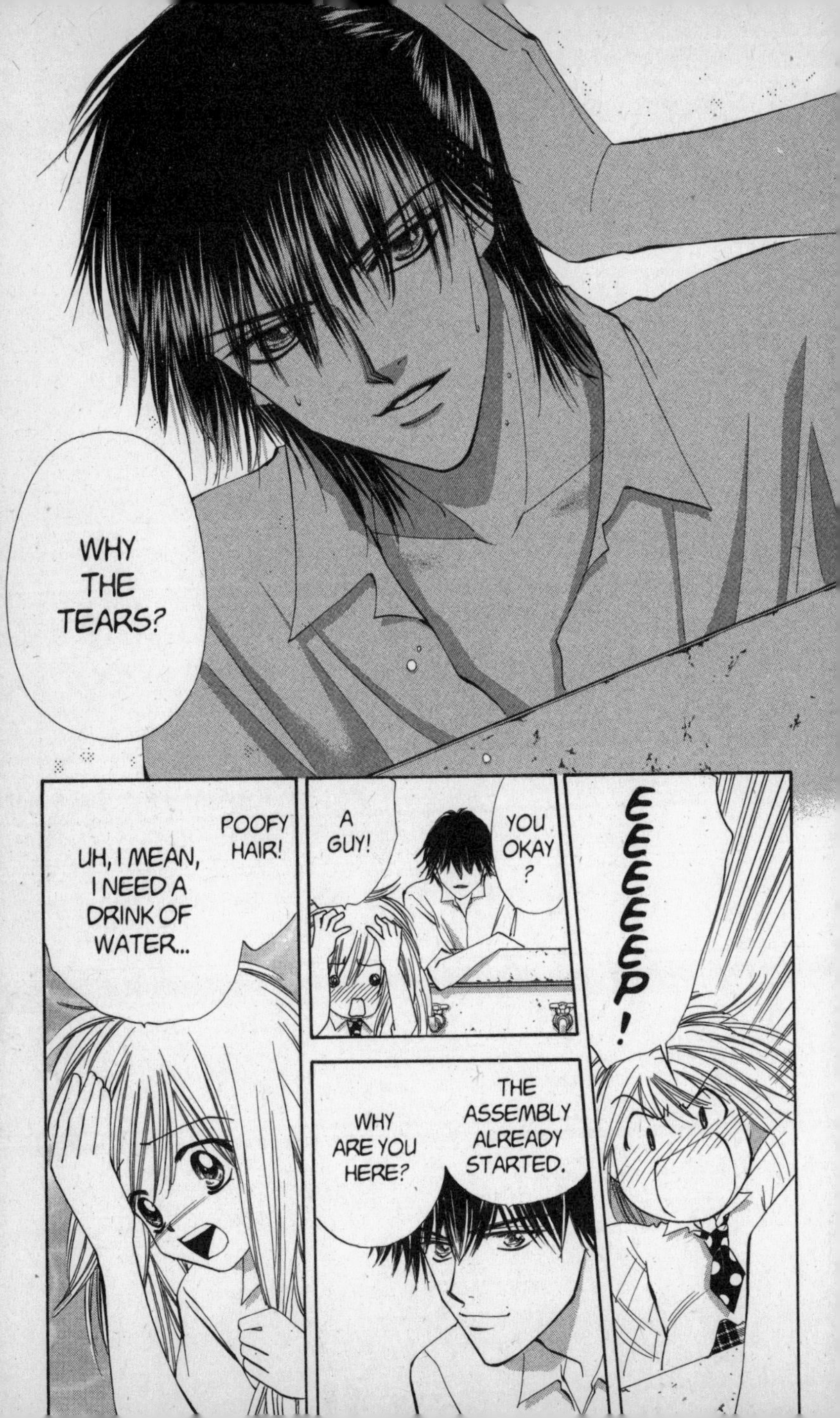
WHY THE TEARS?
EEEEEP!
YOU OKAY?
A GUY!
THE ASSEMBLY ALREADY STARTED.
WHY ARE YOU HERE?
POOFY HAIR!
UH, I MEAN, I NEED A DRINK OF WATER...

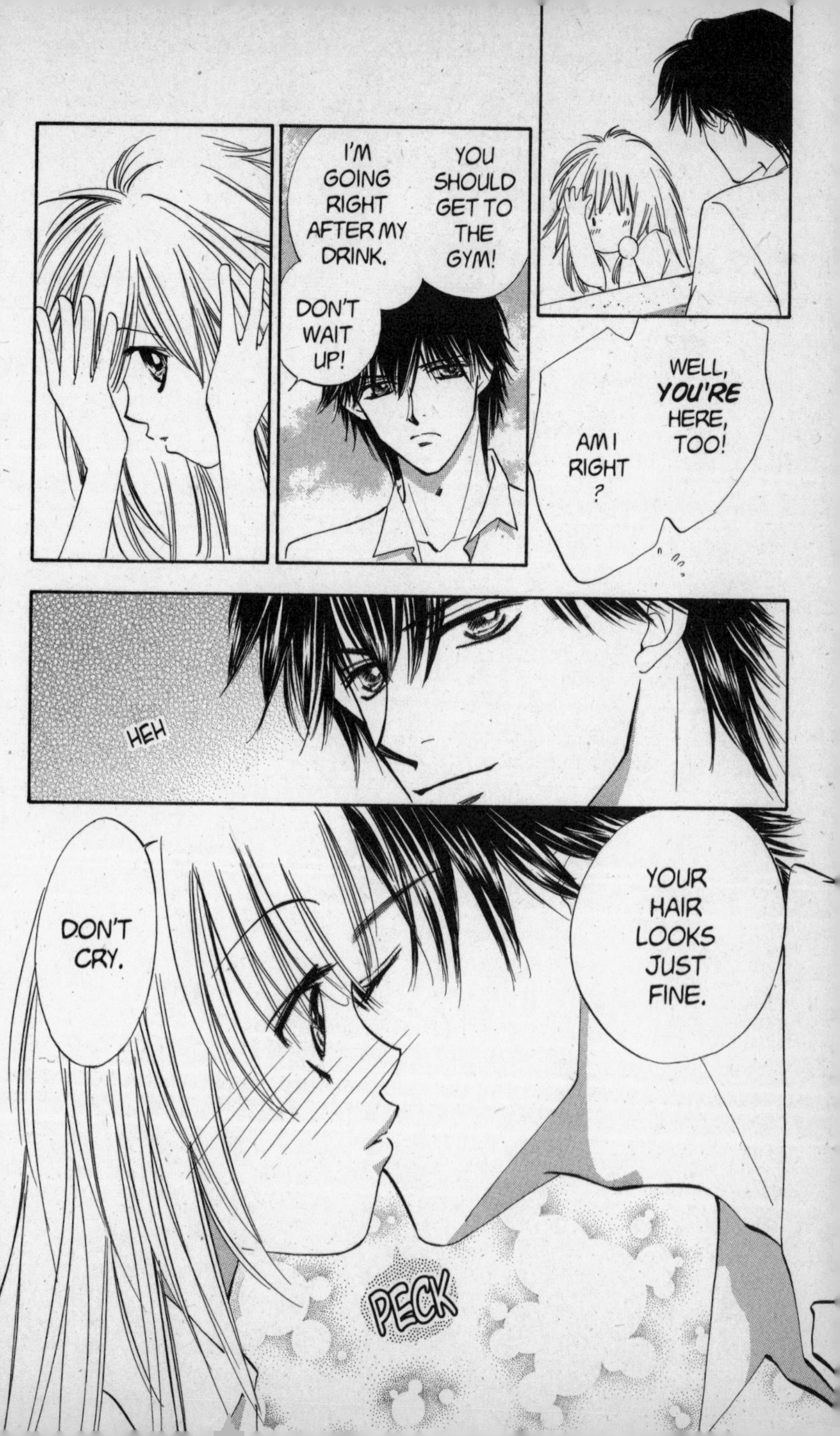
WELL, YOU'RE HERE, TOO!
AM I RIGHT?
YOU SHOULD GET TO THE GYM!
I'M GOING RIGHT AFTER MY DRINK.
DON'T WAIT UP!
HEH
YOUR HAIR LOOKS JUST FINE.
DON'T CRY.
PECK

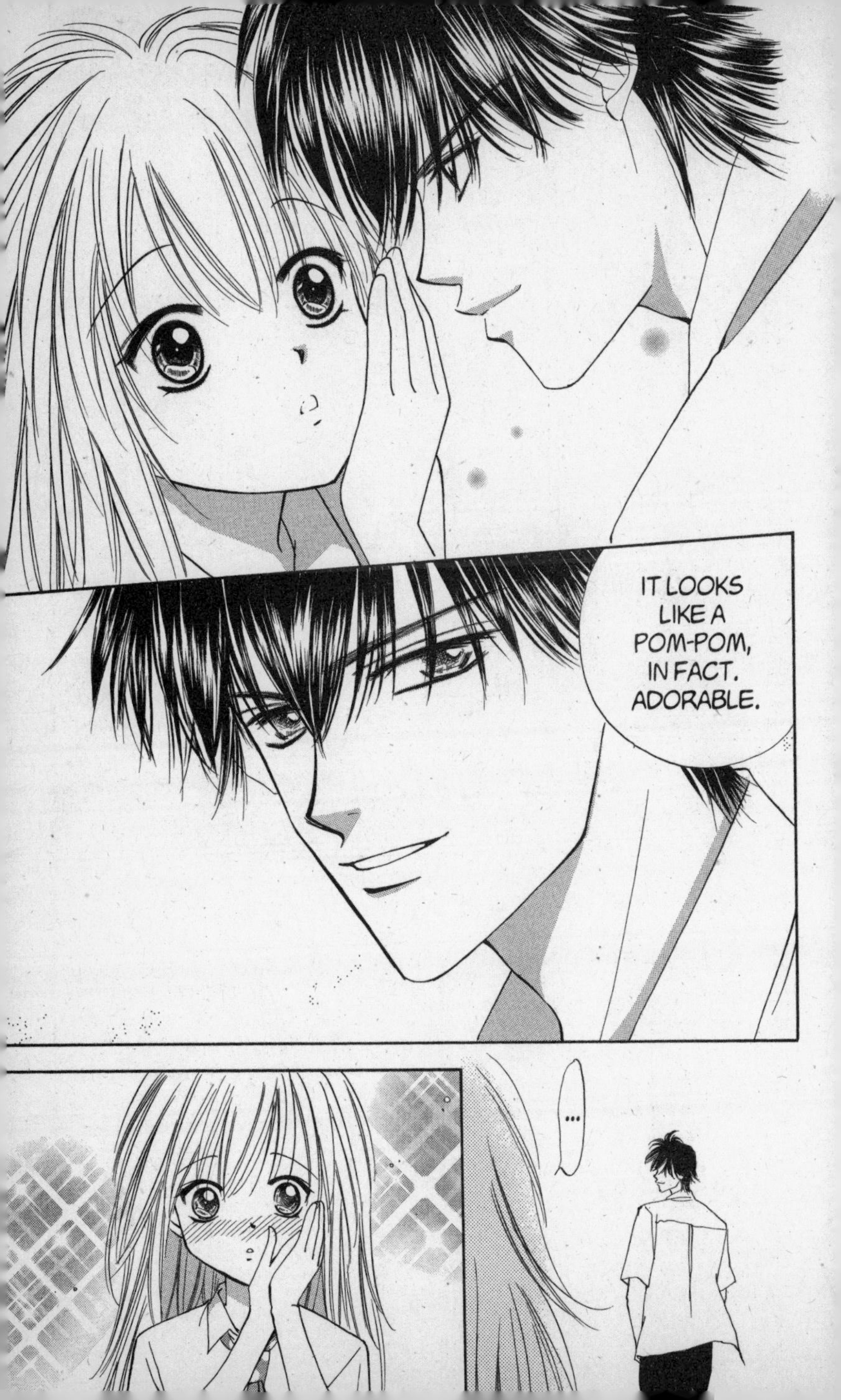
IT LOOKS LIKE A POM-POM, IN FACT. ADORABLE.
...

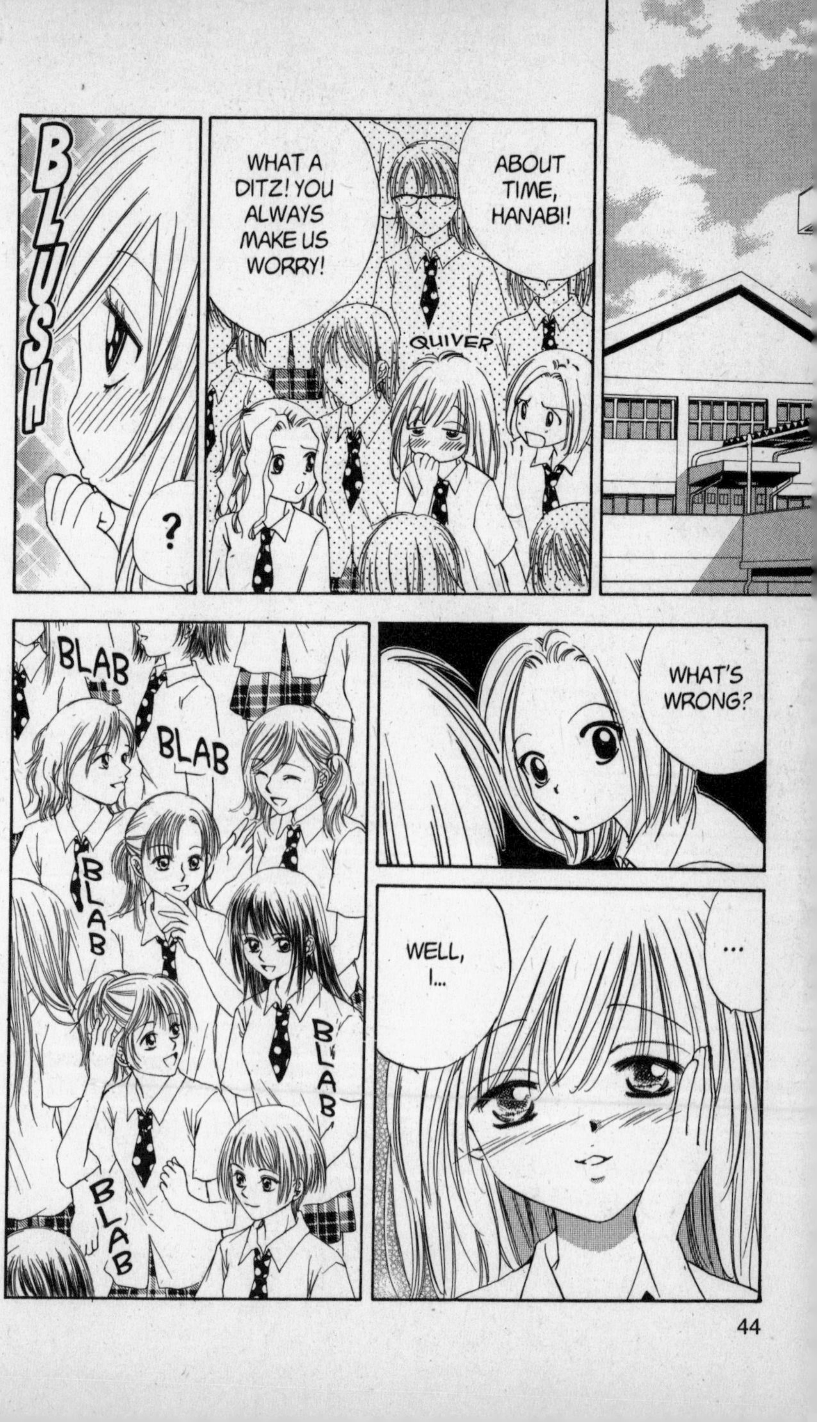
ABOUT TIME, HANABI!
WHAT A DITZ! YOU ALWAYS MAKE US WORRY!
QUIVER
BLUSH
?
WHAT'S WRONG?
...
WELL, I...
BLAB
BLAB
BLAB
BLAB
BLAB

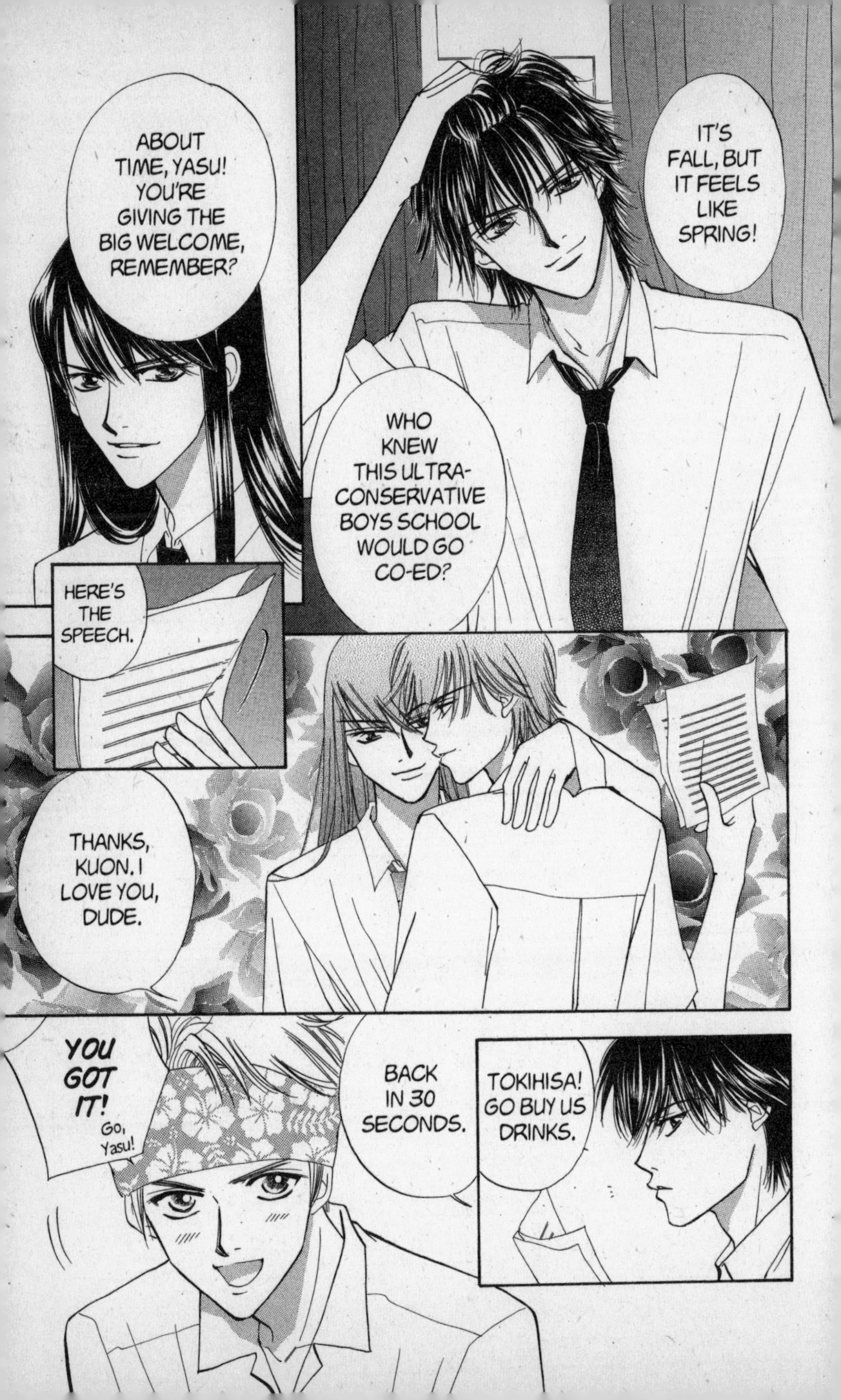
IT'S FALL, BUT IT FEELS LIKE SPRING!
WHO KNEW THIS ULTRA-CONSERVATIVE BOYS SCHOOL WOULD GO CO-ED?
ABOUT TIME, YASU! YOU'RE GIVING THE BIG WELCOME, REMEMBER?
HERE'S THE SPEECH.
THANKS, KUON. I LOVE YOU, DUDE.
TOKIHISA! GO BUY US DRINKS.
BACK IN 30 SECONDS.
YOU GOT IT!
Go, Yasu!

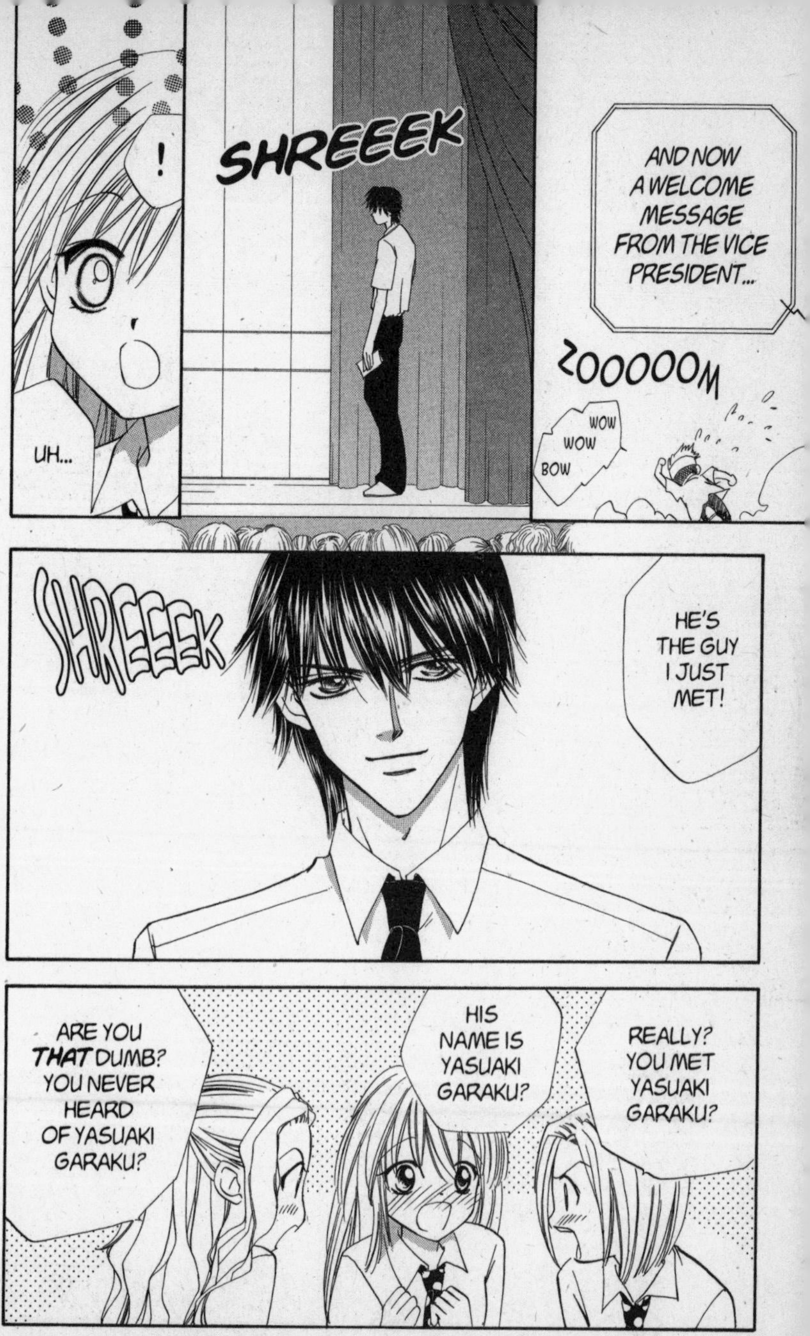
AND NOW A WELCOME MESSAGE FROM THE VICE PRESIDENT...
ZOOOOOM
WOW WOW BOW
SHREEEK
!
UH...
HE'S THE GUY I JUST MET!
SHREEEK
REALLY? YOU MET YASUAKI GARAKU?
HIS NAME IS YASUAKI GARAKU?
ARE YOU THAT DUMB? YOU NEVER HEARD OF YASUAKI GARAKU?

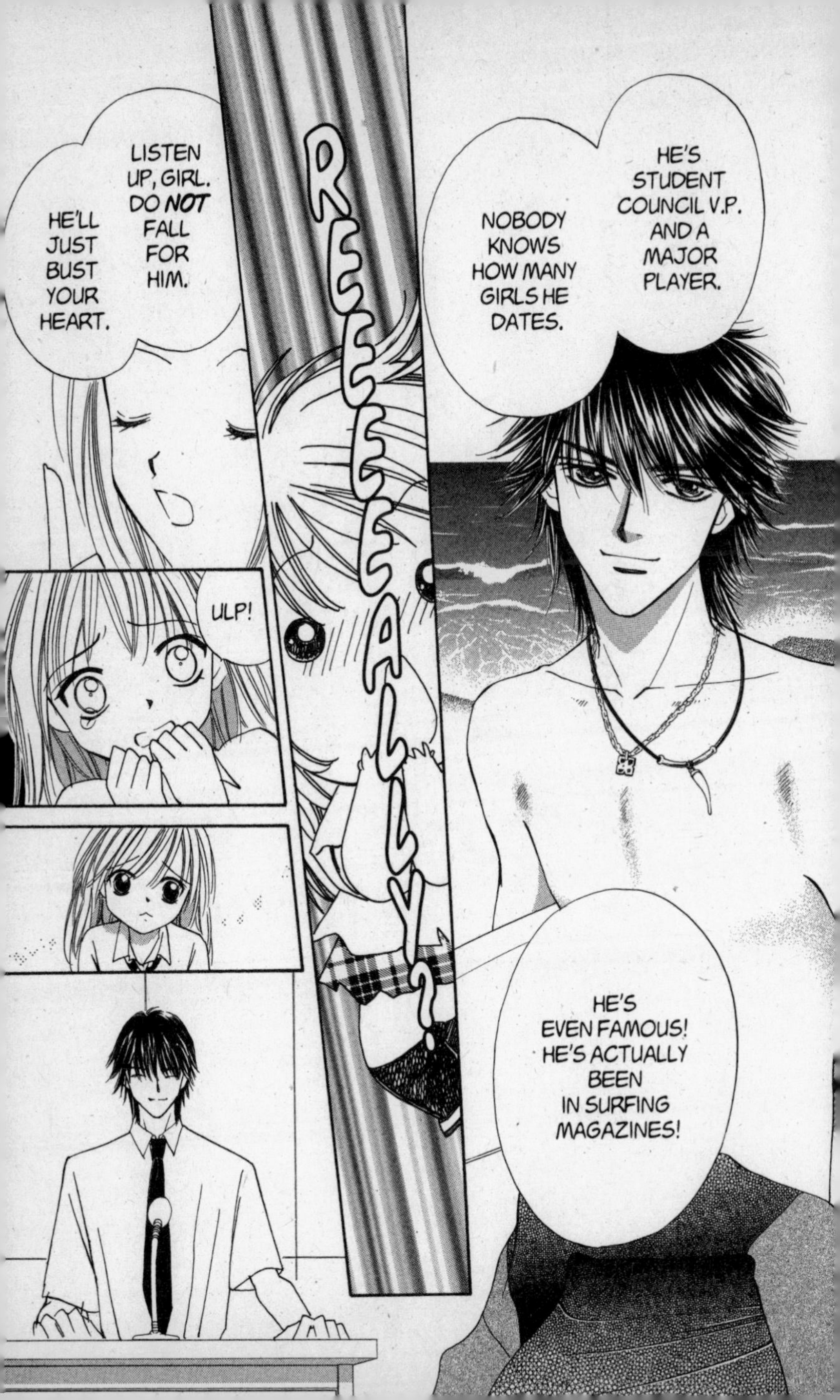
HE'S STUDENT COUNCIL V.P. AND A MAJOR PLAYER.
NOBODY KNOWS HOW MANY GIRLS HE DATES.
REEEEALLY?
LISTEN UP, GIRL. DO NOT FALL FOR HIM.
HE'LL JUST BUST YOUR HEART.
ULP!
HE'S EVEN FAMOUS! HE'S ACTUALLY BEEN IN SURFING MAGAZINES!

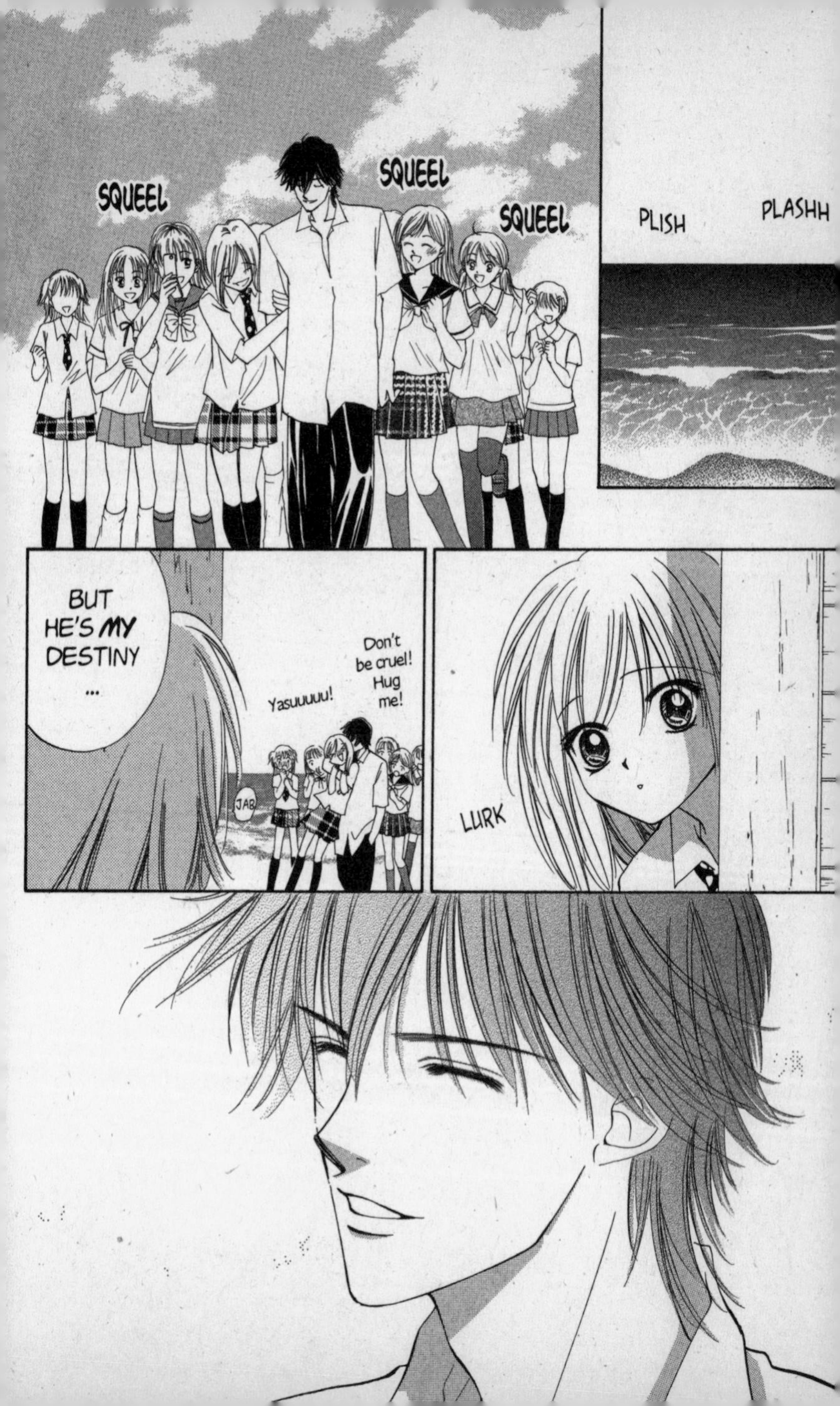

PLASHH
PLISH
SQUEEL
SQUEEL
SQUEEL
LURK
Don't be cruel! Hug me!
Yasuuuuu!
BUT HE'S MY DESTINY ...
JAB

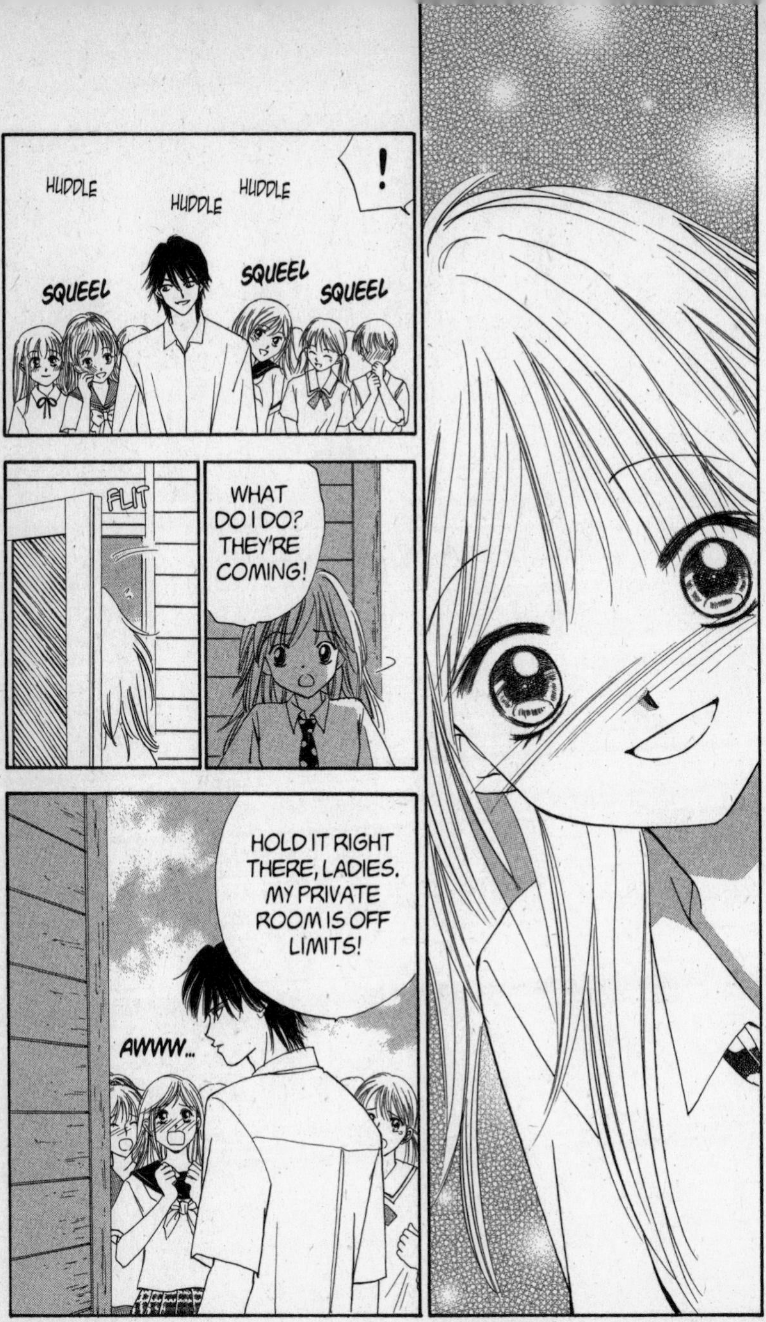
!
HUDDLE
HUDDLE
HUDDLE
SQUEEL
SQUEEL
SQUEEL
WHAT DO I DO? THEY'RE COMING!
FLIT
HOLD IT RIGHT THERE, LADIES. MY PRIVATE ROOM IS OFF LIMITS!
AWWW...

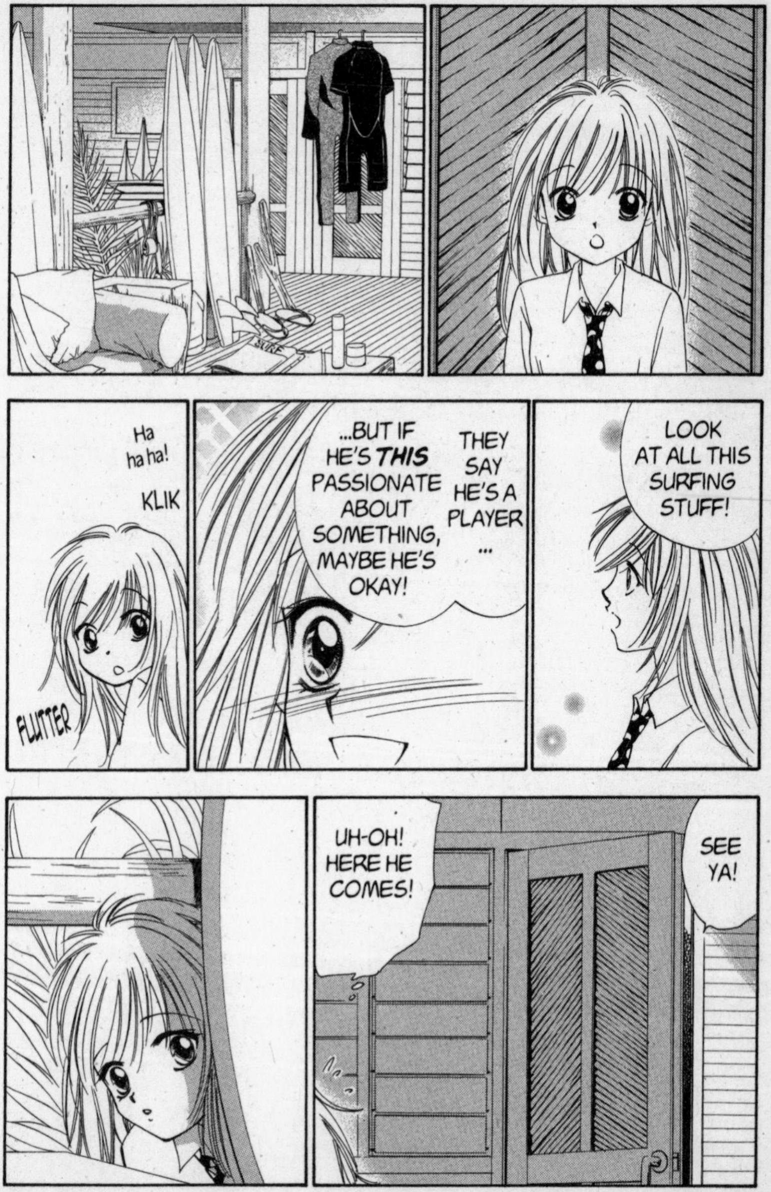
SURF
LOOK AT ALL THIS SURFING STUFF!
THEY SAY HE'S A PLAYER ...
...BUT IF HE'S **THIS** PASSIONATE ABOUT SOMETHING, MAYBE HE'S OKAY!
Ha ha ha!
KLIK
FLUTTER
SEE YA!
UH-OH! HERE HE COMES!

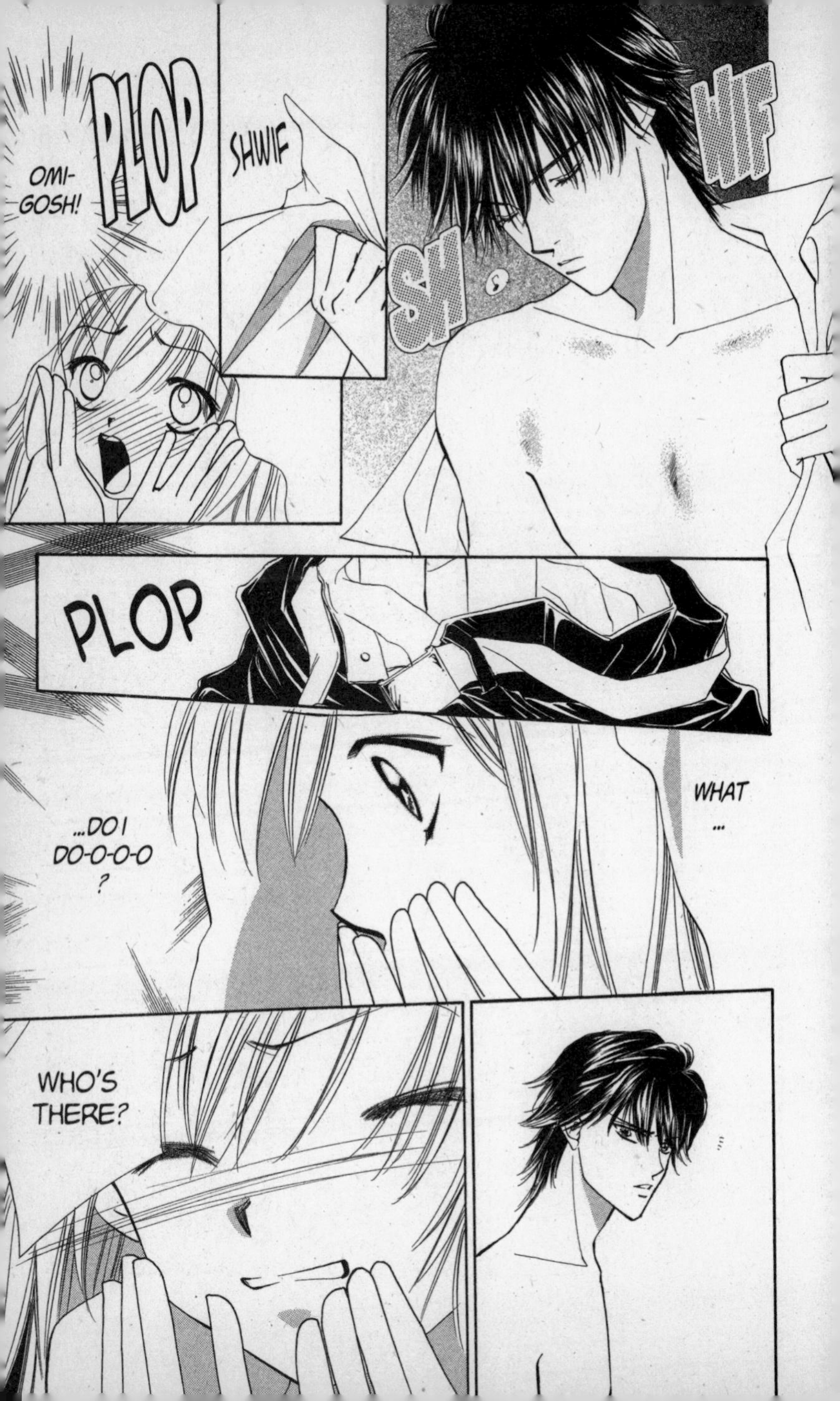
WHIF
SH
SHWIF
PLOP
OMI-GOSH!
PLOP
WHAT ...
...DO I DO-O-O-O ?
WHO'S THERE?

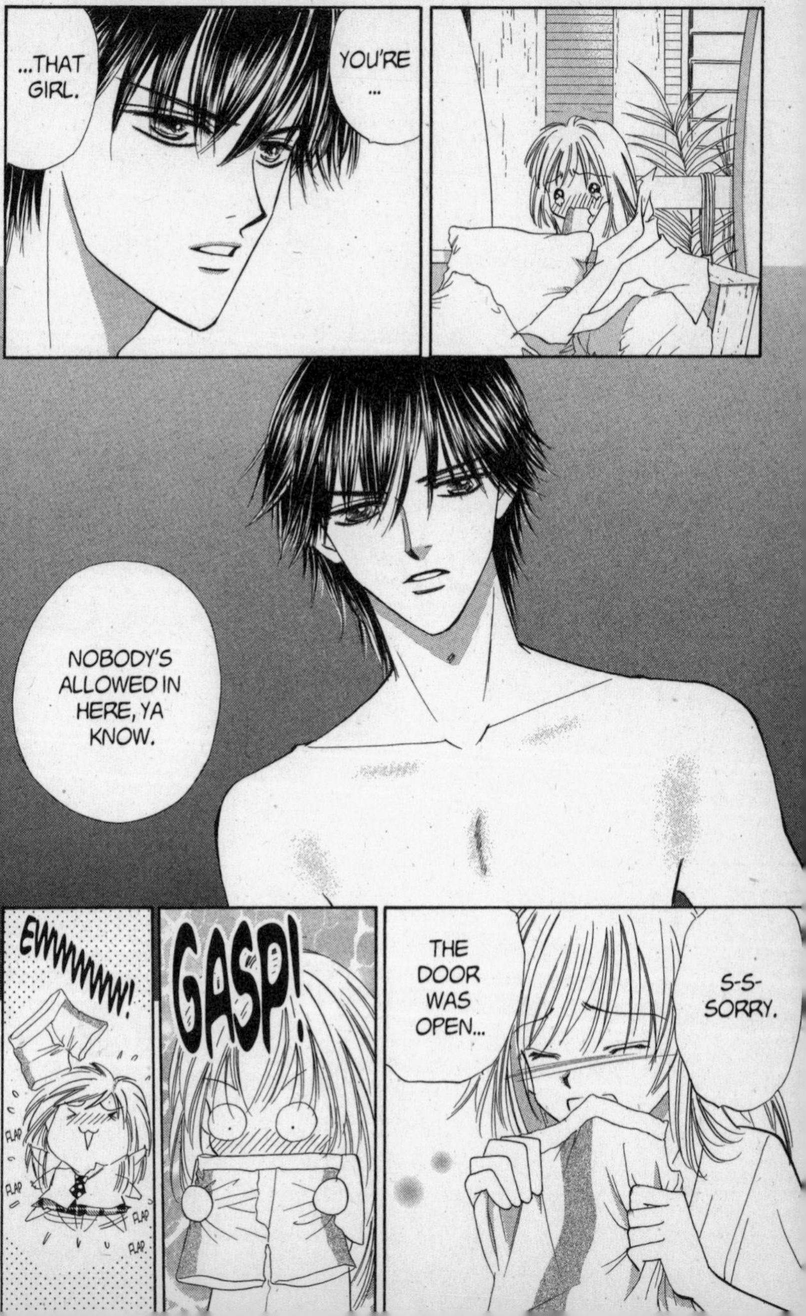
YOU'RE ...
...THAT GIRL.
NOBODY'S ALLOWED IN HERE, YA KNOW.
S-S-SORRY.
THE DOOR WAS OPEN...
GASP!
EWWWWWW!
FLAP
FLAP
FLAP
FLAP

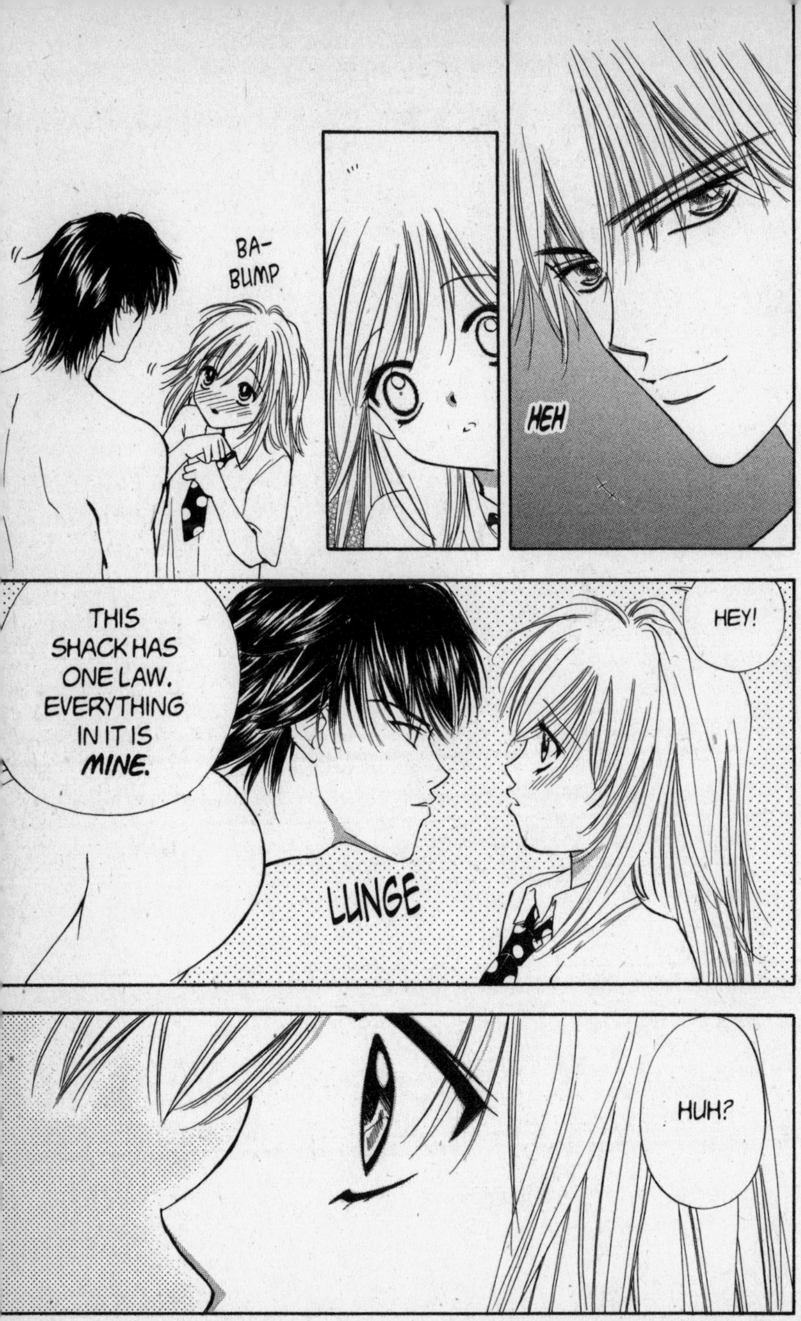
HEH
BA-BUMP
HEY!
THIS SHACK HAS ONE LAW. EVERYTHING IN IT IS *MINE.*
LUNGE
HUH?

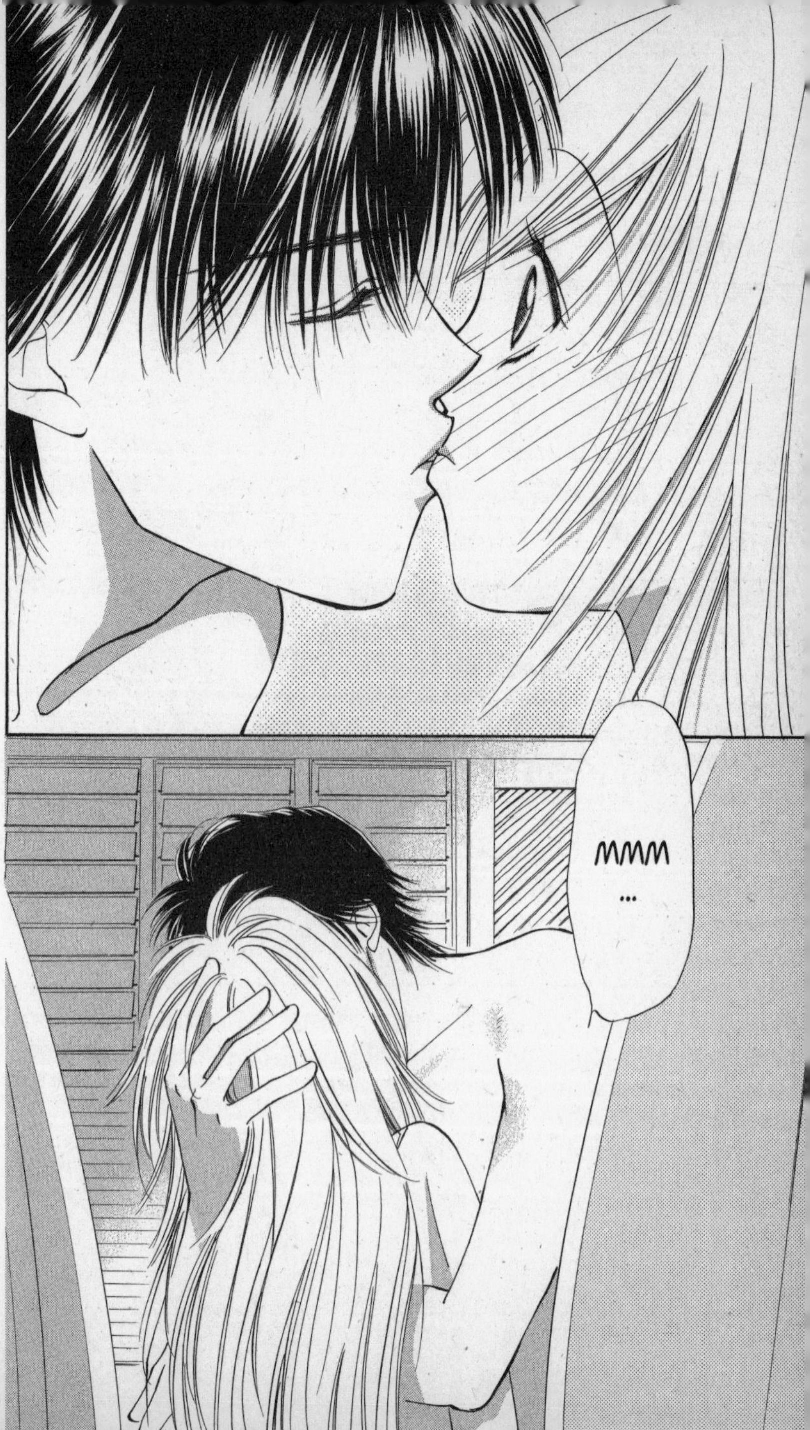
MMM
...

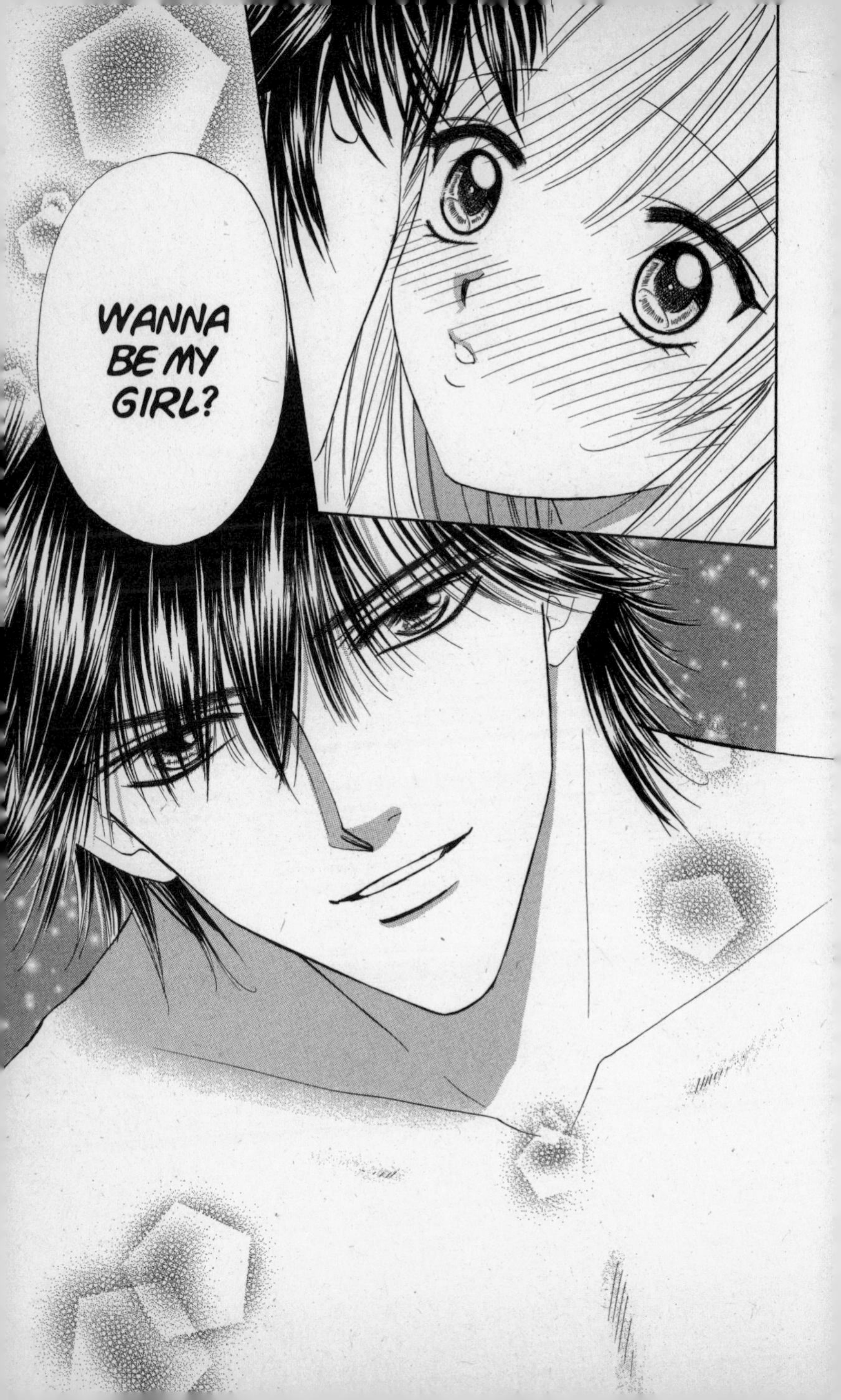
WANNA BE MY GIRL?

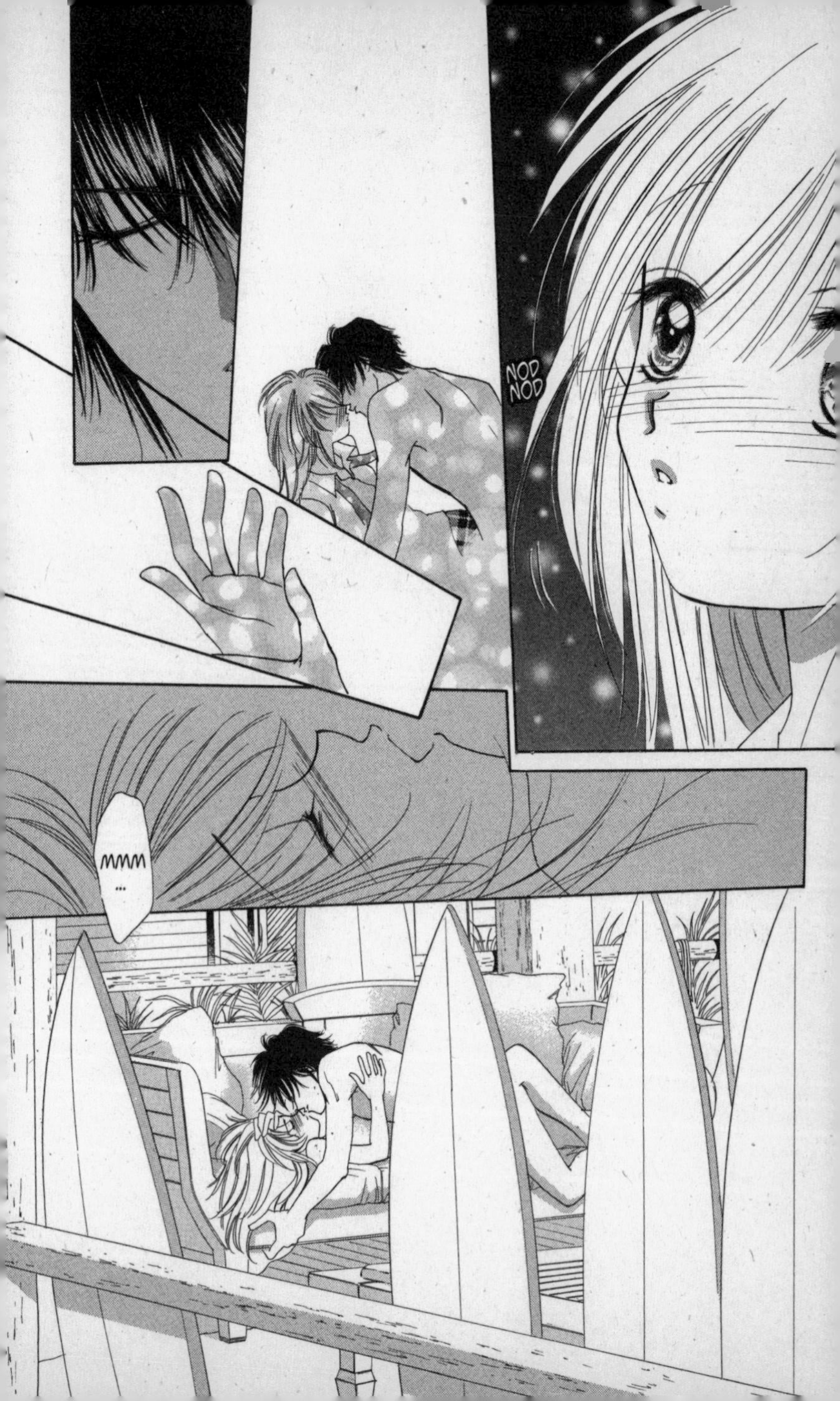
NOD NOD
MMM ...

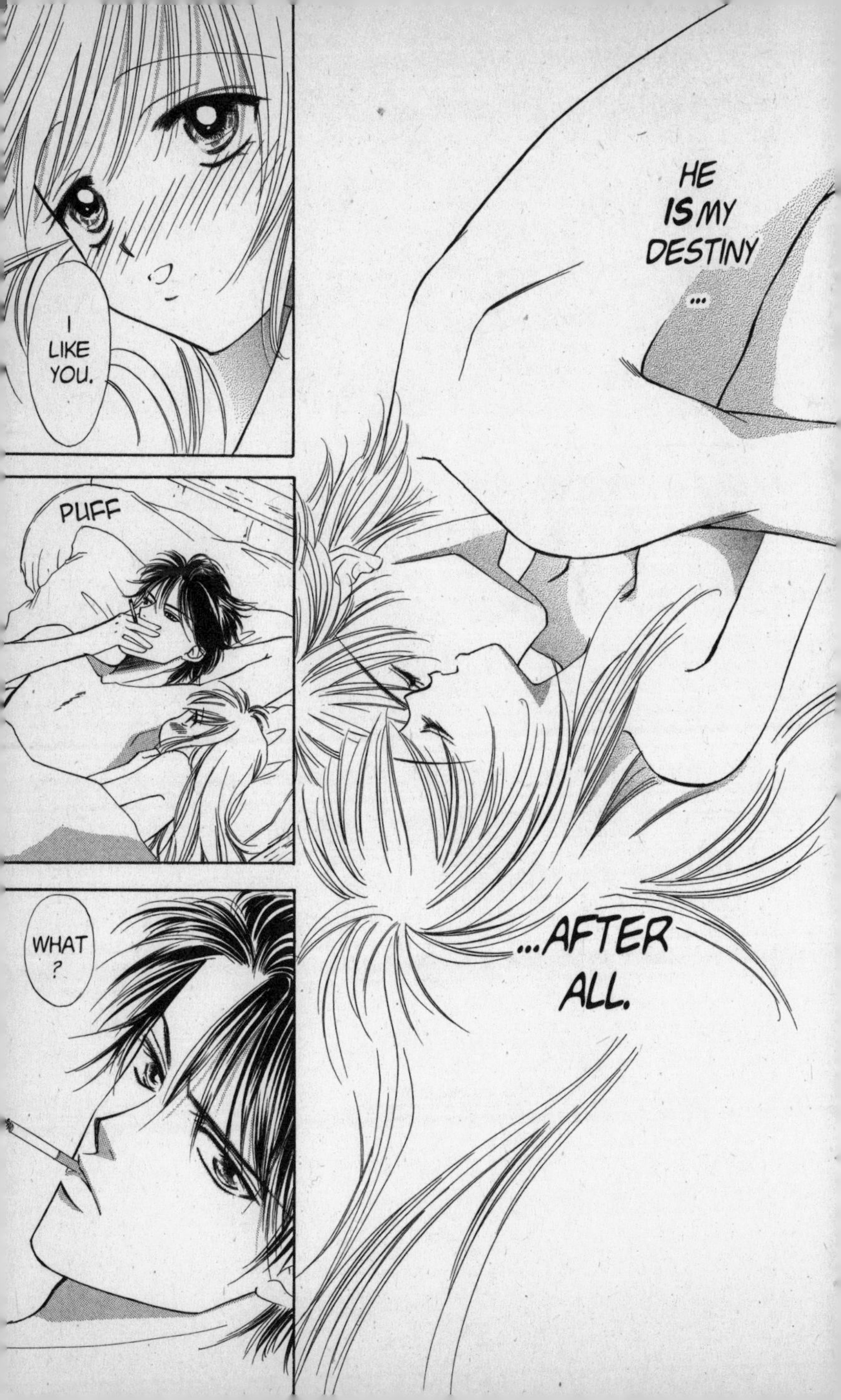
HE IS MY DESTINY ...
...AFTER ALL.
I LIKE YOU.
PUFF
WHAT ?

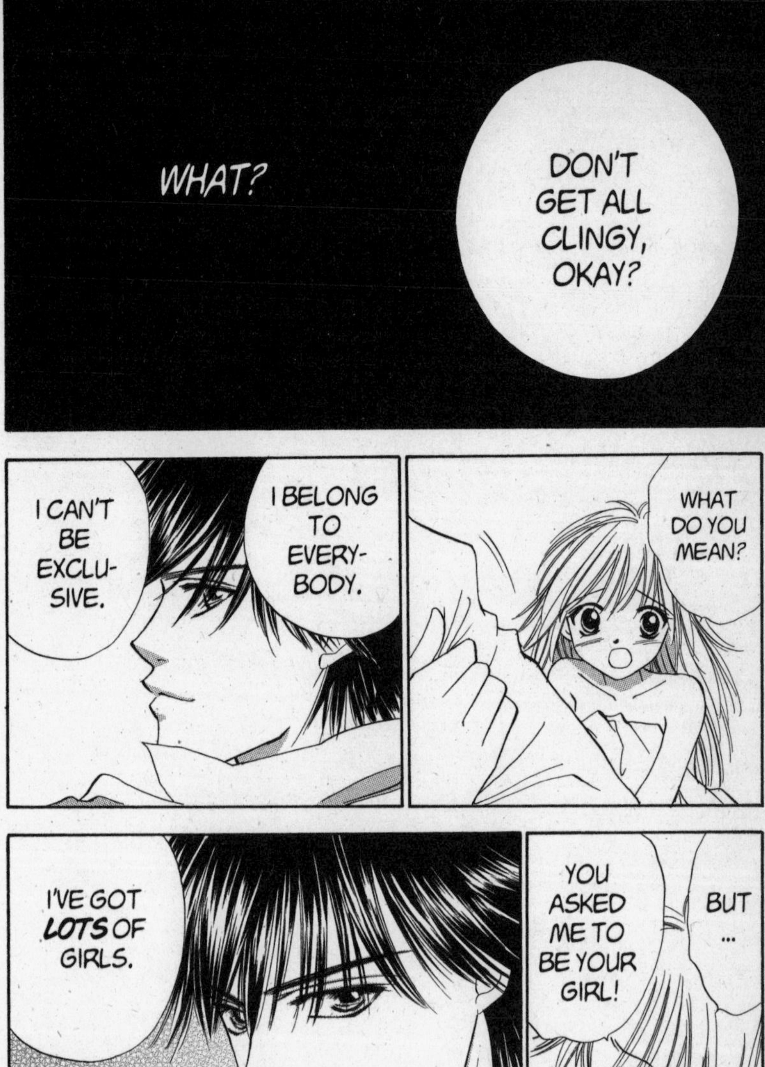
DON'T GET ALL CLINGY, OKAY?
WHAT?
WHAT DO YOU MEAN?
I BELONG TO EVERYBODY.
I CAN'T BE EXCLUSIVE.
BUT ...
YOU ASKED ME TO BE YOUR GIRL!
YEAH ...
I'VE GOT LOTS OF GIRLS.

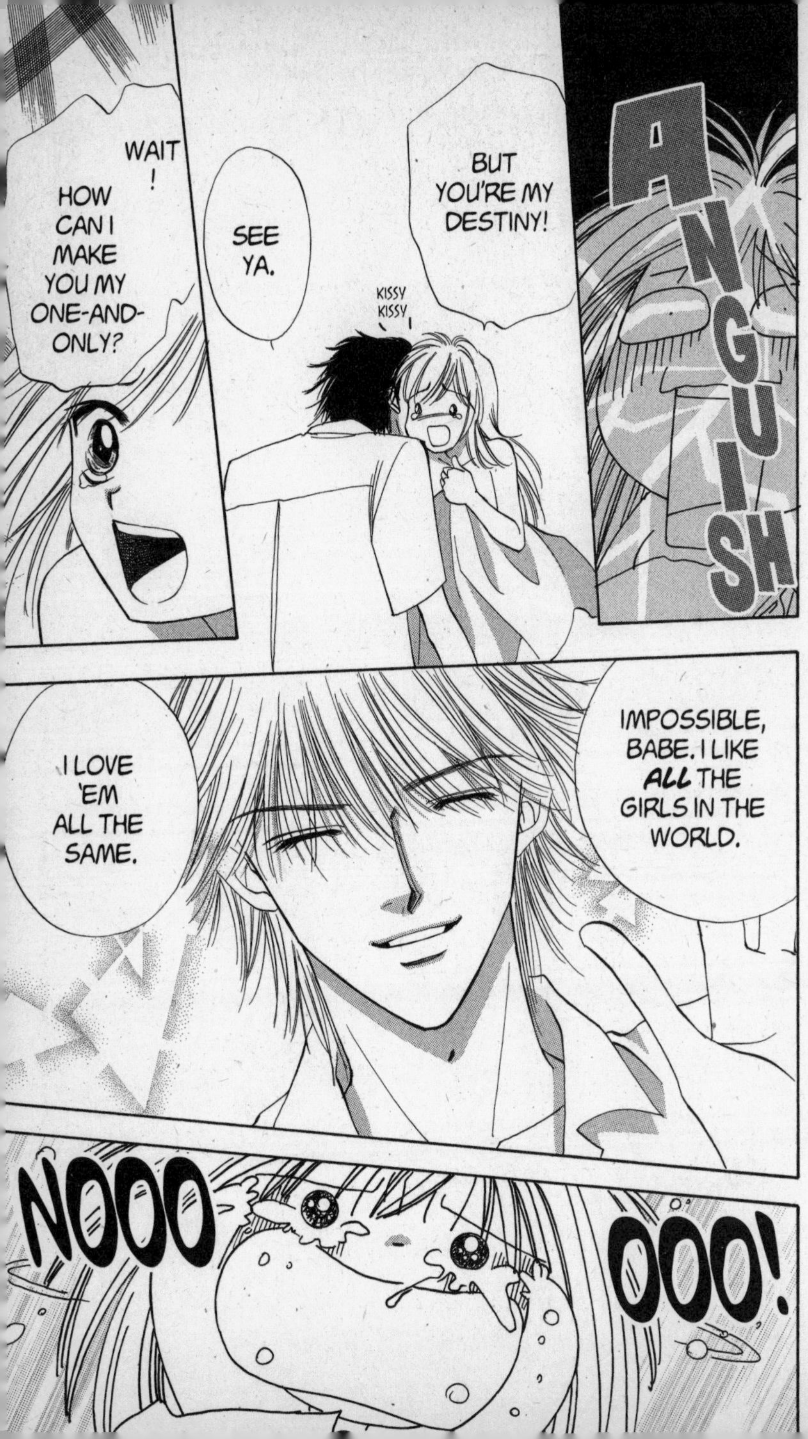
ANGUISH
BUT YOU'RE MY DESTINY!
KISSY KISSY
SEE YA.
WAIT!
HOW CAN I MAKE YOU MY ONE-AND-ONLY?
IMPOSSIBLE, BABE. I LIKE ALL THE GIRLS IN THE WORLD.
I LOVE 'EM ALL THE SAME.
NOOO
OOO!

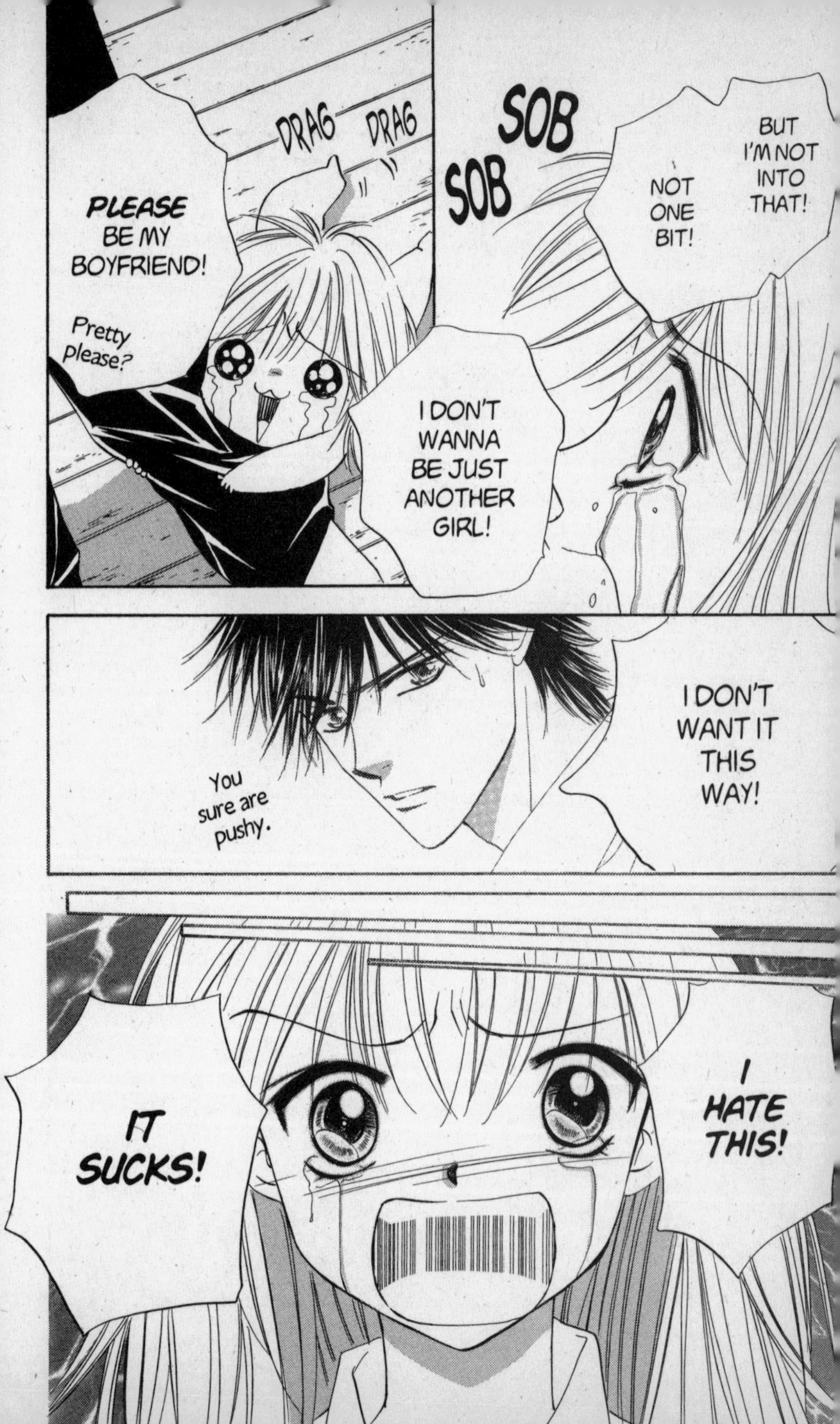
SOB
SOB
BUT I'M NOT INTO THAT!
NOT ONE BIT!
I DON'T WANNA BE JUST ANOTHER GIRL!
DRAG
DRAG
PLEASE BE MY BOYFRIEND!
Pretty please?
I DON'T WANT IT THIS WAY!
You sure are pushy.
I HATE THIS!
IT SUCKS!

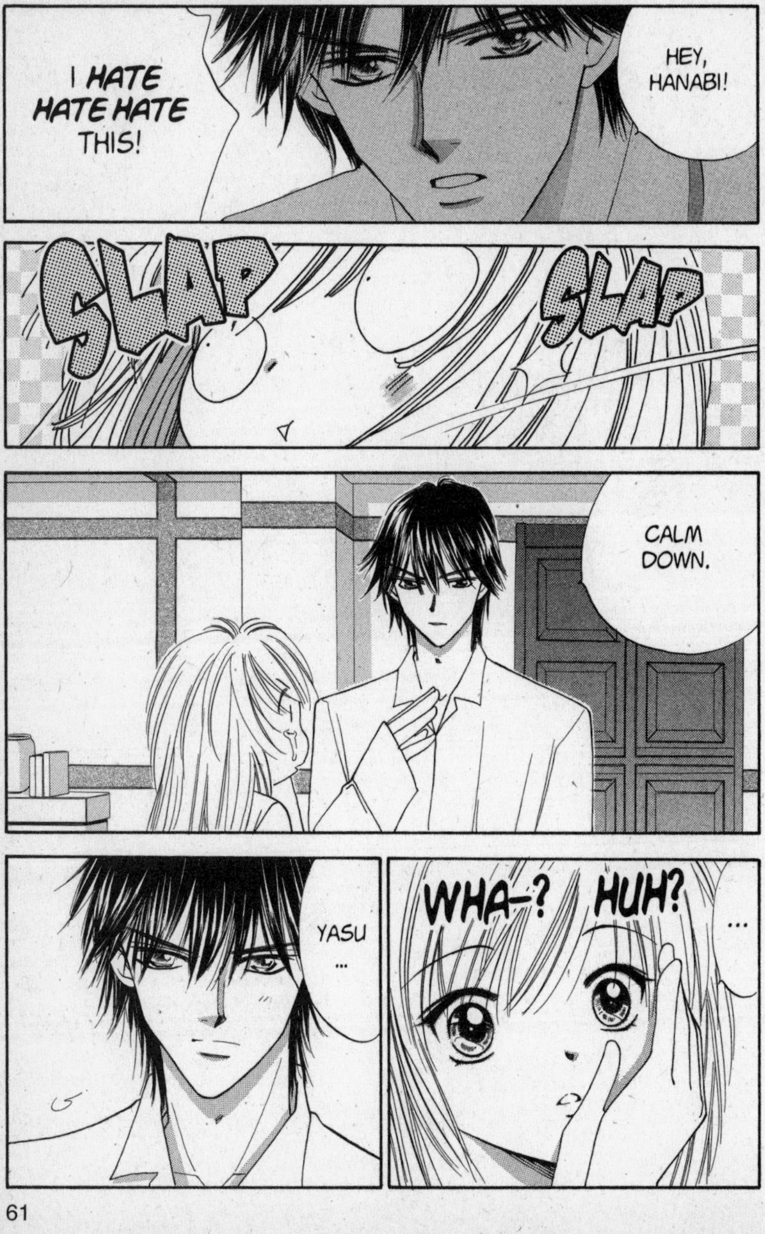
HEY, HANABI!
I HATE HATE HATE THIS!
SLAP
SLAP
CALM DOWN.
...
HUH?
WHA-?
YASU ...

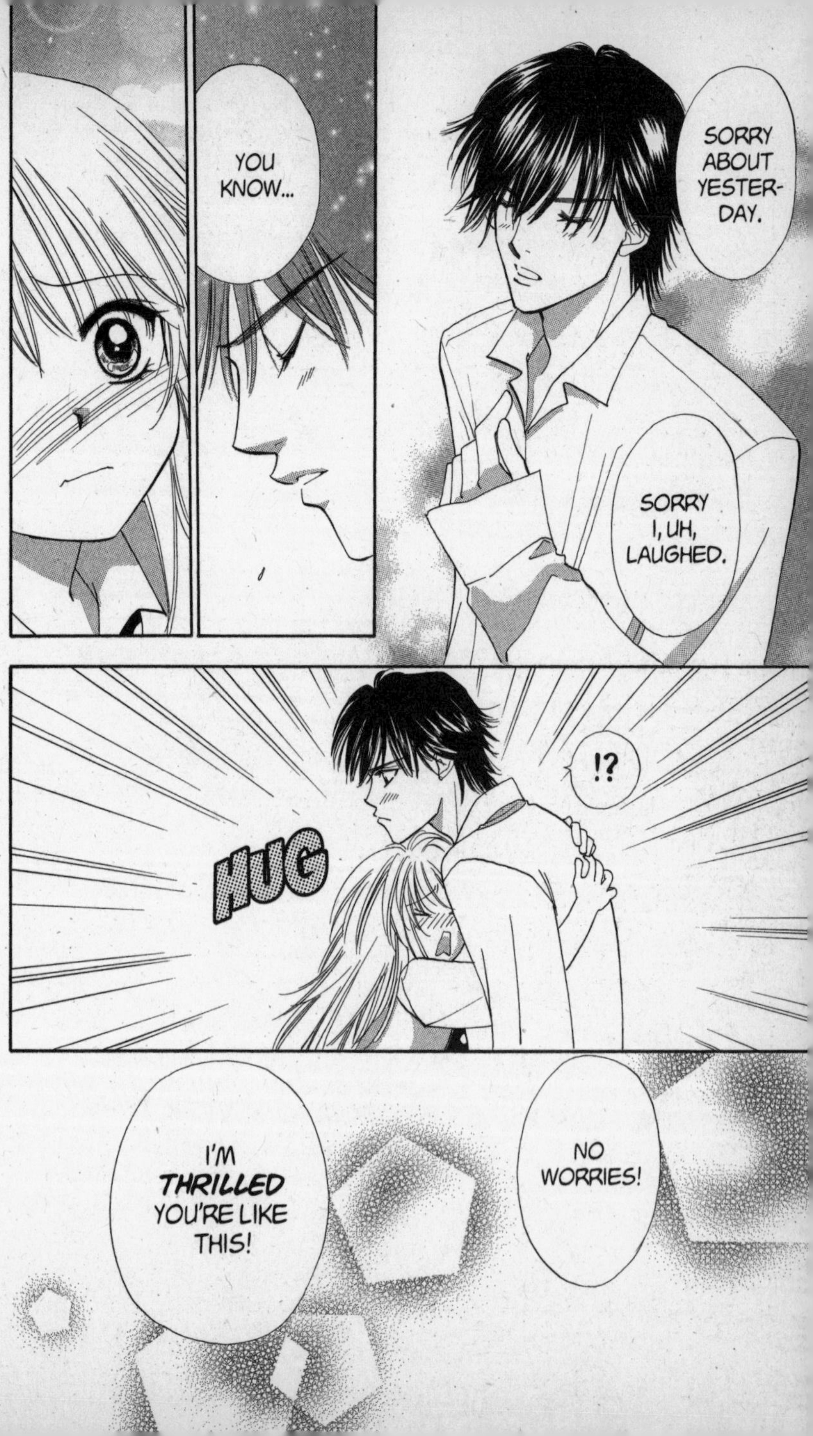
SORRY ABOUT YESTER-DAY.
SORRY I, UH, LAUGHED.
YOU KNOW...
!?
HUG
NO WORRIES!
I'M THRILLED YOU'RE LIKE THIS!

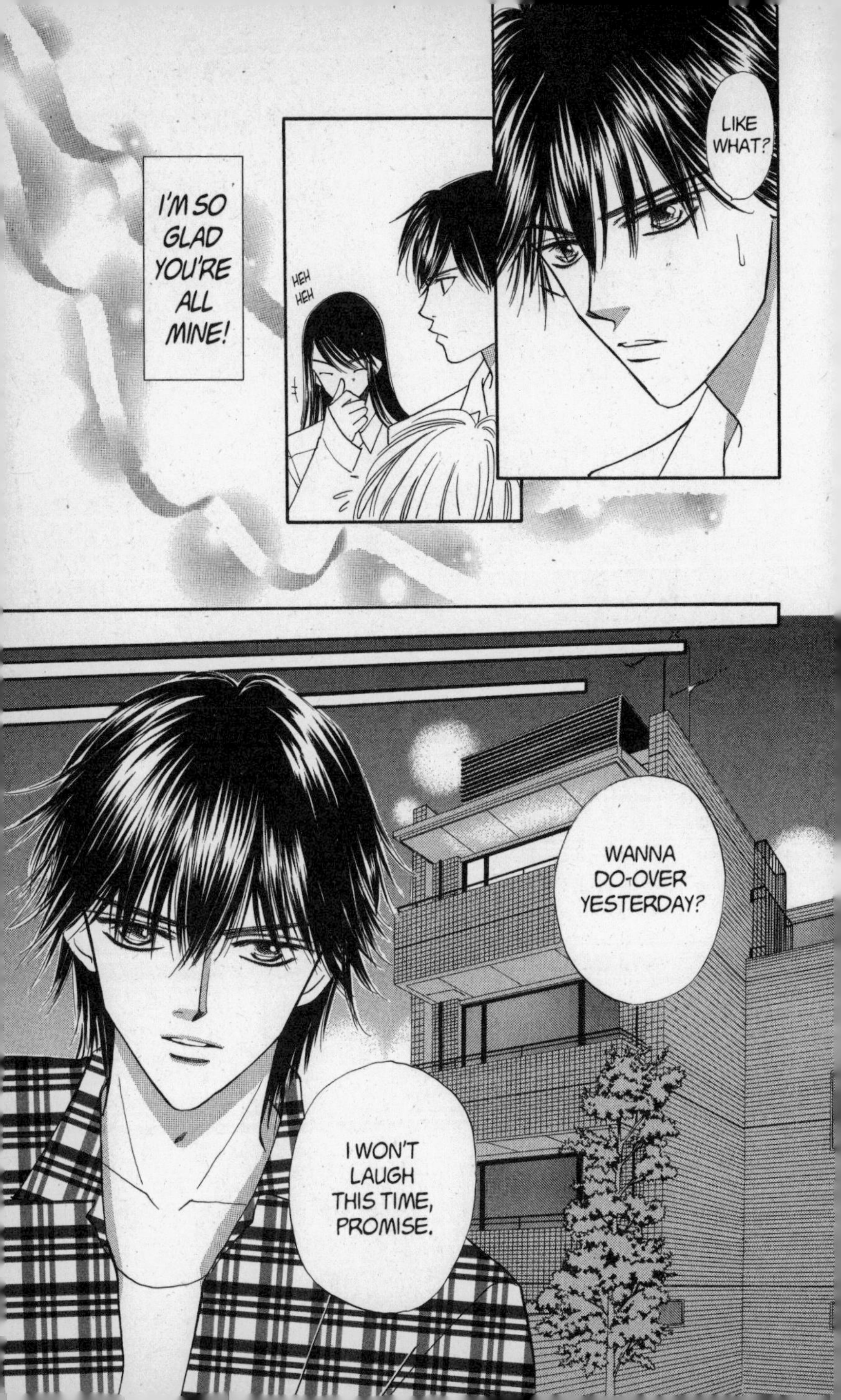
LIKE WHAT?
HEH HEH
I'M SO GLAD YOU'RE ALL MINE!
WANNA DO-OVER YESTERDAY?
I WON'T LAUGH THIS TIME, PROMISE.

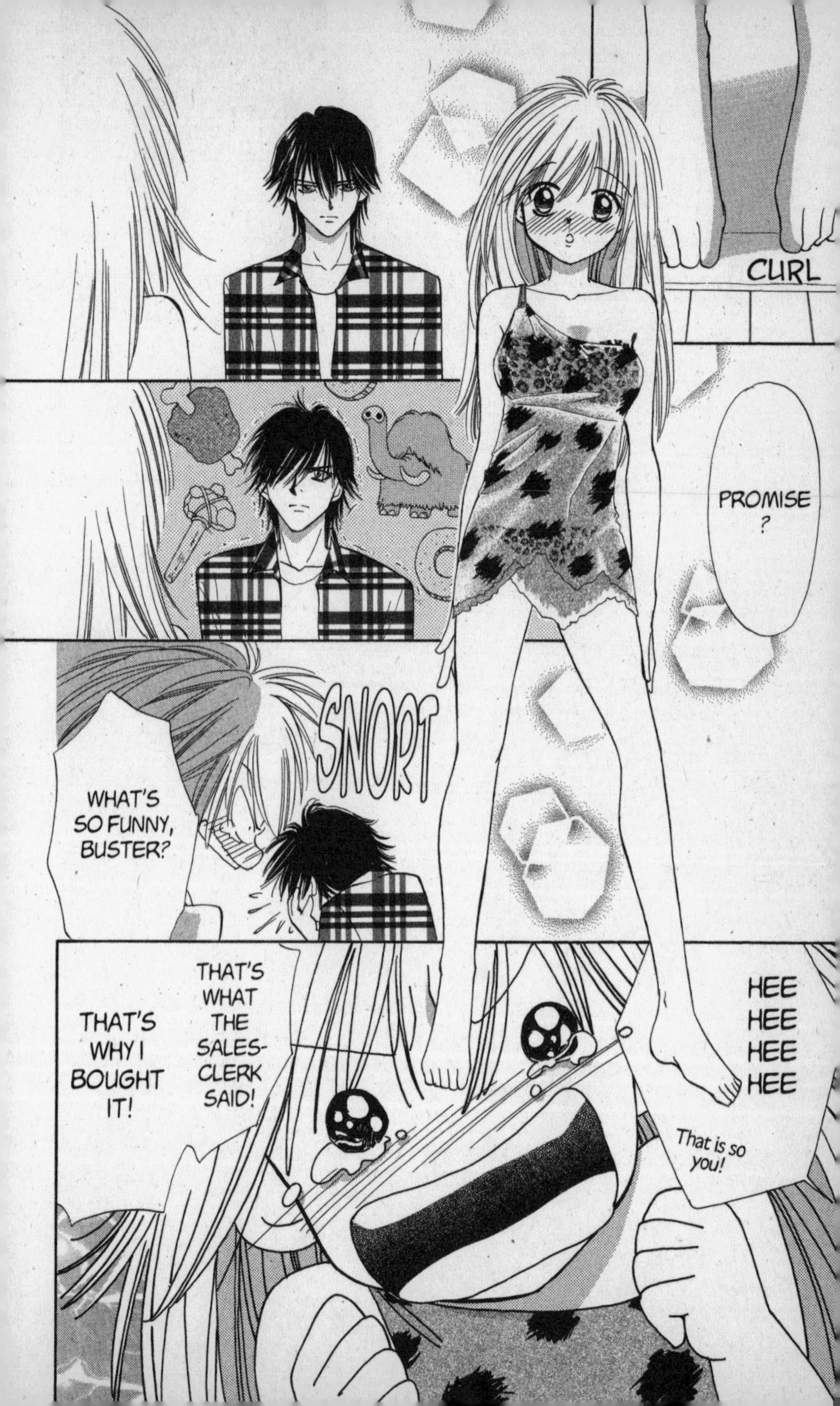
CURL
PROMISE?
SNORT
WHAT'S SO FUNNY, BUSTER?
HEE HEE HEE HEE
That is so you!
THAT'S WHAT THE SALES-CLERK SAID!
THAT'S WHY I BOUGHT IT!

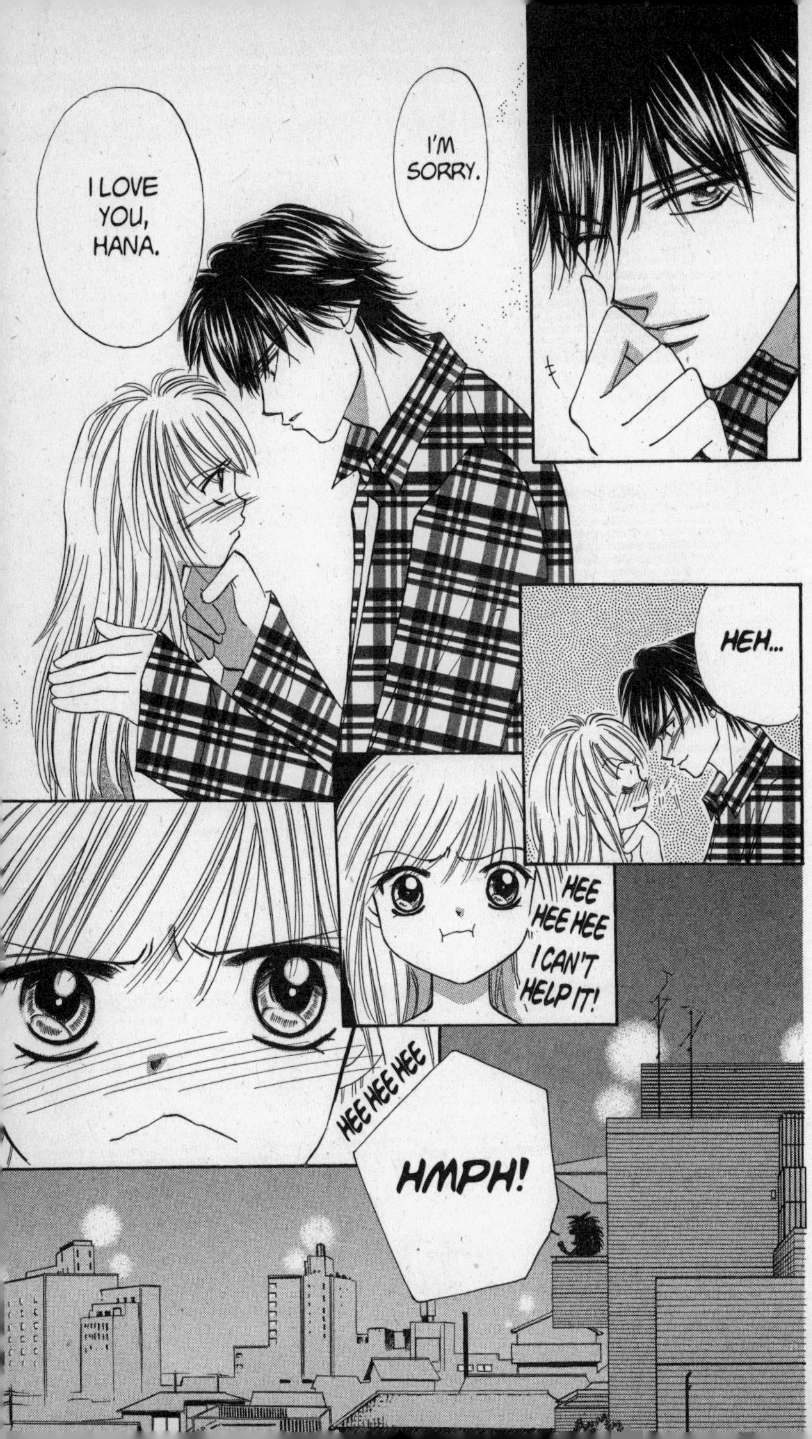
I'M SORRY.
I LOVE YOU, HANA.
HEH...
HEE HEE HEE I CAN'T HELP IT!
HEE HEE HEE
HMPH!

**HAPPY
HUSTLE
HIGH**

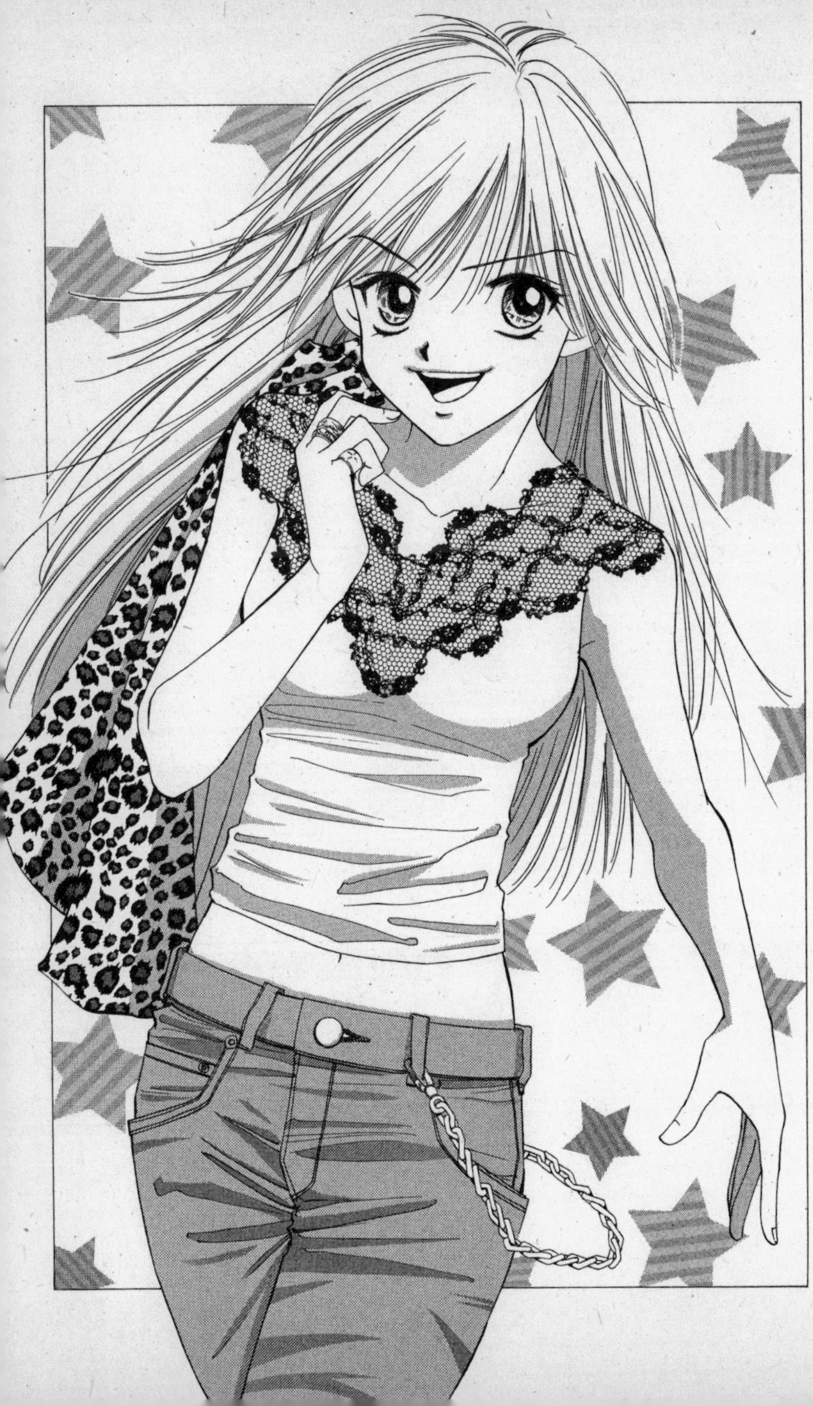

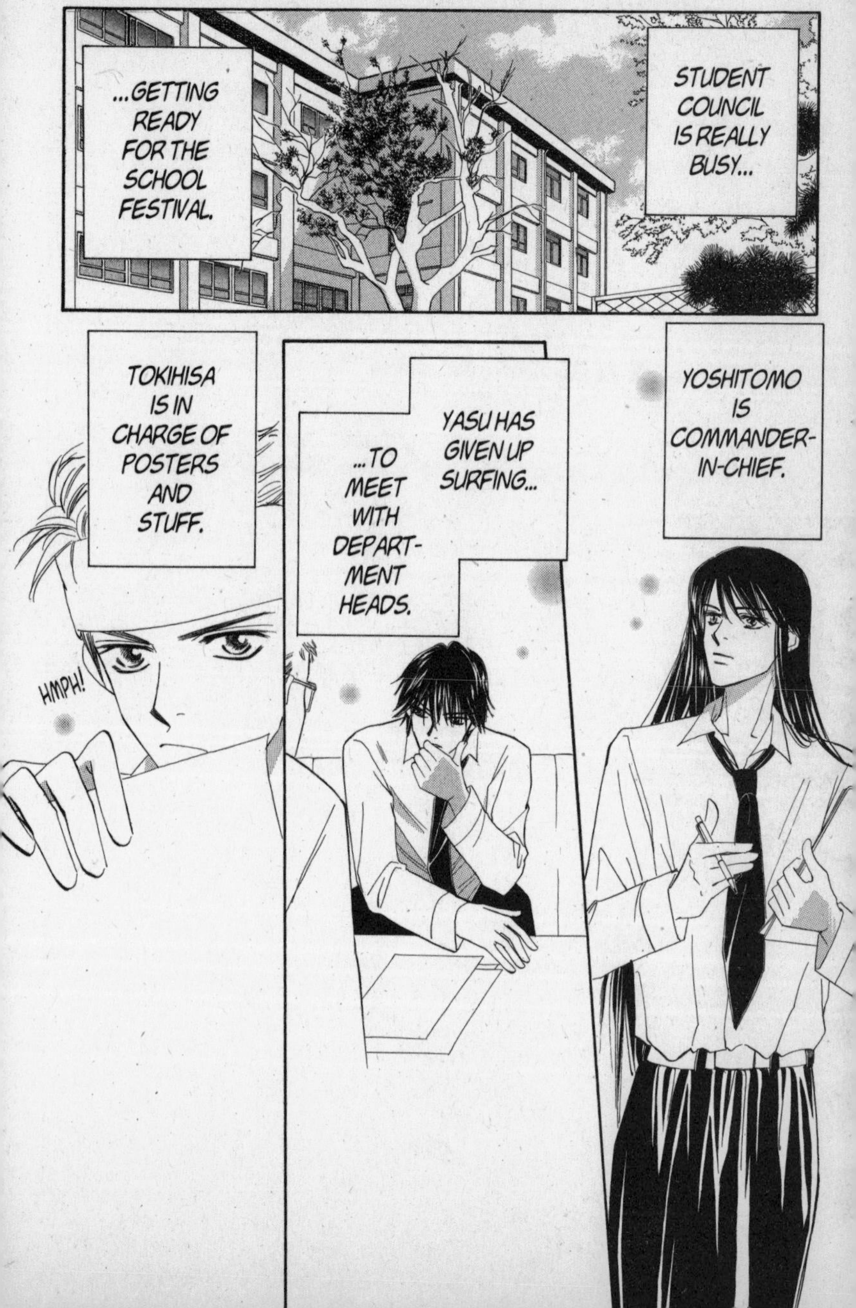
STUDENT COUNCIL IS REALLY BUSY...
...GETTING READY FOR THE SCHOOL FESTIVAL.
YOSHITOMO IS COMMANDER-IN-CHIEF.
YASU HAS GIVEN UP SURFING...
...TO MEET WITH DEPART-MENT HEADS.
TOKIHISA IS IN CHARGE OF POSTERS AND STUFF.
HMPH!

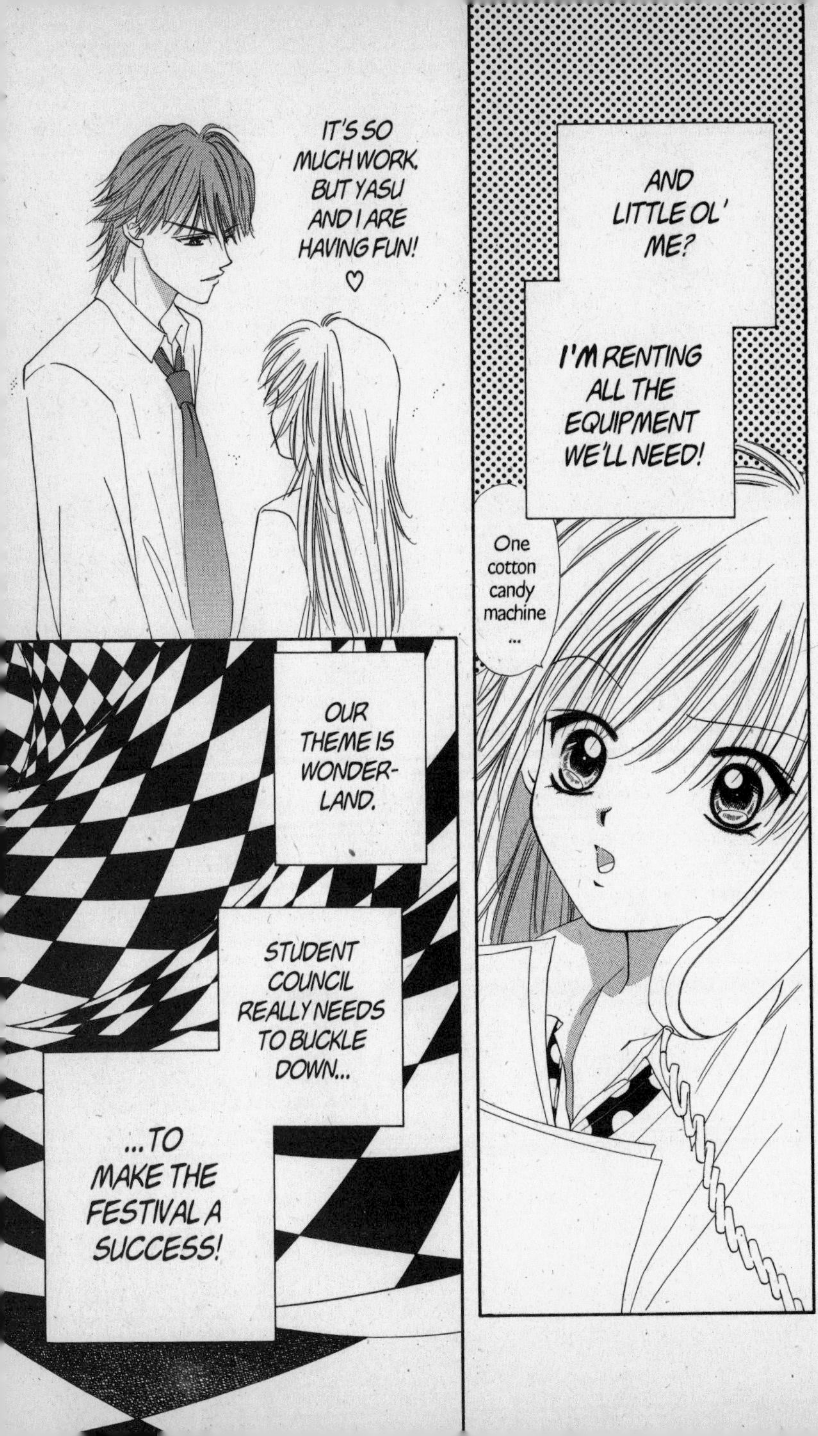
AND LITTLE OL' ME?
I'M RENTING ALL THE EQUIPMENT WE'LL NEED!
One cotton candy machine ...
IT'S SO MUCH WORK. BUT YASU AND I ARE HAVING FUN! ♡
OUR THEME IS WONDER-LAND.
STUDENT COUNCIL REALLY NEEDS TO BUCKLE DOWN...
...TO MAKE THE FESTIVAL A SUCCESS!

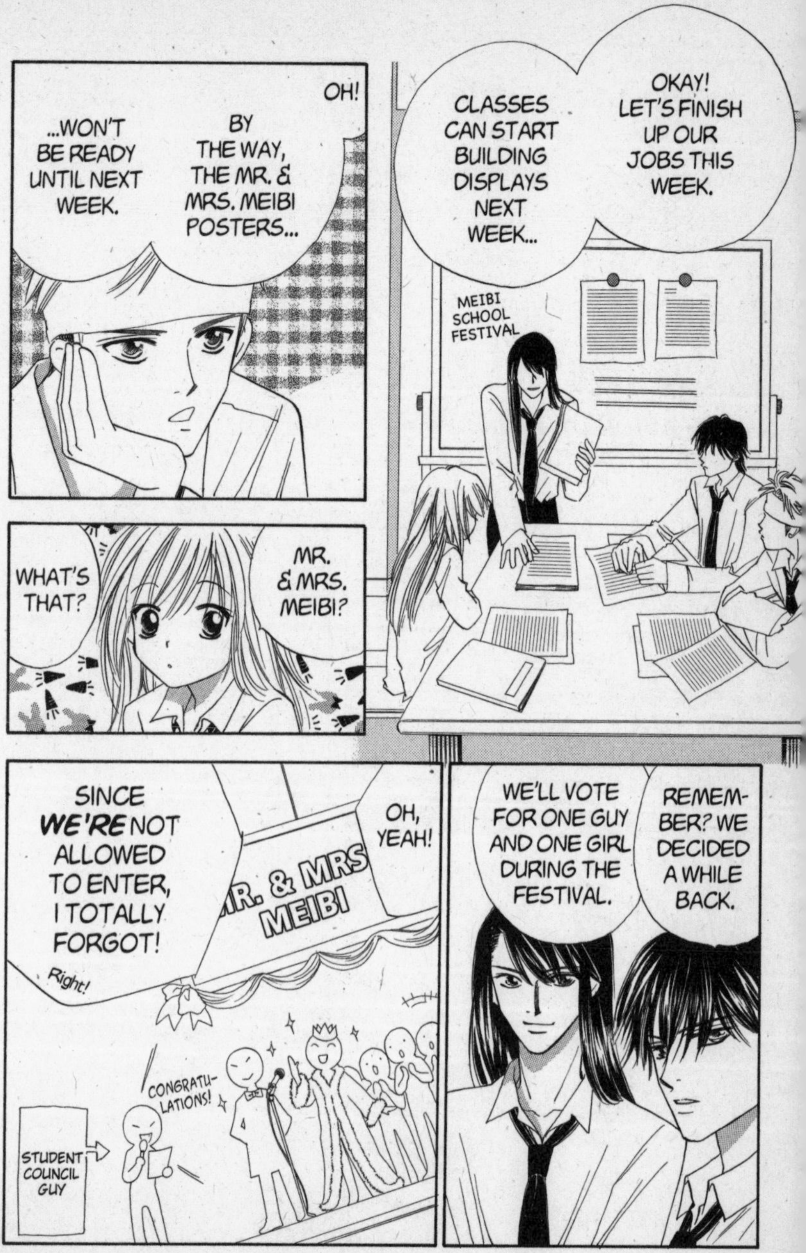
OKAY! LET'S FINISH UP OUR JOBS THIS WEEK.
CLASSES CAN START BUILDING DISPLAYS NEXT WEEK...
MEIBI SCHOOL FESTIVAL
OH!
BY THE WAY, THE MR. & MRS. MEIBI POSTERS...
...WON'T BE READY UNTIL NEXT WEEK.
MR. & MRS. MEIBI?
WHAT'S THAT?
REMEMBER? WE DECIDED A WHILE BACK.
WE'LL VOTE FOR ONE GUY AND ONE GIRL DURING THE FESTIVAL.
OH, YEAH!
SINCE ***WE'RE*** NOT ALLOWED TO ENTER, I TOTALLY FORGOT!
MR. & MRS MEIBI
Right!
CONGRATULATIONS!
STUDENT COUNCIL GUY

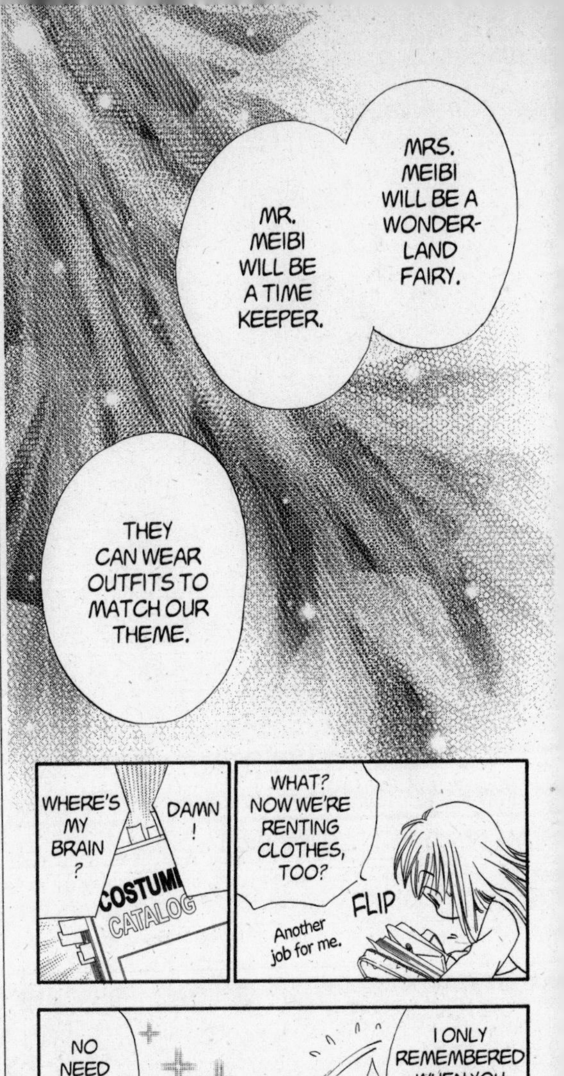
MRS. MEIBI WILL BE A WONDER-LAND FAIRY.
MR. MEIBI WILL BE A TIME KEEPER.
THEY CAN WEAR OUTFITS TO MATCH OUR THEME.
WHAT? NOW WE'RE RENTING CLOTHES, TOO?
FLIP
Another job for me.
DAMN!
WHERE'S MY BRAIN?
COSTUM
CATALOG
I ONLY REMEMBERED WHEN YOU MENTIONED THE POSTERS!
Close one!
NO NEED TO THANK ME...

HELLO 2005

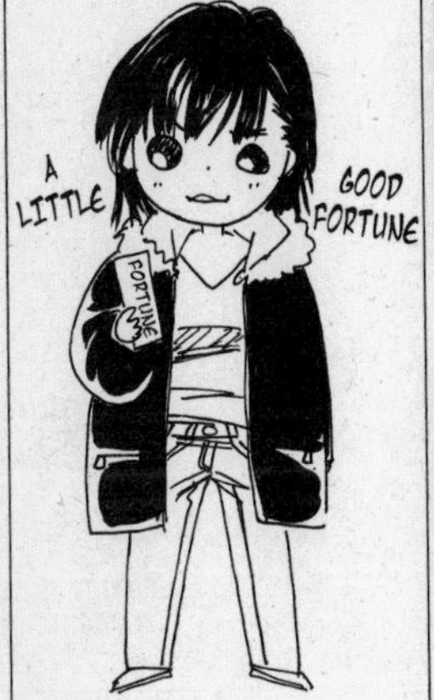
A LITTLE GOOD FORTUNE
FORTUNE

MY FIRST JOB OF 2005 WAS TO READ THROUGH A SPECIAL ISSUE. I ACTUALLY FOUND SOMETHING I WROTE A LONG TIME AGO. (AMAZING! I COULD'VE SWORN I TOSSED IT!) I REALIZED I COULD STILL USE IT, BUT IT DID NEED A LITTLE FIXING. I DIDN'T CHANGE THE STORY MUCH, BUT REVISED THE ARTWORK. WHEN YOU READ IT, PLEASE REMEMBER I WROTE THIS BEFORE MY MANGA DEBUT. THAT OLD STORY REALLY CRACKED ME UP. THE ARTWORK IS PRETTY RISQUÉ, BUT THE PLOT IS SWEET YET AMATEURISH...

(THE SPECIAL ISSUE WENT ON SALE IN MARCH 2005.)

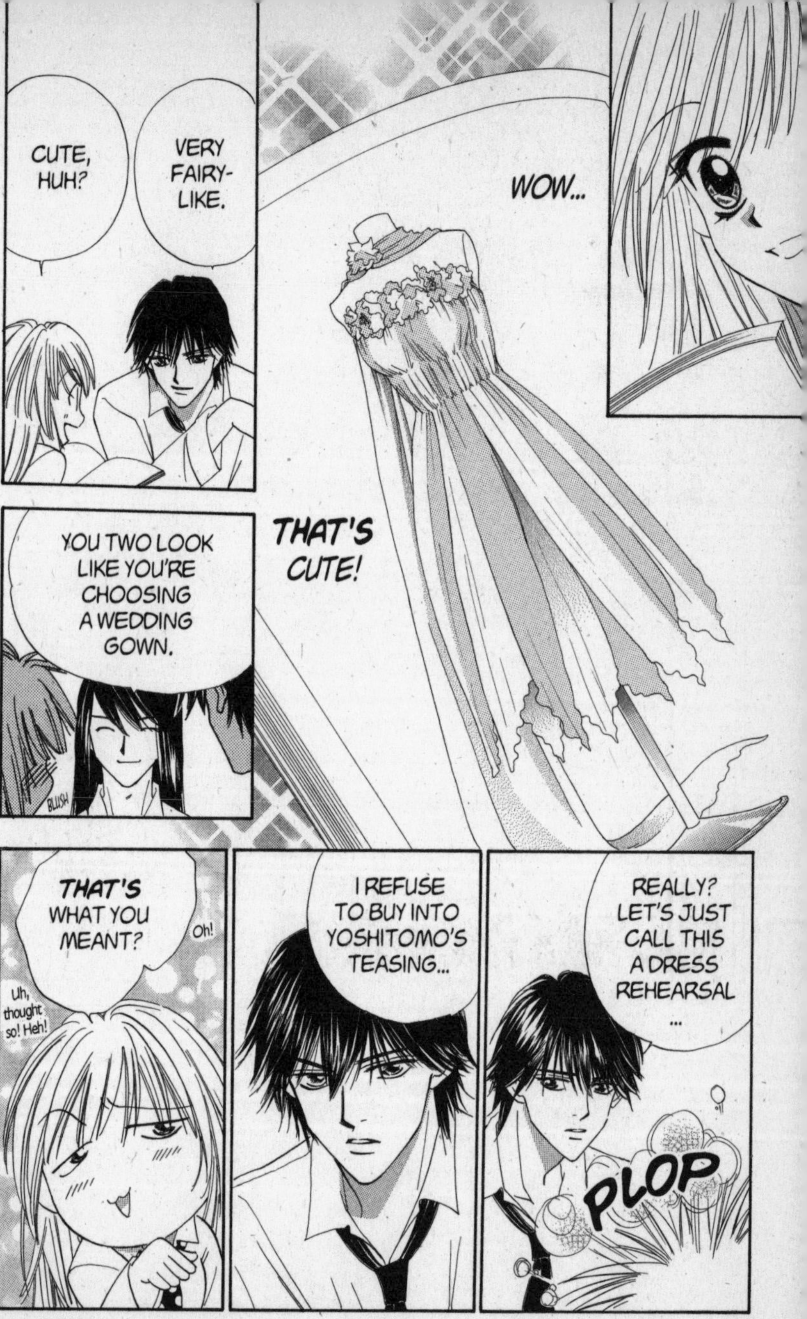
WOW...
VERY FAIRY-LIKE.
CUTE, HUH?
THAT'S CUTE!
YOU TWO LOOK LIKE YOU'RE CHOOSING A WEDDING GOWN.
BLUSH
REALLY? LET'S JUST CALL THIS A DRESS REHEARSAL ...
PLOP
I REFUSE TO BUY INTO YOSHITOMO'S TEASING...
THAT'S WHAT YOU MEANT?
Oh!
Uh, thought so! Heh!

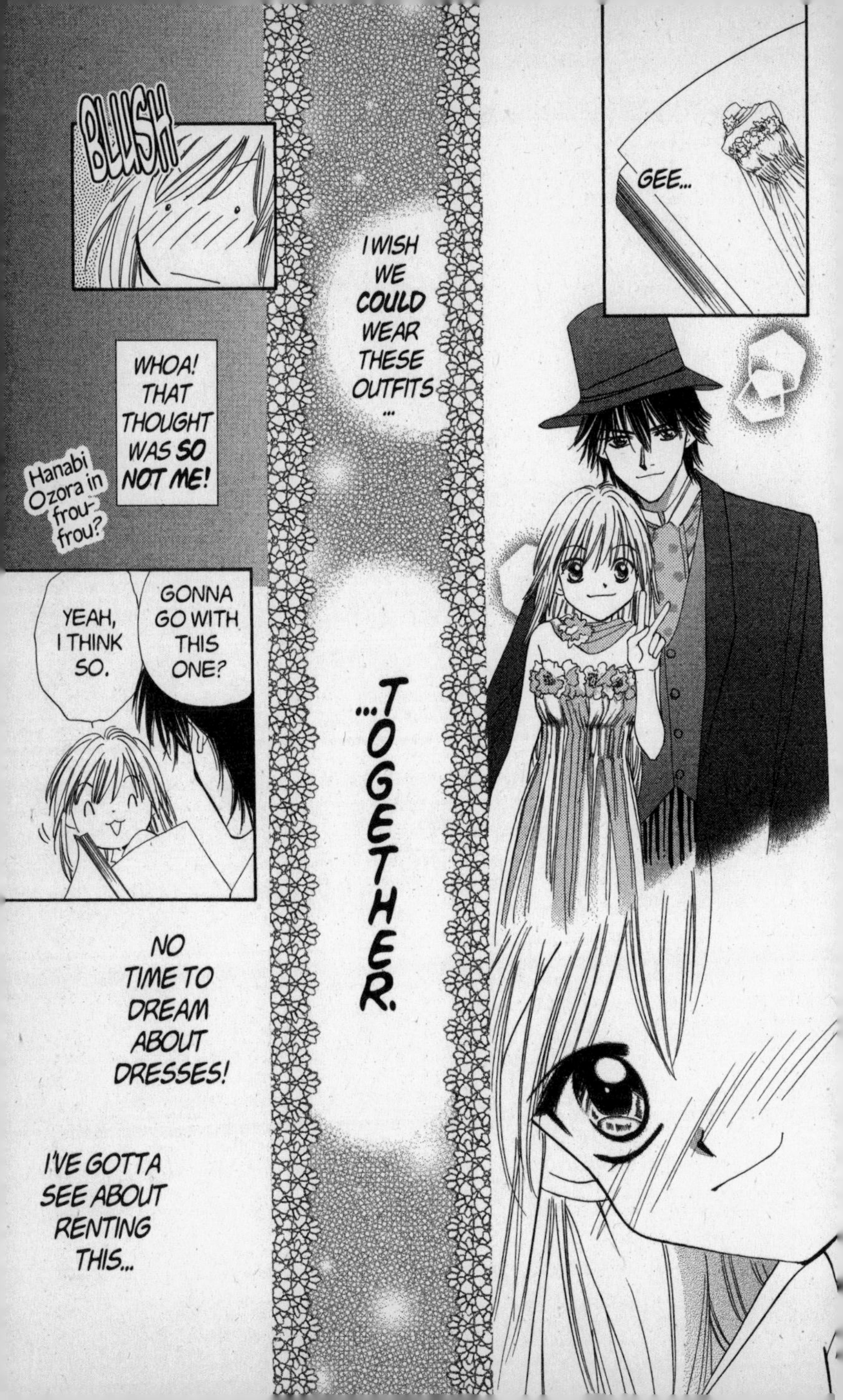
GEE...
I WISH WE COULD WEAR THESE OUTFITS ...
...TOGETHER.
BLUSH
WHOA! THAT THOUGHT WAS SO NOT ME!
Hanabi Ozora in frou-frou?
GONNA GO WITH THIS ONE?
YEAH, I THINK SO.
NO TIME TO DREAM ABOUT DRESSES!
I'VE GOTTA SEE ABOUT RENTING THIS...

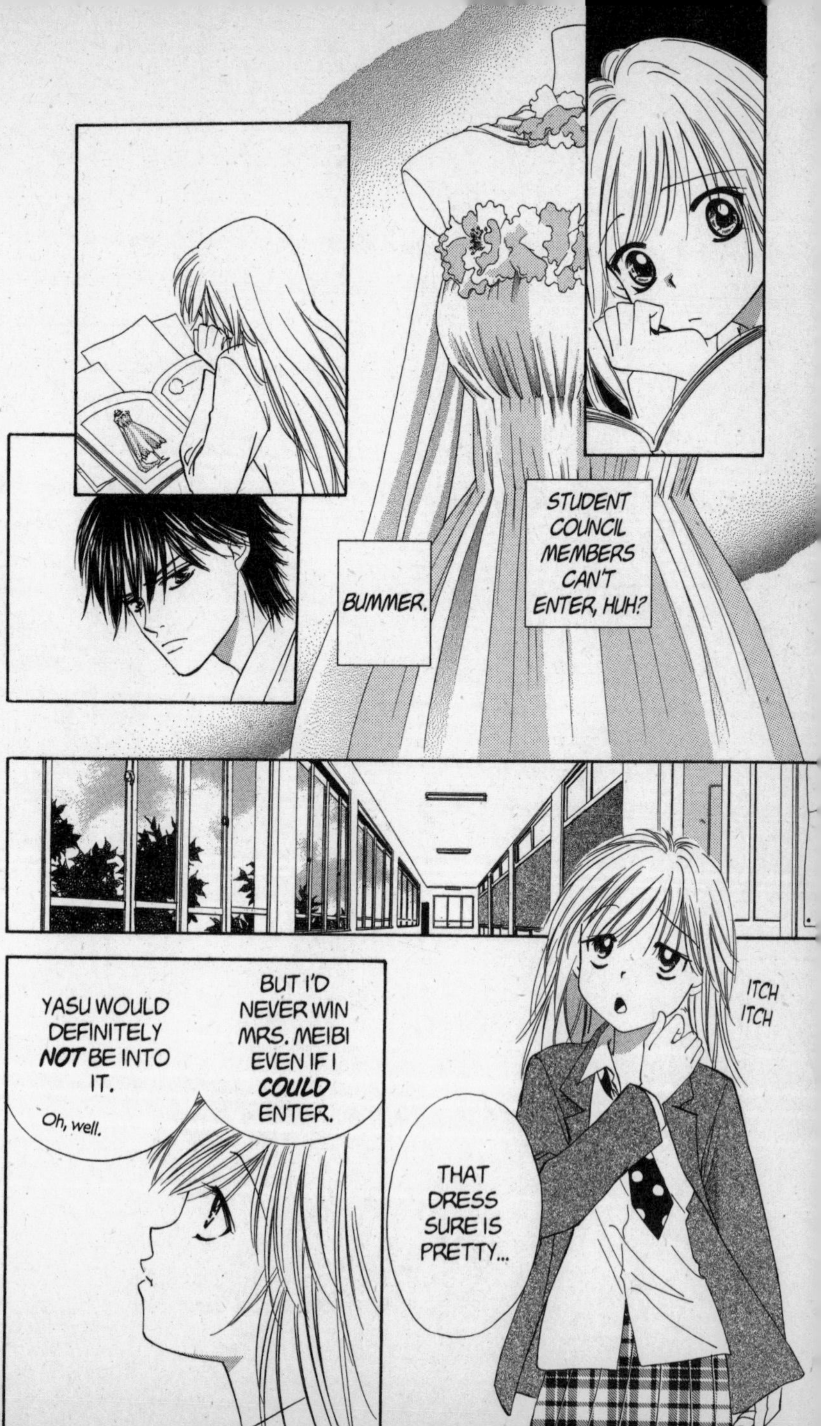
STUDENT COUNCIL MEMBERS CAN'T ENTER, HUH?
BUMMER.
ITCH ITCH
THAT DRESS SURE IS PRETTY...
BUT I'D NEVER WIN MRS. MEIBI EVEN IF I COULD ENTER.
YASU WOULD DEFINITELY NOT BE INTO IT.
Oh, well.

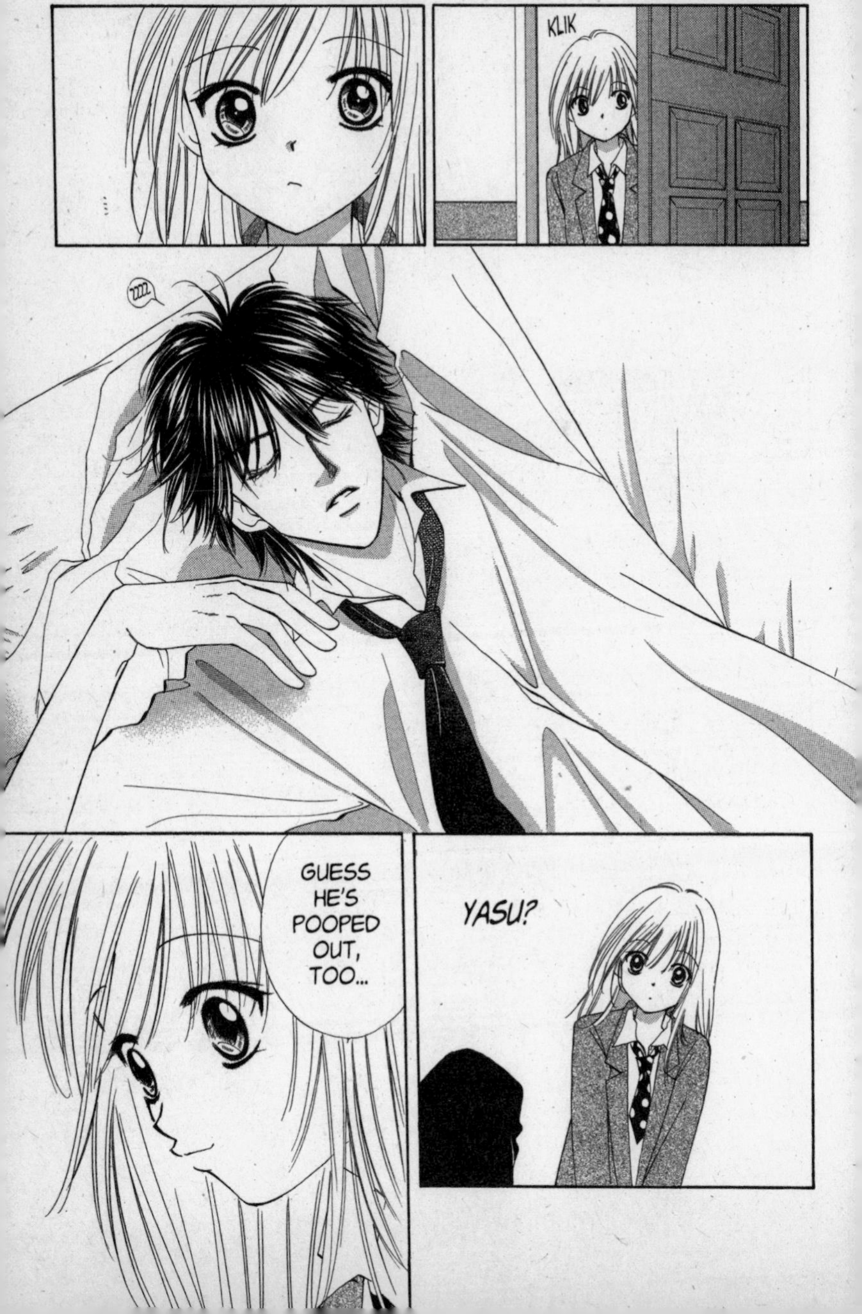
KLIK
ZZZZ
YASU?
GUESS HE'S POOPED OUT, TOO...

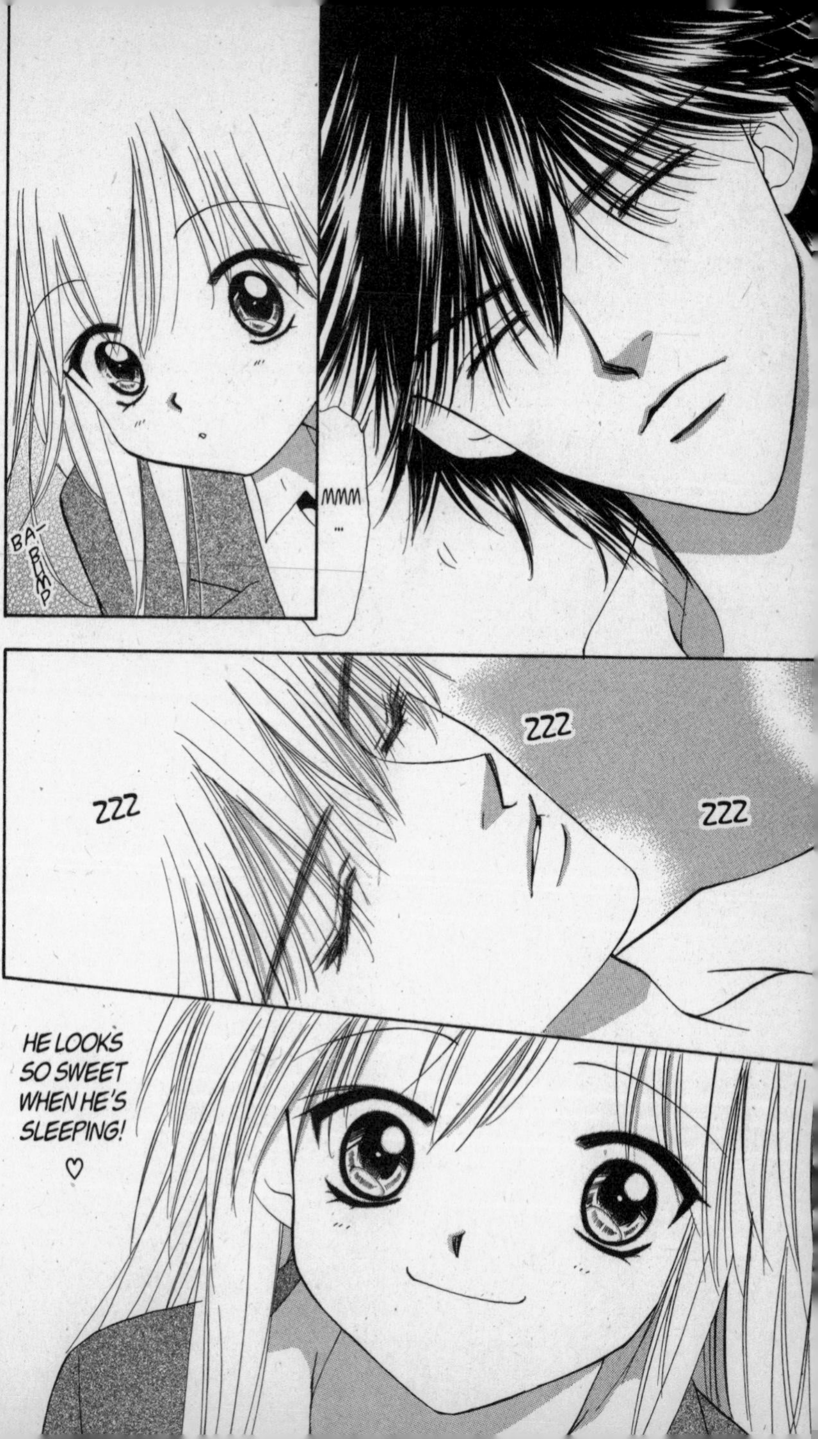
MMMM
...
BA-BUMP
ZZZ
ZZZ
ZZZ
HE LOOKS SO SWEET WHEN HE'S SLEEPING! ♡

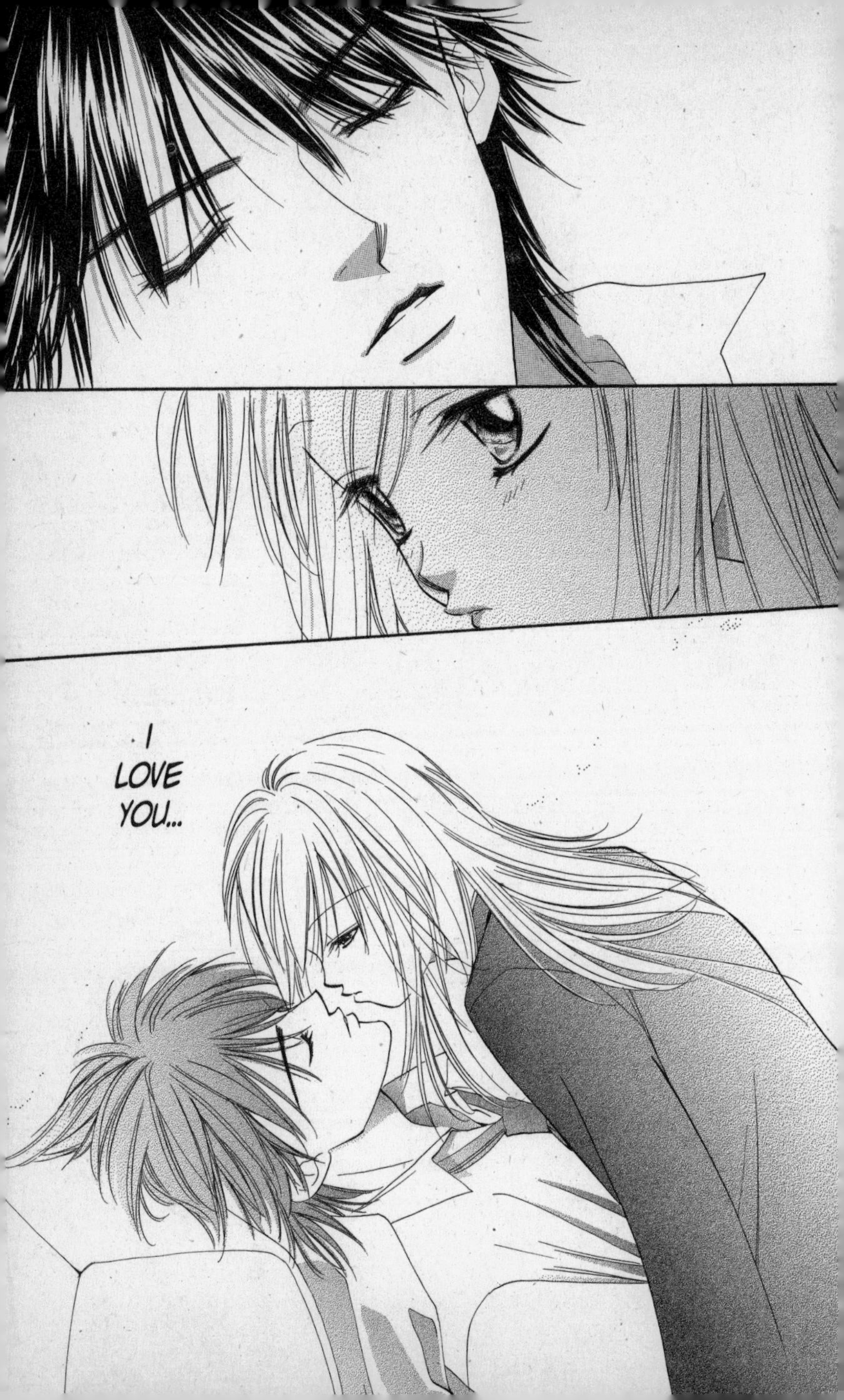
I LOVE YOU...

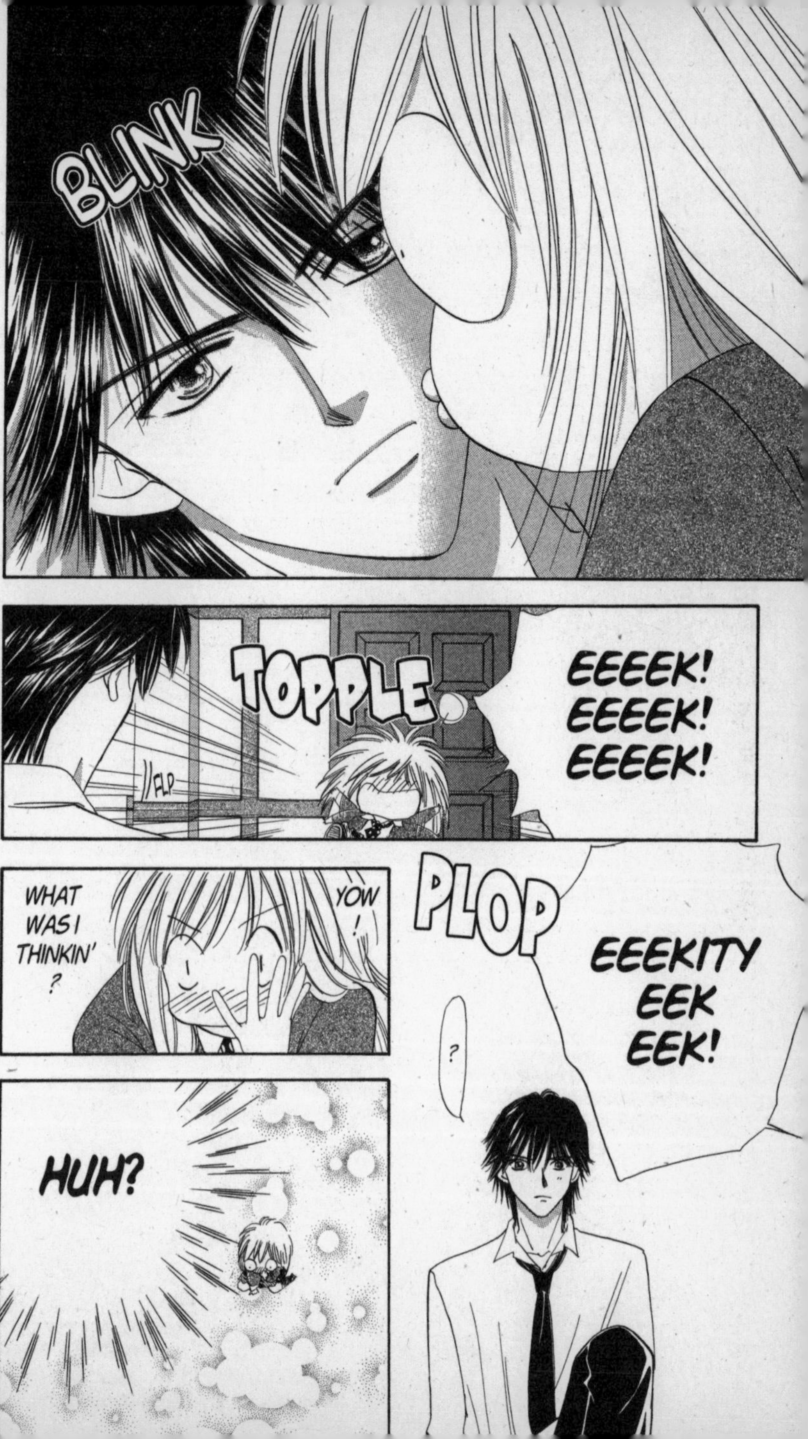
BLINK
EEEEK! EEEEK! EEEEK!
TOPPLE
FLP
PLOP
EEEKITY EEK EEK!
?
YOW!
WHAT WAS I THINKIN'?
HUH?

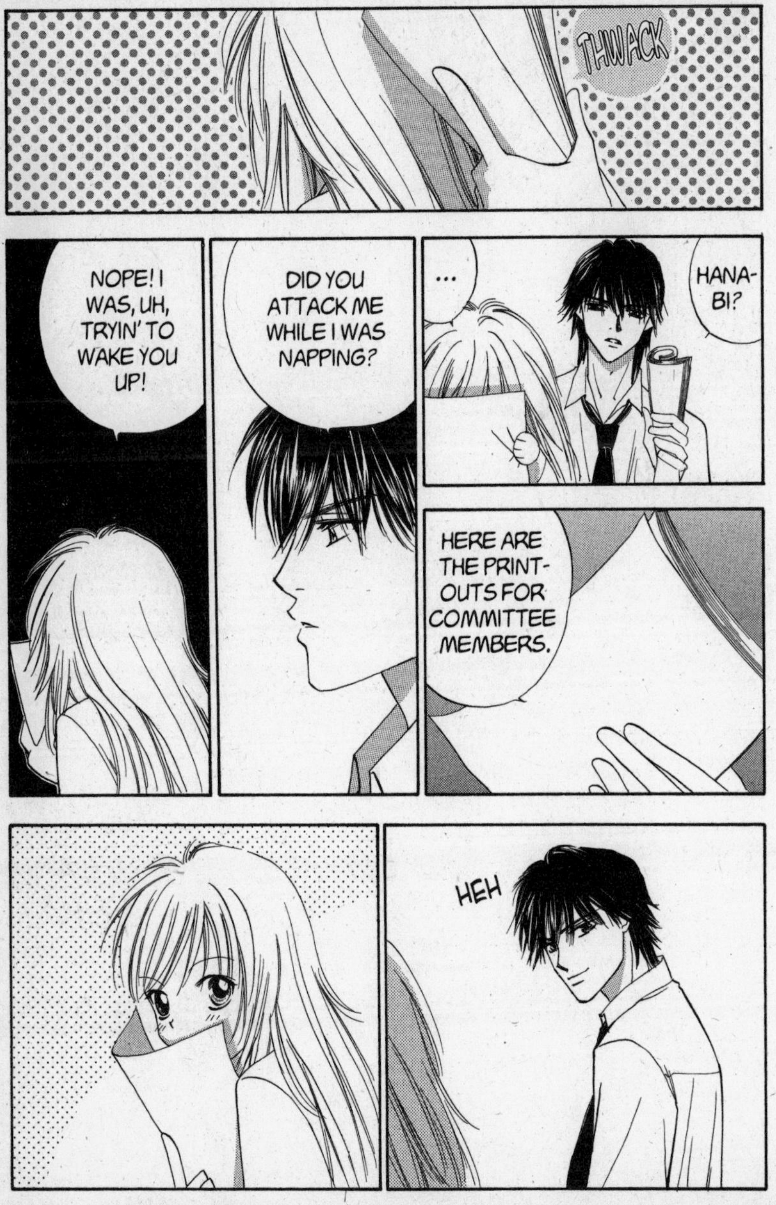
THWACK
HANA-BI?
...
HERE ARE THE PRINT-OUTS FOR COMMITTEE MEMBERS.
DID YOU ATTACK ME WHILE I WAS NAPPING?
NOPE! I WAS, UH, TRYIN' TO WAKE YOU UP!
HEH

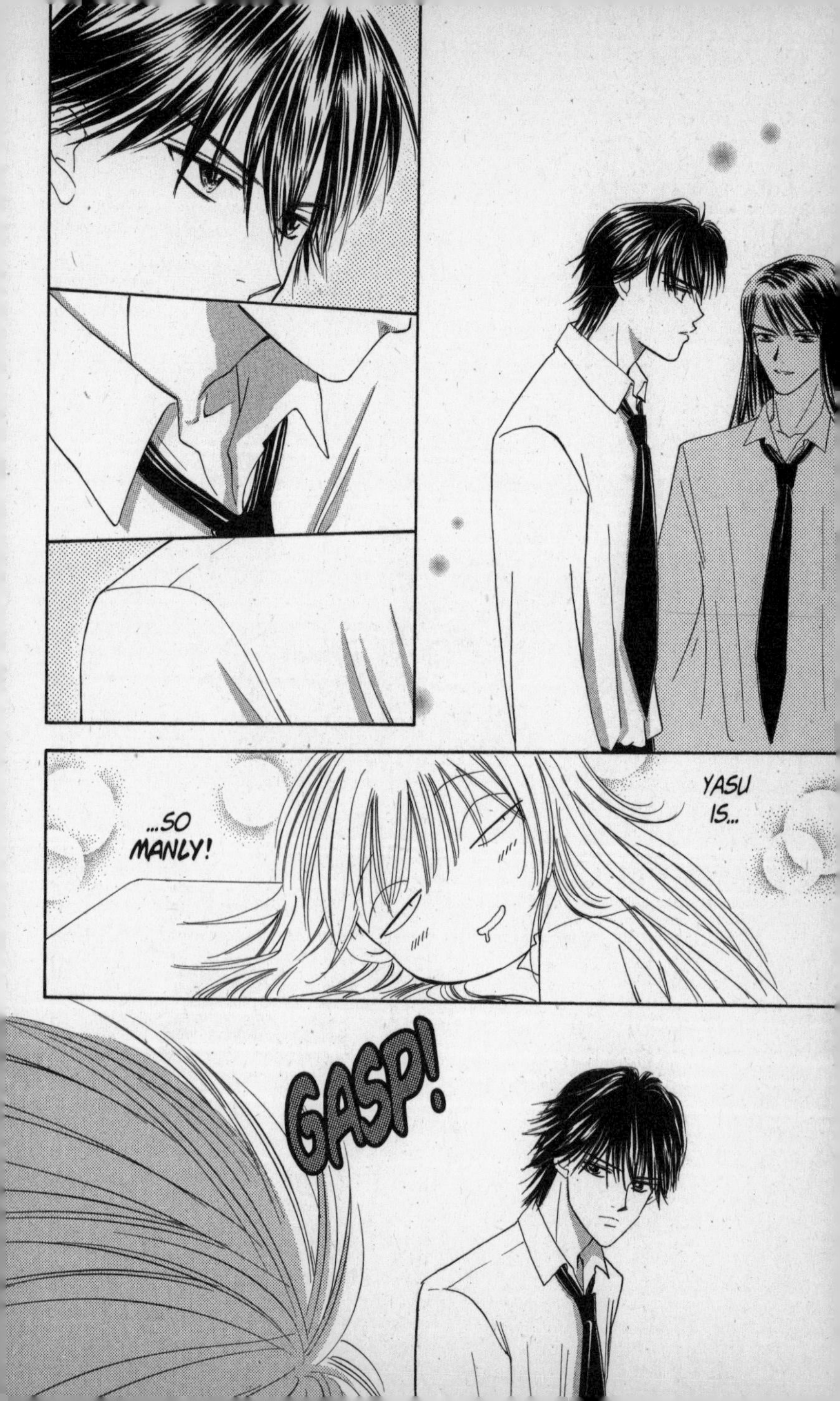
YASU IS...
...SO MANLY!
GASP!

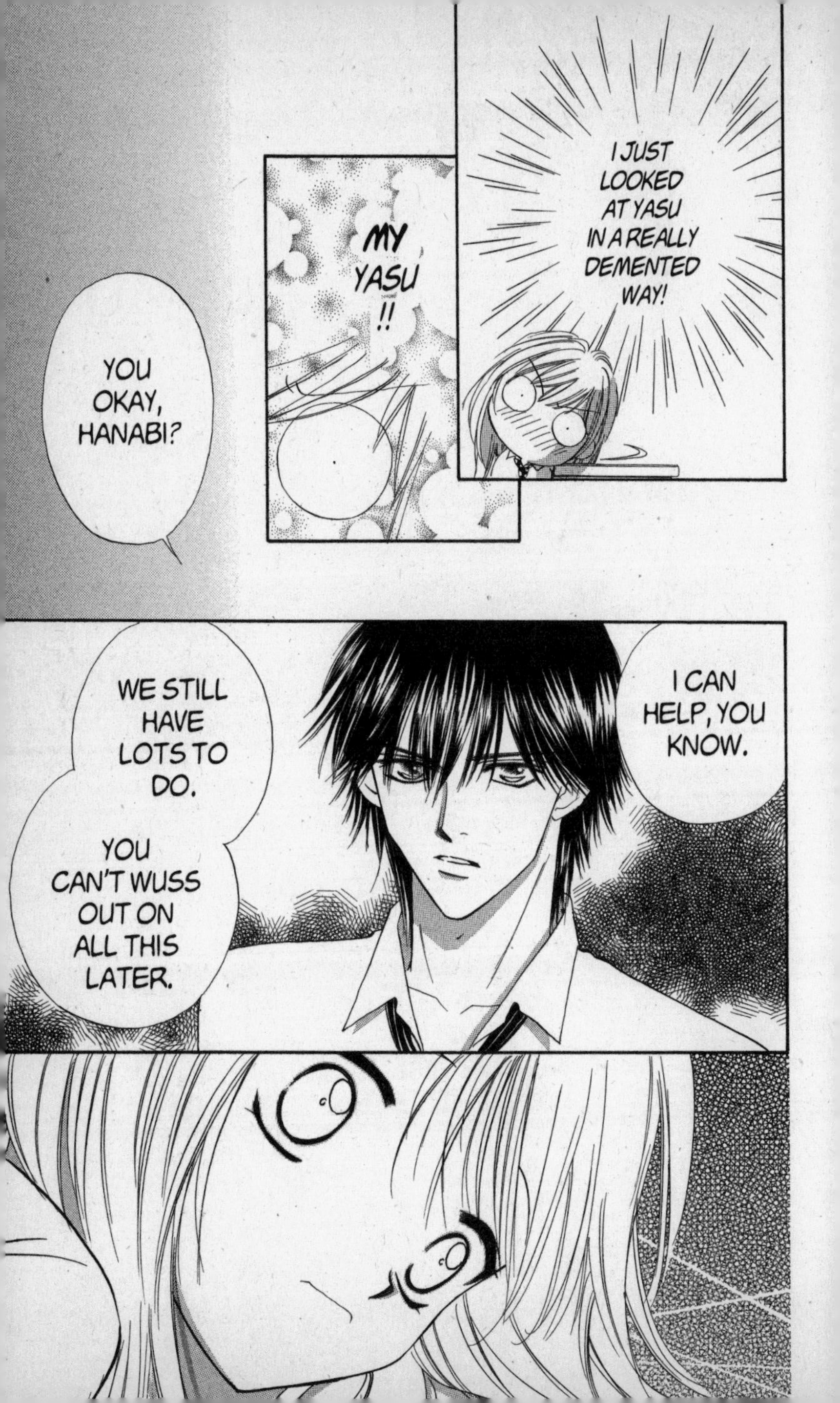
I JUST LOOKED AT YASU IN A REALLY DEMENTED WAY!
MY YASU !!
YOU OKAY, HANABI?
I CAN HELP, YOU KNOW.
WE STILL HAVE LOTS TO DO.
YOU CAN'T WUSS OUT ON ALL THIS LATER.

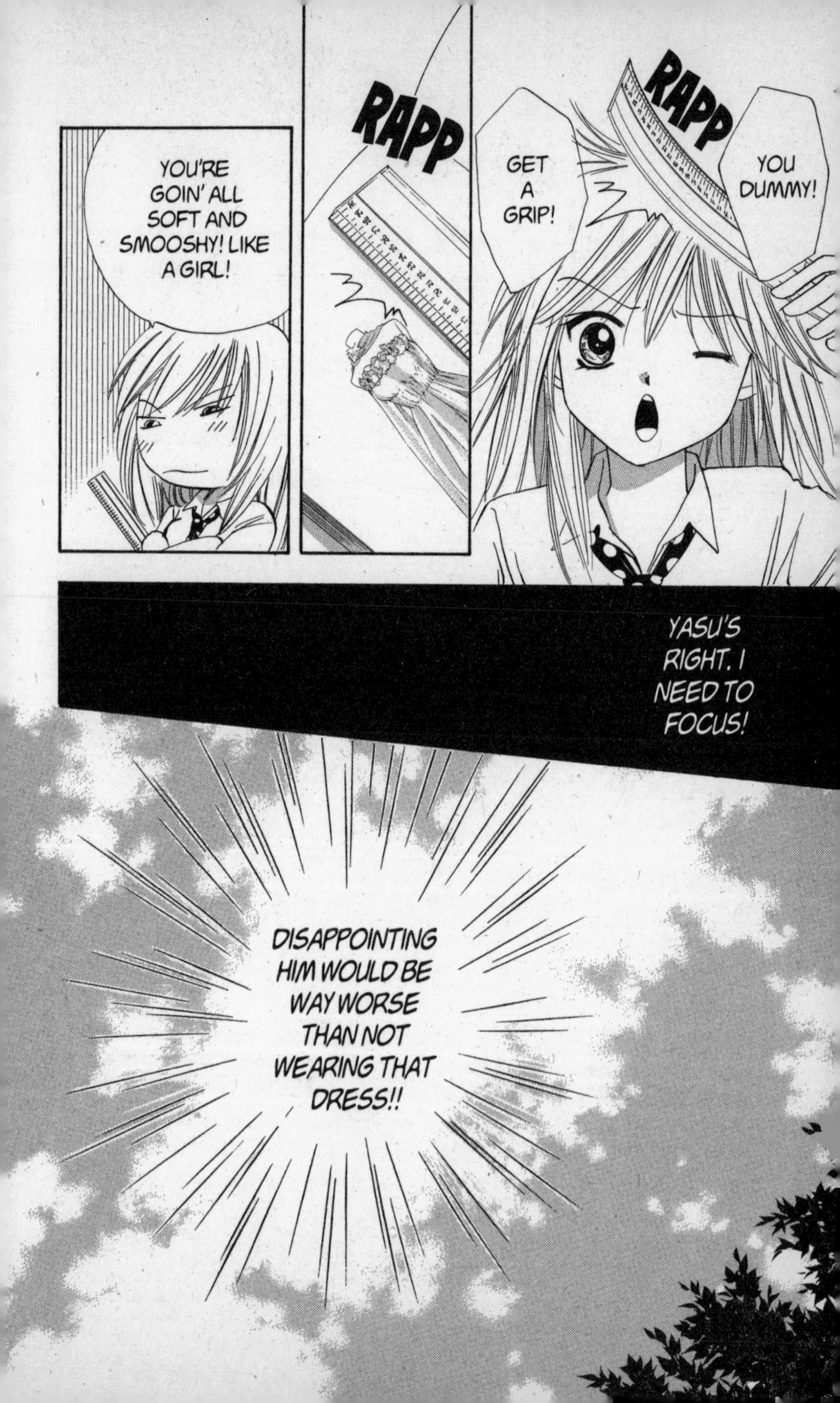
RAPP
YOU DUMMY!
GET A GRIP!
RAPP
YOU'RE GOIN' ALL SOFT AND SMOOSHY! LIKE A GIRL!
YASU'S RIGHT. I NEED TO FOCUS!
DISAPPOINTING HIM WOULD BE WAY WORSE THAN NOT WEARING THAT DRESS!!

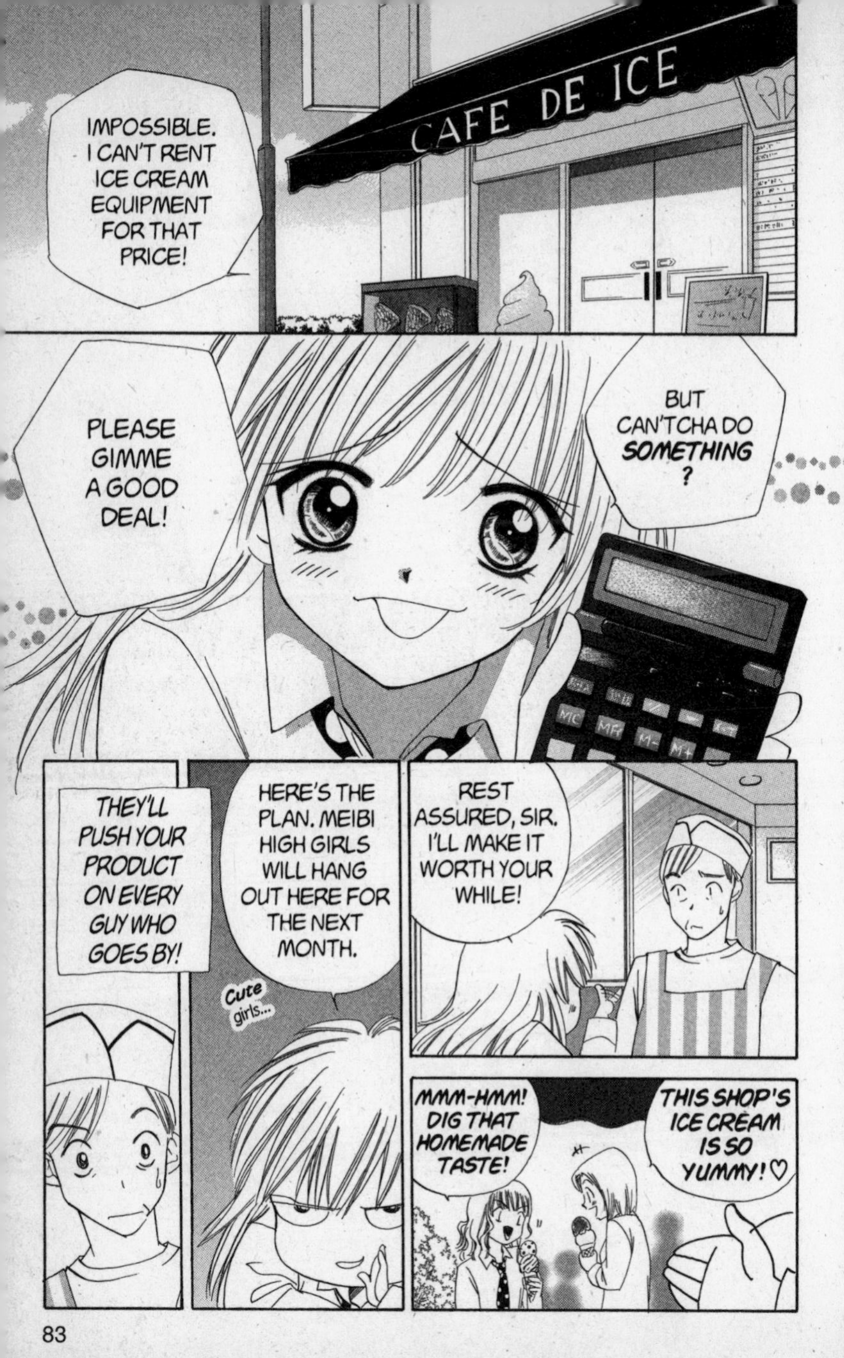
CAFE DE ICE
IMPOSSIBLE. I CAN'T RENT ICE CREAM EQUIPMENT FOR THAT PRICE!
BUT CAN'TCHA DO SOMETHING?
PLEASE GIMME A GOOD DEAL!
REST ASSURED, SIR. I'LL MAKE IT WORTH YOUR WHILE!
THIS SHOP'S ICE CREAM IS SO YUMMY! ♡
MMM-HMM! DIG THAT HOMEMADE TASTE!
HERE'S THE PLAN. MEIBI HIGH GIRLS WILL HANG OUT HERE FOR THE NEXT MONTH.
Cute girls...
THEY'LL PUSH YOUR PRODUCT ON EVERY GUY WHO GOES BY!

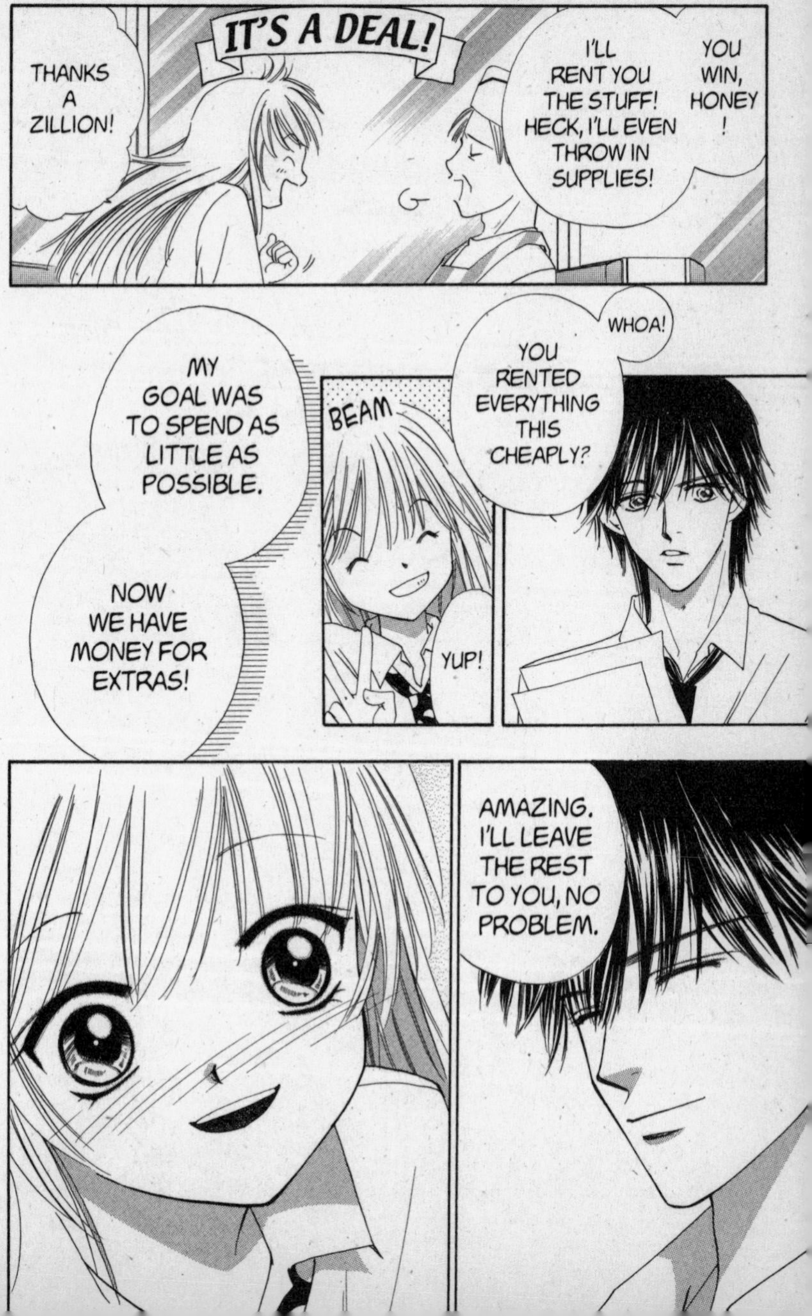
YOU WIN, HONEY!
I'LL RENT YOU THE STUFF! HECK, I'LL EVEN THROW IN SUPPLIES!
IT'S A DEAL!
THANKS A ZILLION!
WHOA!
YOU RENTED EVERYTHING THIS CHEAPLY?
BEAM
YUP!
MY GOAL WAS TO SPEND AS LITTLE AS POSSIBLE.
NOW WE HAVE MONEY FOR EXTRAS!
AMAZING. I'LL LEAVE THE REST TO YOU, NO PROBLEM.

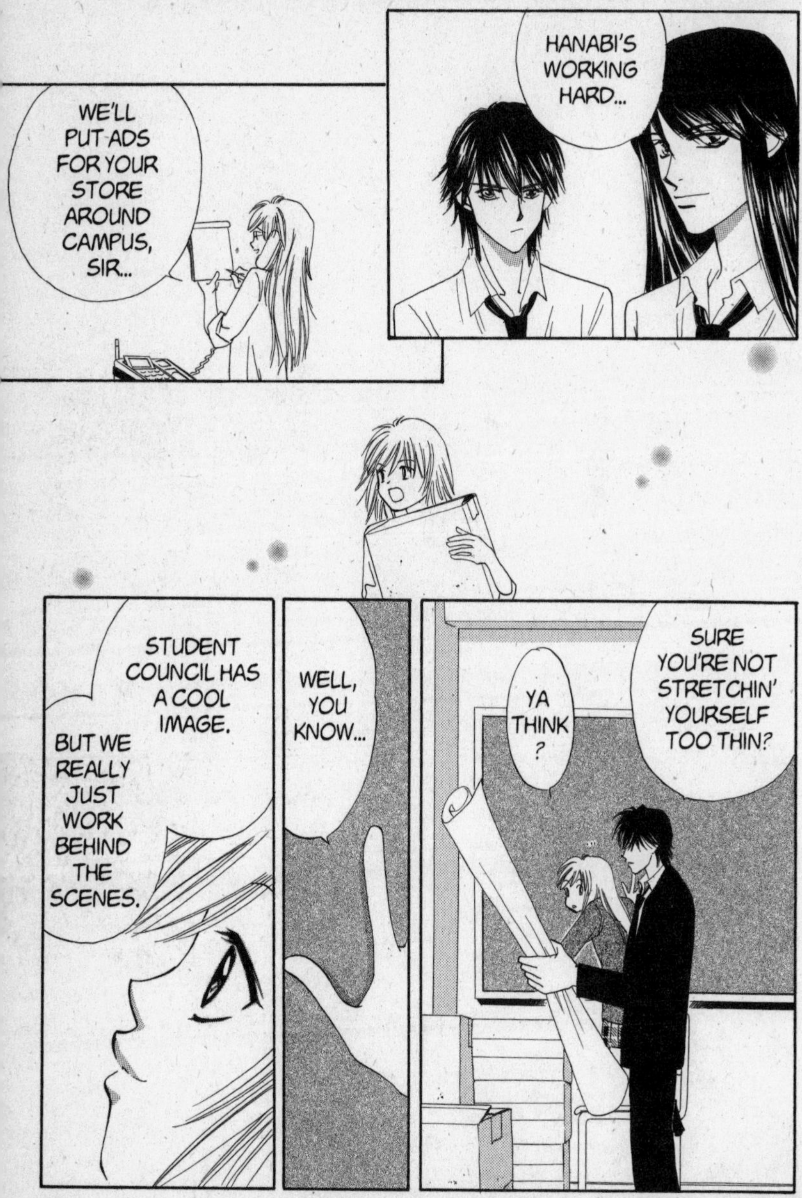
HANABI'S WORKING HARD...
WE'LL PUT ADS FOR YOUR STORE AROUND CAMPUS, SIR...
SURE YOU'RE NOT STRETCHIN' YOURSELF TOO THIN?
YA THINK ?
WELL, YOU KNOW...
STUDENT COUNCIL HAS A COOL IMAGE.
BUT WE REALLY JUST WORK BEHIND THE SCENES.

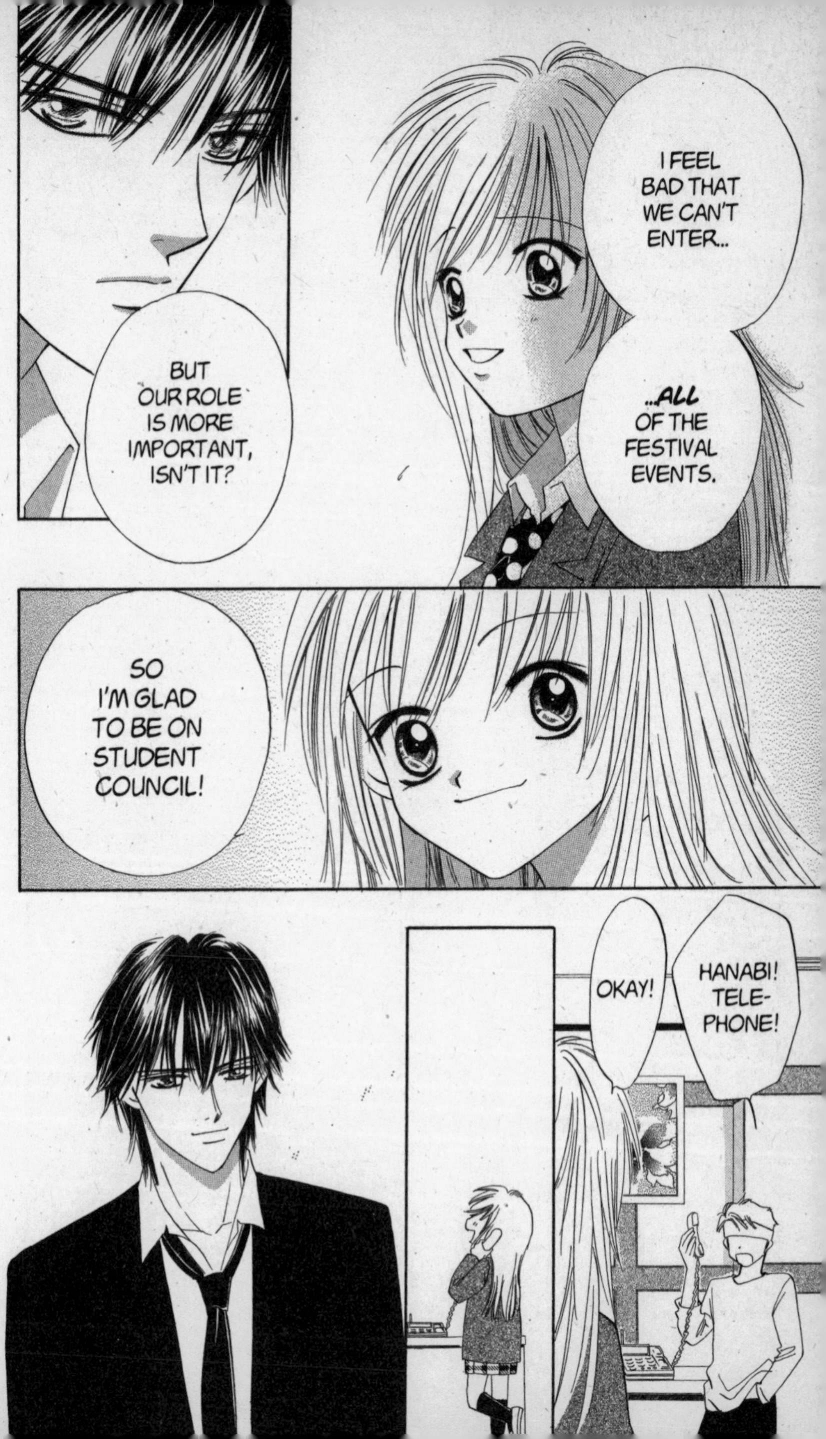
I FEEL BAD THAT WE CAN'T ENTER...
...ALL OF THE FESTIVAL EVENTS.
BUT OUR ROLE IS MORE IMPORTANT, ISN'T IT?
SO I'M GLAD TO BE ON STUDENT COUNCIL!
HANABI! TELE-PHONE!
OKAY!

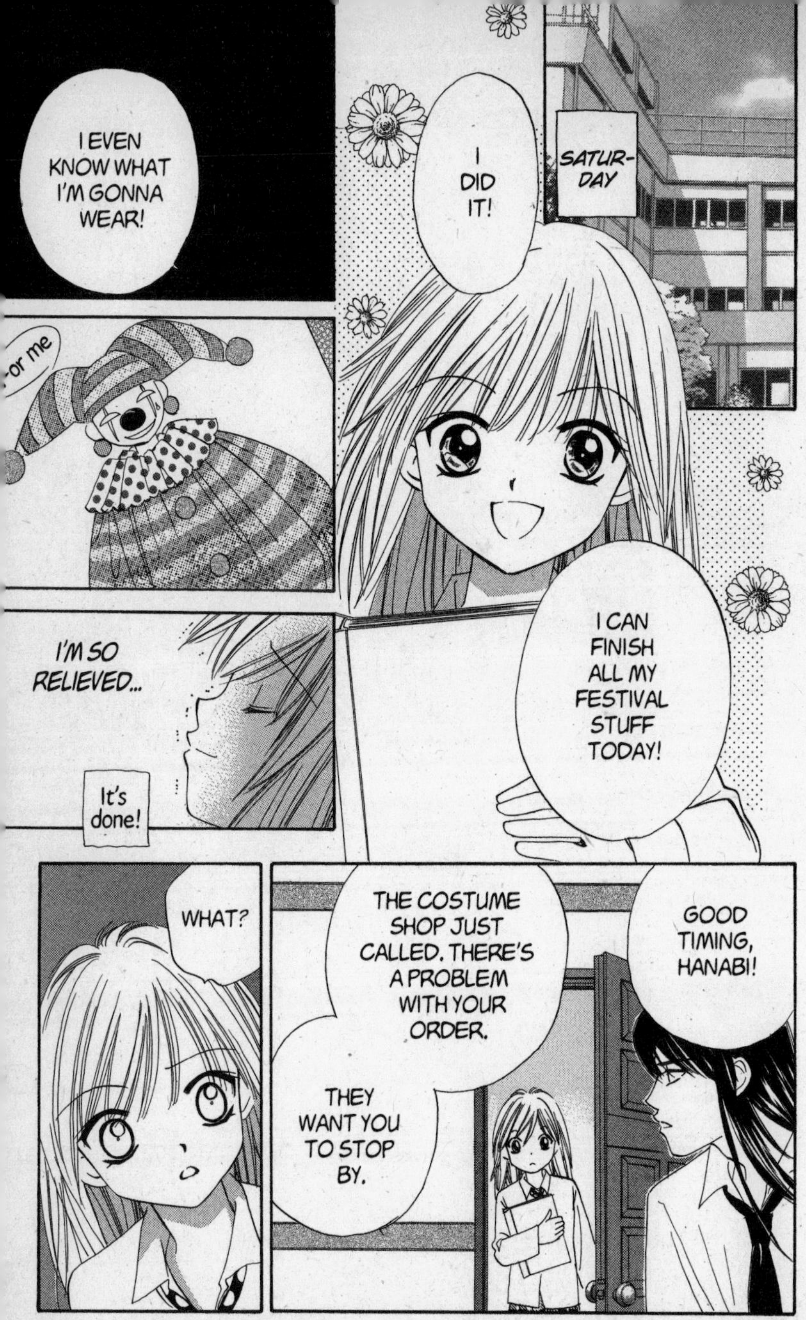
SATUR-DAY
I DID IT!
I CAN FINISH ALL MY FESTIVAL STUFF TODAY!
I EVEN KNOW WHAT I'M GONNA WEAR!
or me
I'M SO RELIEVED...
It's done!
GOOD TIMING, HANABI!
THE COSTUME SHOP JUST CALLED. THERE'S A PROBLEM WITH YOUR ORDER.
THEY WANT YOU TO STOP BY.
WHAT?

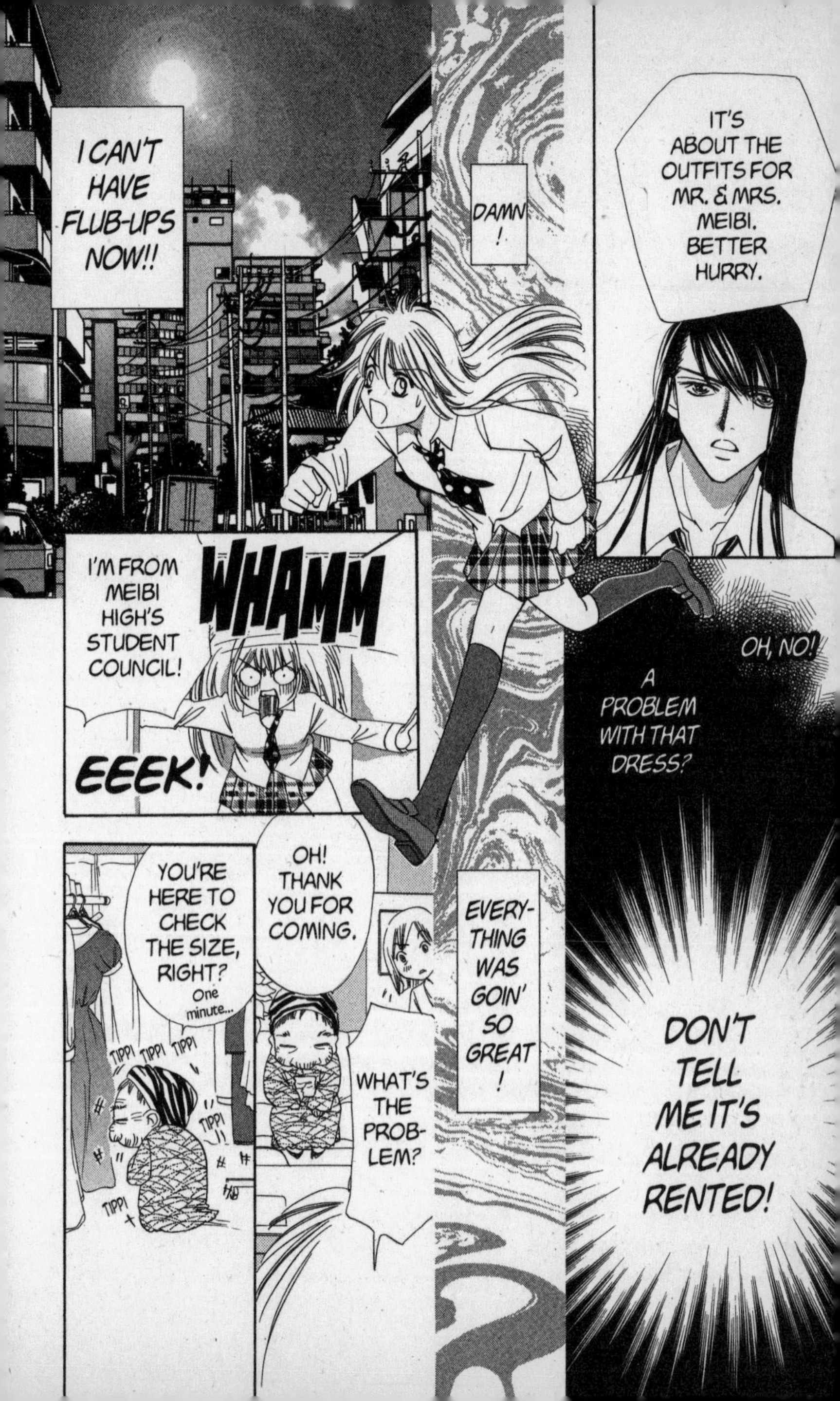
IT'S ABOUT THE OUTFITS FOR MR. & MRS. MEIBI. BETTER HURRY.
DAMN!
I CAN'T HAVE FLUB-UPS NOW!!
OH, NO!
A PROBLEM WITH THAT DRESS?
DON'T TELL ME IT'S ALREADY RENTED!
EVERY-THING WAS GOIN' SO GREAT!
WHAMM
I'M FROM MEIBI HIGH'S STUDENT COUNCIL!
EEEK!
OH! THANK YOU FOR COMING.
WHAT'S THE PROB-LEM?
YOU'RE HERE TO CHECK THE SIZE, RIGHT?
One minute...
TIPPI TIPPI TIPPI
TIPPI
TIPPI

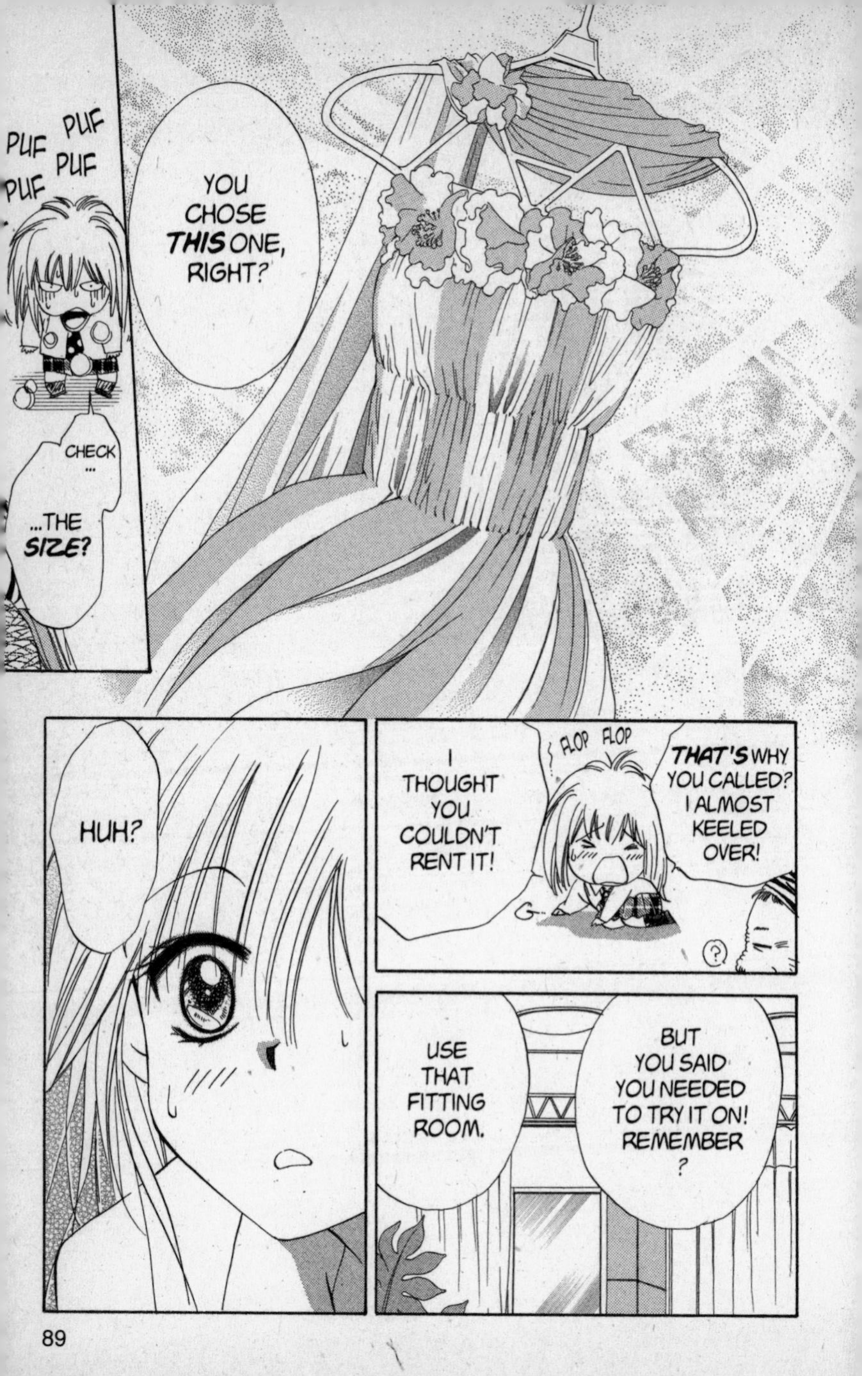
YOU CHOSE THIS ONE, RIGHT?
PUF PUF PUF PUF
CHECK... ...THE SIZE?
THAT'S WHY YOU CALLED? I ALMOST KEELED OVER!
FLOP FLOP
I THOUGHT YOU COULDN'T RENT IT!
?
BUT YOU SAID YOU NEEDED TO TRY IT ON! REMEMBER?
USE THAT FITTING ROOM.
HUH?

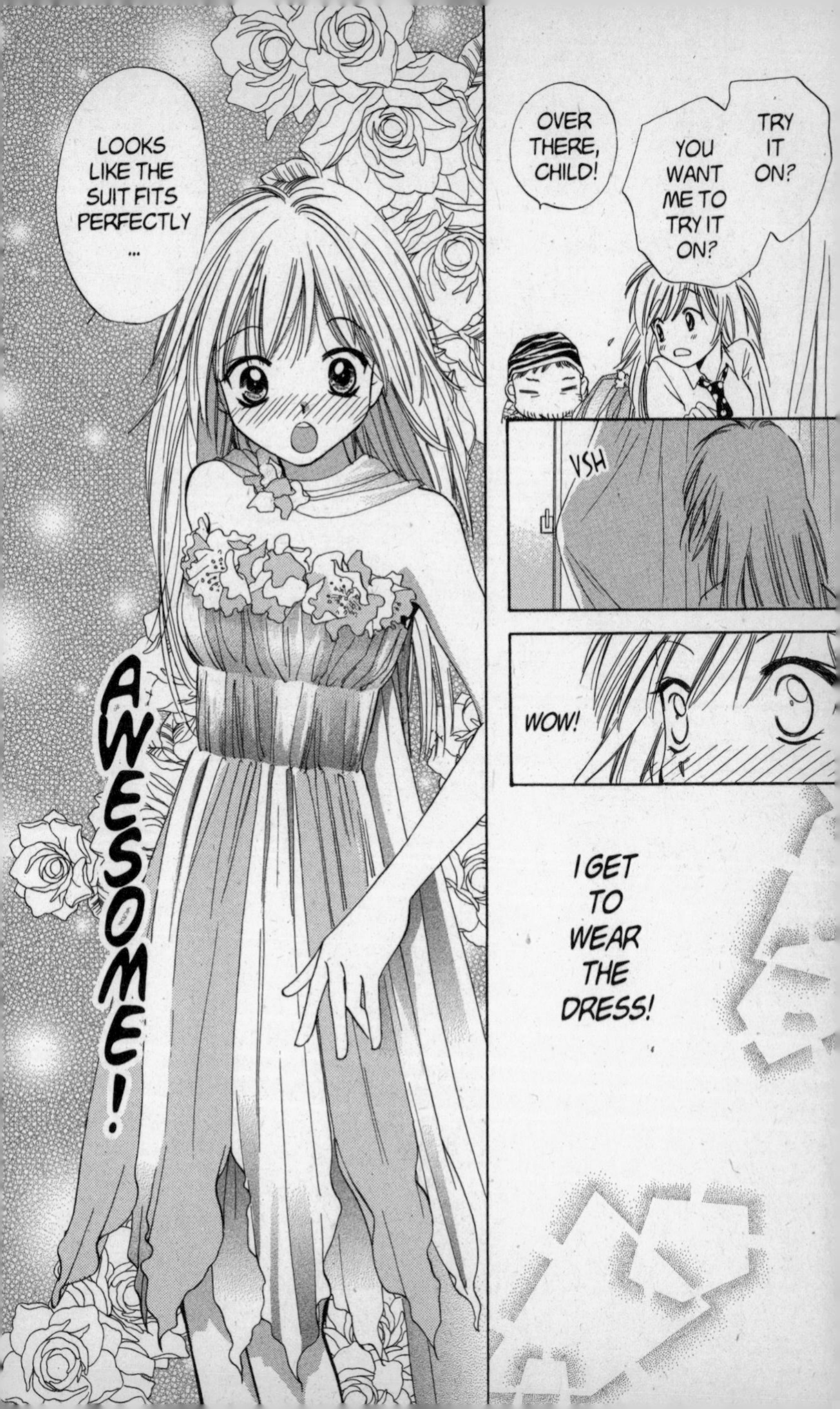
TRY IT ON? YOU WANT ME TO TRY IT ON?
OVER THERE, CHILD!
VSH
WOW!
I GET TO WEAR THE DRESS!
LOOKS LIKE THE SUIT FITS PERFECTLY ...
AWESOME!

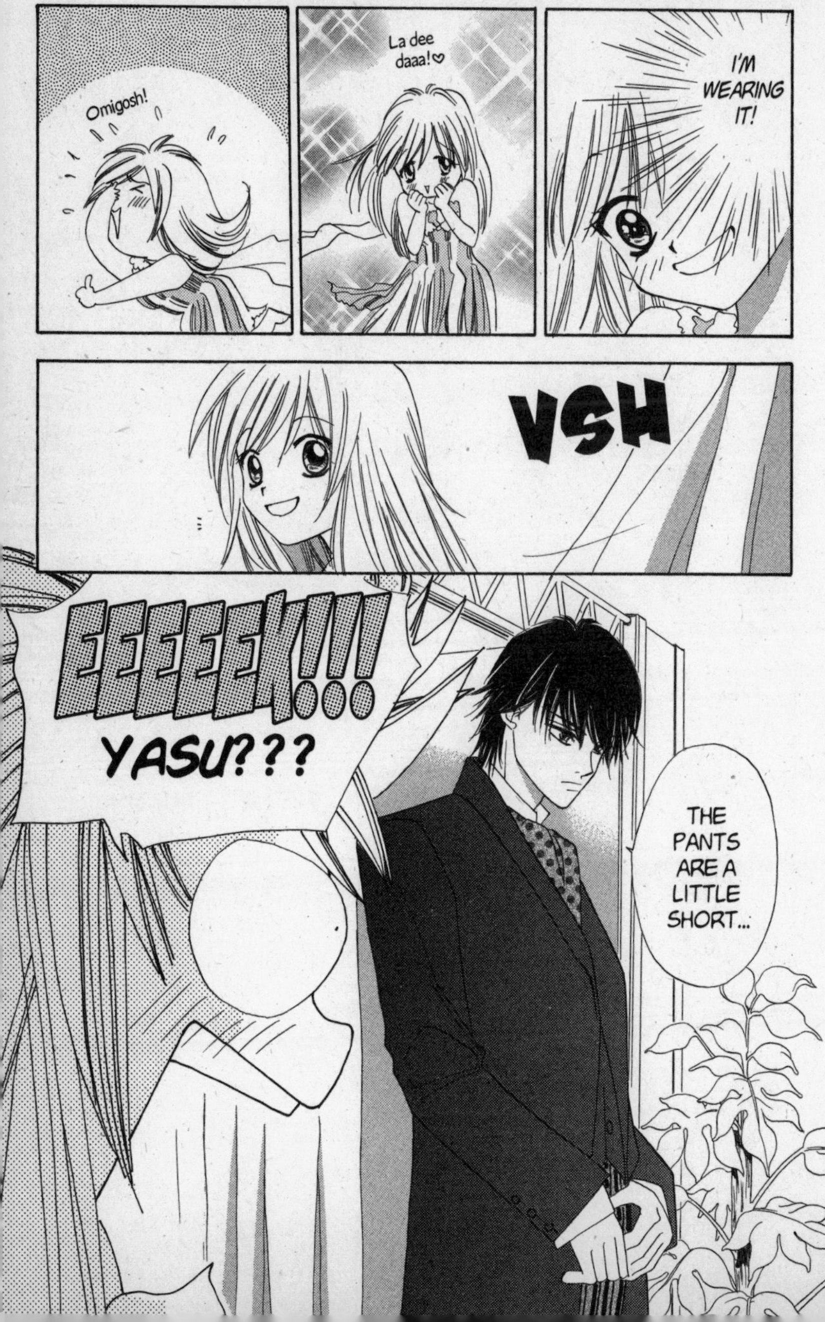
I'M WEARING IT!
La dee daaa!♡
Omigosh!
VSH
THE PANTS ARE A LITTLE SHORT...
EEEEEK!!!
YASU???

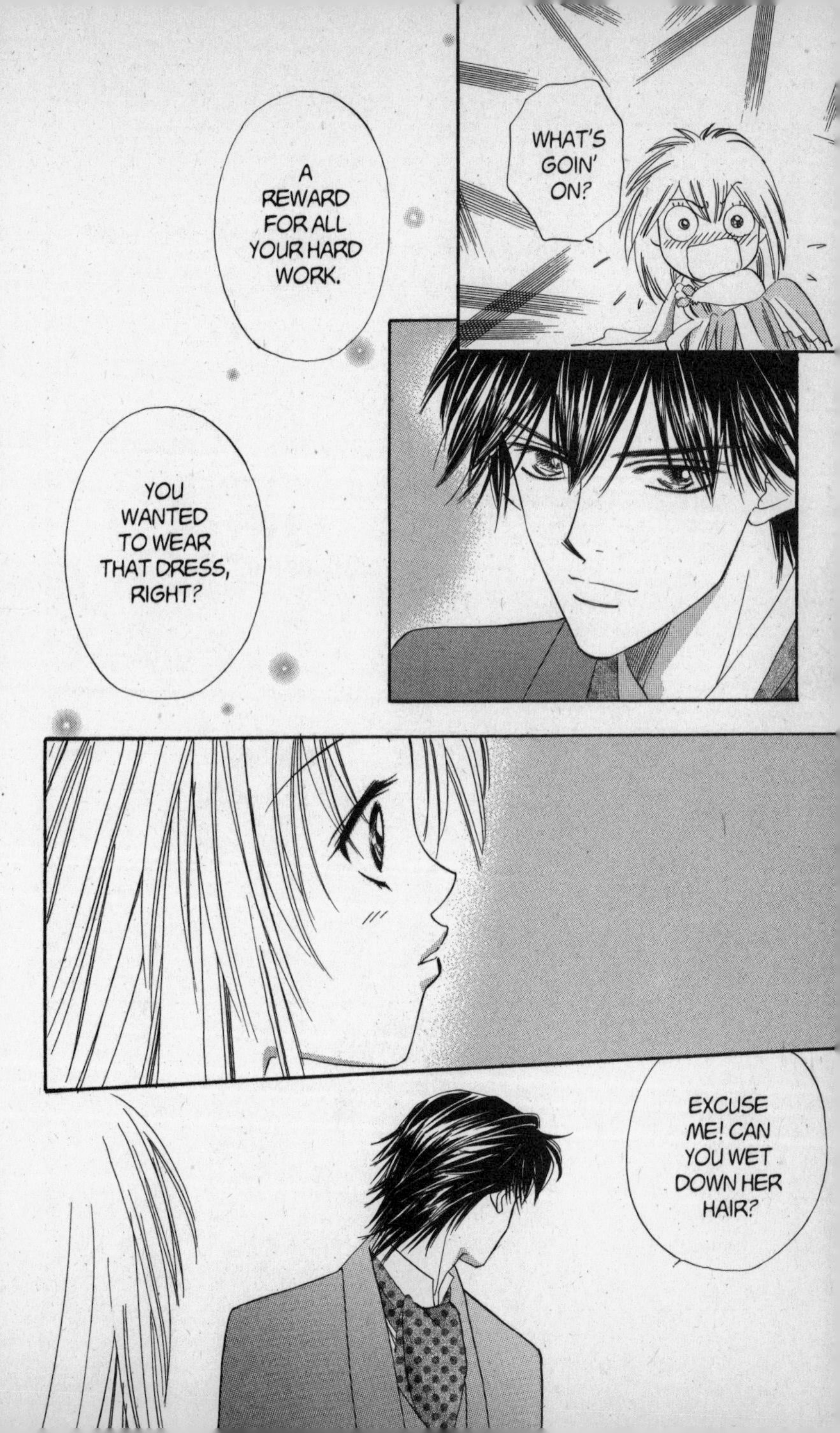
WHAT'S GOIN' ON?
A REWARD FOR ALL YOUR HARD WORK.
YOU WANTED TO WEAR THAT DRESS, RIGHT?
EXCUSE ME! CAN YOU WET DOWN HER HAIR?

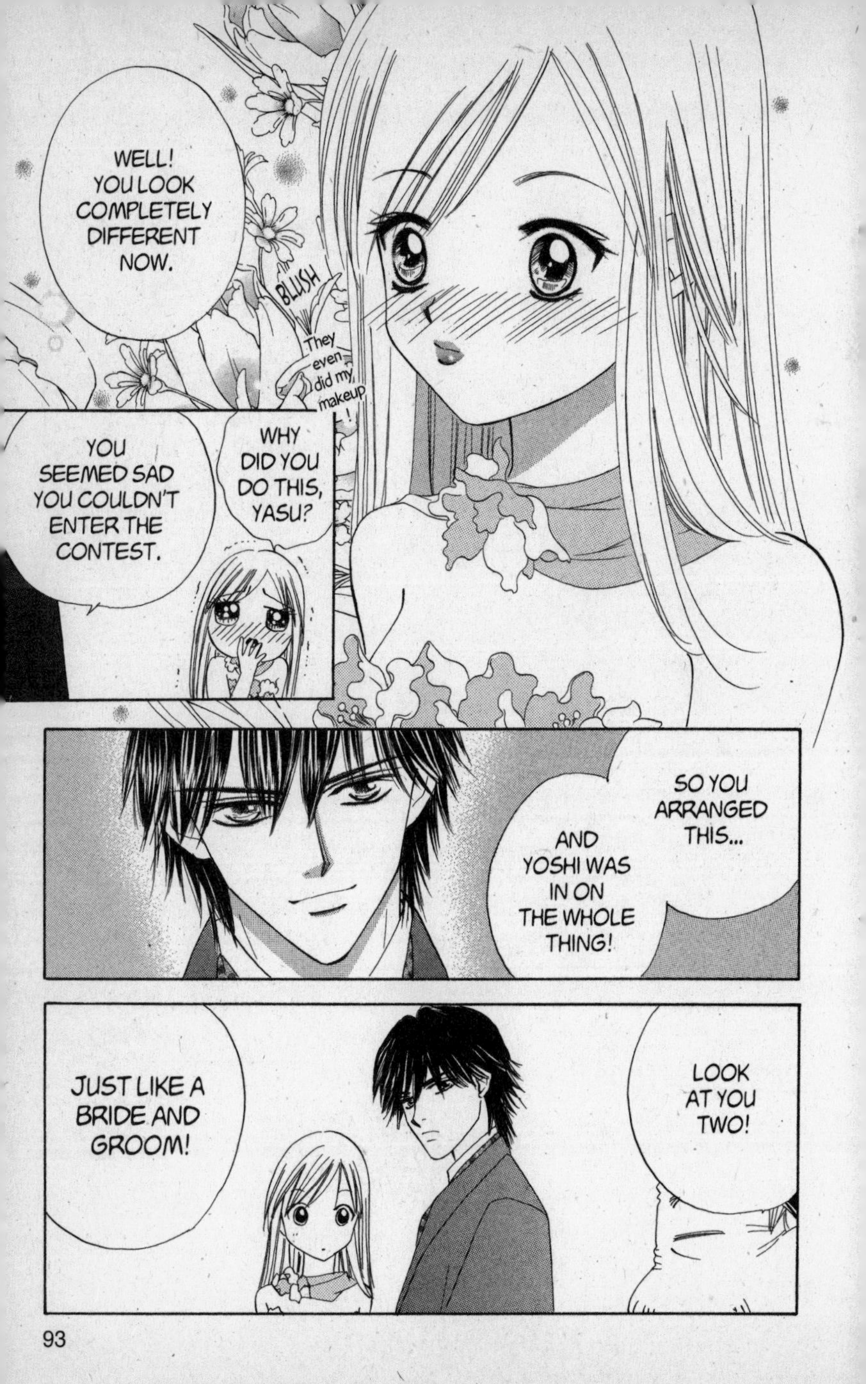
WELL! YOU LOOK COMPLETELY DIFFERENT NOW.
BLUSH
They even did my makeup!
WHY DID YOU DO THIS, YASU?
YOU SEEMED SAD YOU COULDN'T ENTER THE CONTEST.
SO YOU ARRANGED THIS...
AND YOSHI WAS IN ON THE WHOLE THING!
LOOK AT YOU TWO!
JUST LIKE A BRIDE AND GROOM!

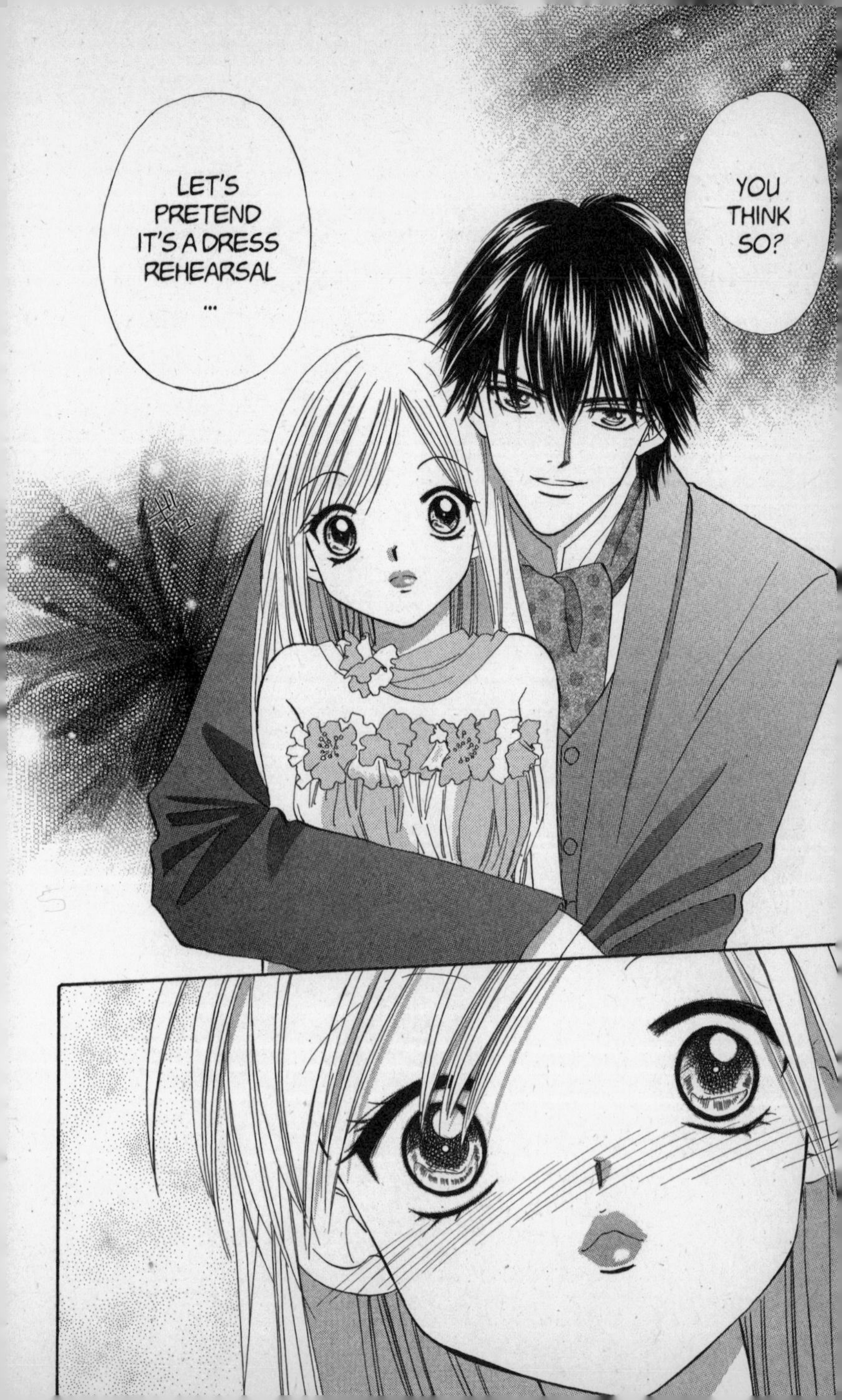
YOU THINK SO?
LET'S PRETEND IT'S A DRESS REHEARSAL ...

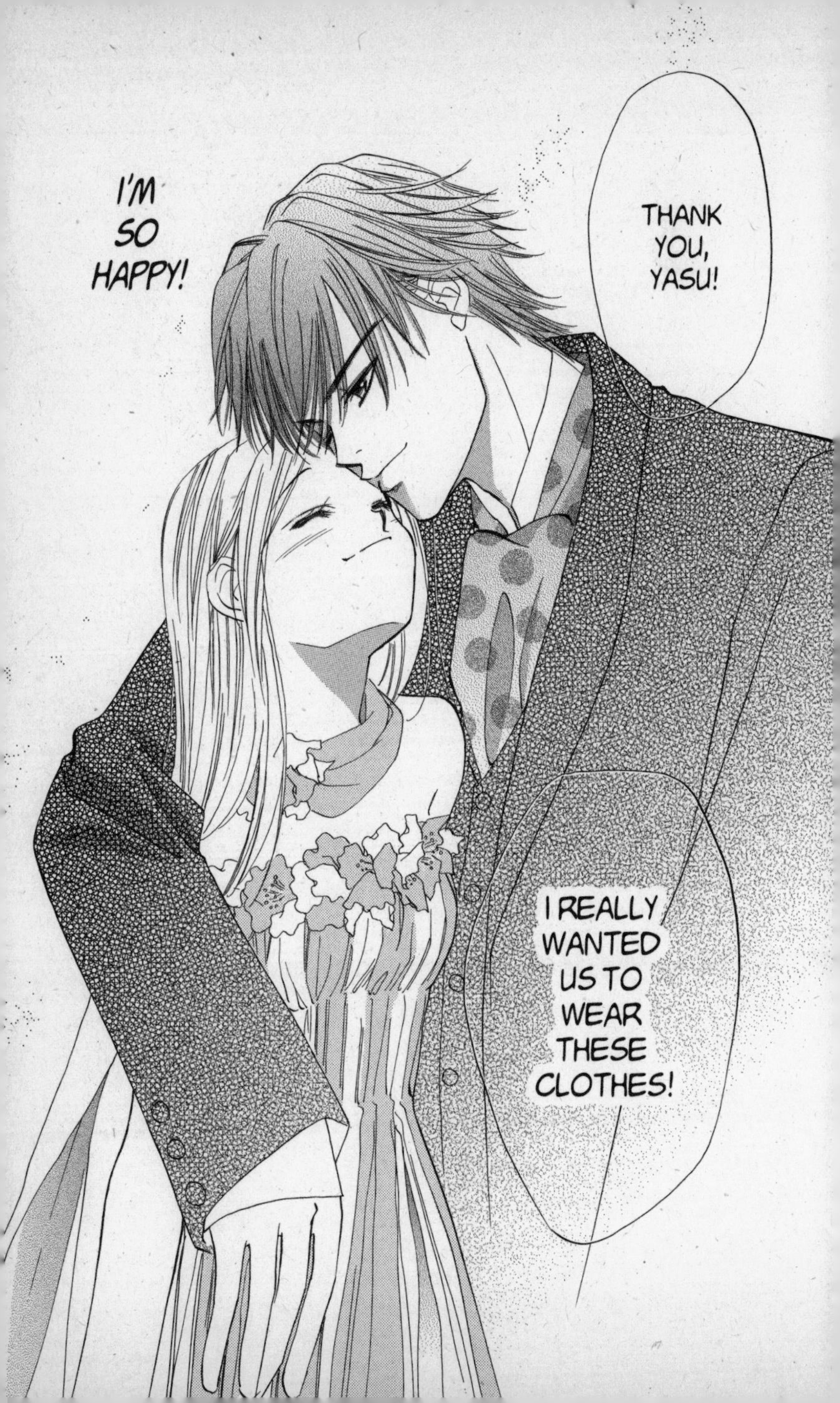
THANK YOU, YASU!
I'M SO HAPPY!
I REALLY WANTED US TO WEAR THESE CLOTHES!

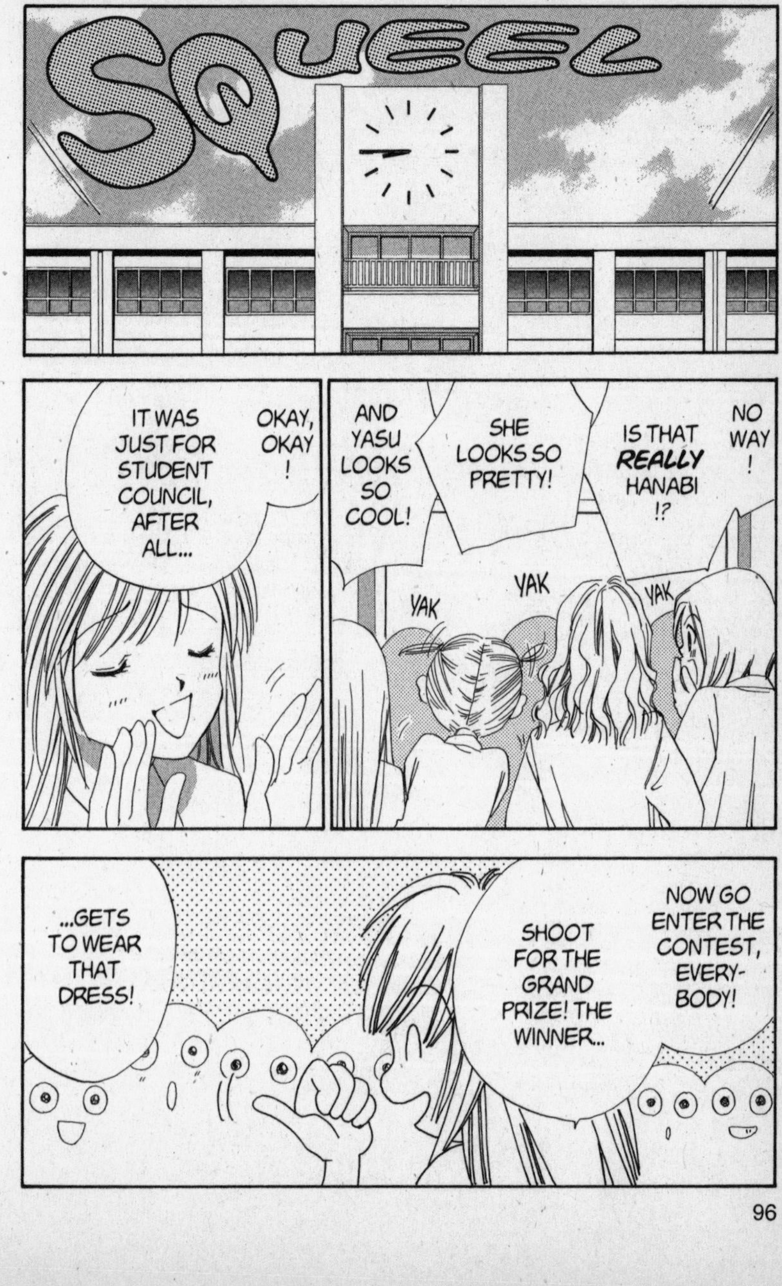
SQUEEL
NO WAY!
IS THAT **REALLY** HANABI!?
SHE LOOKS SO PRETTY!
AND YASU LOOKS SO COOL!
YAK
YAK
YAK
OKAY, OKAY!
IT WAS JUST FOR STUDENT COUNCIL, AFTER ALL...
NOW GO ENTER THE CONTEST, EVERY-BODY!
SHOOT FOR THE GRAND PRIZE! THE WINNER...
...GETS TO WEAR THAT DRESS!

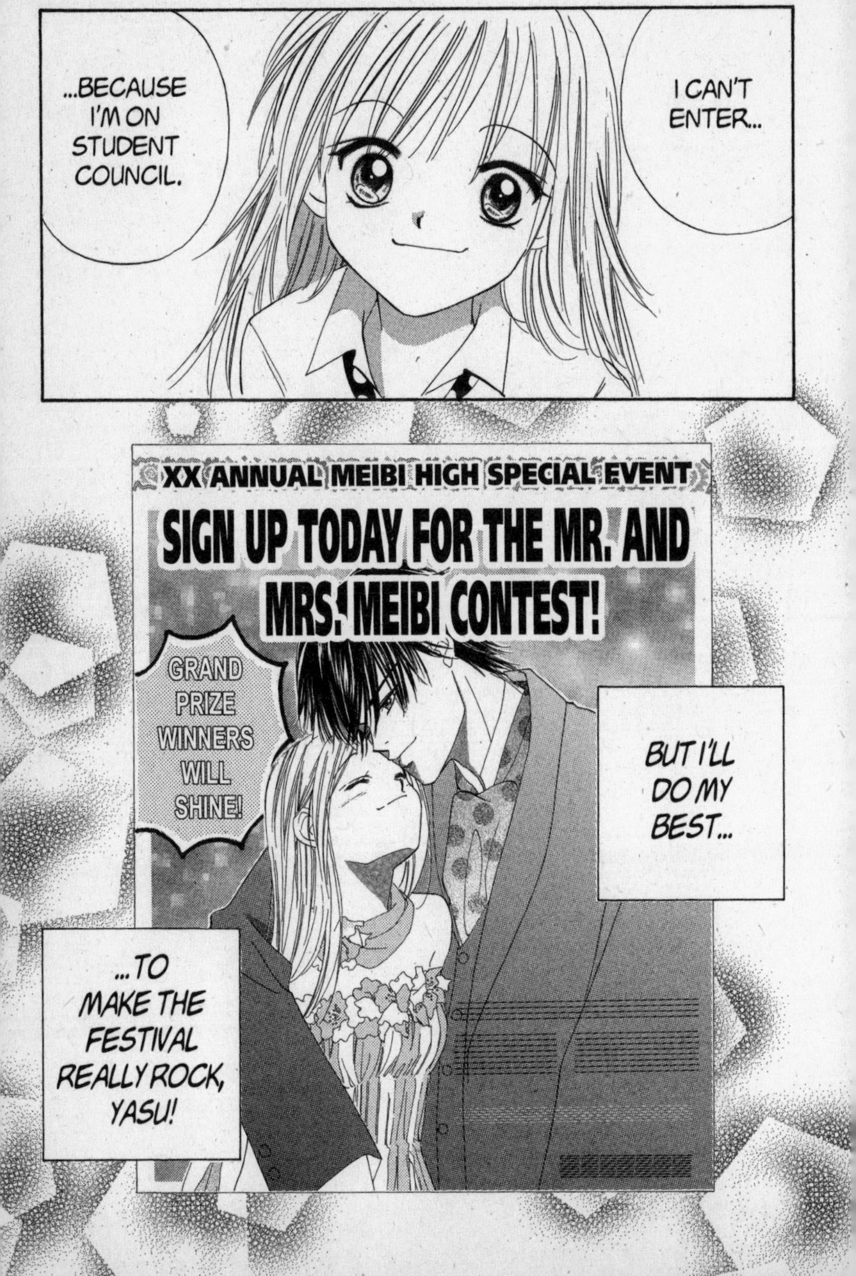
I CAN'T ENTER...
...BECAUSE I'M ON STUDENT COUNCIL.
XX ANNUAL MEIBI HIGH SPECIAL EVENT
SIGN UP TODAY FOR THE MR. AND MRS. MEIBI CONTEST!
GRAND PRIZE WINNERS WILL SHINE!
BUT I'LL DO MY BEST...
...TO MAKE THE FESTIVAL REALLY ROCK, YASU!

HAPPY
HUST
HIGH

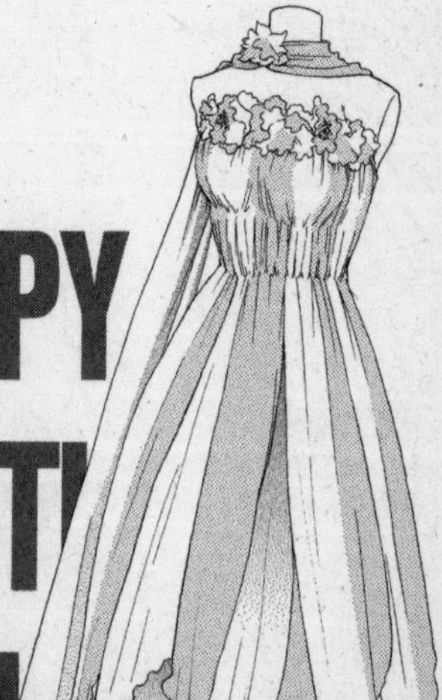

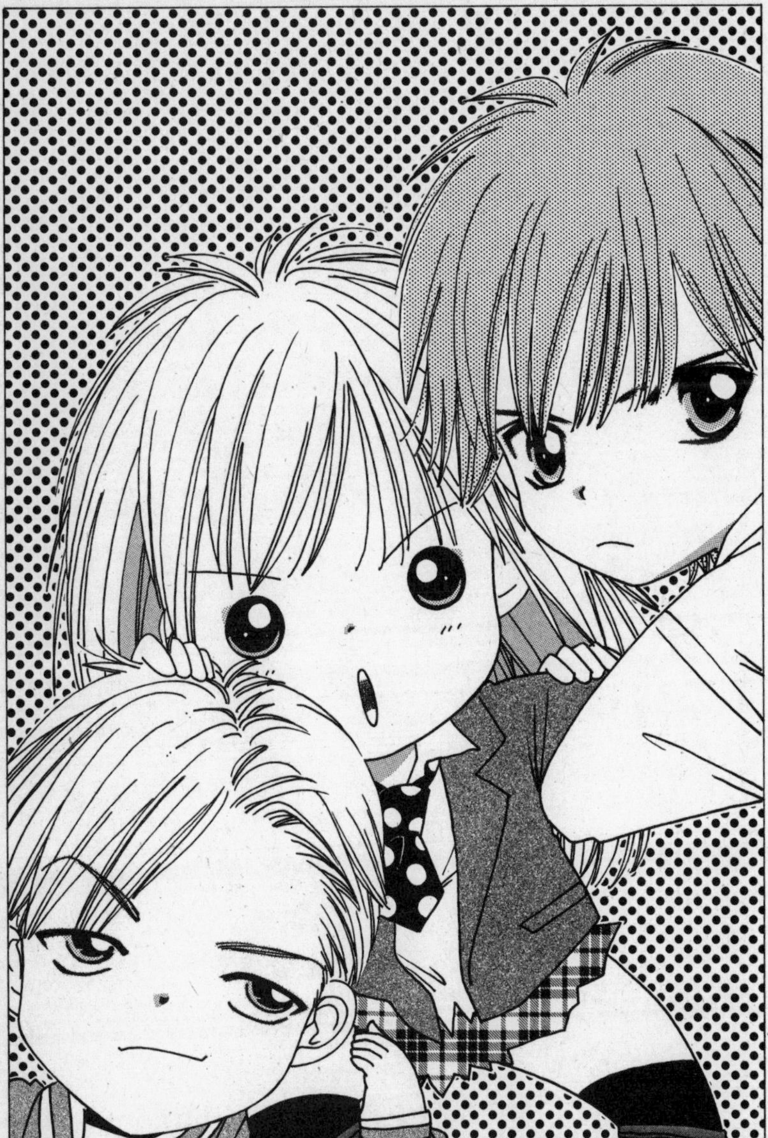

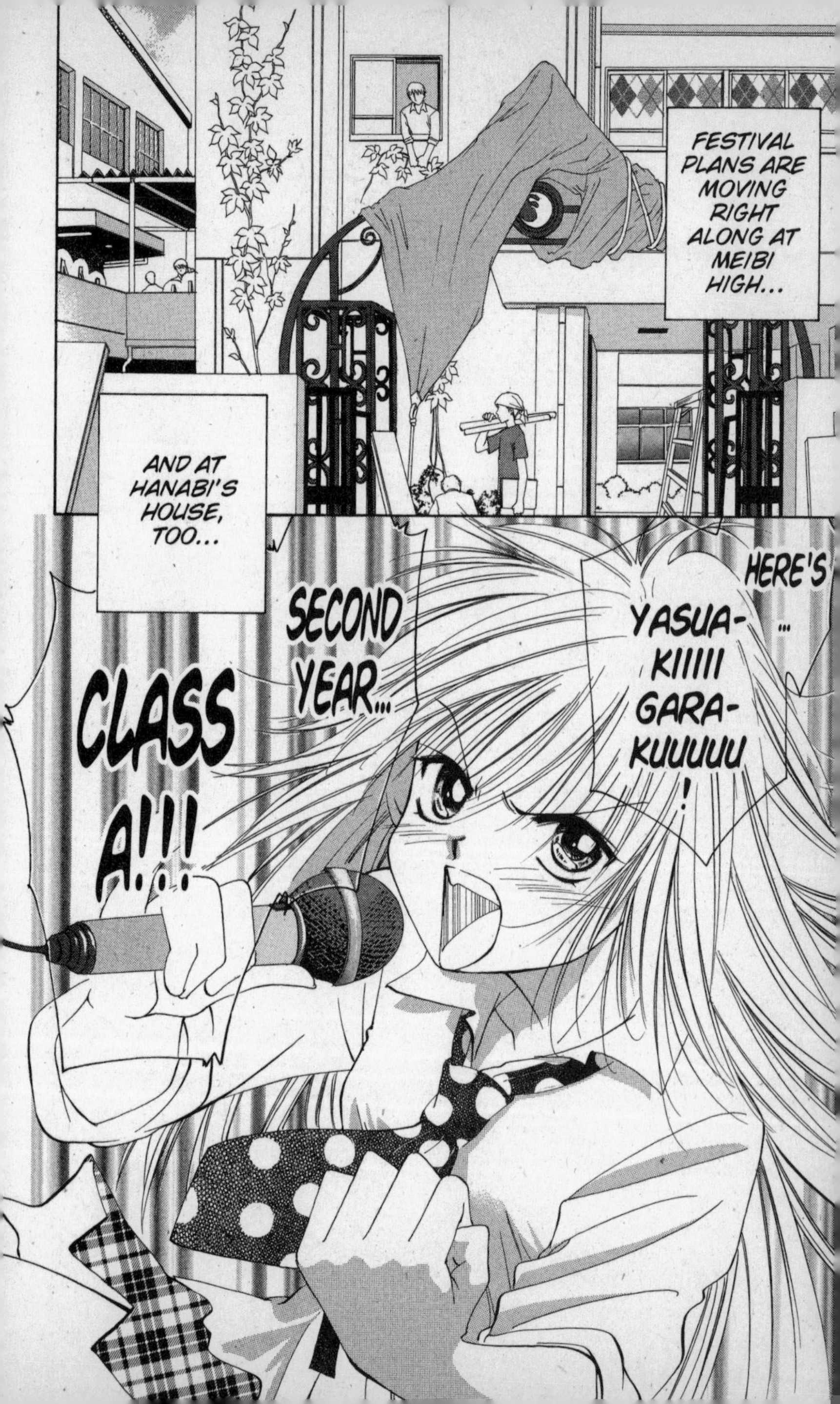
FESTIVAL PLANS ARE MOVING RIGHT ALONG AT MEIBI HIGH...
AND AT HANABI'S HOUSE, TOO...
HERE'S ...
YASUA-KIIIII GARA-KUUUUU!
SECOND YEAR...
CLASS A!!!

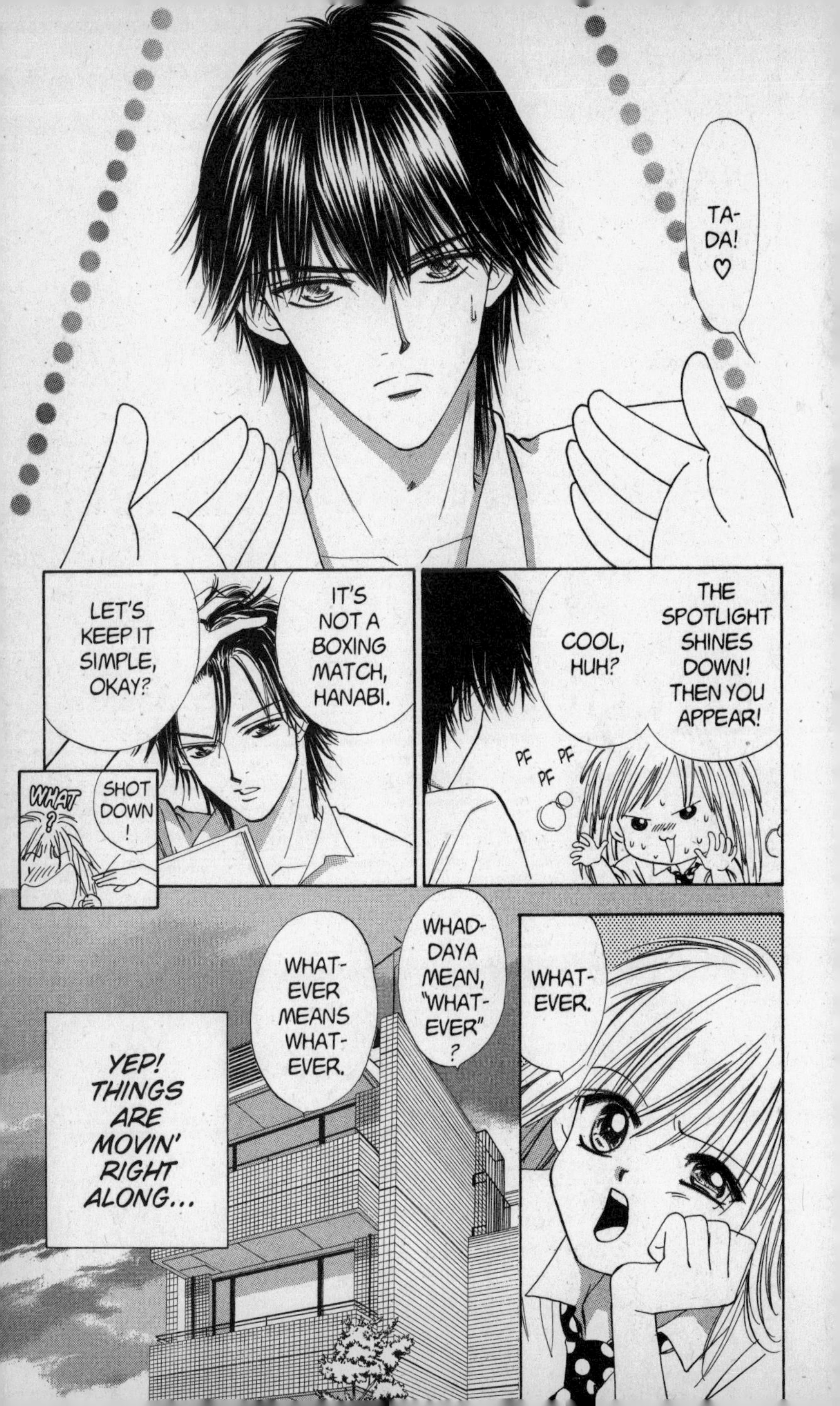
TA-DA! ♡
THE SPOTLIGHT SHINES DOWN! THEN YOU APPEAR!
COOL, HUH?
PF PF PF
IT'S NOT A BOXING MATCH, HANABI.
LET'S KEEP IT SIMPLE, OKAY?
SHOT DOWN!
WHAT ?
WHAT-EVER.
WHAD-DAYA MEAN, "WHAT-EVER"?
WHAT-EVER MEANS WHAT-EVER.
YEP! THINGS ARE MOVIN' RIGHT ALONG...

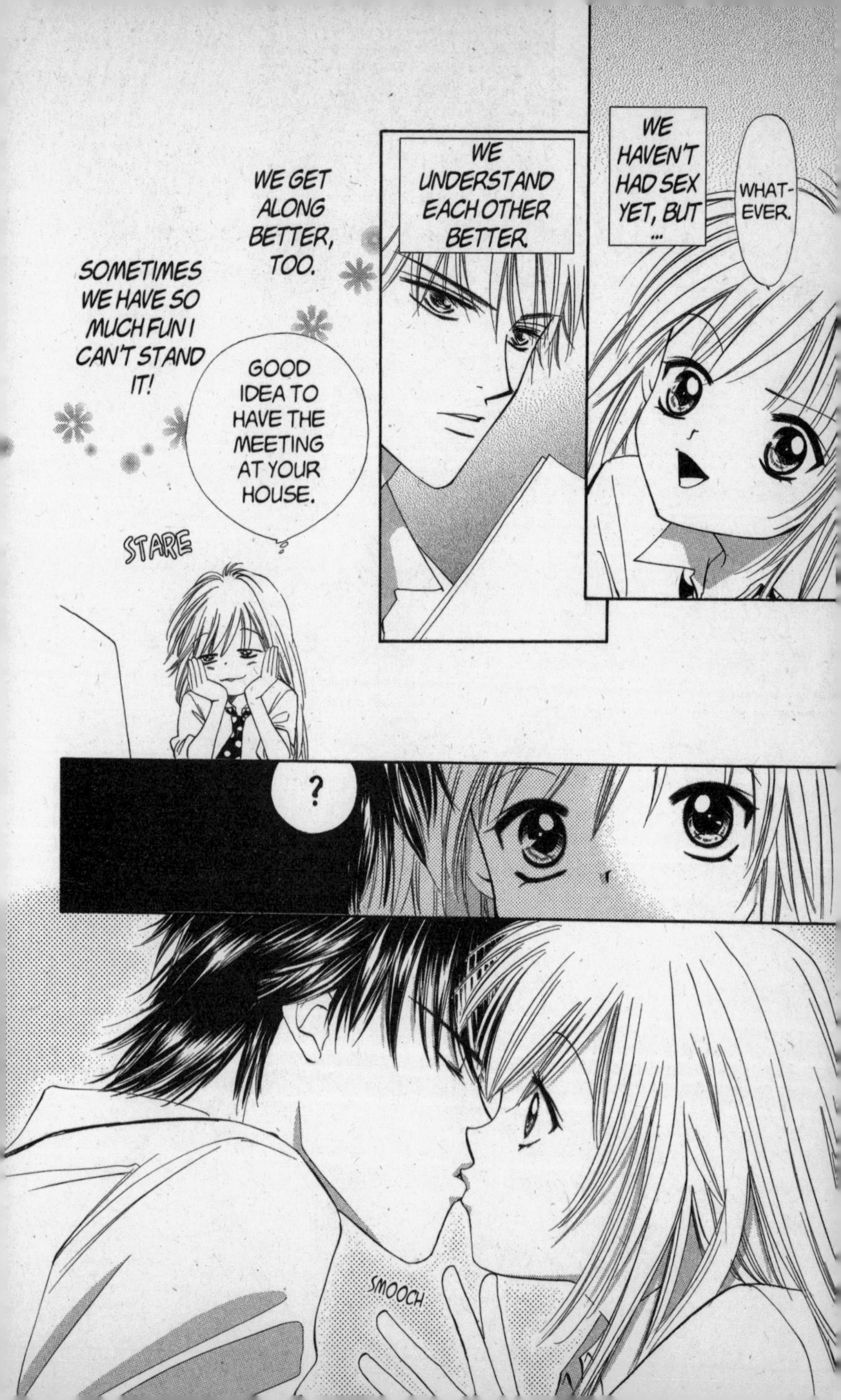
WHAT-EVER.
WE HAVEN'T HAD SEX YET, BUT ...
WE UNDERSTAND EACH OTHER BETTER.
WE GET ALONG BETTER, TOO.
SOMETIMES WE HAVE SO MUCH FUN I CAN'T STAND IT!
GOOD IDEA TO HAVE THE MEETING AT YOUR HOUSE.
STARE
?
SMOOCH

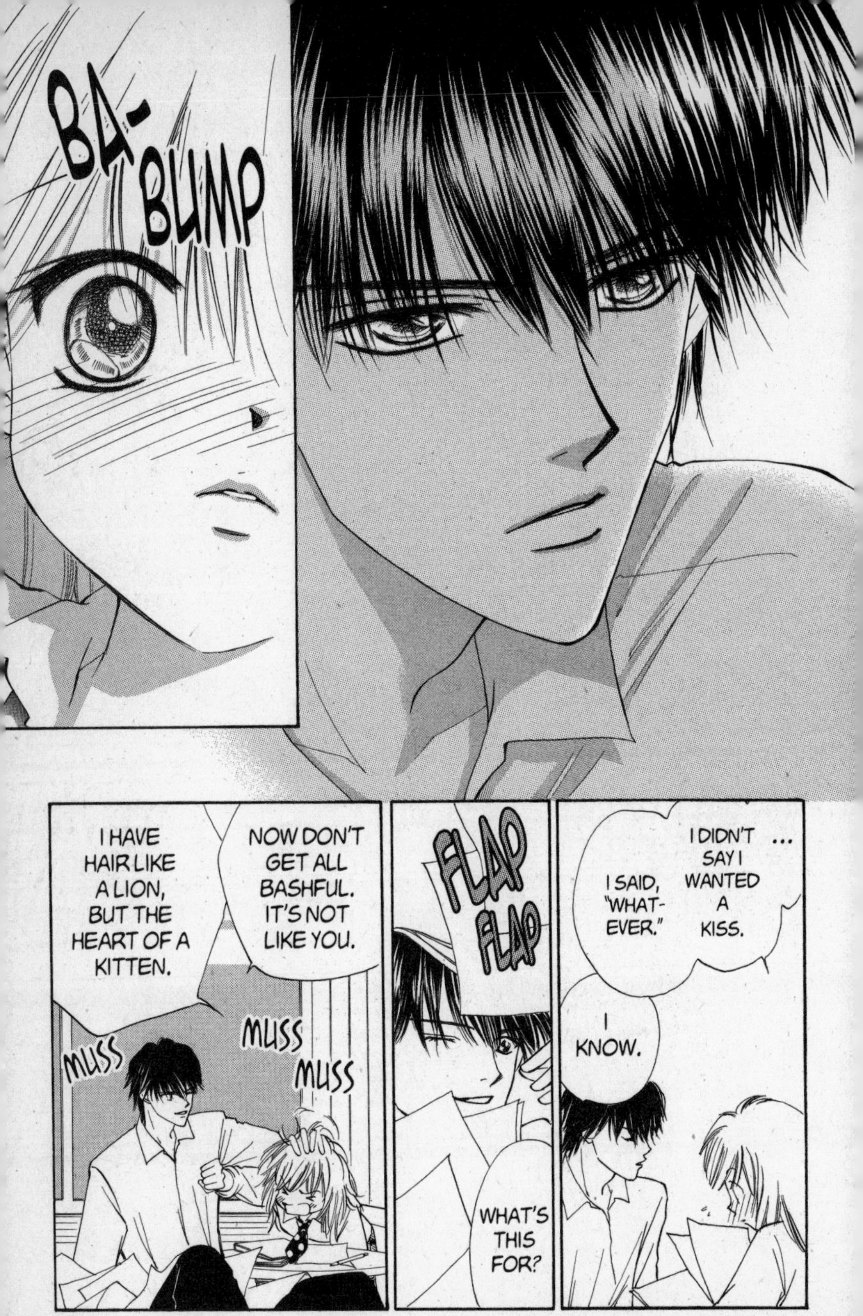
BA-BUMP
...
I DIDN'T SAY I WANTED A KISS.
I SAID, "WHATEVER."
I KNOW.
FLAP FLAP
WHAT'S THIS FOR?
NOW DON'T GET ALL BASHFUL. IT'S NOT LIKE YOU.
I HAVE HAIR LIKE A LION, BUT THE HEART OF A KITTEN.
MUSS MUSS MUSS

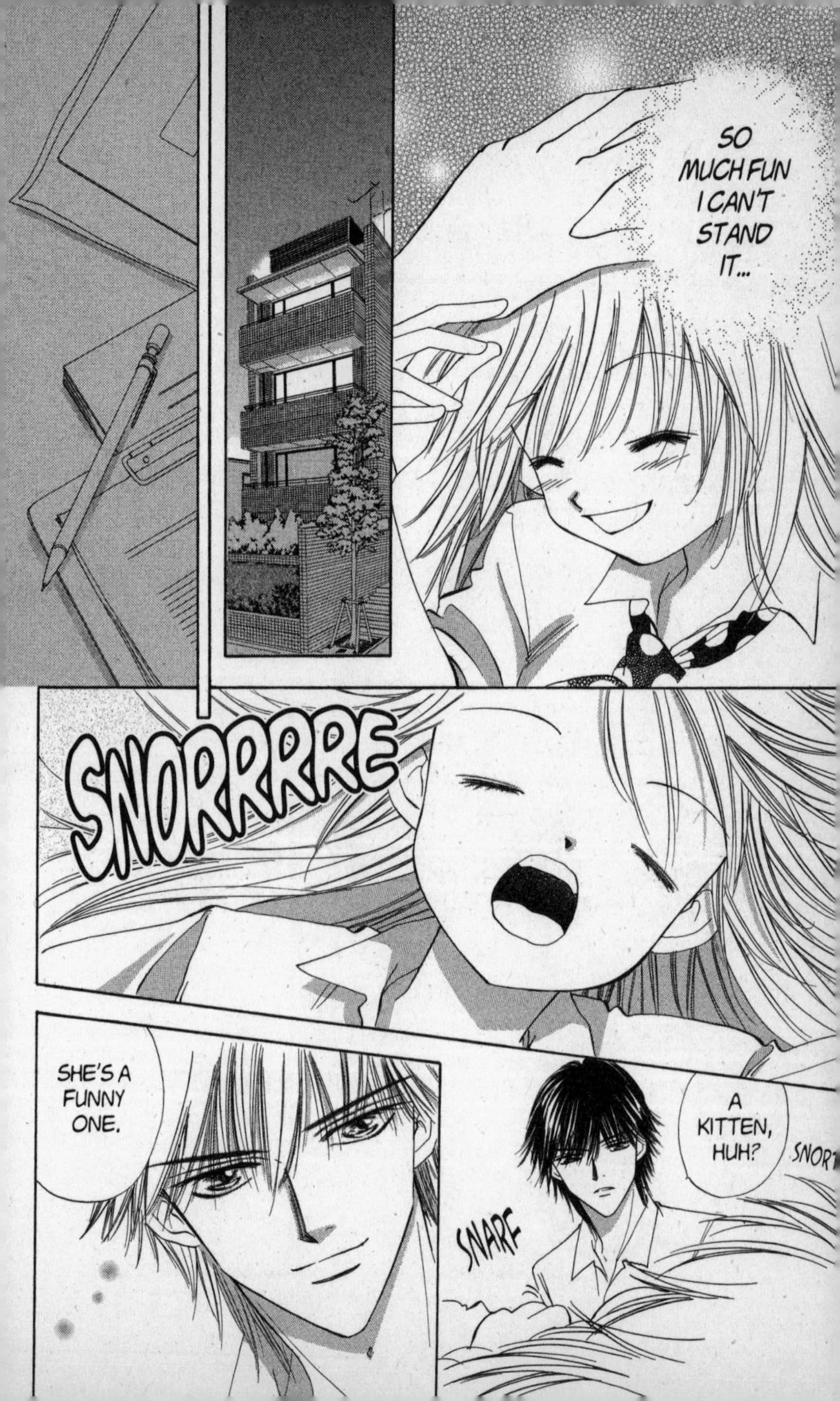
SO MUCH FUN I CAN'T STAND IT...
SNORRRRE
A KITTEN, HUH?
SNORT
SNARF
SHE'S A FUNNY ONE.

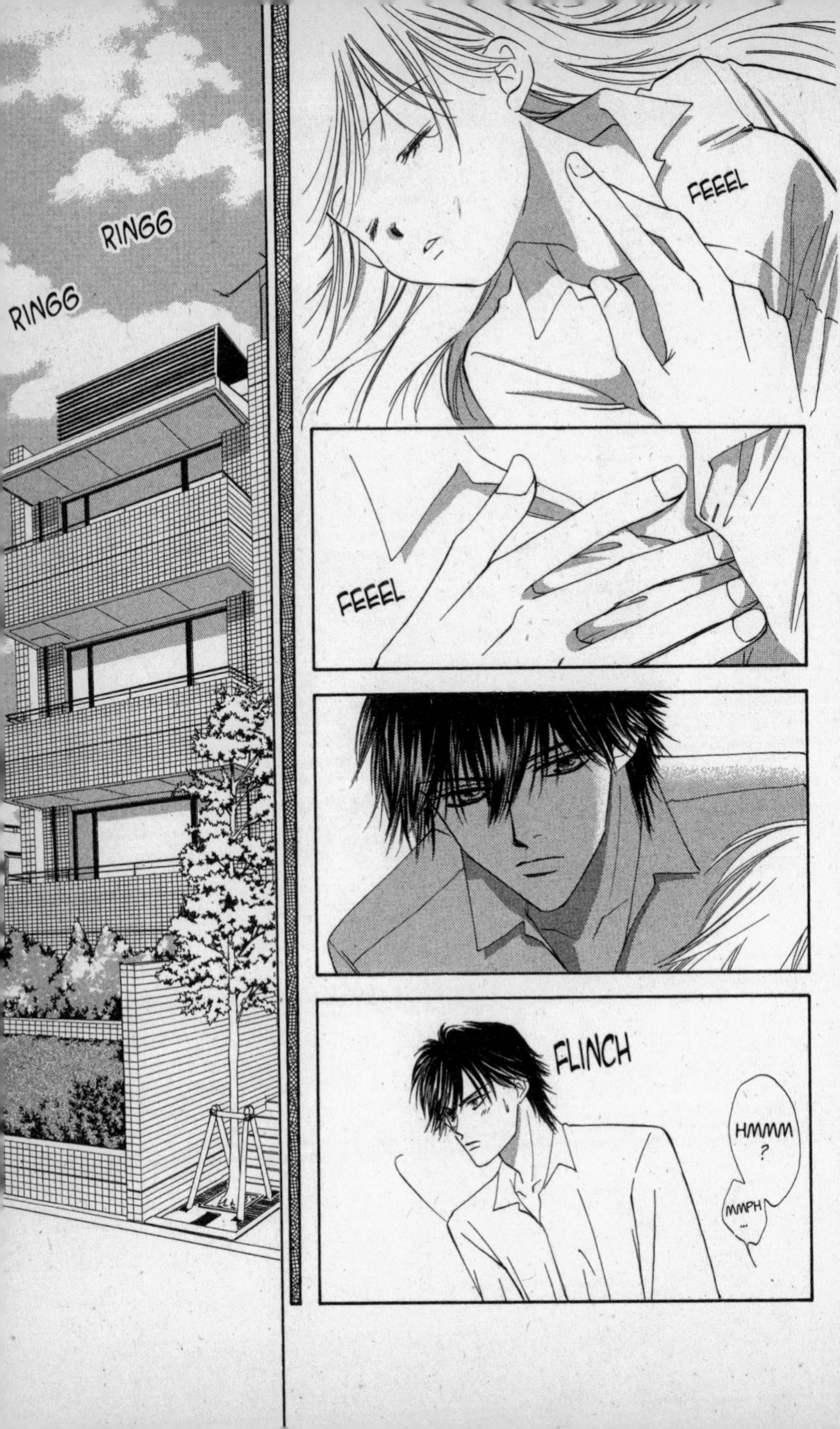
FEEEL
FEEEL
FLINCH
HMMM ?
MMPH ...
RINGG
RINGG

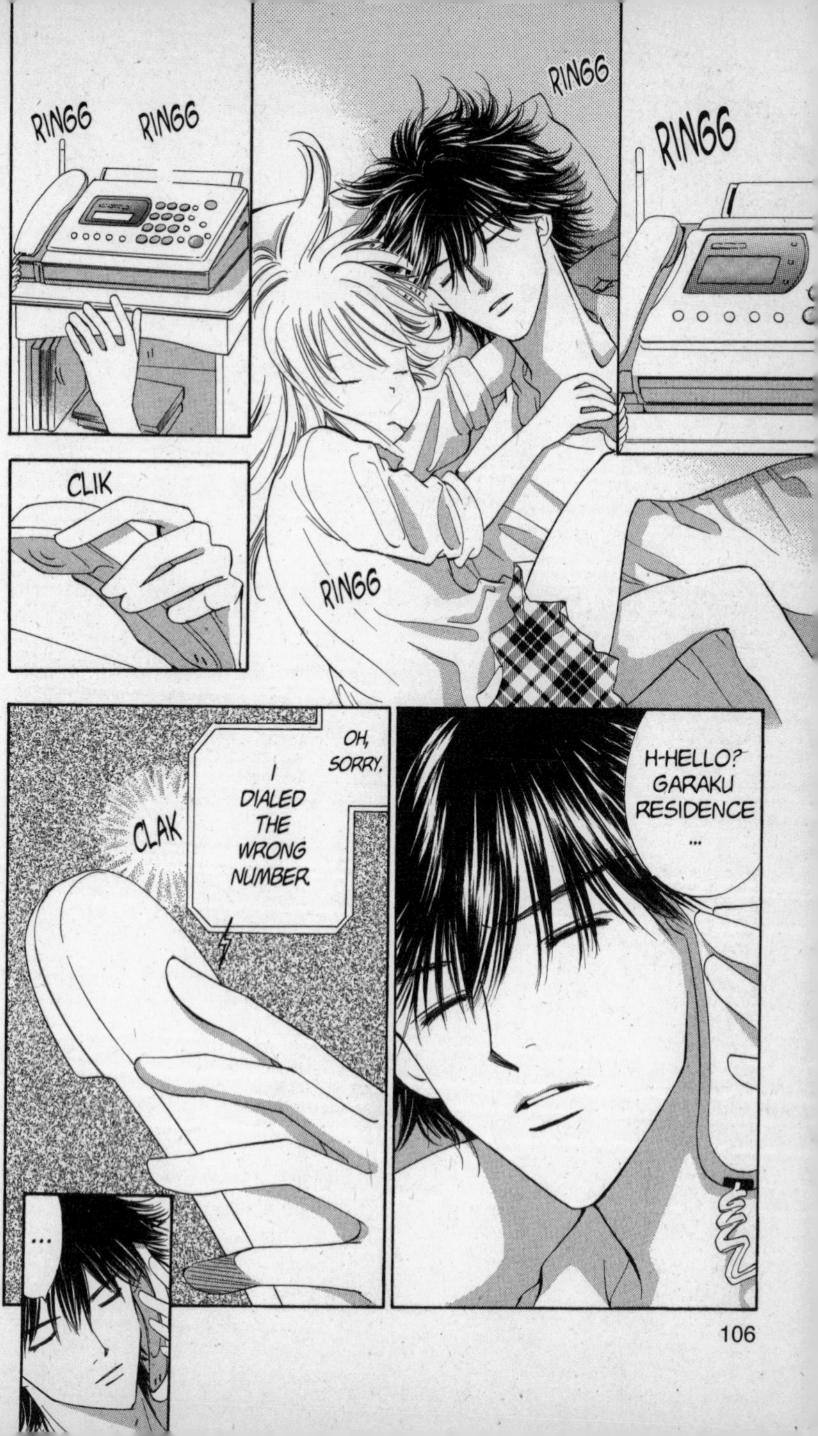

RINGG
RINGG
RINGG
RINGG
RINGG
CLIK
H-HELLO? GARAKU RESIDENCE ...
OH, SORRY.
I DIALED THE WRONG NUMBER.
CLAK
...

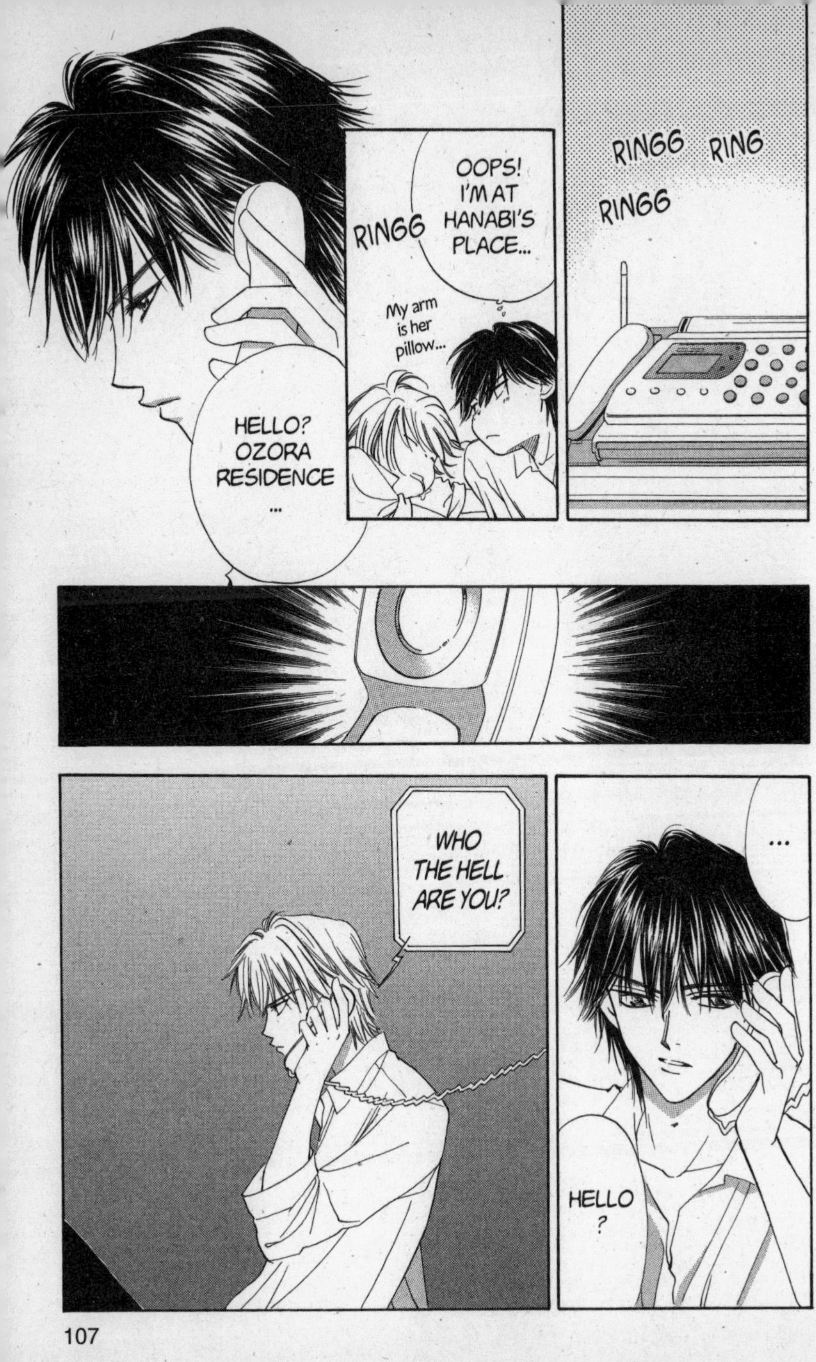
RINGG RING
RINGG
OOPS! I'M AT HANABI'S PLACE...
RINGG
My arm is her pillow...
HELLO? OZORA RESIDENCE ...
...
HELLO ?
WHO THE HELL ARE YOU?

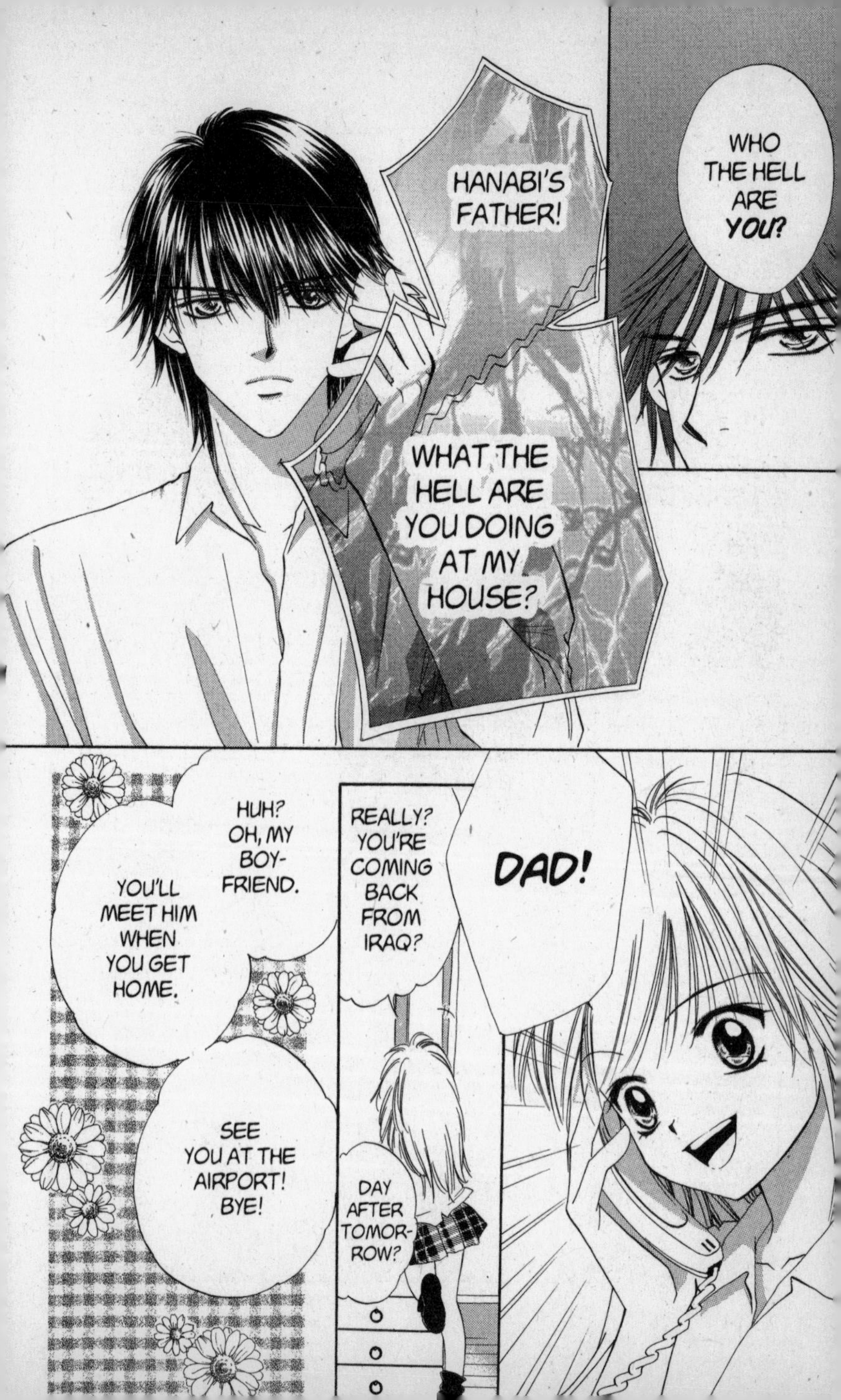
WHO THE HELL ARE YOU?
HANABI'S FATHER!
WHAT THE HELL ARE YOU DOING AT MY HOUSE?
DAD!
REALLY? YOU'RE COMING BACK FROM IRAQ?
DAY AFTER TOMOR-ROW?
HUH? OH, MY BOY-FRIEND.
YOU'LL MEET HIM WHEN YOU GET HOME.
SEE YOU AT THE AIRPORT! BYE!

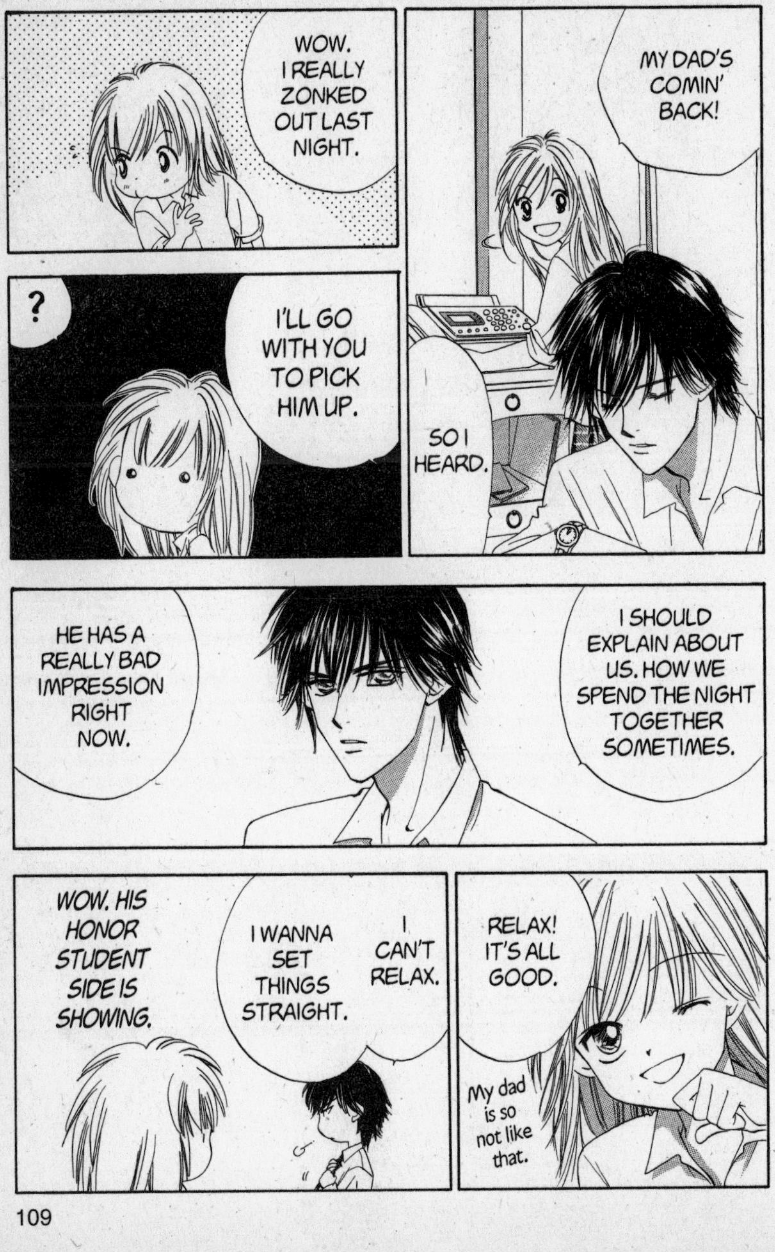
MY DAD'S COMIN' BACK!
SO I HEARD.
WOW. I REALLY ZONKED OUT LAST NIGHT.
?
I'LL GO WITH YOU TO PICK HIM UP.
I SHOULD EXPLAIN ABOUT US. HOW WE SPEND THE NIGHT TOGETHER SOMETIMES.
HE HAS A REALLY BAD IMPRESSION RIGHT NOW.
RELAX! IT'S ALL GOOD.
My dad is so not like that.
I CAN'T RELAX.
I WANNA SET THINGS STRAIGHT.
WOW. HIS HONOR STUDENT SIDE IS SHOWING.

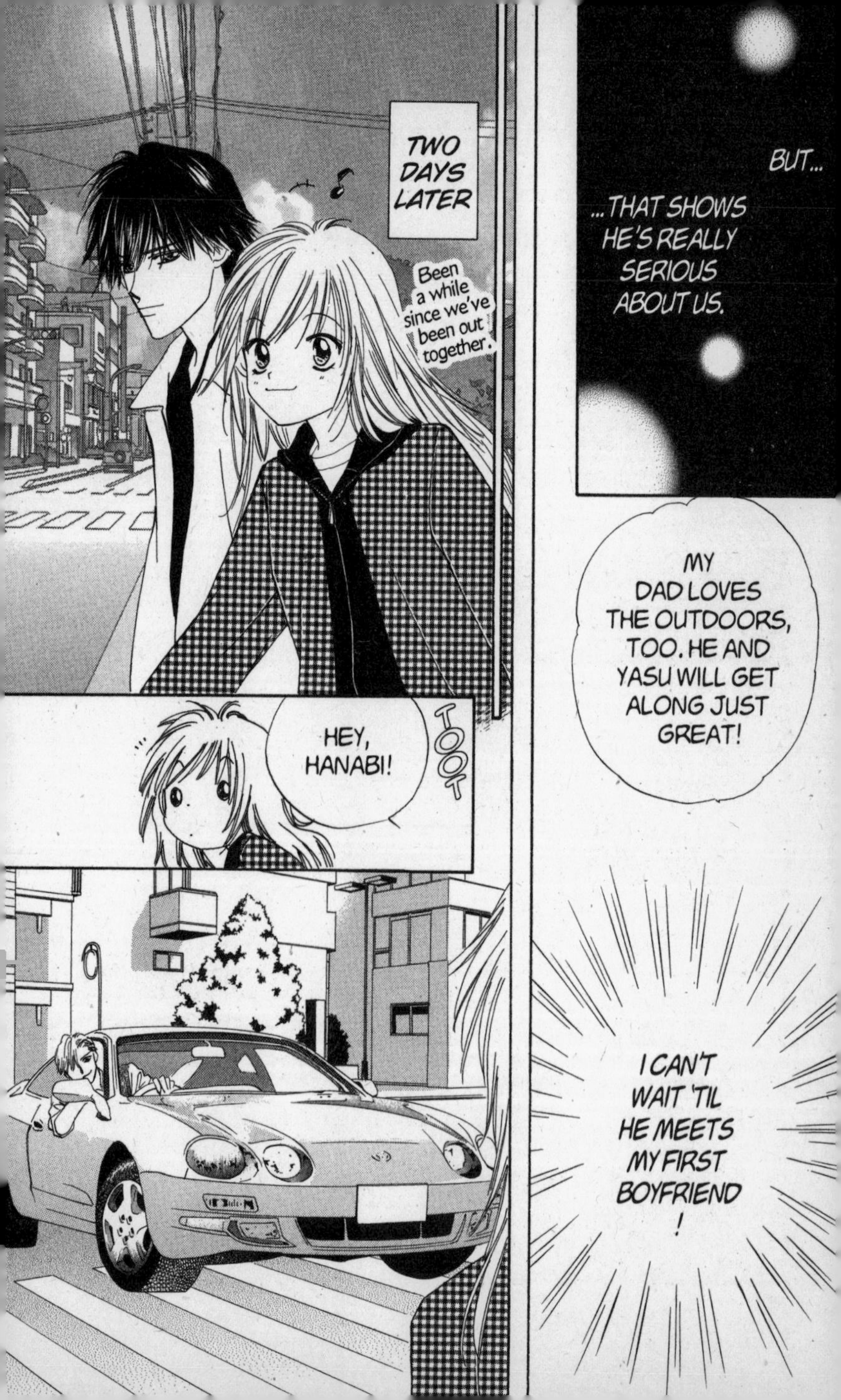
BUT...
...THAT SHOWS HE'S REALLY SERIOUS ABOUT US.
MY DAD LOVES THE OUTDOORS, TOO. HE AND YASU WILL GET ALONG JUST GREAT!
I CAN'T WAIT 'TIL HE MEETS MY FIRST BOYFRIEND!
TWO DAYS LATER
Been a while since we've been out together.
TOOT
HEY, HANABI!

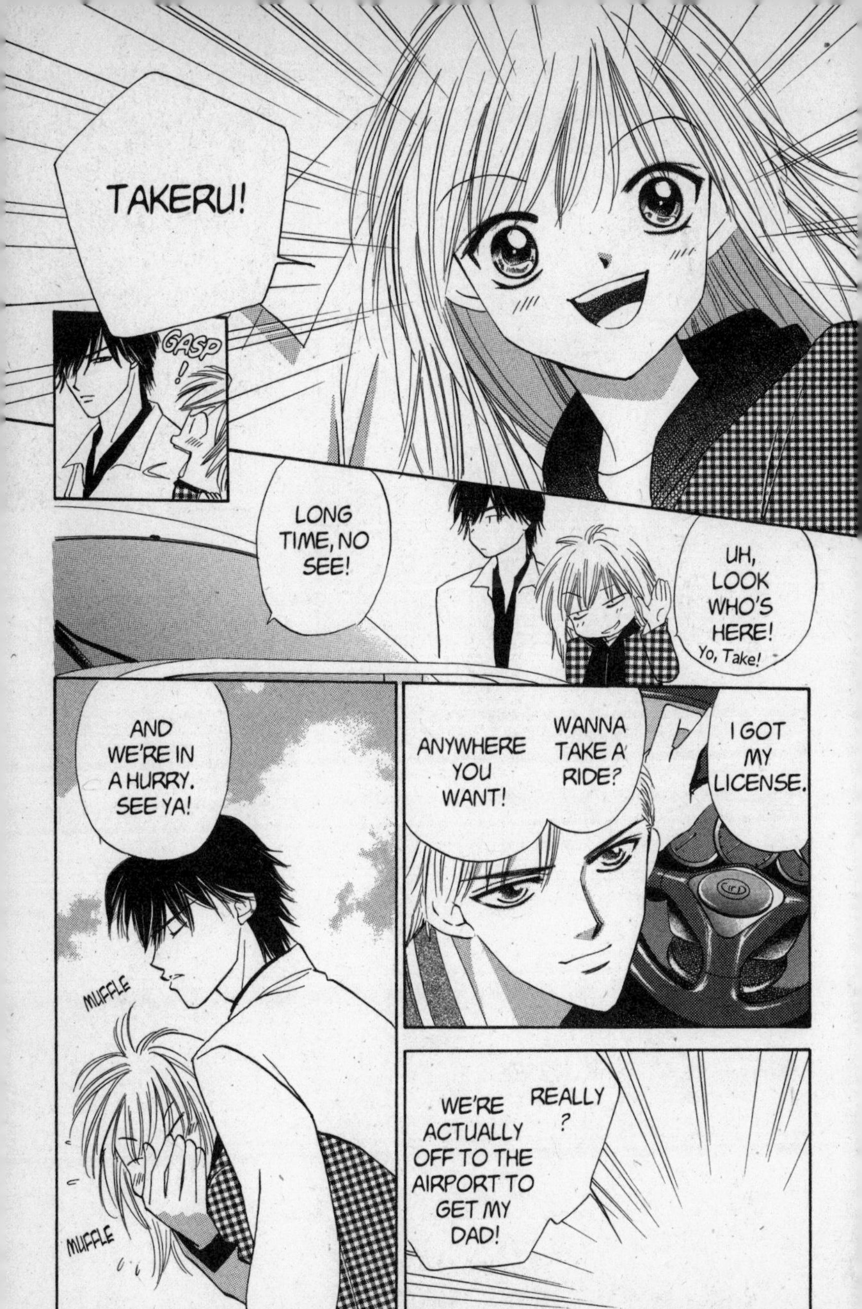

TAKERU!
GASP !
UH, LOOK WHO'S HERE!
Yo, Take!
LONG TIME, NO SEE!
I GOT MY LICENSE.
WANNA TAKE A RIDE?
ANYWHERE YOU WANT!
REALLY ?
WE'RE ACTUALLY OFF TO THE AIRPORT TO GET MY DAD!
AND WE'RE IN A HURRY. SEE YA!
MUFFLE
MUFFLE

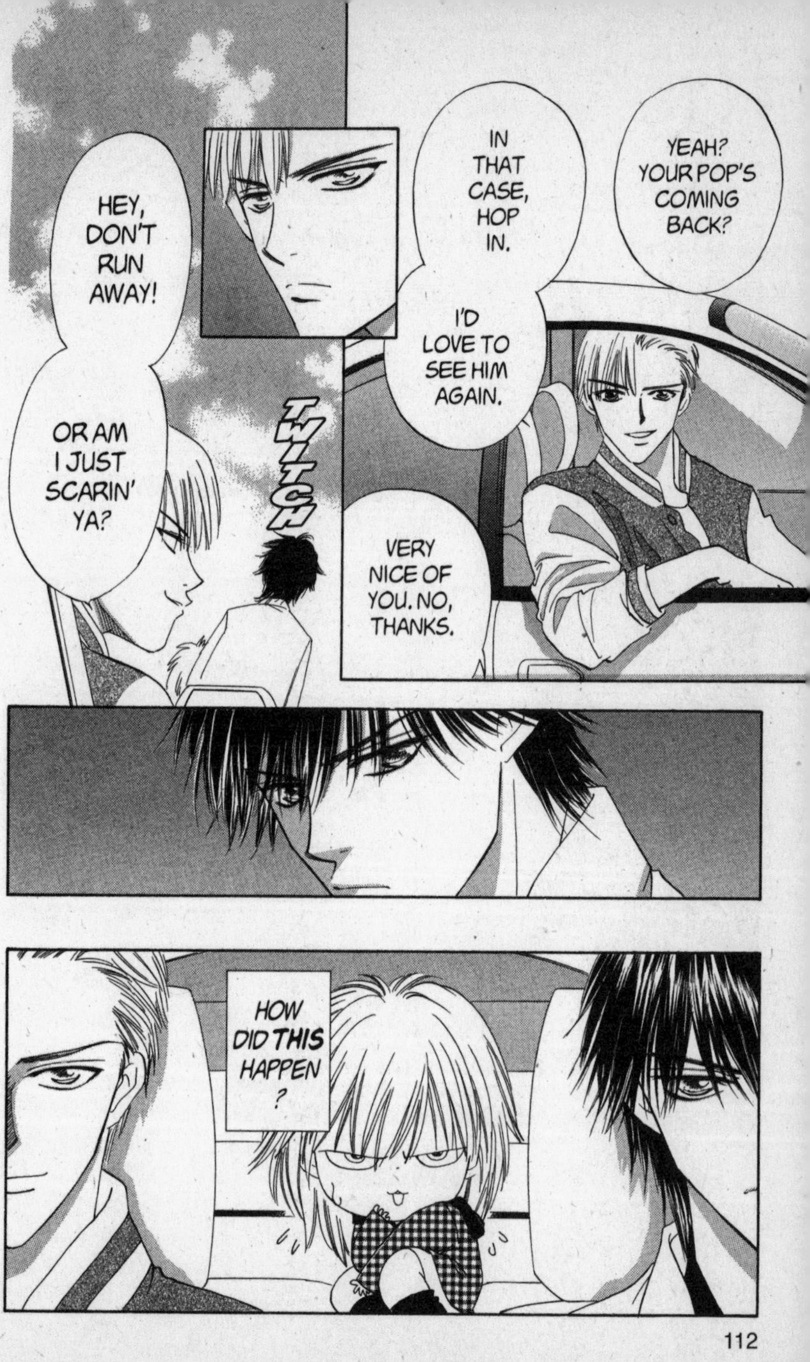
YEAH? YOUR POP'S COMING BACK?
I'D LOVE TO SEE HIM AGAIN.
IN THAT CASE, HOP IN.
VERY NICE OF YOU. NO, THANKS.
HEY, DON'T RUN AWAY!
OR AM I JUST SCARIN' YA?
TWITCH
HOW DID THIS HAPPEN?

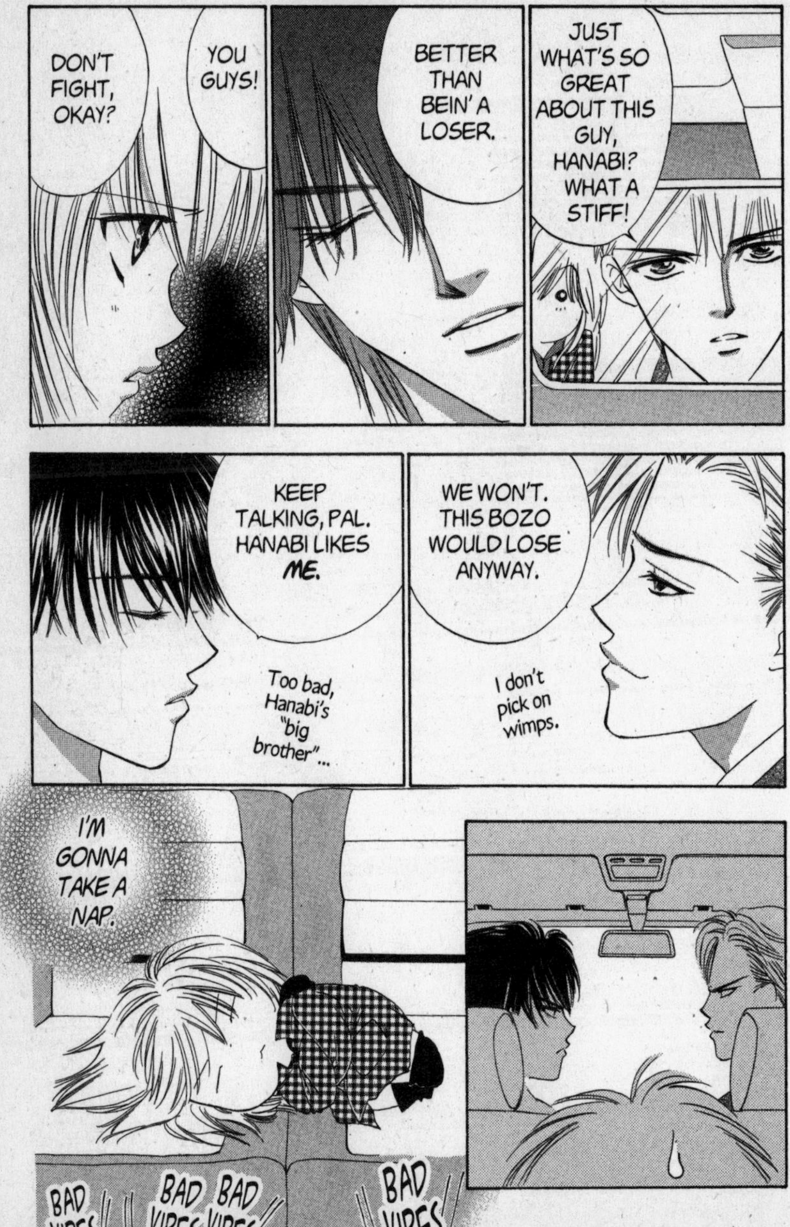
JUST WHAT'S SO GREAT ABOUT THIS GUY, HANABI? WHAT A STIFF!
BETTER THAN BEIN' A LOSER.
YOU GUYS!
DON'T FIGHT, OKAY?
WE WON'T. THIS BOZO WOULD LOSE ANYWAY.
I don't pick on wimps.
KEEP TALKING, PAL. HANABI LIKES ME.
Too bad, Hanabi's "big brother"...
BAD VIBES
I'M GONNA TAKE A NAP.
BAD VIBES
BAD VIBES
BAD VIBES

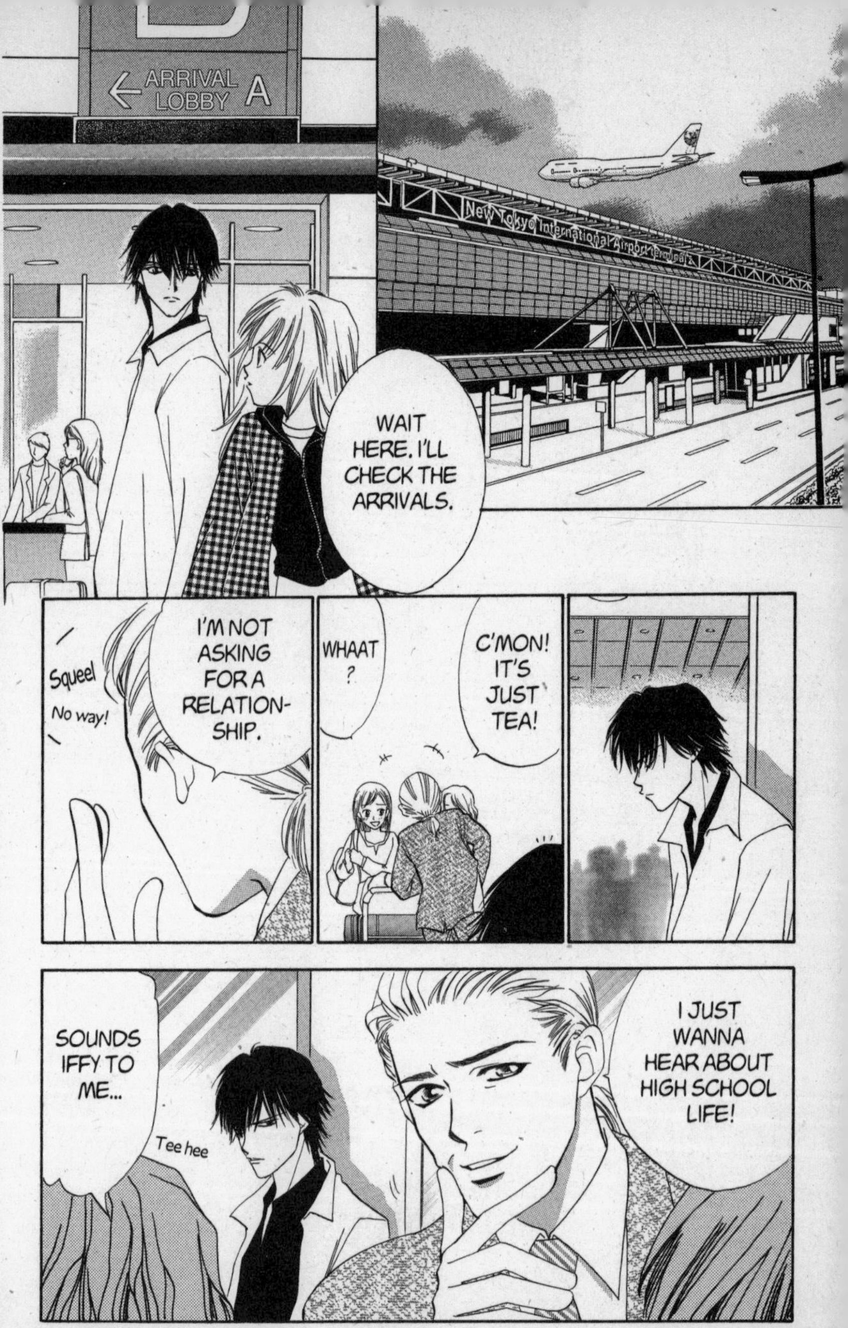
New Tokyo International Airport
ARRIVAL LOBBY A
WAIT HERE. I'LL CHECK THE ARRIVALS.
C'MON! IT'S JUST TEA!
WHAAT?
I'M NOT ASKING FOR A RELATION-SHIP.
Squeel
No way!
I JUST WANNA HEAR ABOUT HIGH SCHOOL LIFE!
SOUNDS IFFY TO ME...
Tee hee

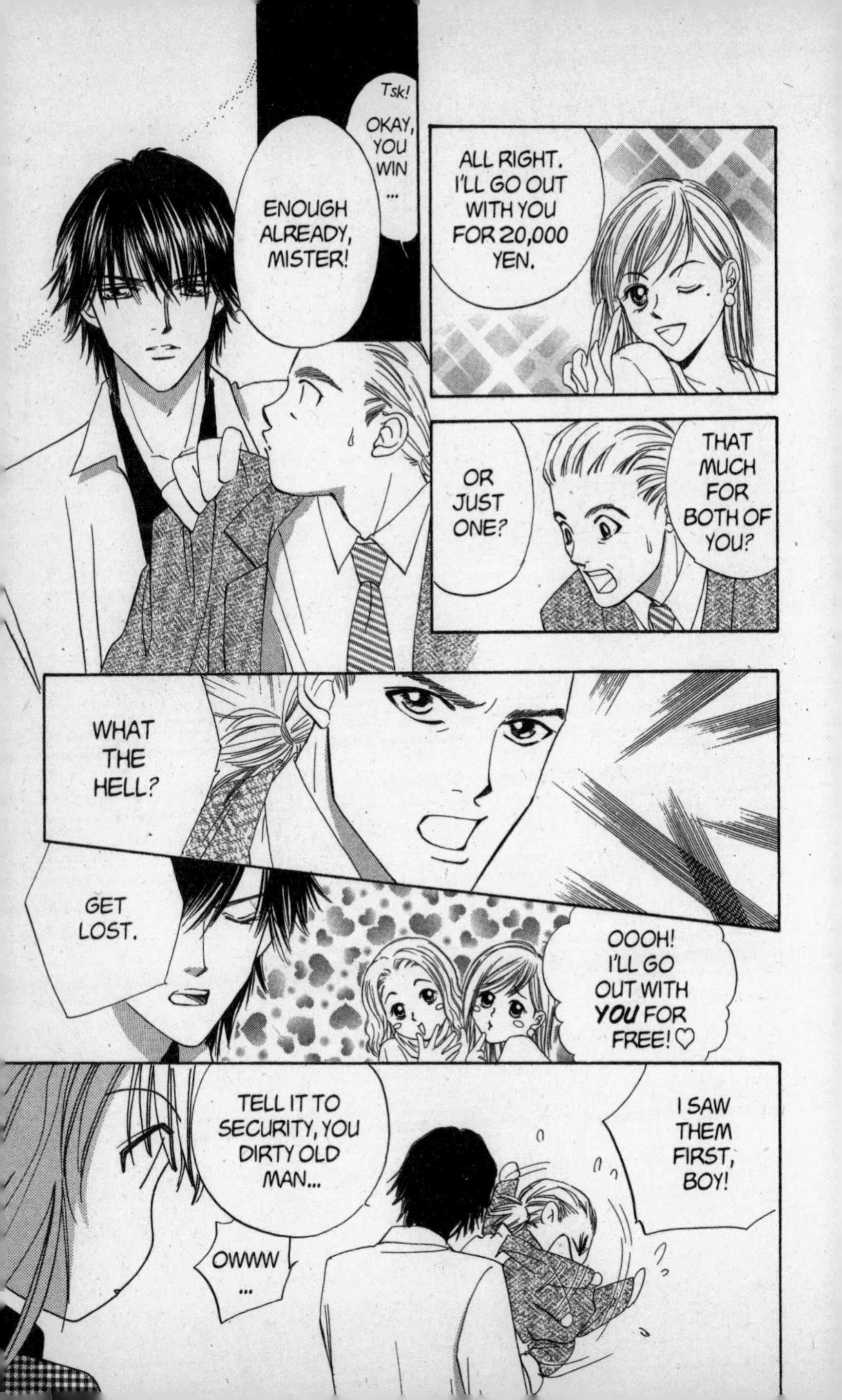
ALL RIGHT. I'LL GO OUT WITH YOU FOR 20,000 YEN.
THAT MUCH FOR BOTH OF YOU?
OR JUST ONE?
Tsk!
OKAY, YOU WIN ...
ENOUGH ALREADY, MISTER!
WHAT THE HELL?
OOOH! I'LL GO OUT WITH **YOU** FOR FREE! ♡
GET LOST.
I SAW THEM FIRST, BOY!
TELL IT TO SECURITY, YOU DIRTY OLD MAN...
OWWW ...

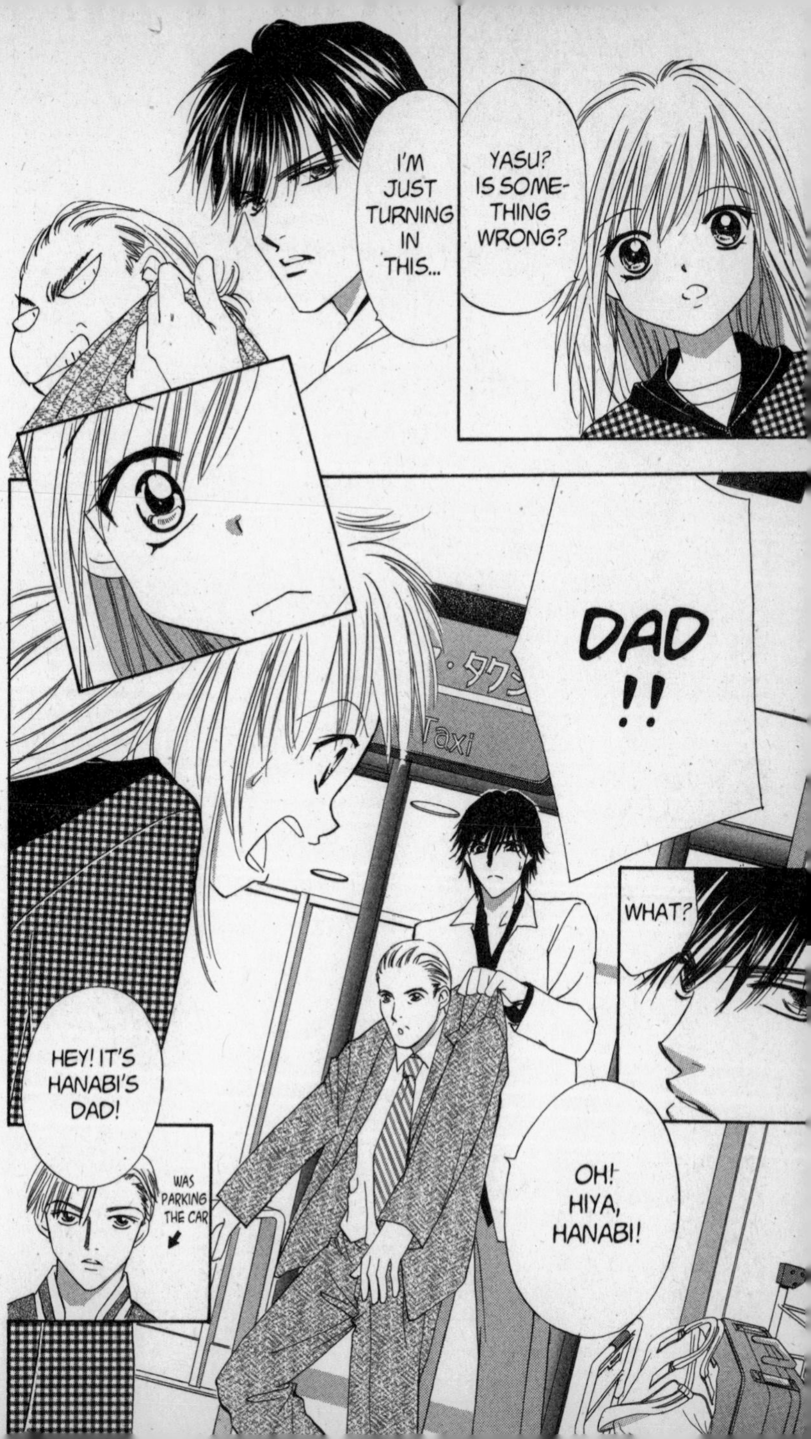
YASU? IS SOME-THING WRONG?
I'M JUST TURNING IN THIS...
DAD!!
Taxi
WHAT?
OH! HIYA, HANABI!
HEY! IT'S HANABI'S DAD!
WAS PARKING THE CAR

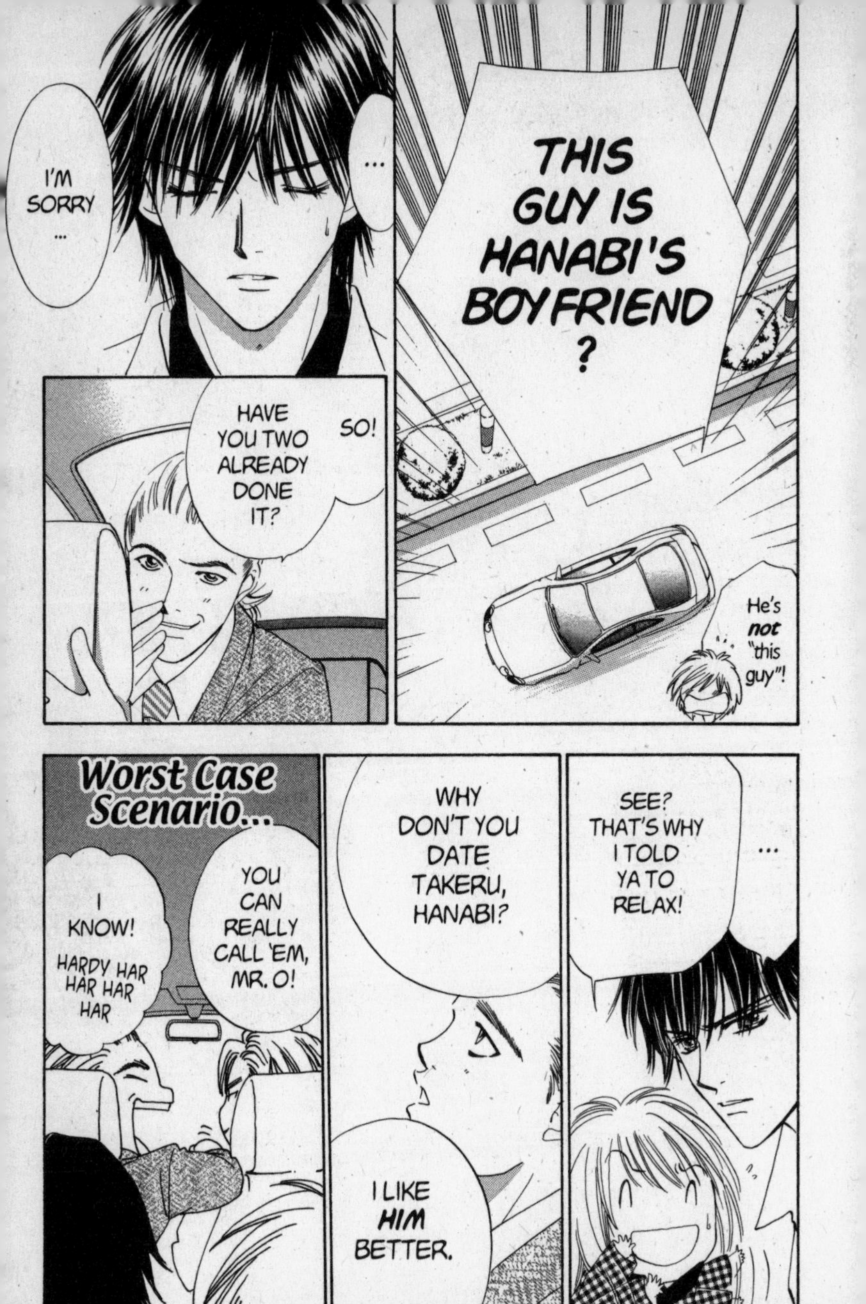
THIS GUY IS HANABI'S BOYFRIEND?
He's **not** "this guy"!
...
I'M SORRY ...
SO!
HAVE YOU TWO ALREADY DONE IT?
...
SEE? THAT'S WHY I TOLD YA TO RELAX!
WHY DON'T YOU DATE TAKERU, HANABI?
I LIKE ***HIM*** BETTER.
Worst Case Scenario...
YOU CAN REALLY CALL 'EM, MR. O!
I KNOW!
HARDY HAR HAR HAR HAR

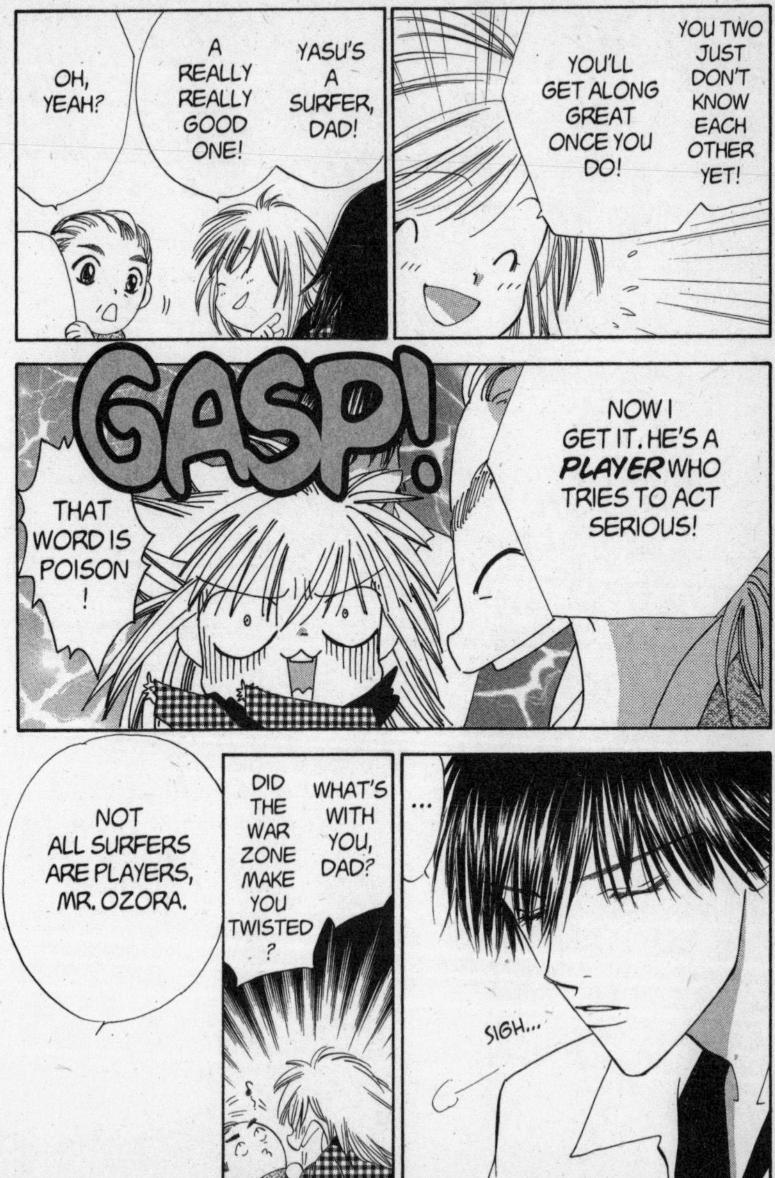
YOU TWO JUST DON'T KNOW EACH OTHER YET!
YOU'LL GET ALONG GREAT ONCE YOU DO!
YASU'S A SURFER, DAD!
A REALLY REALLY GOOD ONE!
OH, YEAH?
NOW I GET IT. HE'S A *PLAYER* WHO TRIES TO ACT SERIOUS!
GASP!
THAT WORD IS POISON!
...
SIGH...
WHAT'S WITH YOU, DAD?
DID THE WAR ZONE MAKE YOU TWISTED?
NOT ALL SURFERS ARE PLAYERS, MR. OZORA.

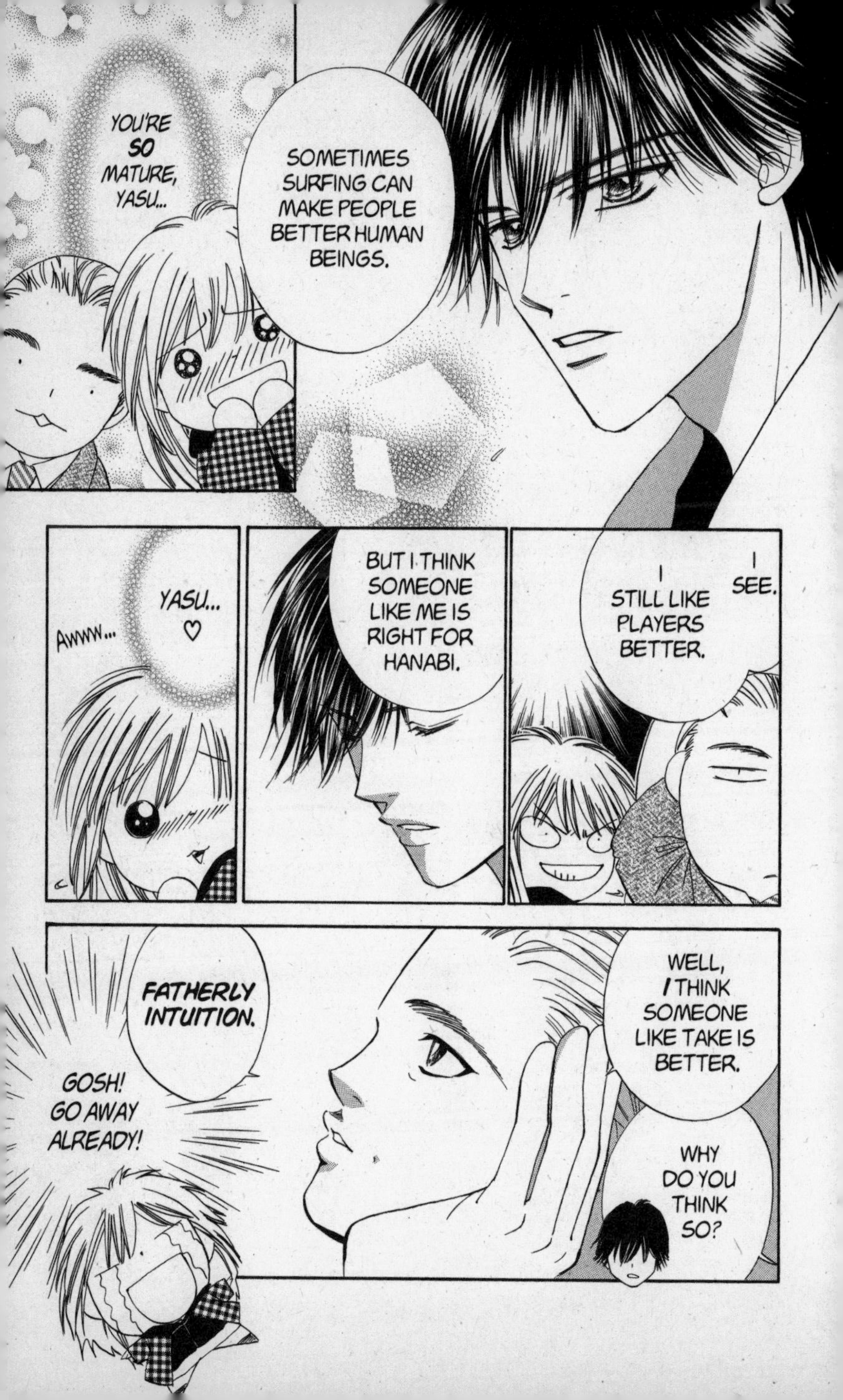
SOMETIMES SURFING CAN MAKE PEOPLE BETTER HUMAN BEINGS.
YOU'RE SO MATURE, YASU...
I SEE.
I STILL LIKE PLAYERS BETTER.
BUT I THINK SOMEONE LIKE ME IS RIGHT FOR HANABI.
YASU... ♡
AWWW...
WELL, I THINK SOMEONE LIKE TAKE IS BETTER.
WHY DO YOU THINK SO?
FATHERLY INTUITION.
GOSH! GO AWAY ALREADY!

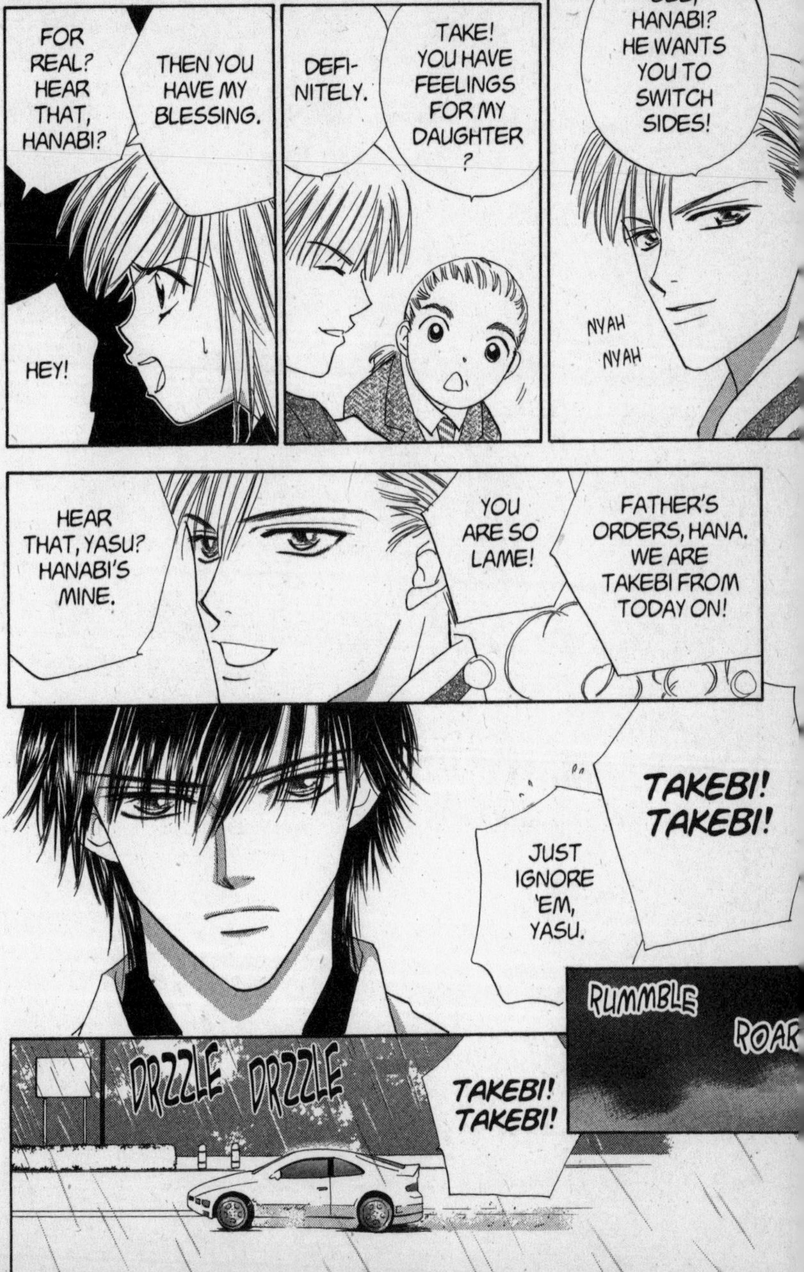
SEE, HANABI? HE WANTS YOU TO SWITCH SIDES!
NYAH NYAH
TAKE! YOU HAVE FEELINGS FOR MY DAUGHTER?
DEFI-NITELY.
THEN YOU HAVE MY BLESSING.
FOR REAL? HEAR THAT, HANABI?
HEY!
FATHER'S ORDERS, HANA. WE ARE TAKEBI FROM TODAY ON!
YOU ARE SO LAME!
HEAR THAT, YASU? HANABI'S MINE.
TAKEBI! TAKEBI!
JUST IGNORE 'EM, YASU.
RUMMBLE
ROAR
TAKEBI! TAKEBI!
DRZZLE DRZZLE

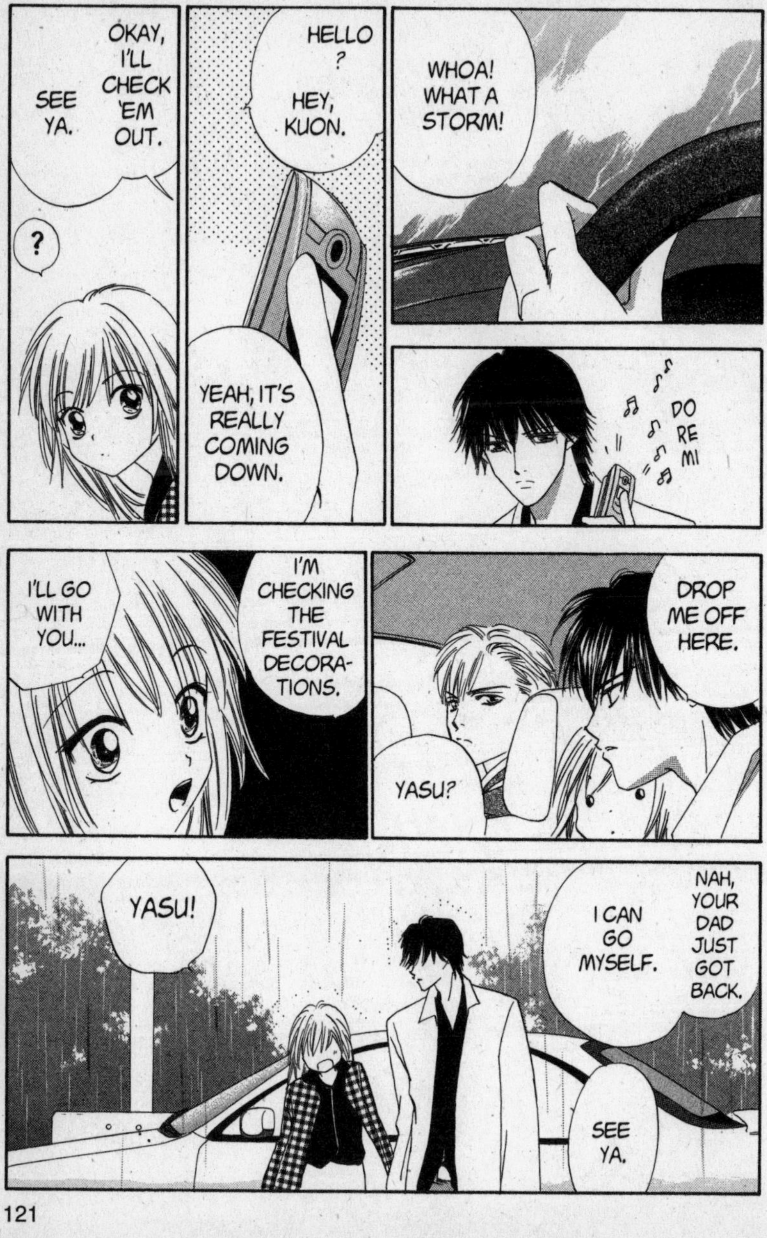
WHOA! WHAT A STORM!
DO RE MI
HELLO?
HEY, KUON.
YEAH, IT'S REALLY COMING DOWN.
OKAY, I'LL CHECK 'EM OUT.
SEE YA.
?
DROP ME OFF HERE.
YASU?
I'M CHECKING THE FESTIVAL DECORATIONS.
I'LL GO WITH YOU...
NAH, YOUR DAD JUST GOT BACK.
I CAN GO MYSELF.
SEE YA.
YASU!

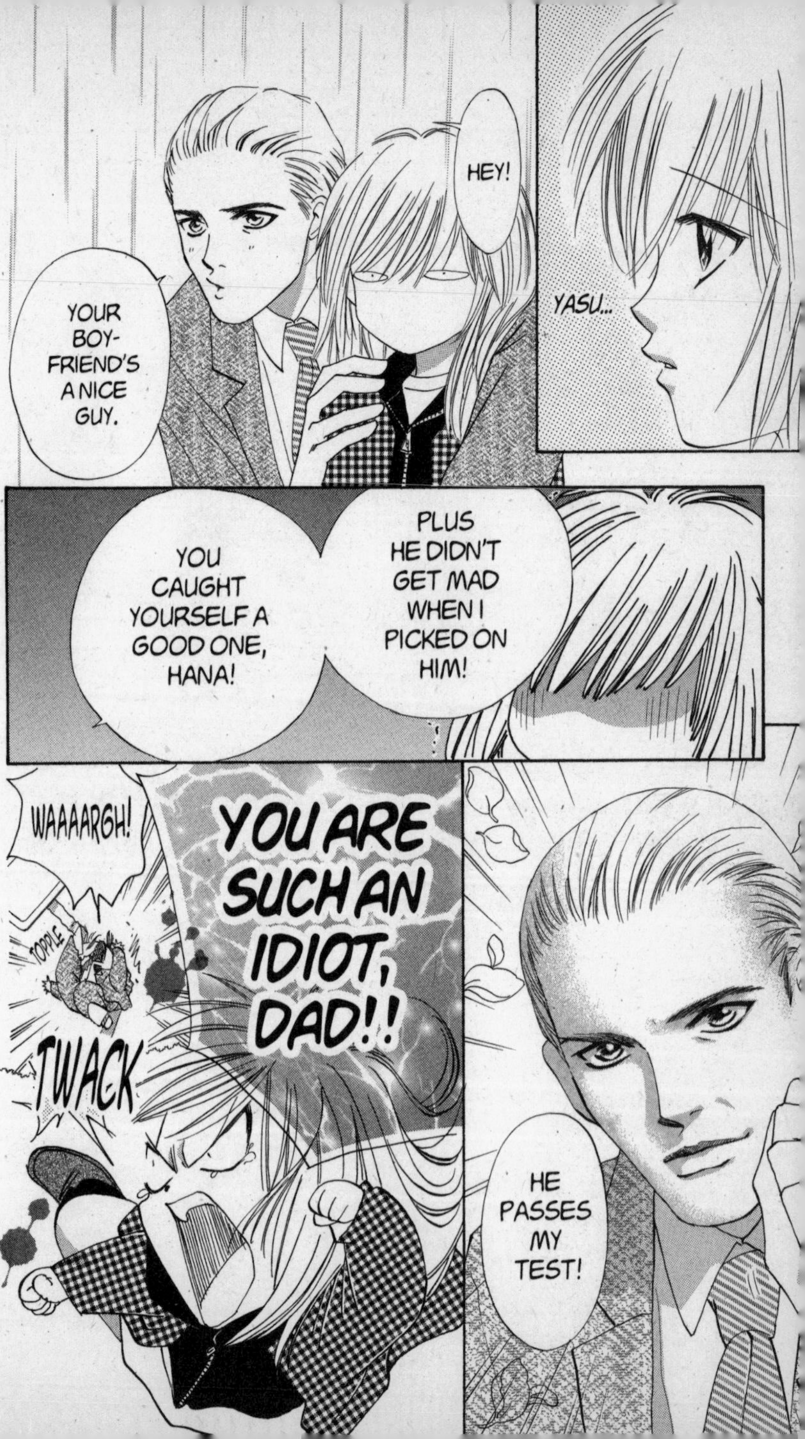
YASU...
HEY!
YOUR BOY-FRIEND'S A NICE GUY.
PLUS HE DIDN'T GET MAD WHEN I PICKED ON HIM!
YOU CAUGHT YOURSELF A GOOD ONE, HANA!
HE PASSES MY TEST!
YOU ARE SUCH AN IDIOT, DAD!!
WAAAARGH!
TOPPLE
TWACK

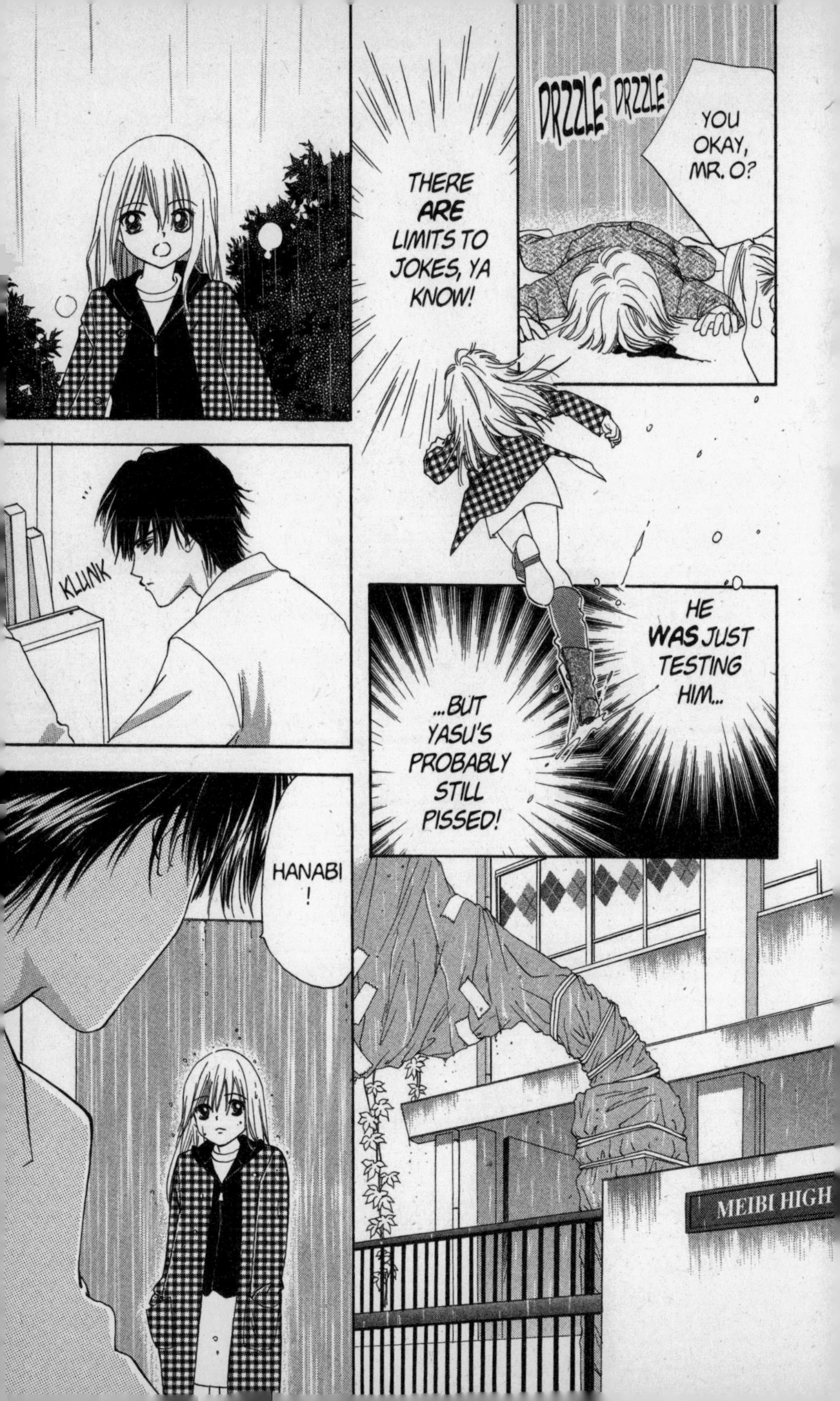
DRZZLE DRZZLE
YOU OKAY, MR. O?
THERE ARE LIMITS TO JOKES, YA KNOW!
HE WAS JUST TESTING HIM...
...BUT YASU'S PROBABLY STILL PISSED!
KLUNK
MEIBI HIGH
HANABI!

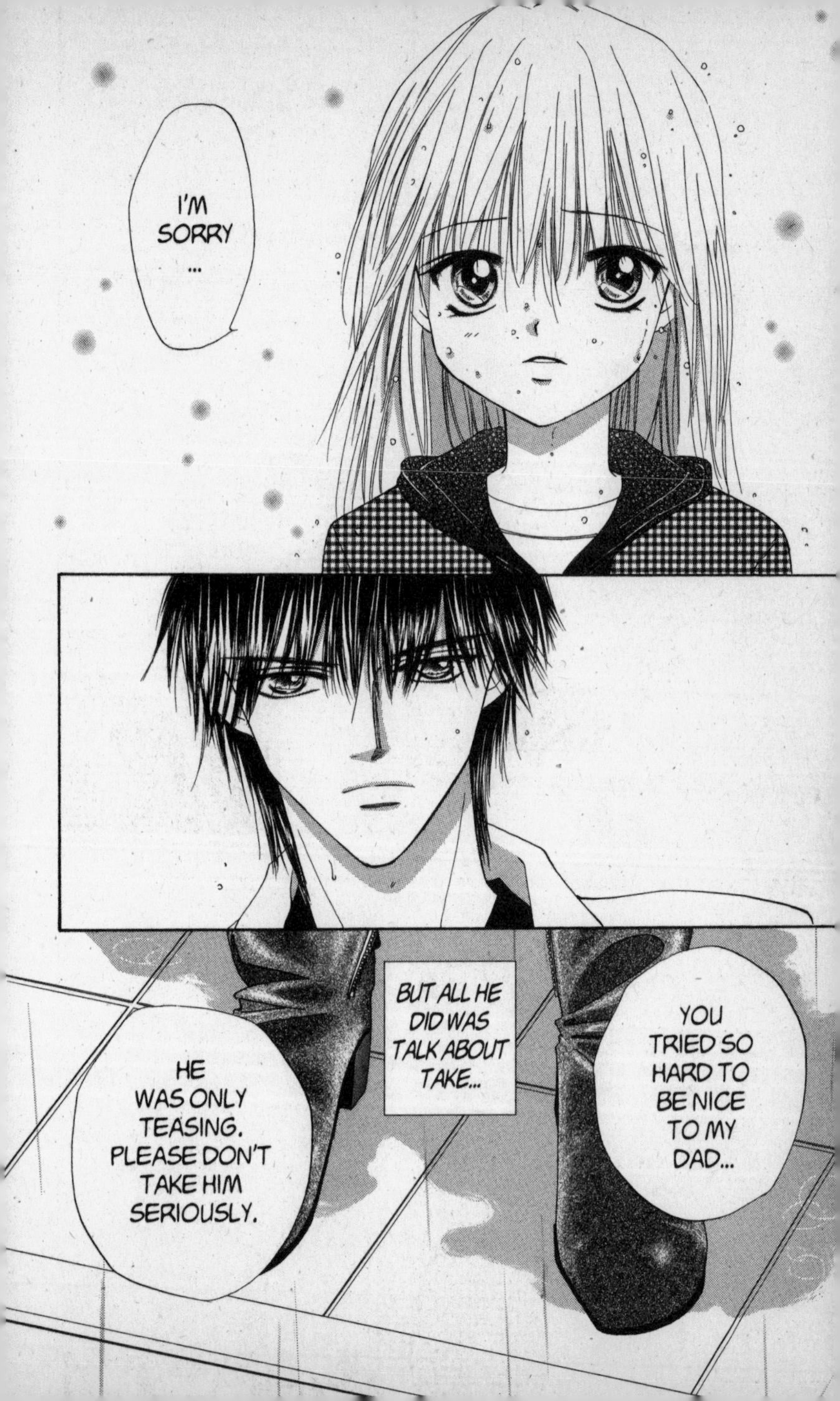
I'M SORRY ...
YOU TRIED SO HARD TO BE NICE TO MY DAD...
BUT ALL HE DID WAS TALK ABOUT TAKE...
HE WAS ONLY TEASING. PLEASE DON'T TAKE HIM SERIOUSLY.

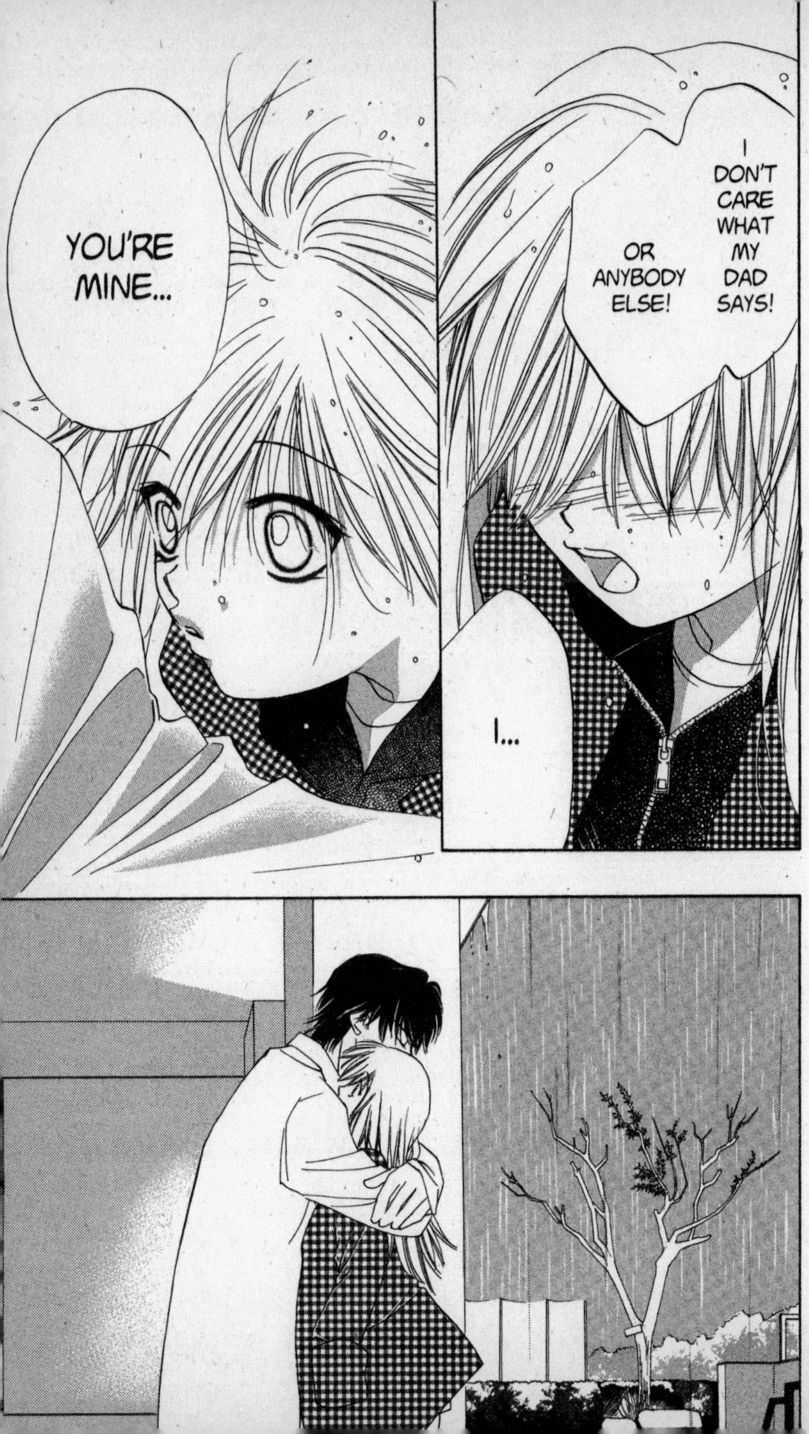
I DON'T CARE WHAT MY DAD SAYS!
OR ANYBODY ELSE!
I...
YOU'RE MINE...

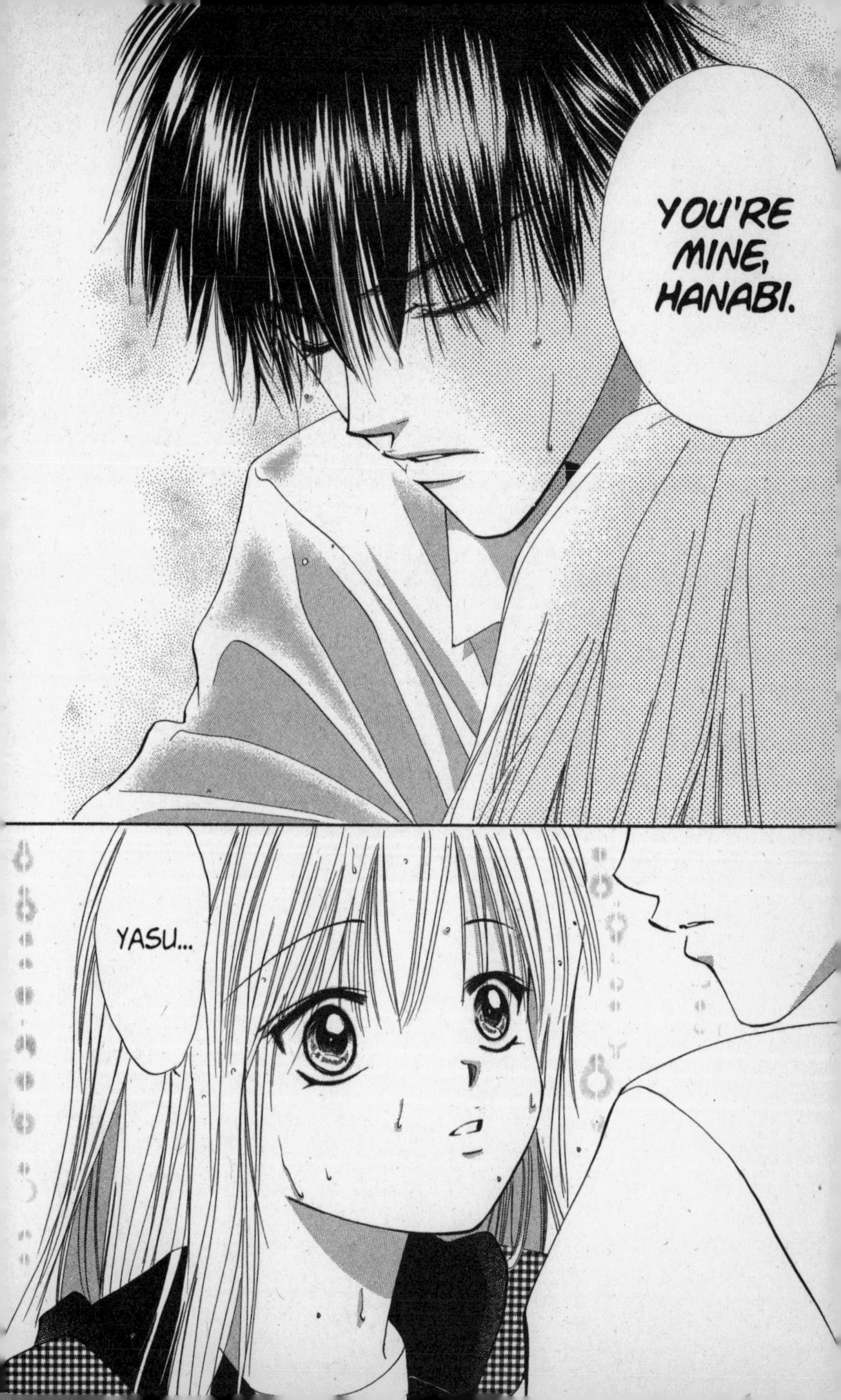
YOU'RE MINE, HANABI.
YASU...

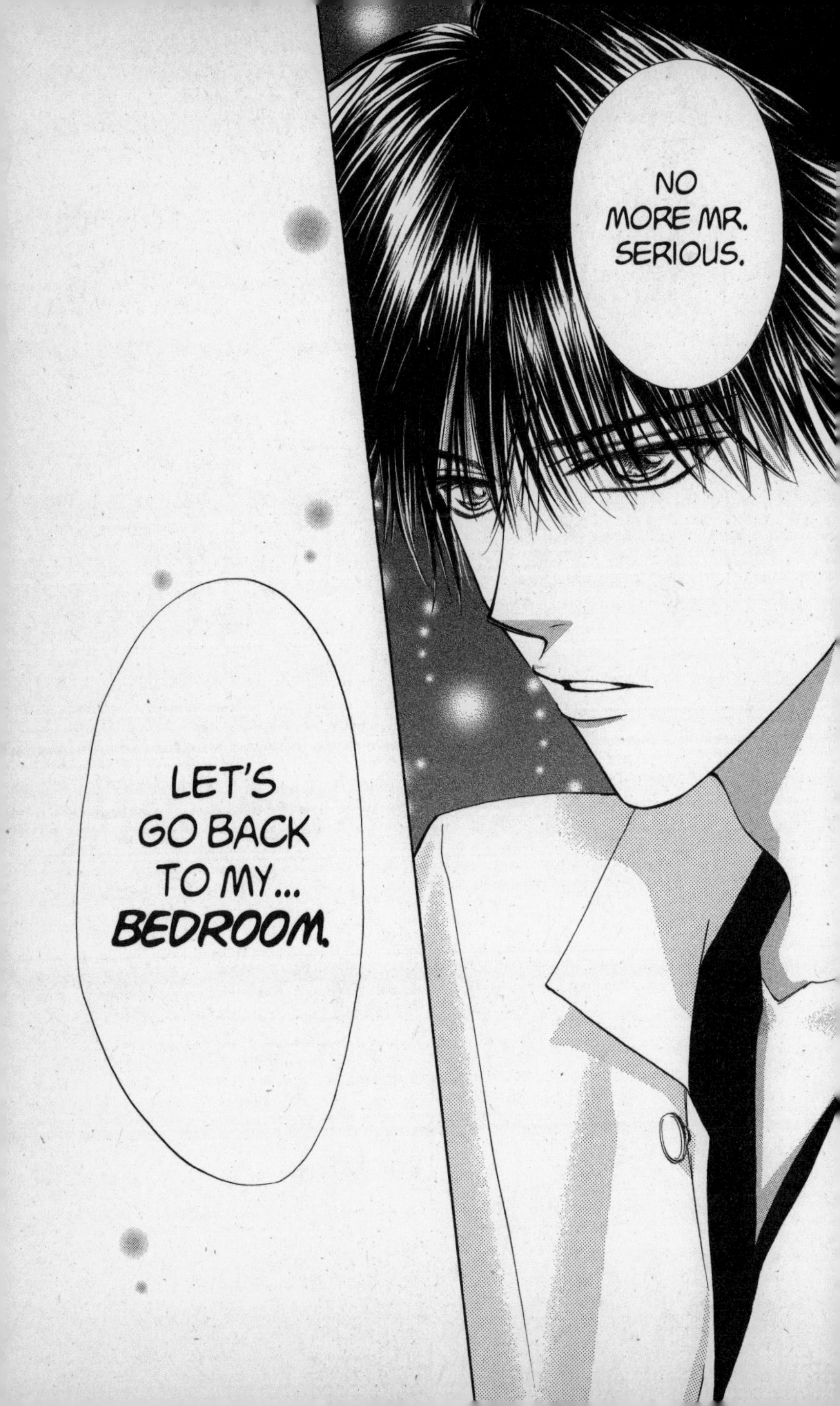
NO MORE MR. SERIOUS.
LET'S GO BACK TO MY... BEDROOM.

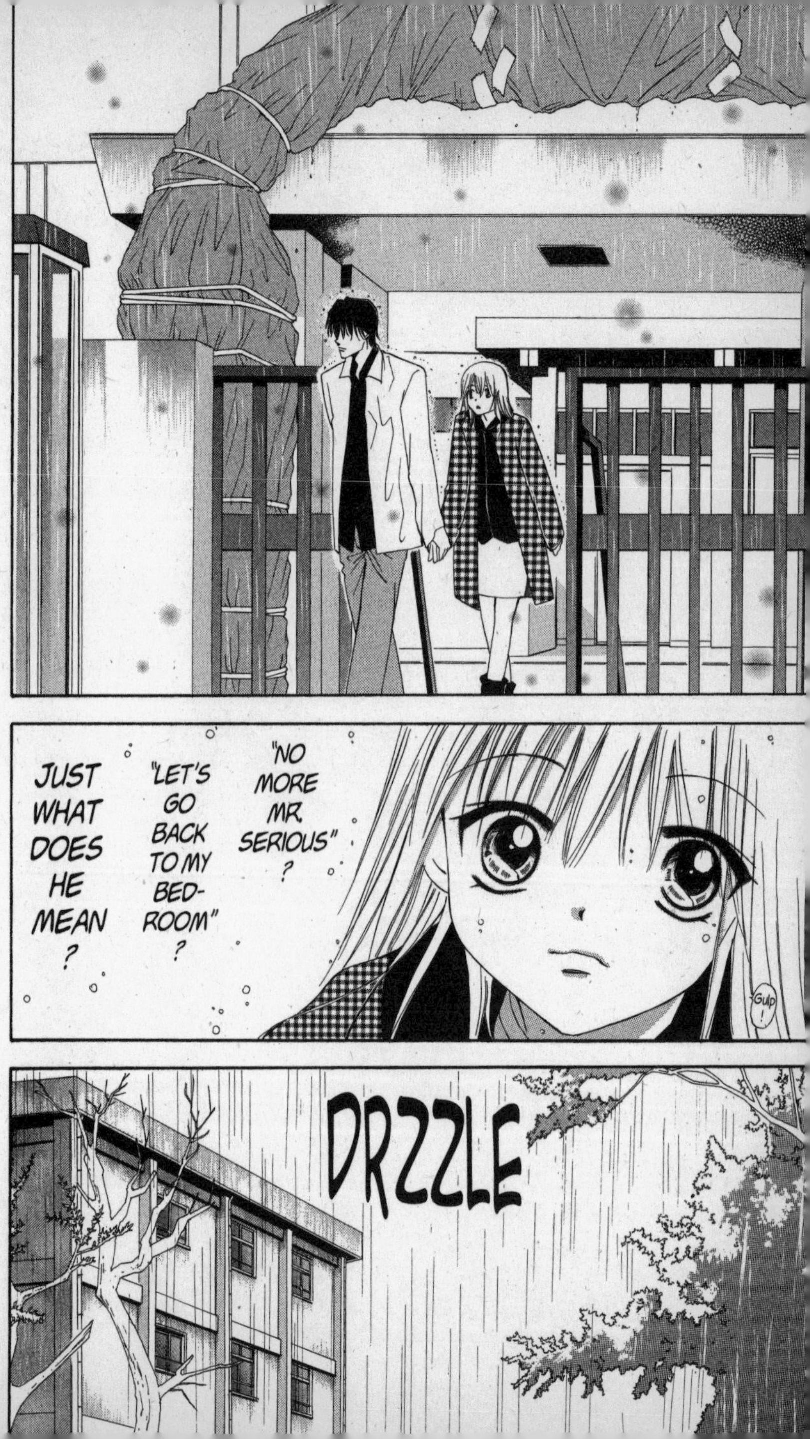
"NO MORE MR. SERIOUS" ?
"LET'S GO BACK TO MY BEDROOM" ?
JUST WHAT DOES HE MEAN ?
GULP!
DRZZLE

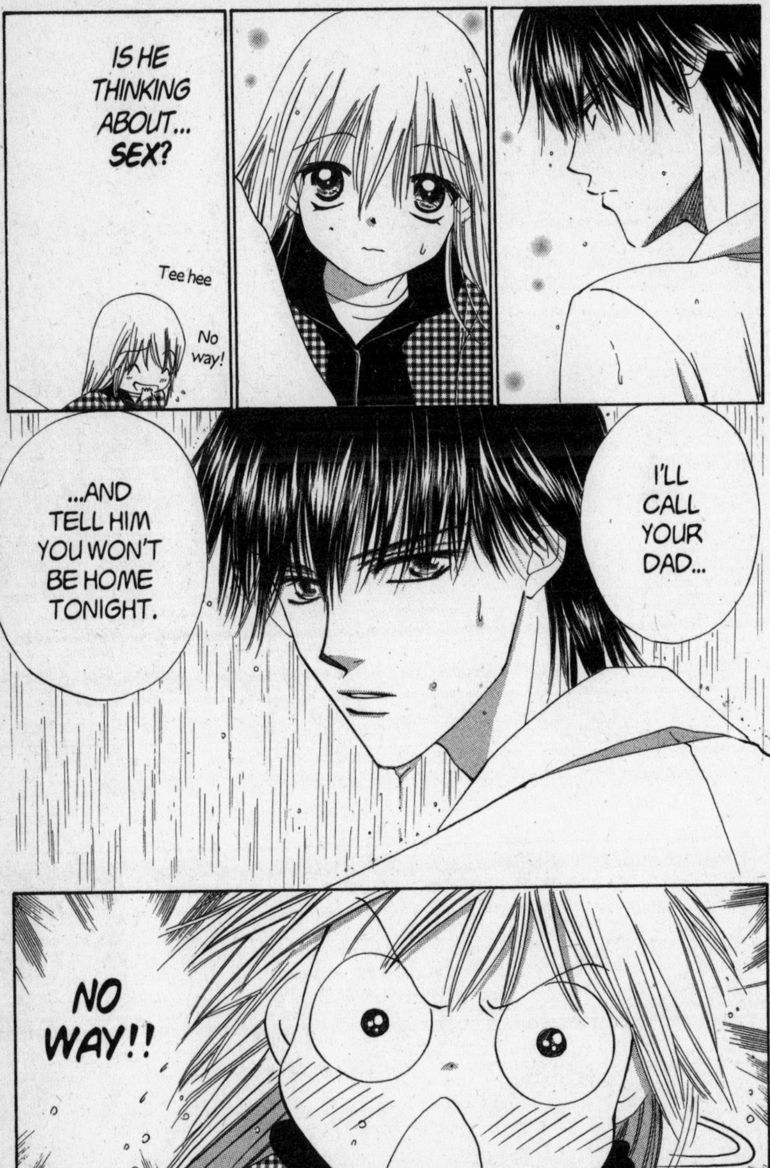
IS HE THINKING ABOUT... SEX?
Tee hee
No way!
I'LL CALL YOUR DAD...
...AND TELL HIM YOU WON'T BE HOME TONIGHT.
NO WAY!!

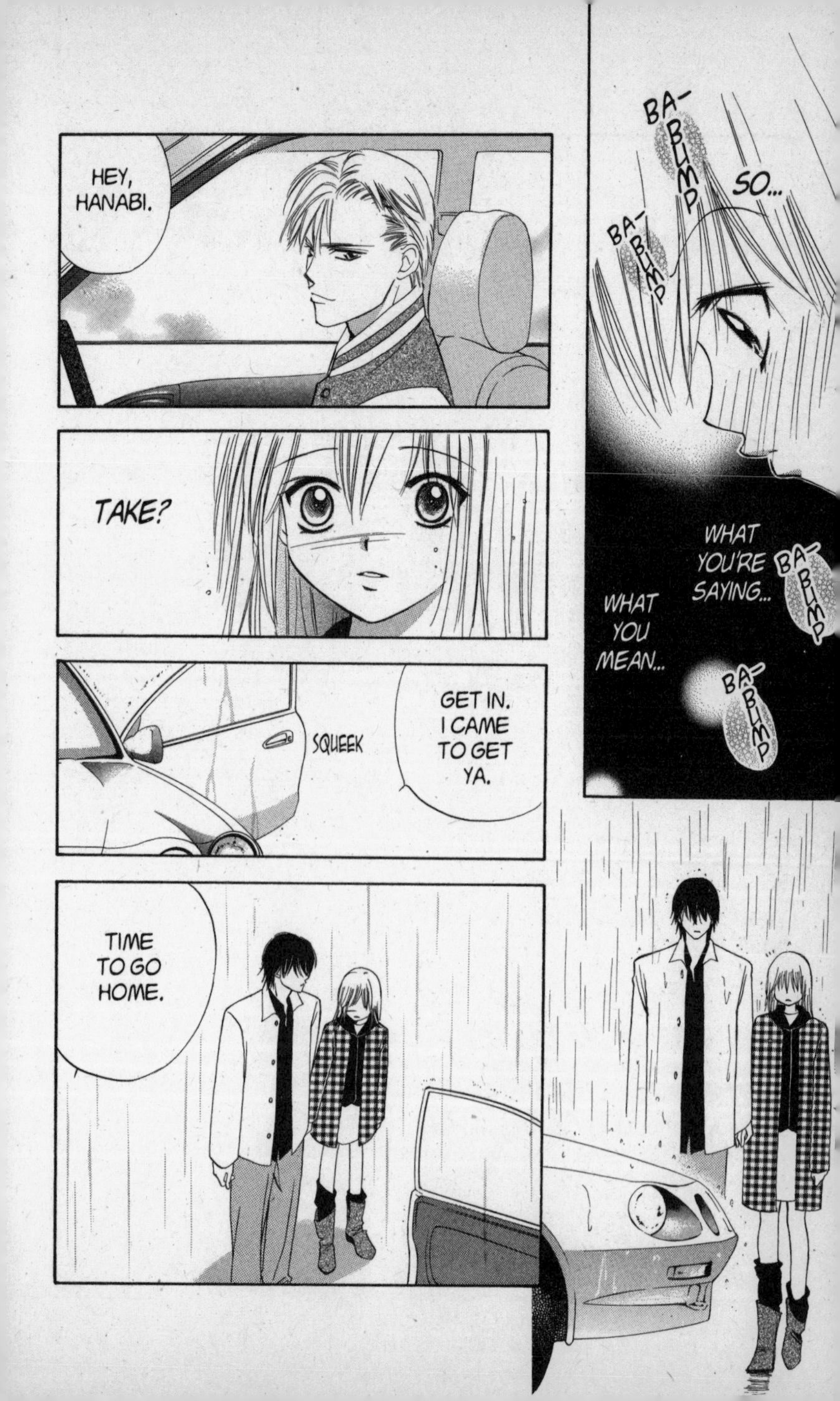
BA-BUMP
SO...
BA-BUMP
WHAT YOU'RE SAYING...
BA-BUMP
WHAT YOU MEAN...
BA-BUMP
HEY, HANABI.
TAKE?
GET IN. I CAME TO GET YA.
SQUEEK
TIME TO GO HOME.

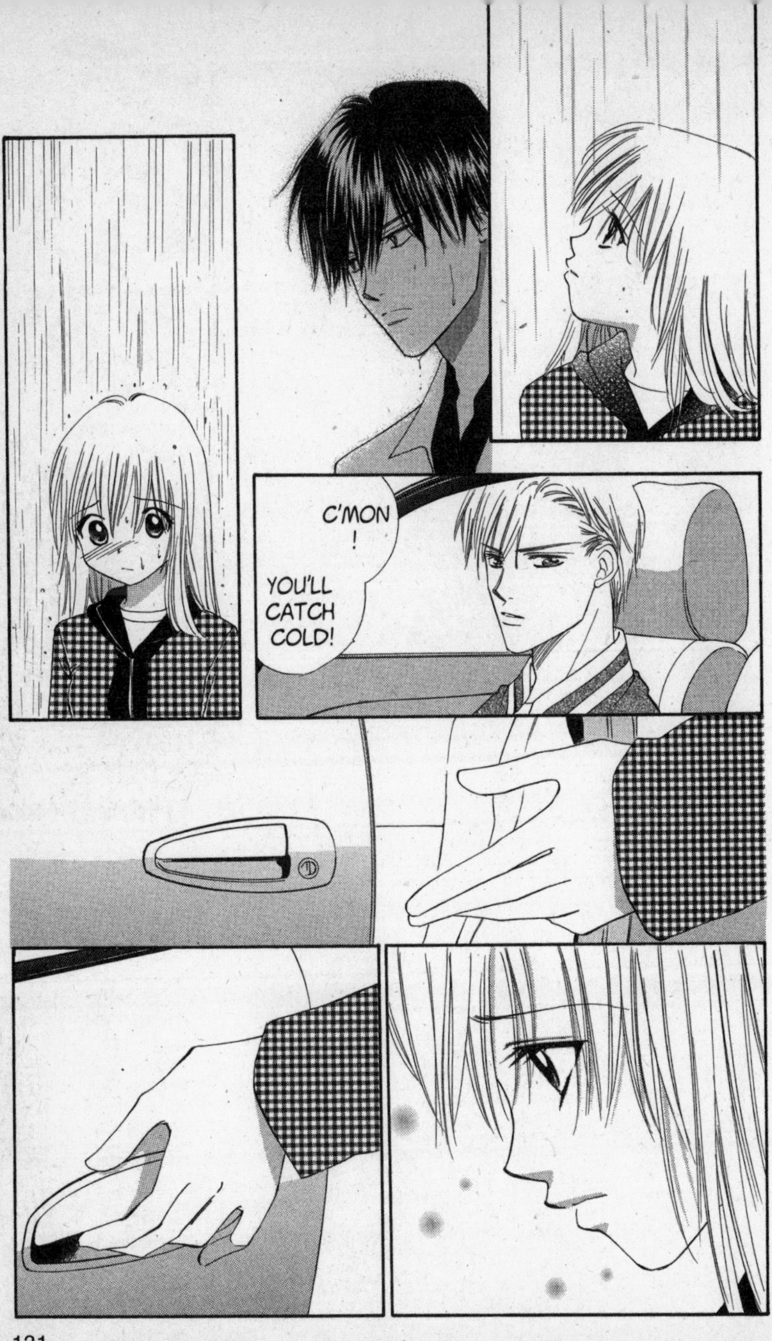
C'MON!
YOU'LL CATCH COLD!

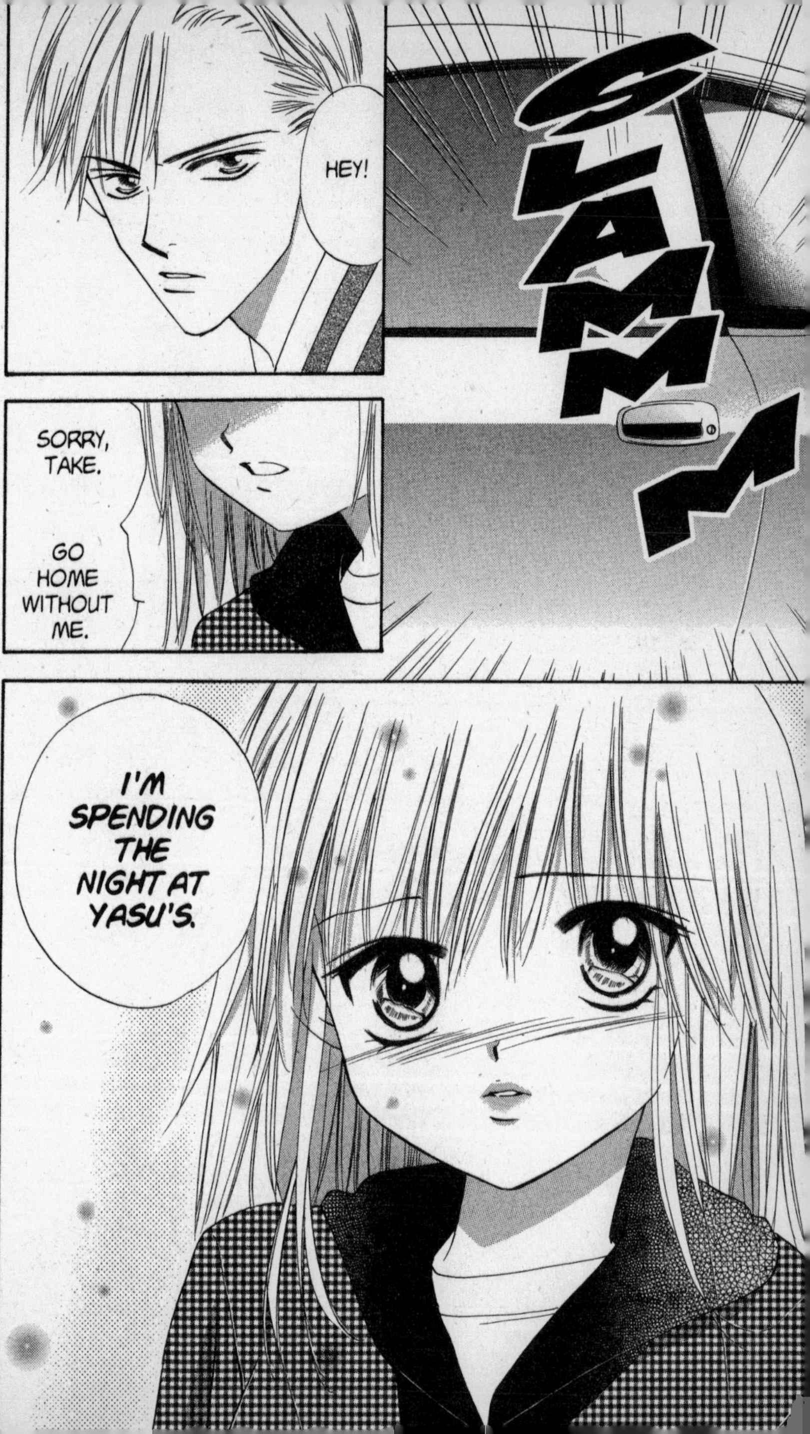
SLAMM
HEY!
SORRY, TAKE.
GO HOME WITHOUT ME.
I'M SPENDING THE NIGHT AT YASU'S.

LET'S GO.

HANABI!

I FINALLY STOOD UP TO TAKE!

THROB

THROB

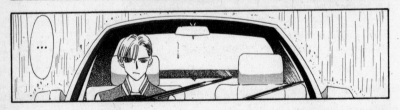

...

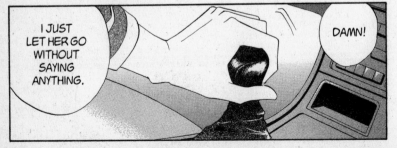

I JUST LET HER GO WITHOUT SAYING ANYTHING.

DAMN!

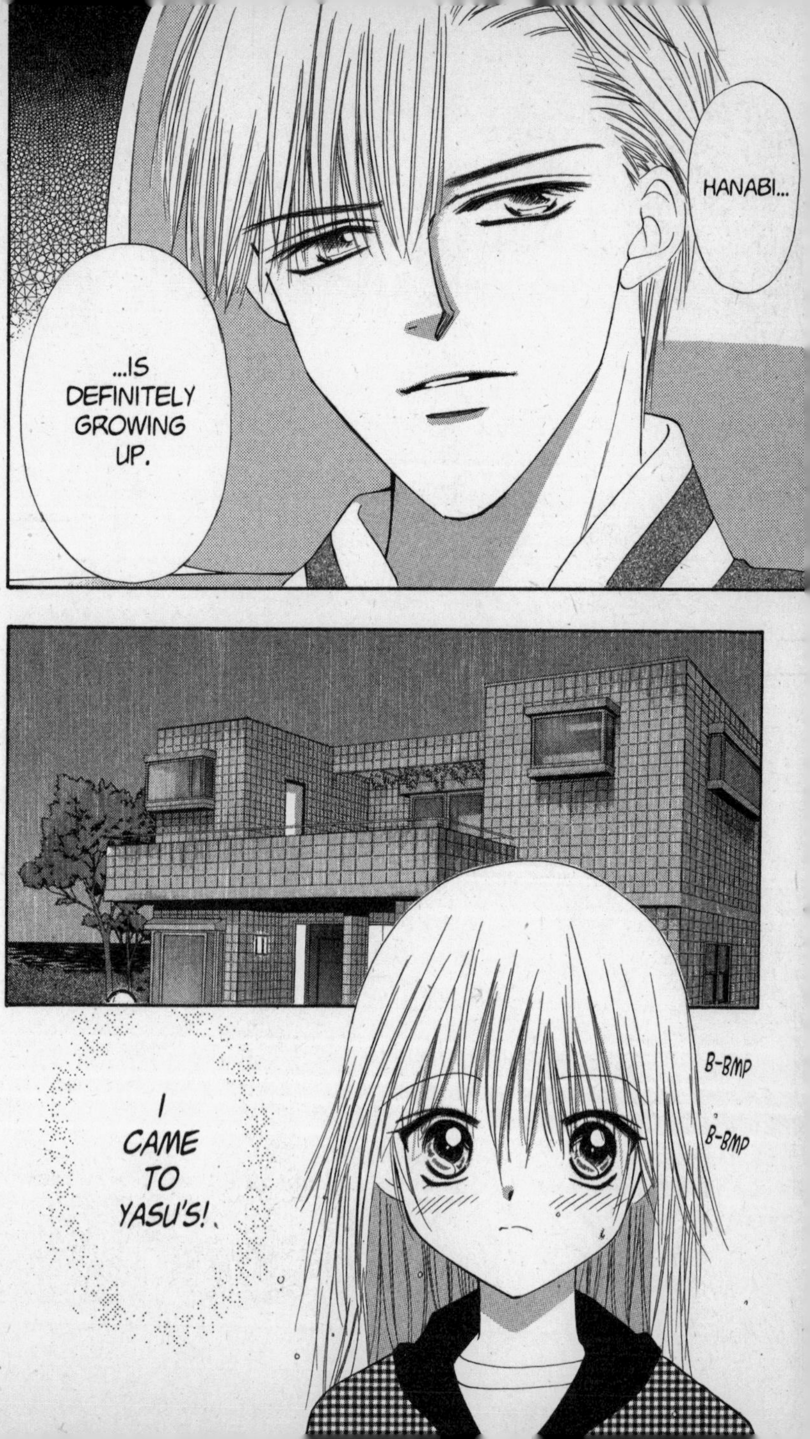
HANABI...
...IS DEFINITELY GROWING UP.
B-BMP
B-BMP
I CAME TO YASU'S!

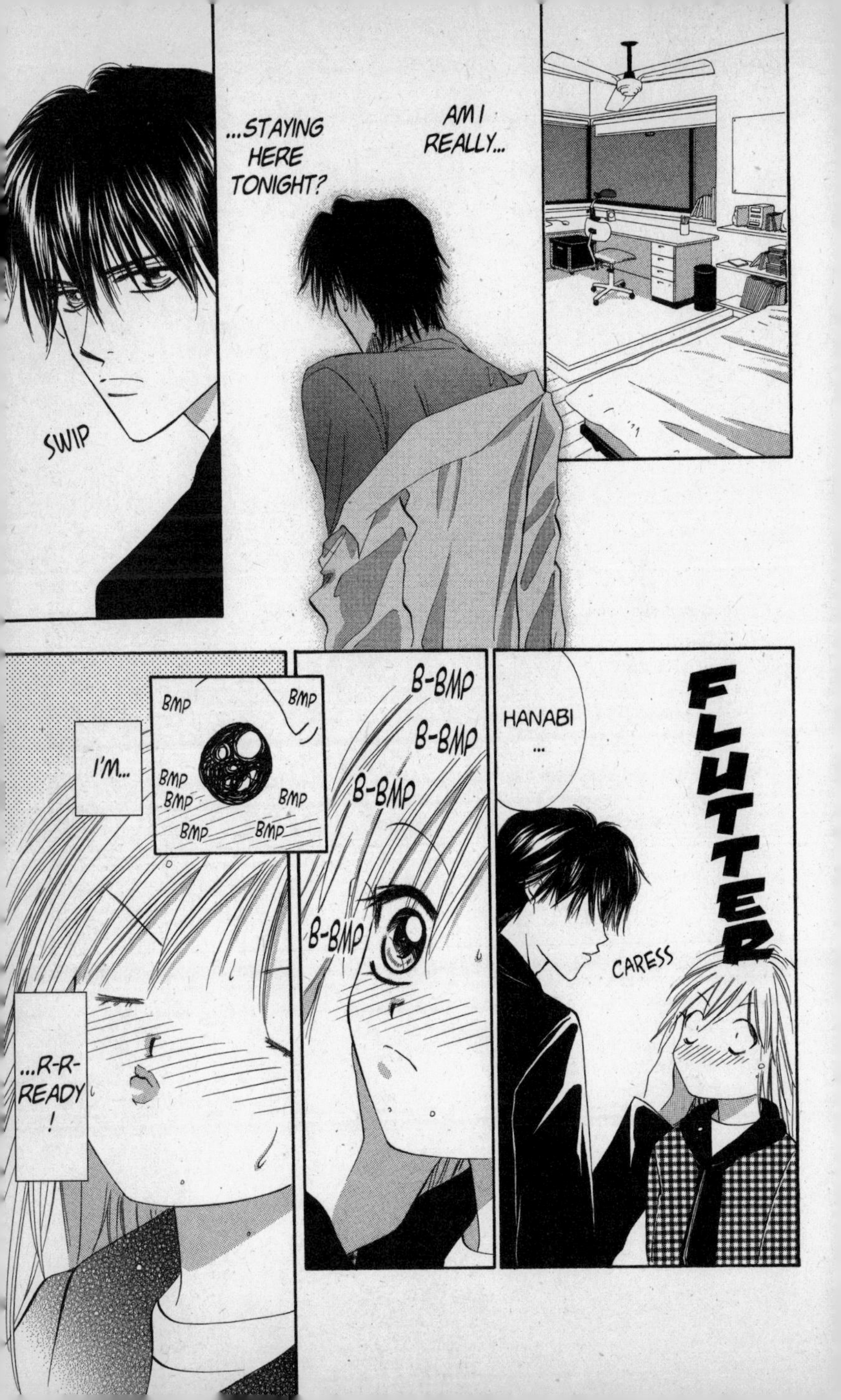

AM I REALLY...
...STAYING HERE TONIGHT?
SWIP
HANABI...
FLUTTER
CARESS
B-BMP
B-BMP
B-BMP
B-BMP
BMP
BMP
BMP
BMP
BMP
BMP
BMP
I'M...
...R-R-READY!

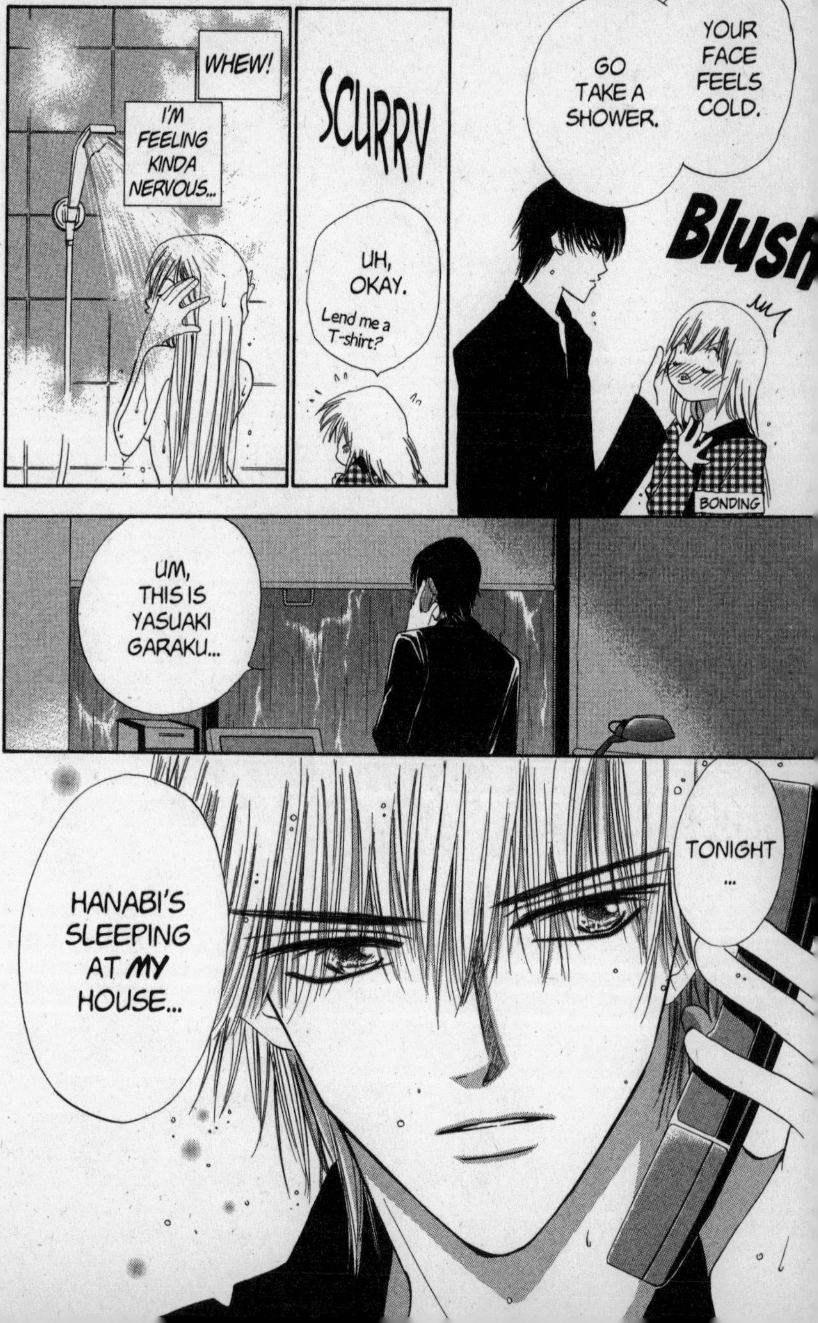
YOUR FACE FEELS COLD.
GO TAKE A SHOWER.
Blush
BONDING
SCURRY
UH, OKAY.
Lend me a T-shirt?
WHEW!
I'M FEELING KINDA NERVOUS...
UM, THIS IS YASUAKI GARAKU...
TONIGHT ...
HANABI'S SLEEPING AT MY HOUSE...

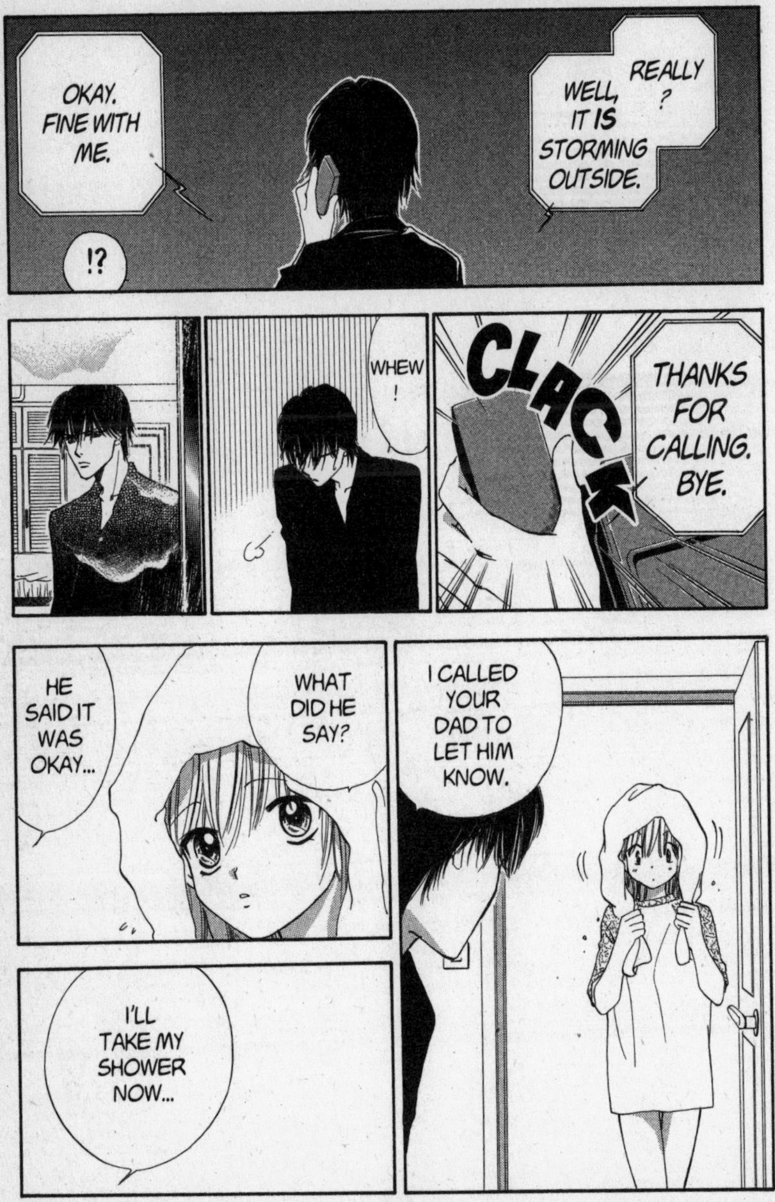
REALLY? WELL, IT IS STORMING OUTSIDE.
OKAY. FINE WITH ME.
!?
THANKS FOR CALLING. BYE.
CLACK
WHEW!
I CALLED YOUR DAD TO LET HIM KNOW.
WHAT DID HE SAY?
HE SAID IT WAS OKAY...
I'LL TAKE MY SHOWER NOW...

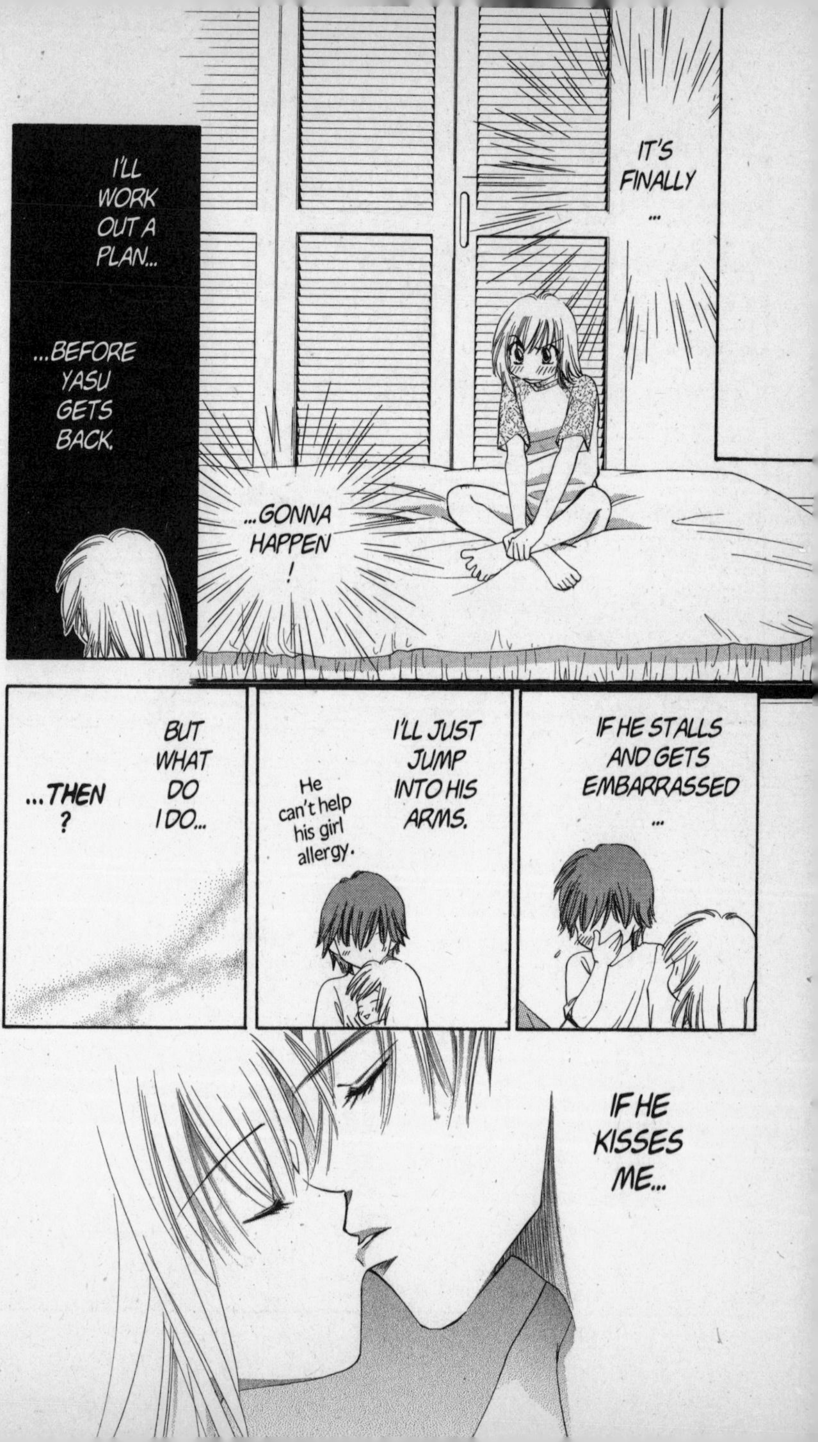

IT'S FINALLY ...
...GONNA HAPPEN!
I'LL WORK OUT A PLAN...
...BEFORE YASU GETS BACK.
IF HE STALLS AND GETS EMBARRASSED ...
I'LL JUST JUMP INTO HIS ARMS.
He can't help his girl allergy.
BUT WHAT DO I DO...
...THEN ?
IF HE KISSES ME...

WHAT DO I DO...
...WITH MY HAND ?
I COULD ...
...TOUCH HIS FACE.
SWISH
SWISH
SWISH
SWISH
SWISH

NOTICE

FREE SCREENTONE!

I BOUGHT SOME SCREENTONE A WHILE BACK THAT I REALLY DON'T NEED, BUT I HATE TO TOSS IT. ANYBODY INTERESTED? JUST SEND ME A LETTER. I'D LIKE TO GIVE IT TO A YOUNG STUDENT WHO'S INTERESTED IN DRAWING MANGA OR DOUJINSHI.

SCREENTONE ISN'T CHEAP! PLUS THERE ARE NO DO-OVERS WHEN USING IT. BUT REMEMBER, I COULDN'T USE THIS STUFF, SO PLEASE DON'T SAY "I CAN'T USE THIS CRAP!" IF YOU GET IT. A WINNER WILL **NOT** BE ANNOUNCED. I'LL JUST SHIP THEM THE SCREENTONE. IF I GET LOTS OF LETTERS, I'LL PICK ONE FROM THE PILE. IF JUST A FEW PEOPLE WRITE, I'LL DIVVY IT UP EQUALLY.

(EDITOR'S NOTE: SORRY! THIS OFFER EXPIRED ON JUNE 20, 2005.)

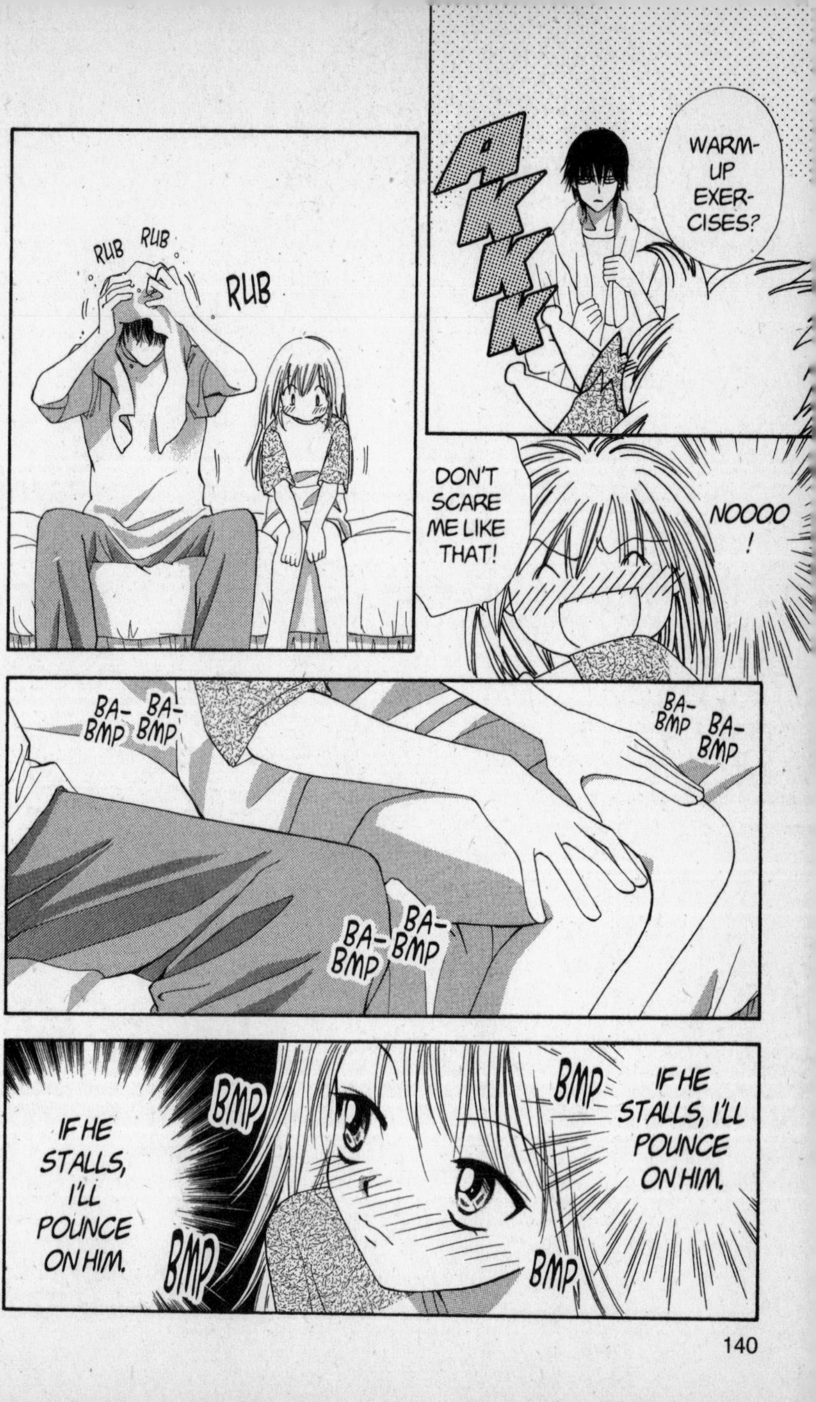
WARM-UP EXERCISES?
AKKK
NOOOO!
DON'T SCARE ME LIKE THAT!
RUB RUB
RUB
BA-BMP BA-BMP
BA-BMP BA-BMP
BA-BMP BA-BMP
IF HE STALLS, I'LL POUNCE ON HIM.
BMP
BMP
IF HE STALLS, I'LL POUNCE ON HIM.
BMP
BMP

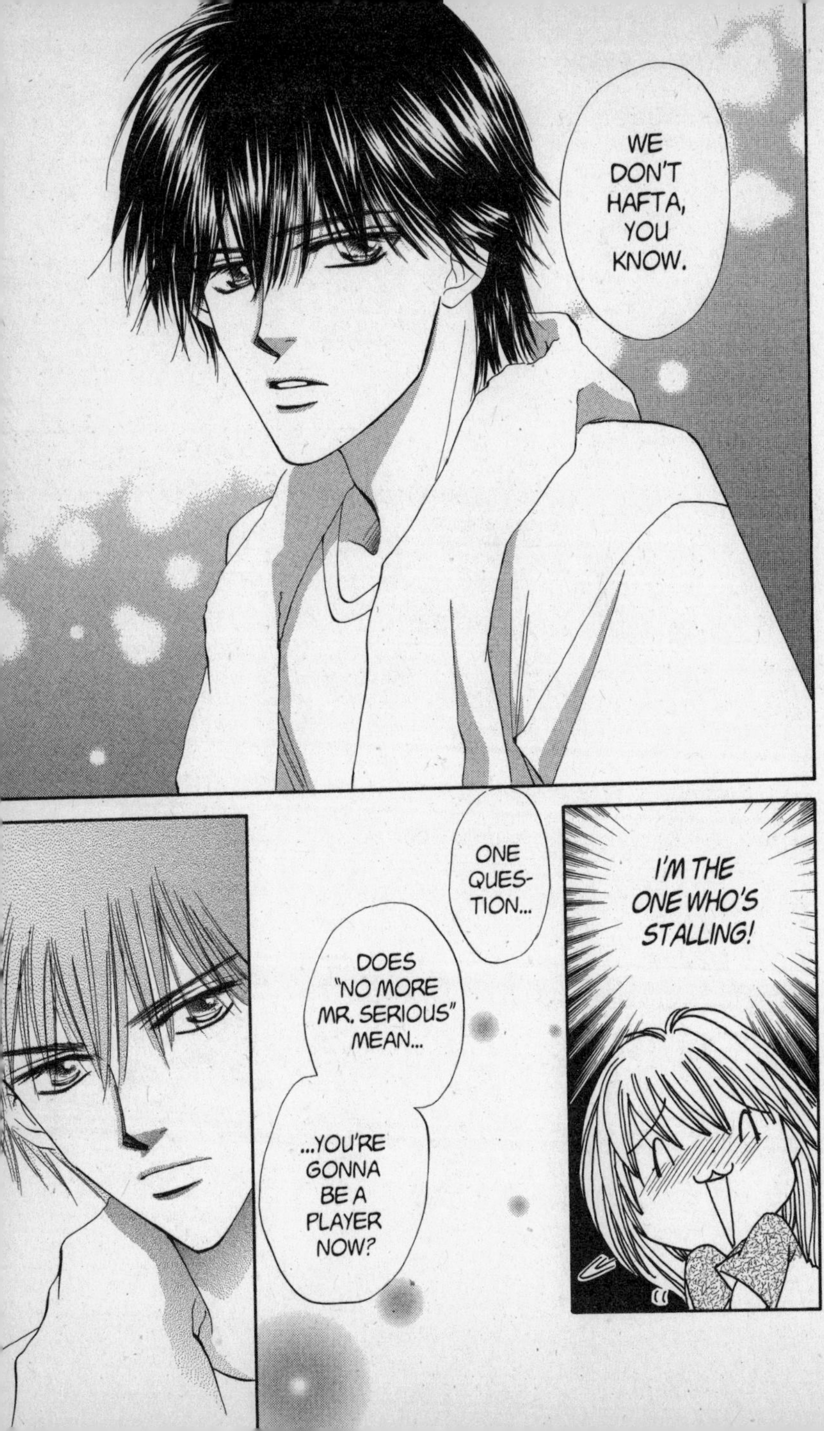
WE DON'T HAFTA, YOU KNOW.
I'M THE ONE WHO'S STALLING!
ONE QUES-TION...
DOES "NO MORE MR. SERIOUS" MEAN...
...YOU'RE GONNA BE A PLAYER NOW?

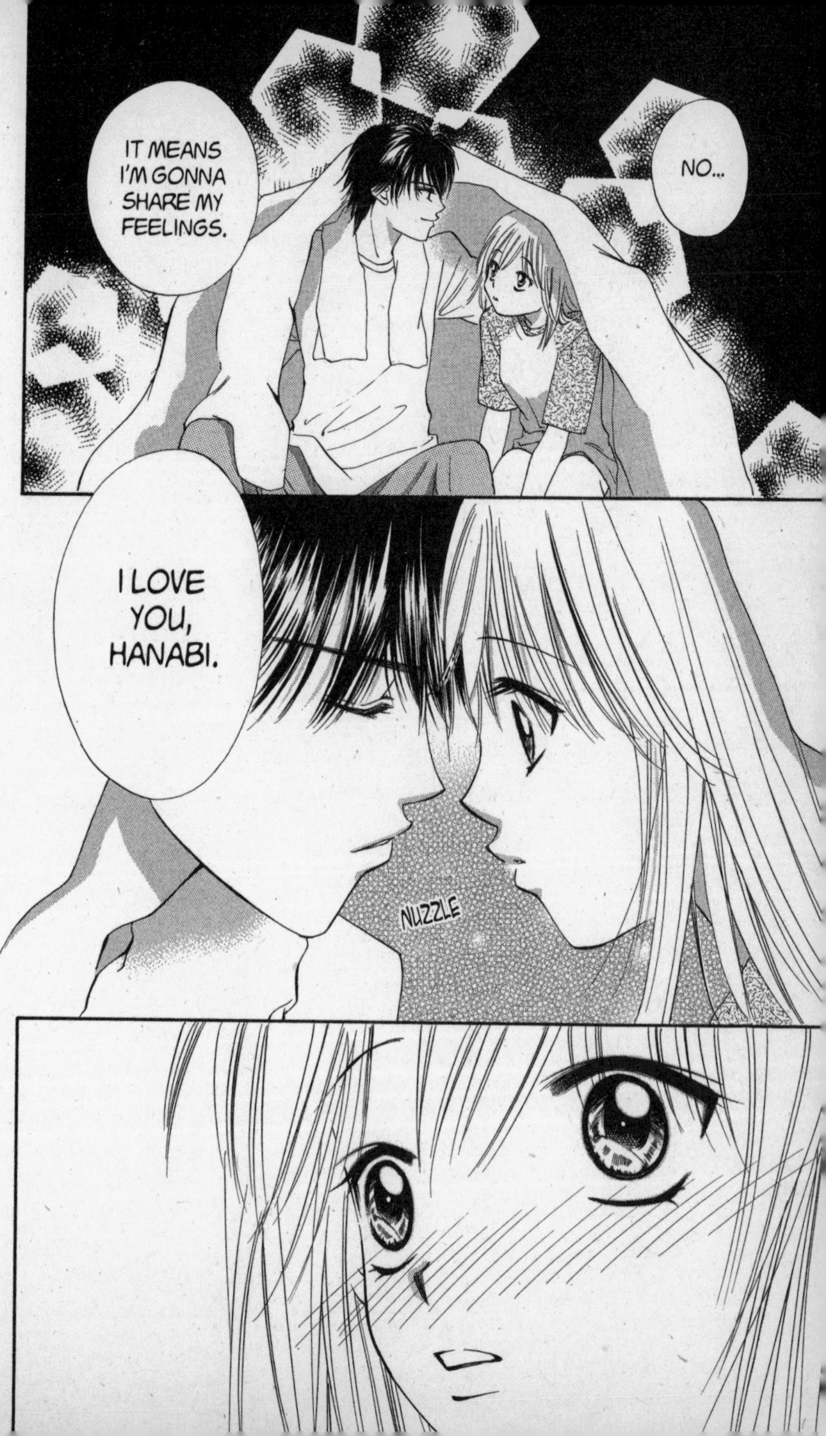
NO...
IT MEANS I'M GONNA SHARE MY FEELINGS.
I LOVE YOU, HANABI.
NUZZLE

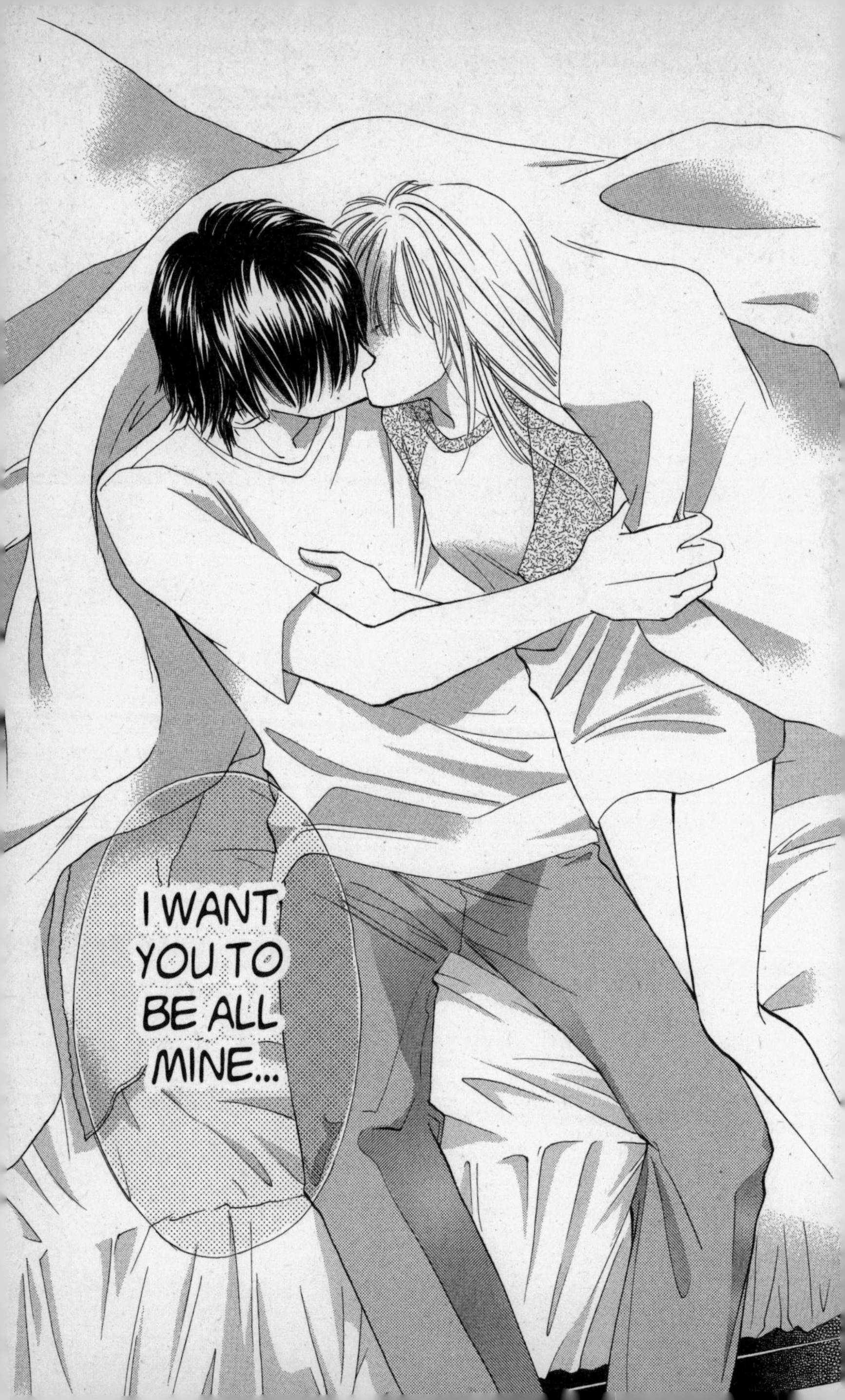
I WANT YOU TO BE ALL MINE...

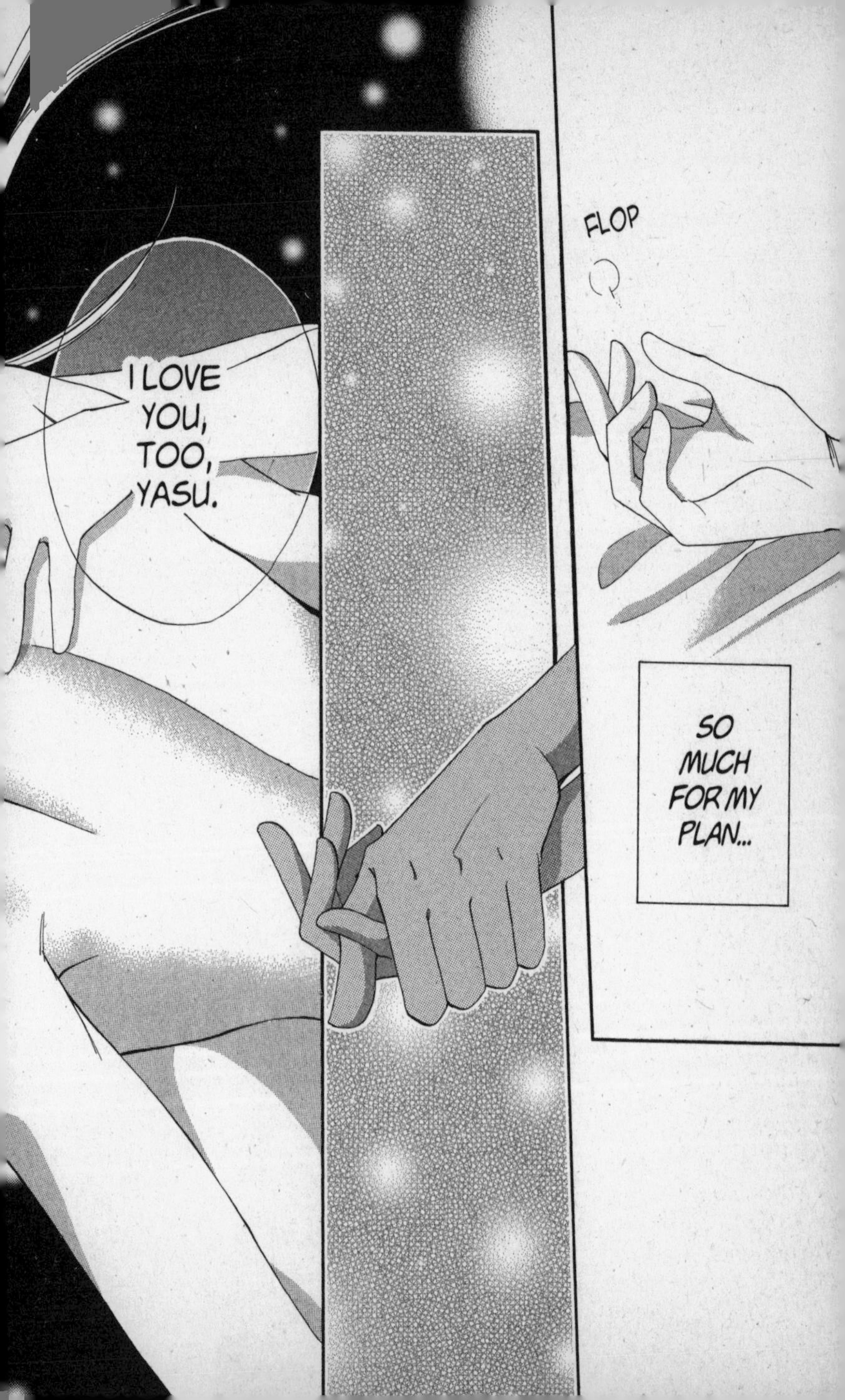
FLOP
SO MUCH FOR MY PLAN...
I LOVE YOU, TOO, YASU.

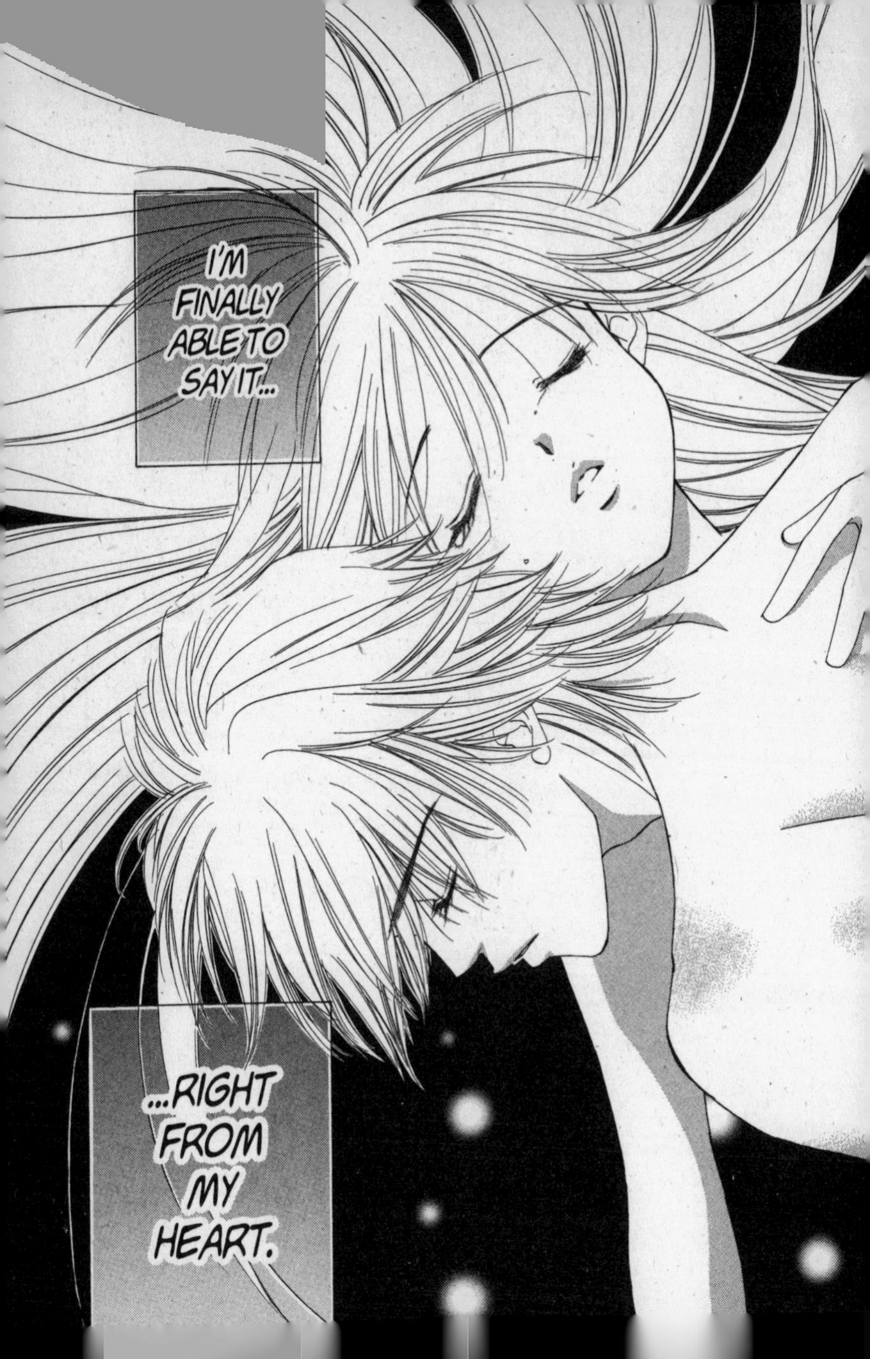
I'M FINALLY ABLE TO SAY IT...
...RIGHT FROM MY HEART.

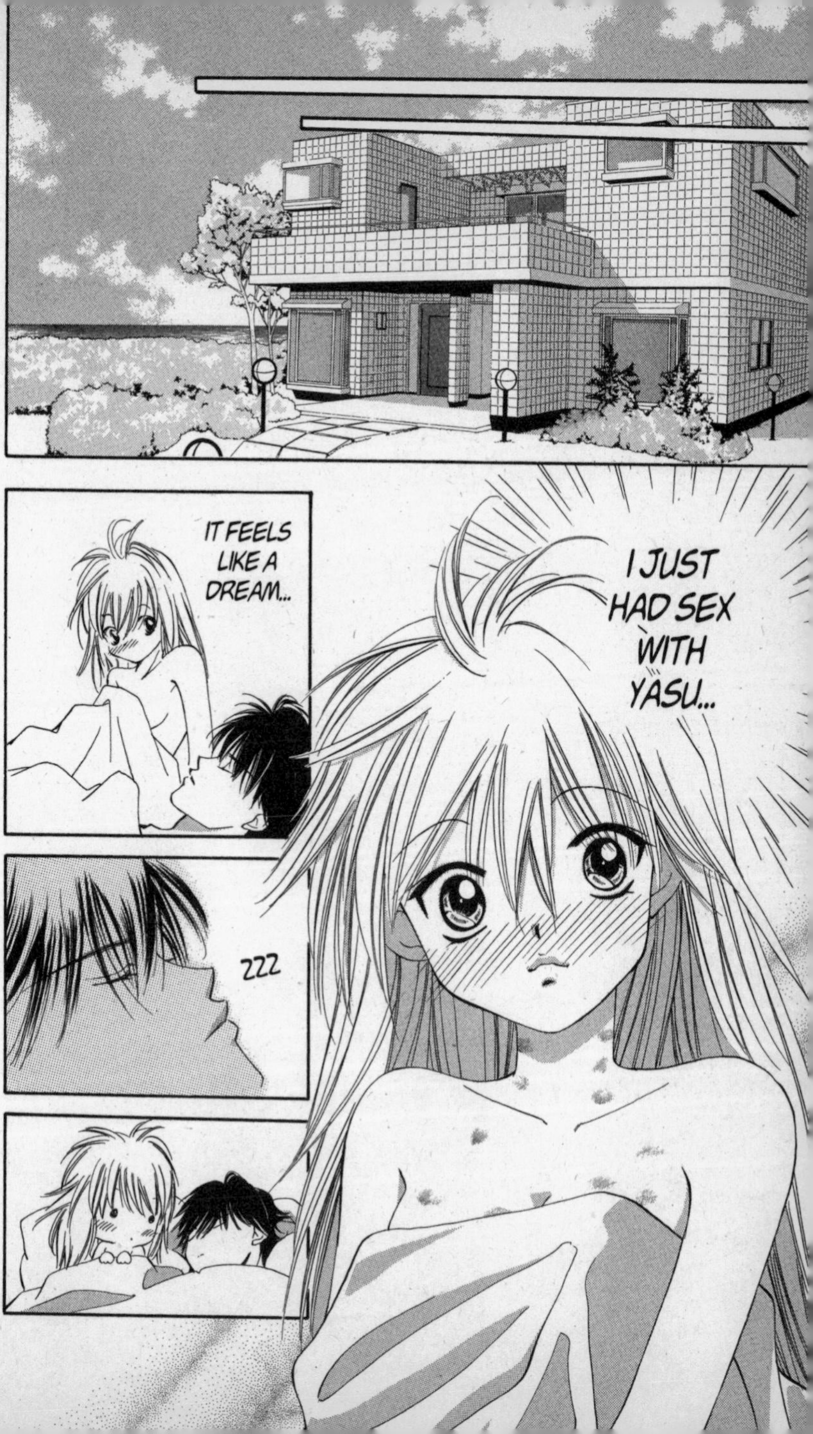
I JUST HAD SEX WITH YASU...
IT FEELS LIKE A DREAM...
ZZZ

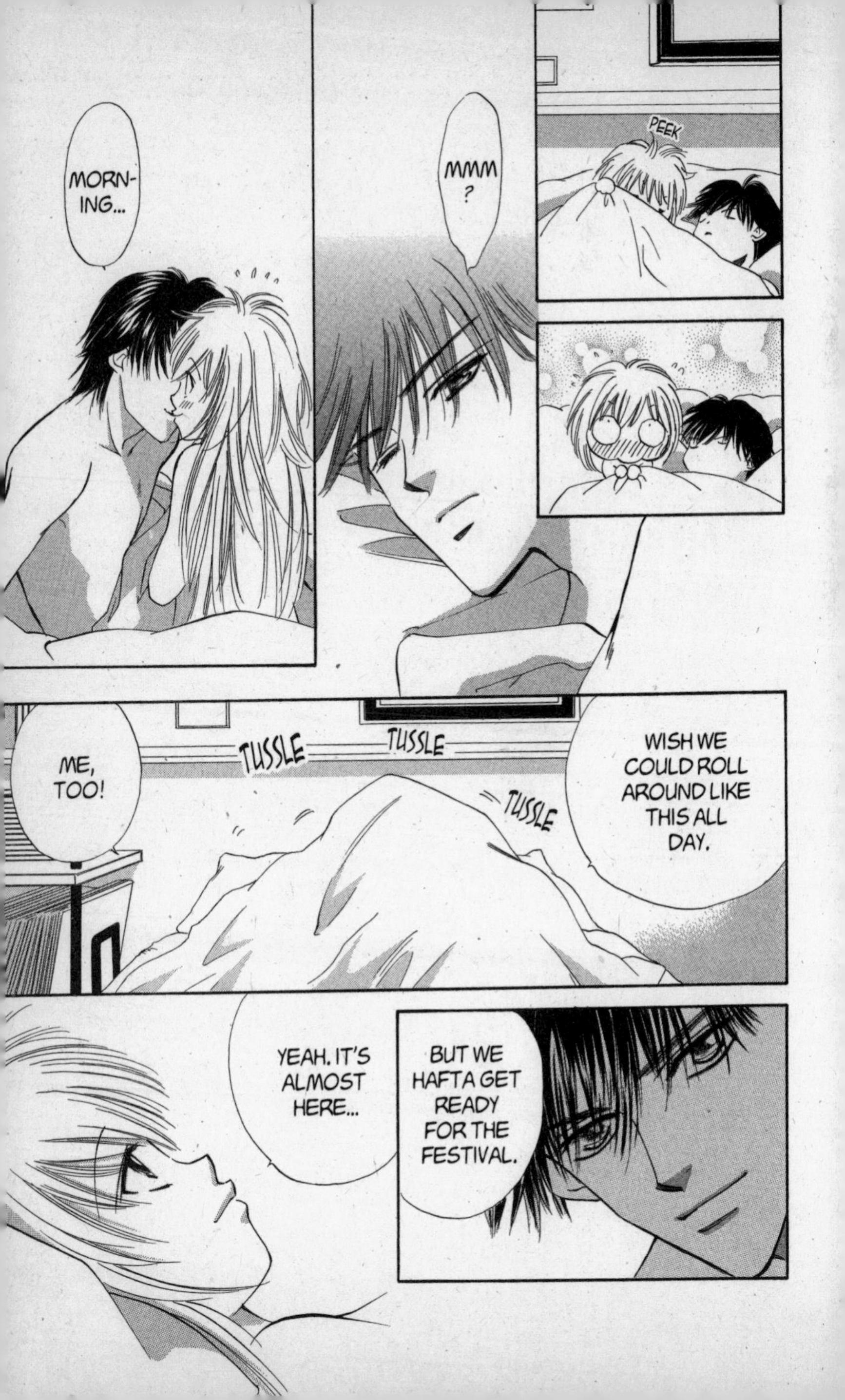
PEEK
MMM ?
MORNING...
WISH WE COULD ROLL AROUND LIKE THIS ALL DAY.
TUSSLE
TUSSLE
TUSSLE
ME, TOO!
BUT WE HAFTA GET READY FOR THE FESTIVAL.
YEAH. IT'S ALMOST HERE...

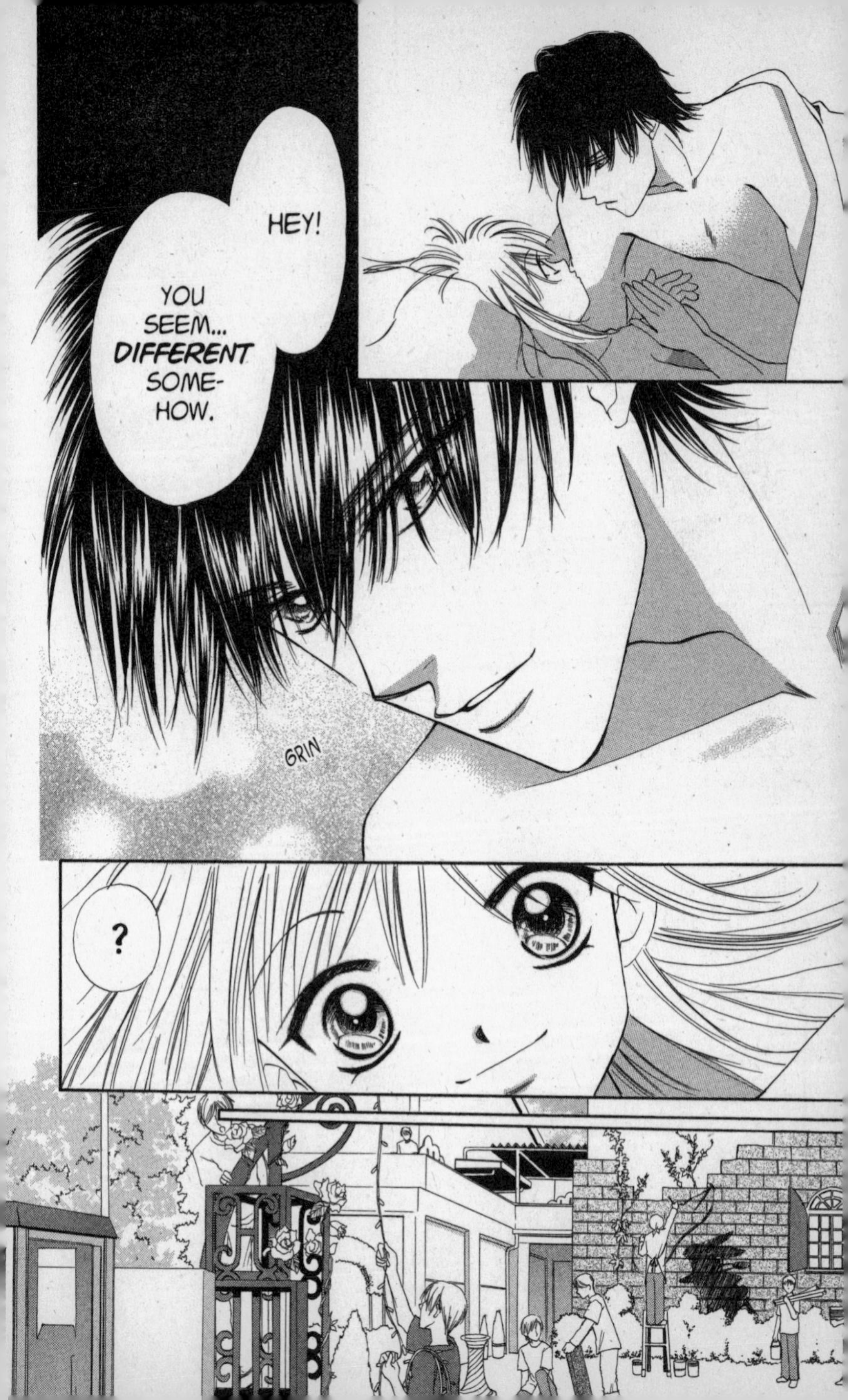
HEY!
YOU SEEM... DIFFERENT SOME-HOW.
GRIN
?

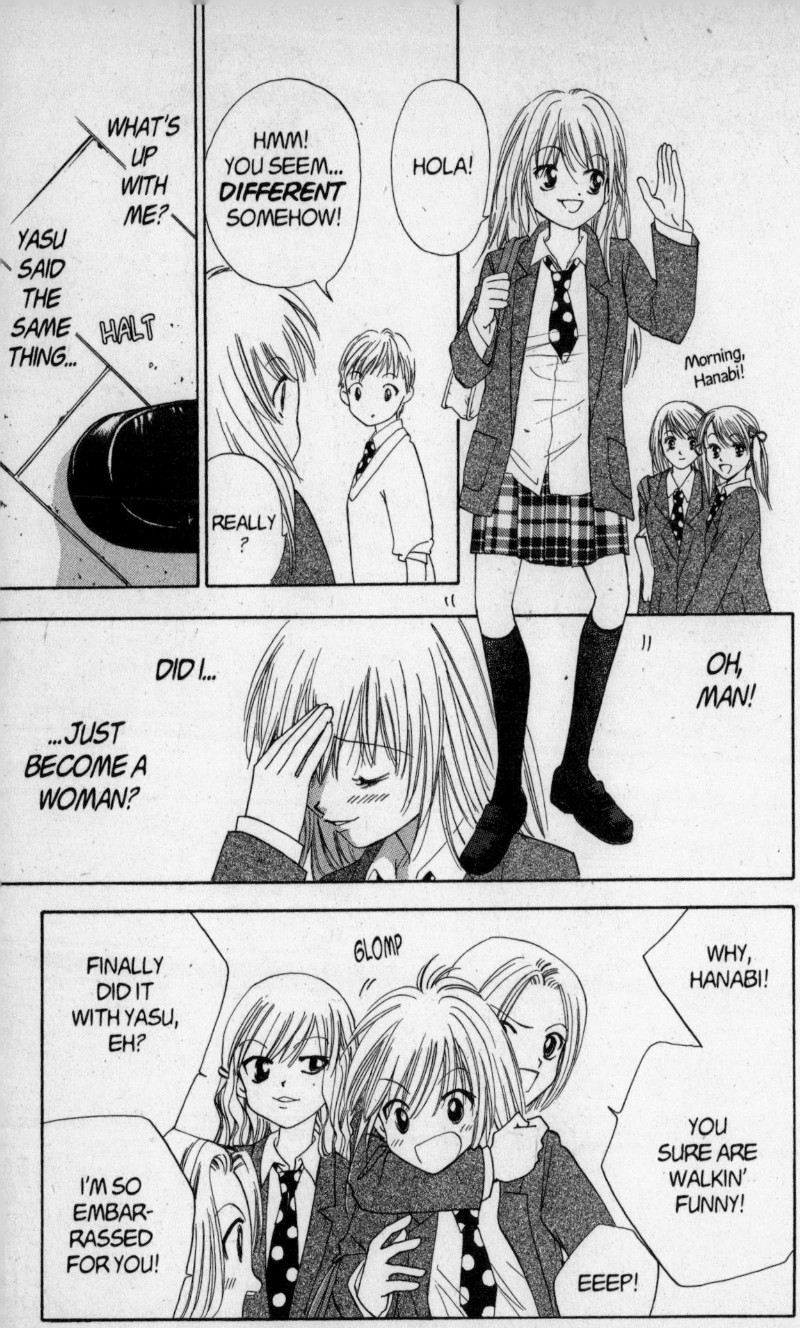

HOLA!
Morning, Hanabi!
HMM! YOU SEEM... DIFFERENT SOMEHOW!
REALLY?
HALT
WHAT'S UP WITH ME?
YASU SAID THE SAME THING...
OH, MAN!
DID I...
...JUST BECOME A WOMAN?
WHY, HANABI!
GLOMP
YOU SURE ARE WALKIN' FUNNY!
EEEP!
FINALLY DID IT WITH YASU, EH?
I'M SO EMBARRASSED FOR YOU!

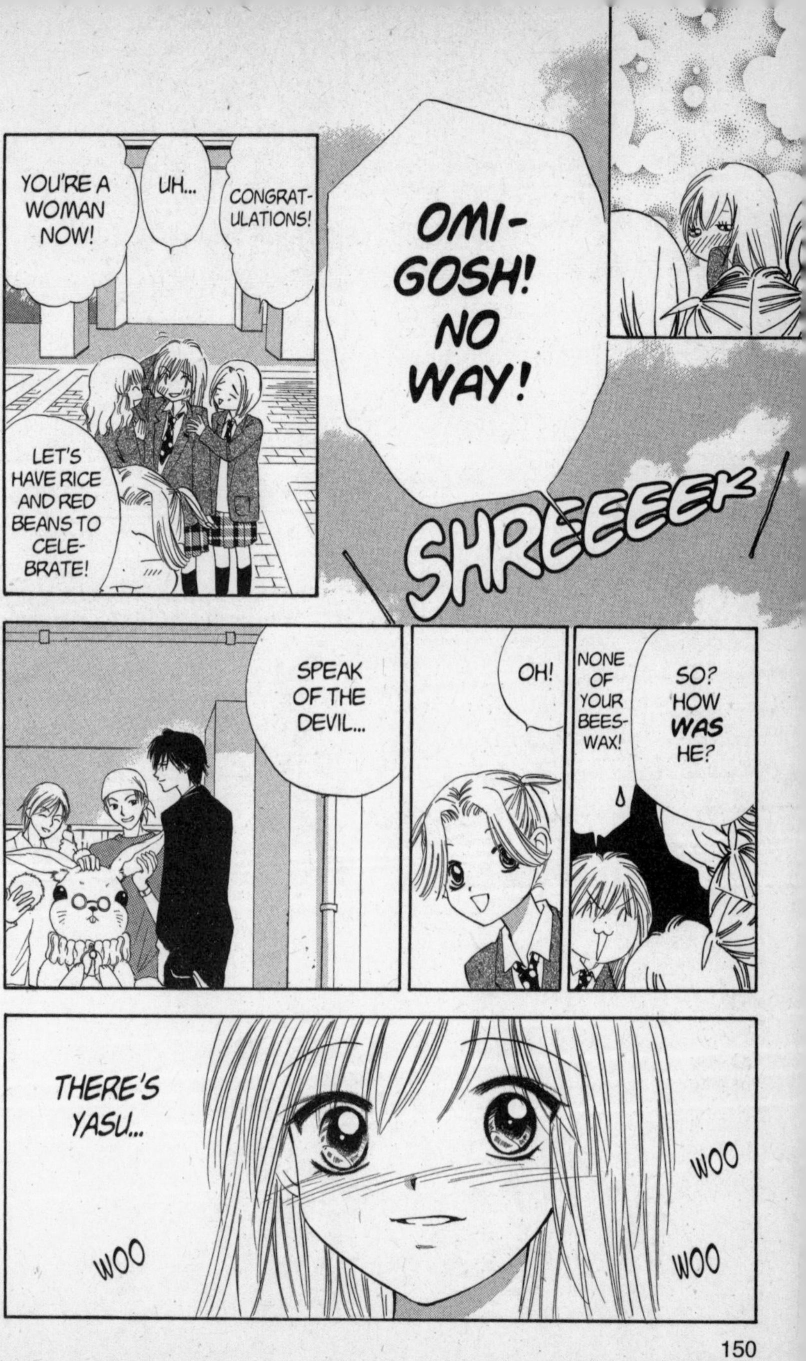
OMI-GOSH! NO WAY!
SHREEEEK
CONGRAT-ULATIONS!
UH...
YOU'RE A WOMAN NOW!
LET'S HAVE RICE AND RED BEANS TO CELE-BRATE!
SO? HOW WAS HE?
NONE OF YOUR BEES-WAX!
OH!
SPEAK OF THE DEVIL...
WOO
THERE'S YASU...
WOO
WOO

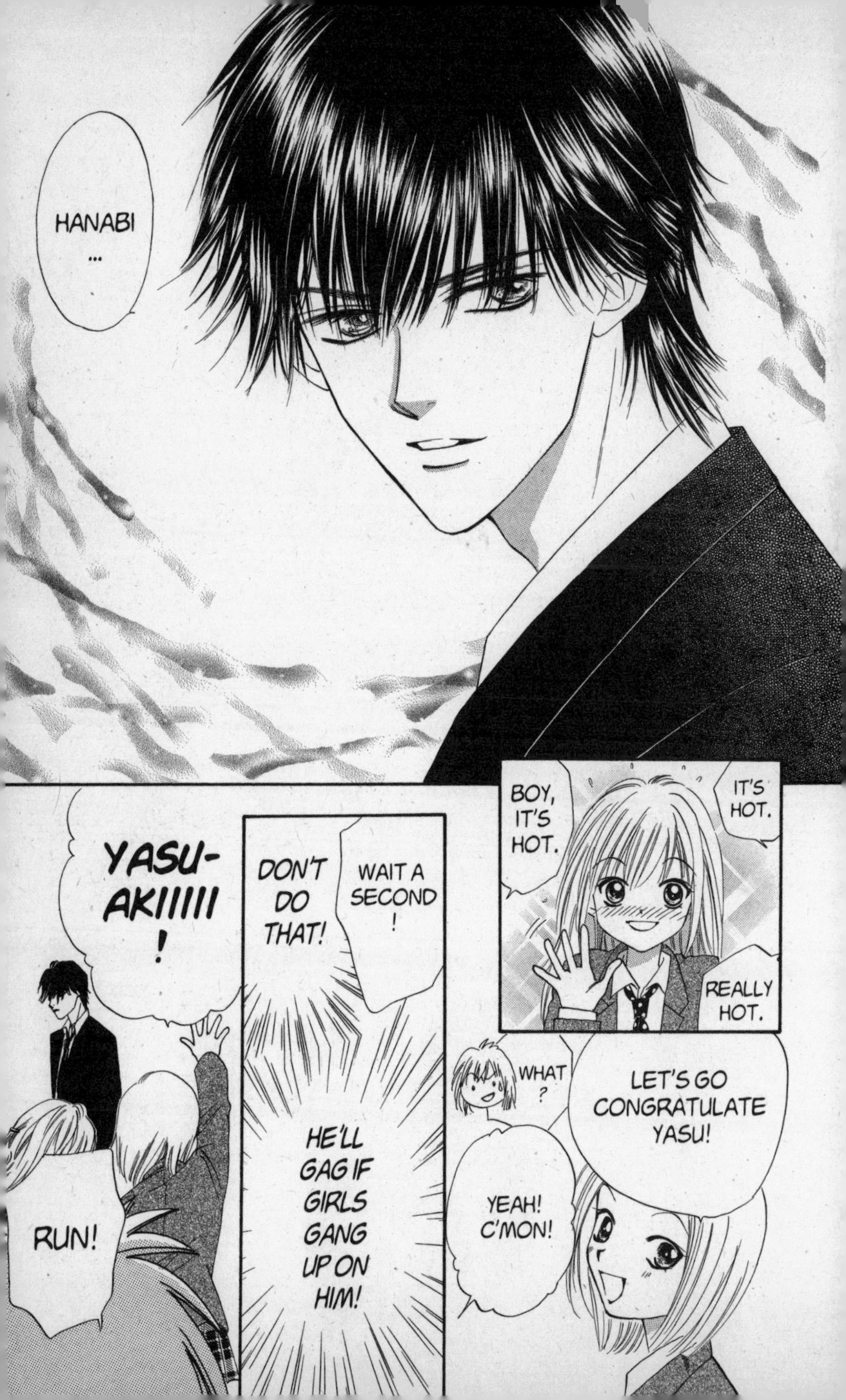
HANABI ...
IT'S HOT.
BOY, IT'S HOT.
REALLY HOT.
LET'S GO CONGRATULATE YASU!
WHAT?
YEAH! C'MON!
WAIT A SECOND!
DON'T DO THAT!
HE'LL GAG IF GIRLS GANG UP ON HIM!
YASU-AKIIIIII!
RUN!

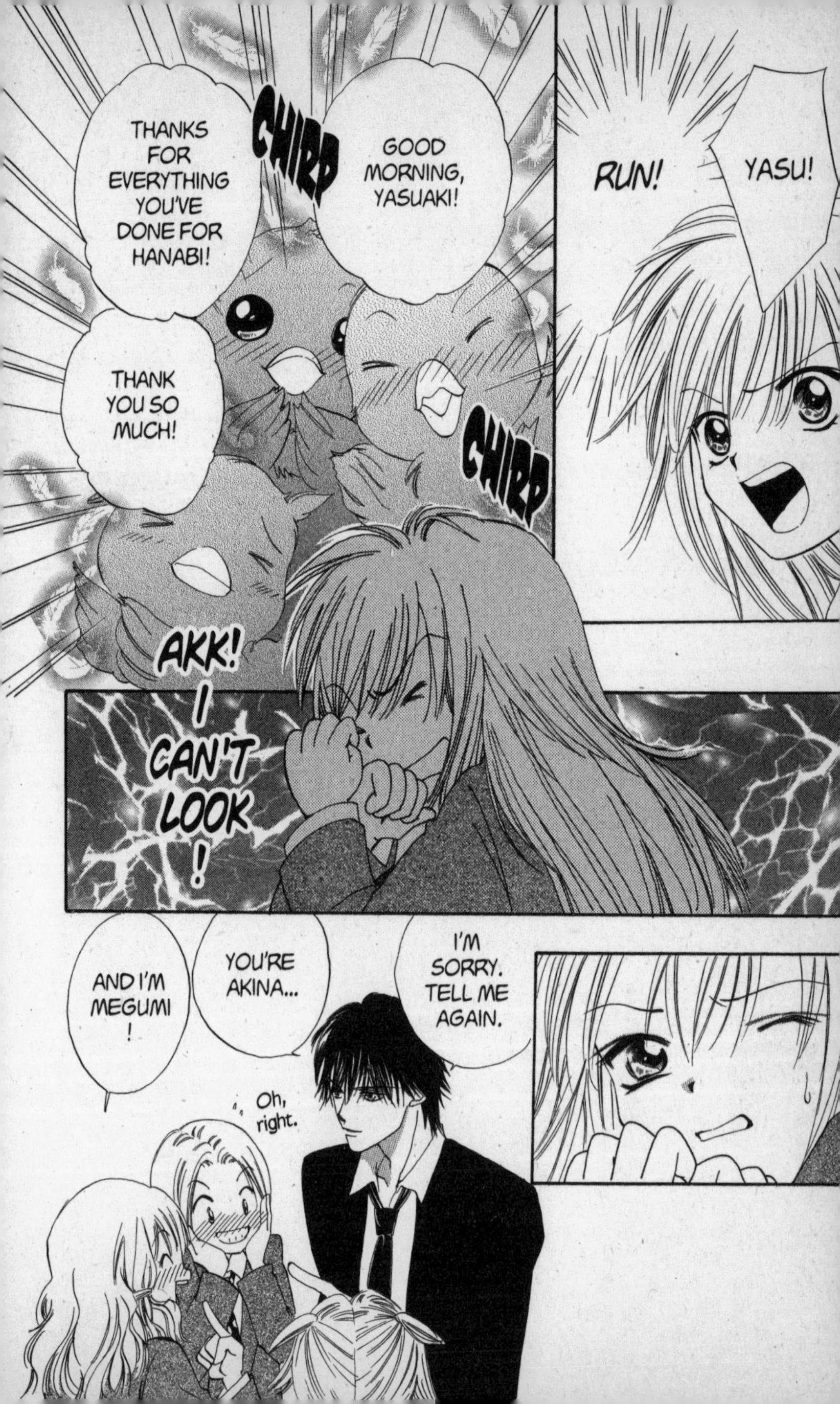
YASU!
RUN!
CHIRP
GOOD MORNING, YASUAKI!
THANKS FOR EVERYTHING YOU'VE DONE FOR HANABI!
THANK YOU SO MUCH!
CHIRP
AKK! I CAN'T LOOK!
I'M SORRY. TELL ME AGAIN.
YOU'RE AKINA...
AND I'M MEGUMI!
Oh, right.

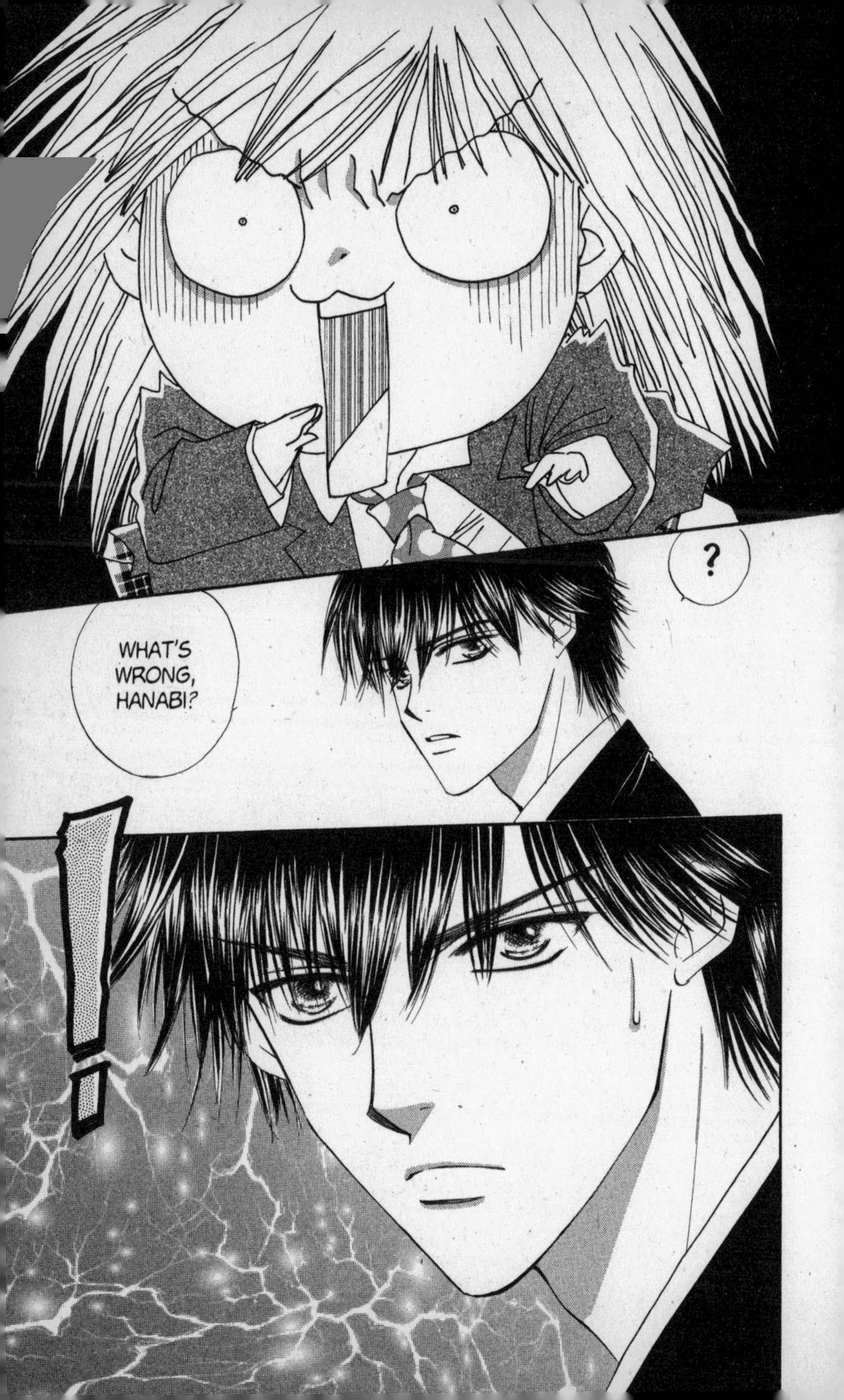
?
WHAT'S WRONG, HANABI?
!

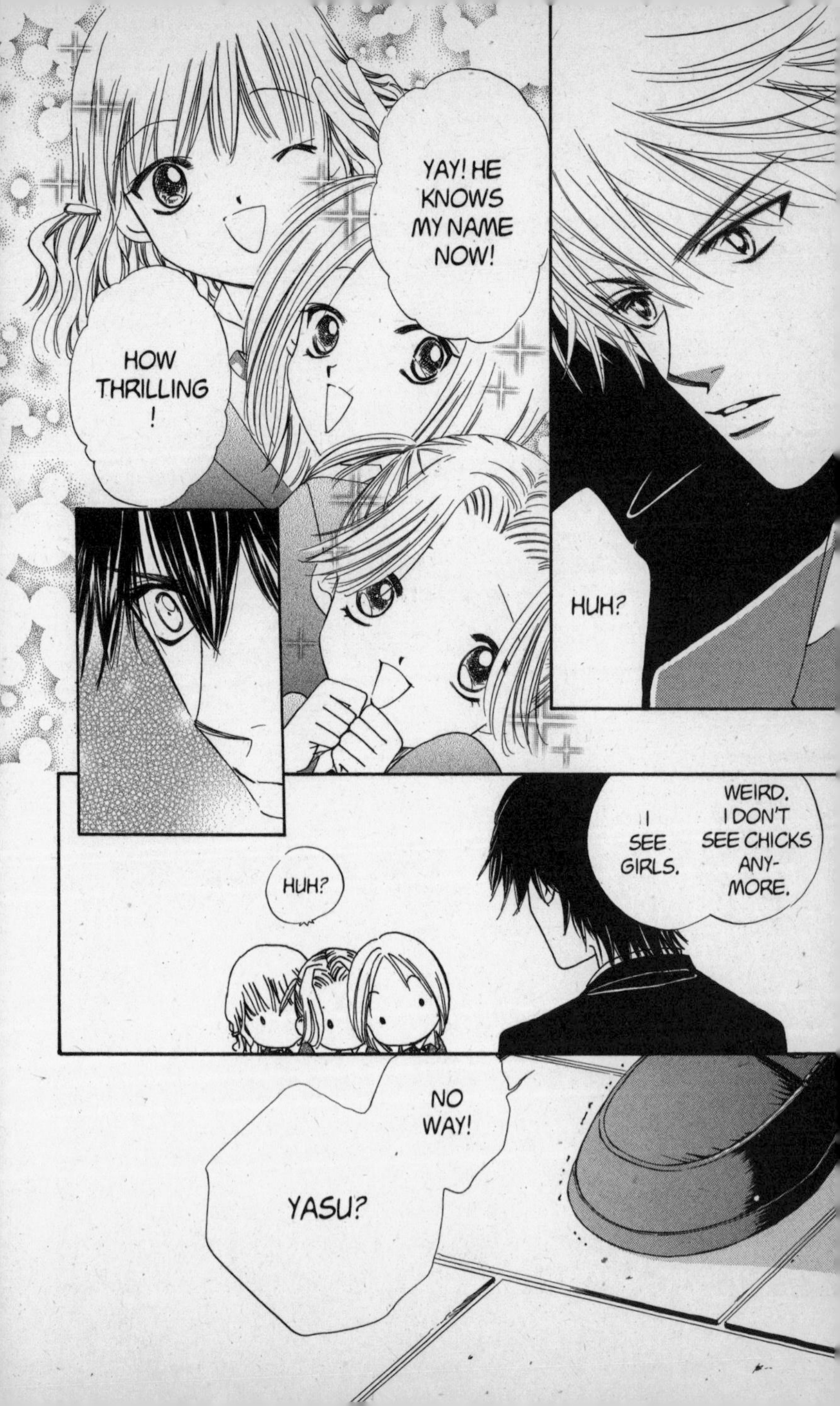
HUH?
YAY! HE KNOWS MY NAME NOW!
HOW THRILLING!
WEIRD. I DON'T SEE CHICKS ANY-MORE.
I SEE GIRLS.
HUH?
NO WAY!
YASU?

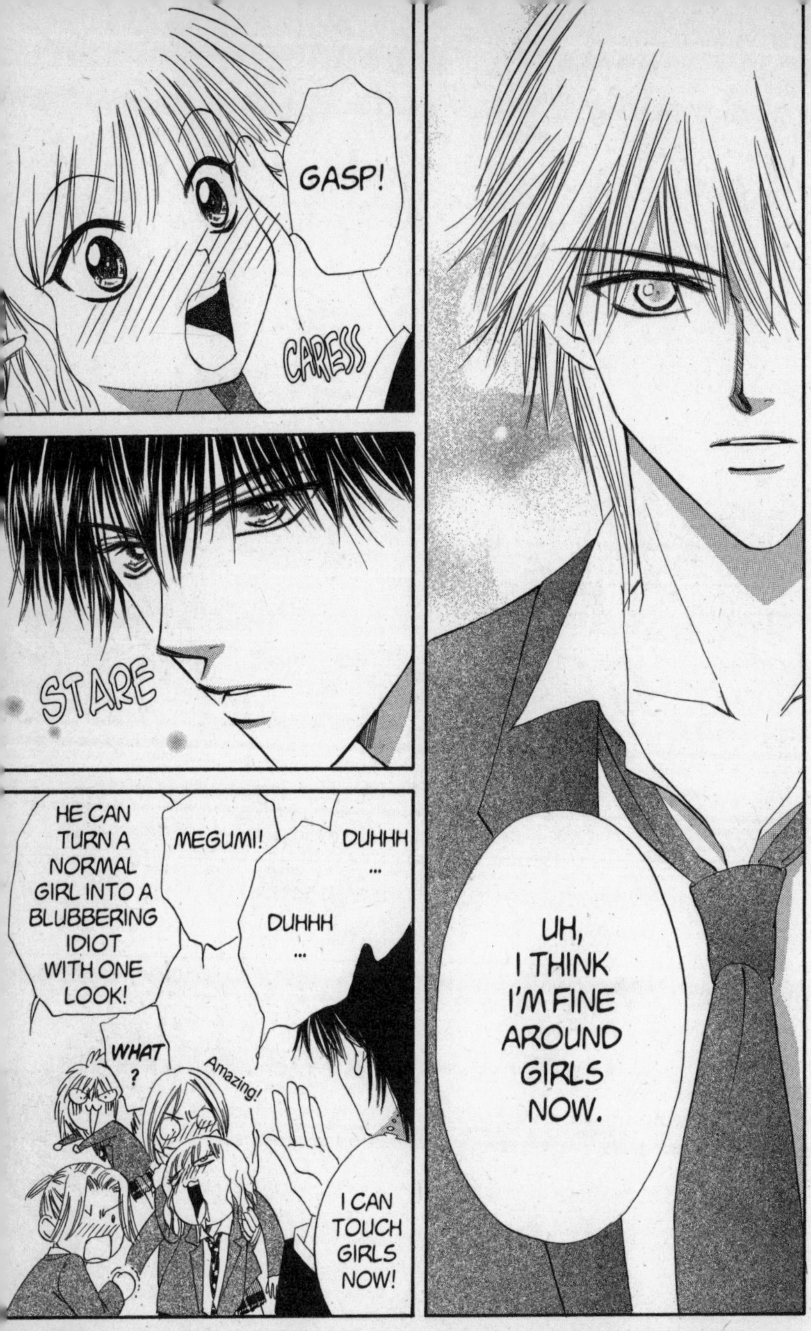
UH, I THINK I'M FINE AROUND GIRLS NOW.
GASP!
CARESS
STARE
DUHHH ...
MEGUMI!
HE CAN TURN A NORMAL GIRL INTO A BLUBBERING IDIOT WITH ONE LOOK!
DUHHH ...
I CAN TOUCH GIRLS NOW!
Amazing!
WHAT?

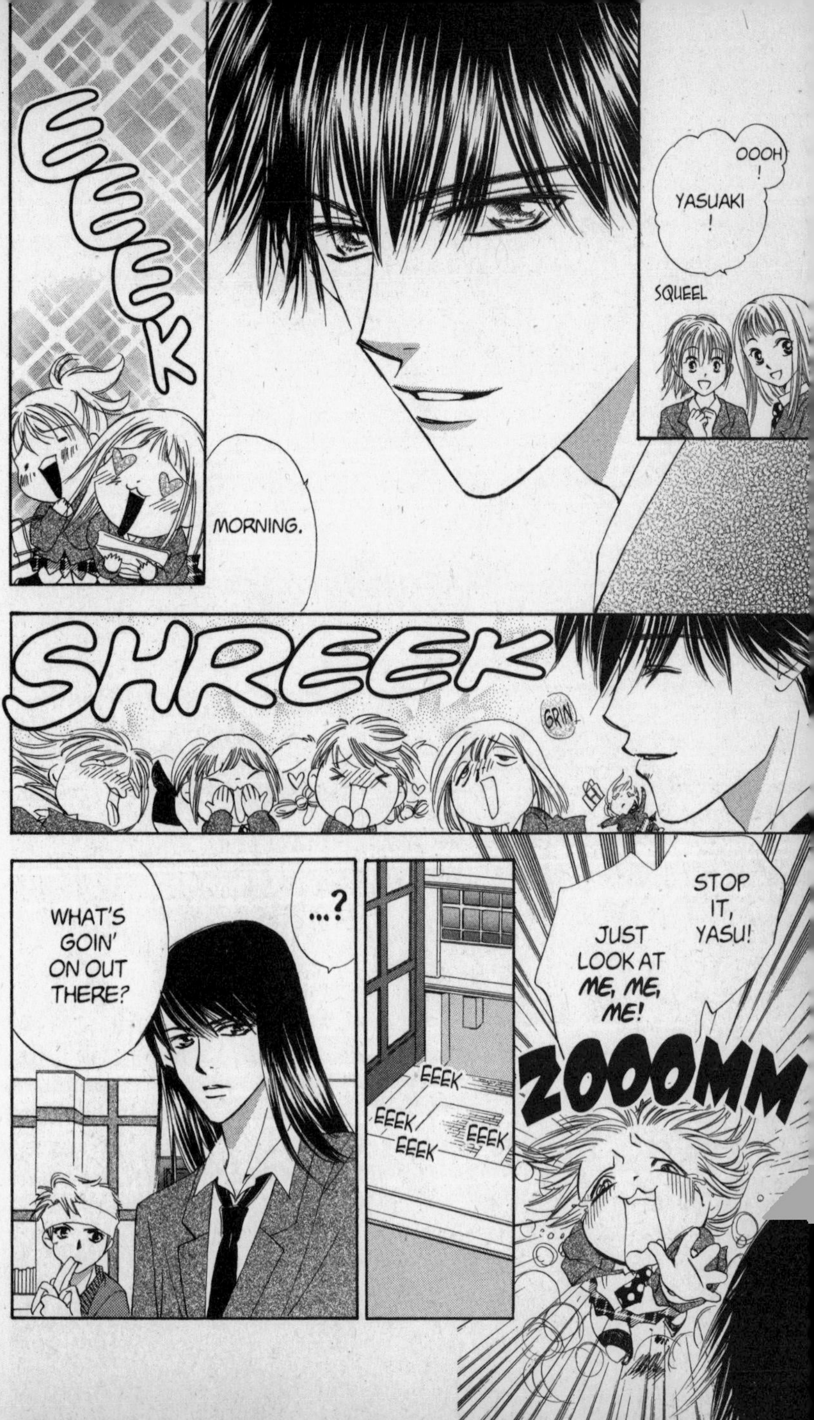
OOOH! YASUAKI!
SQUEEL
MORNING.
EEEK
GRIN
SHREEK
STOP IT, YASU!
JUST LOOK AT ME, ME, ME!
ZOOOMM
...?
EEEK
EEEK
EEEK
EEEK
WHAT'S GOIN' ON OUT THERE?

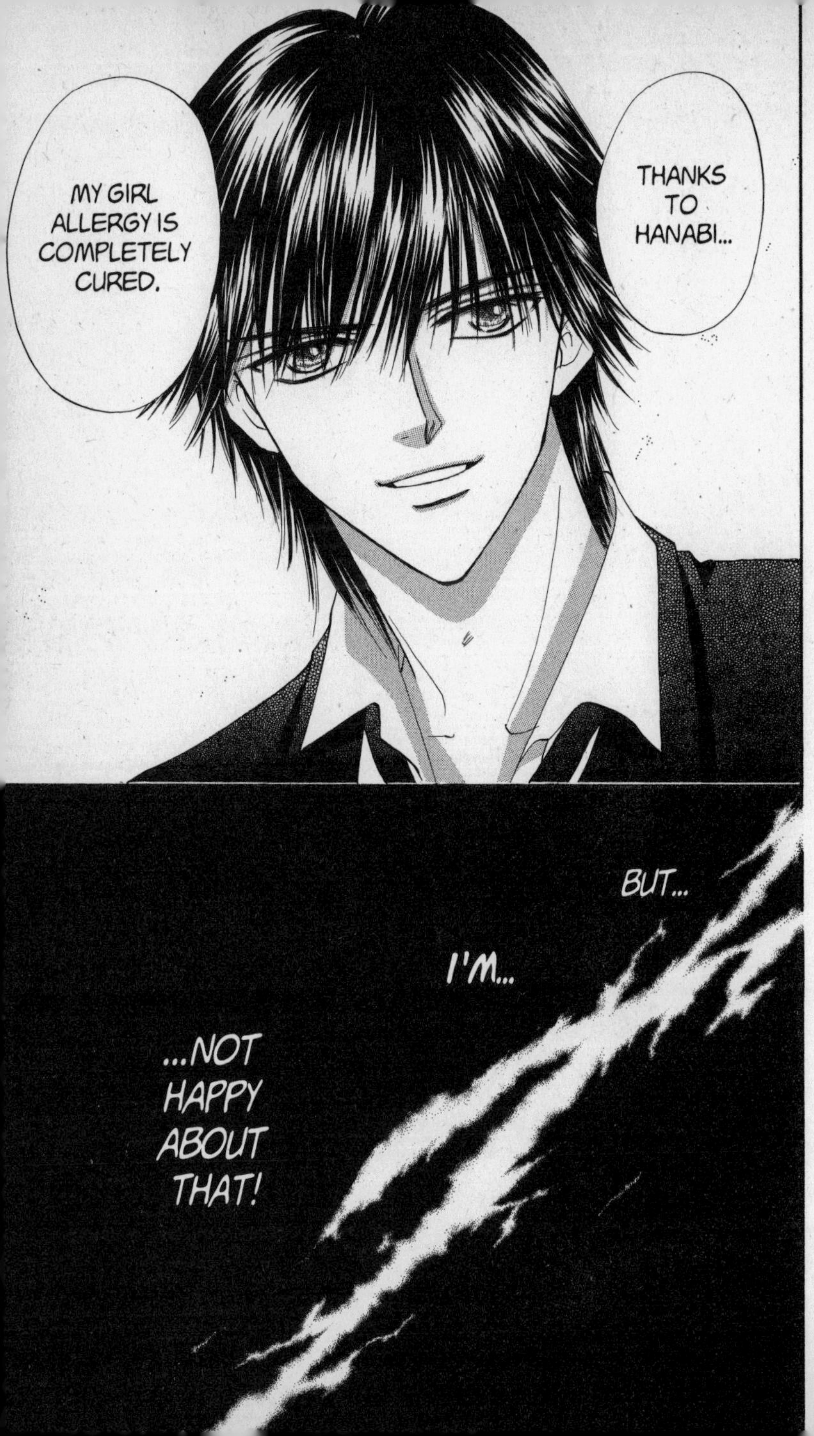
THANKS TO HANABI...
MY GIRL ALLERGY IS COMPLETELY CURED.
BUT...
I'M...
...NOT HAPPY ABOUT THAT!

HAPPY HUSTLE HIGH

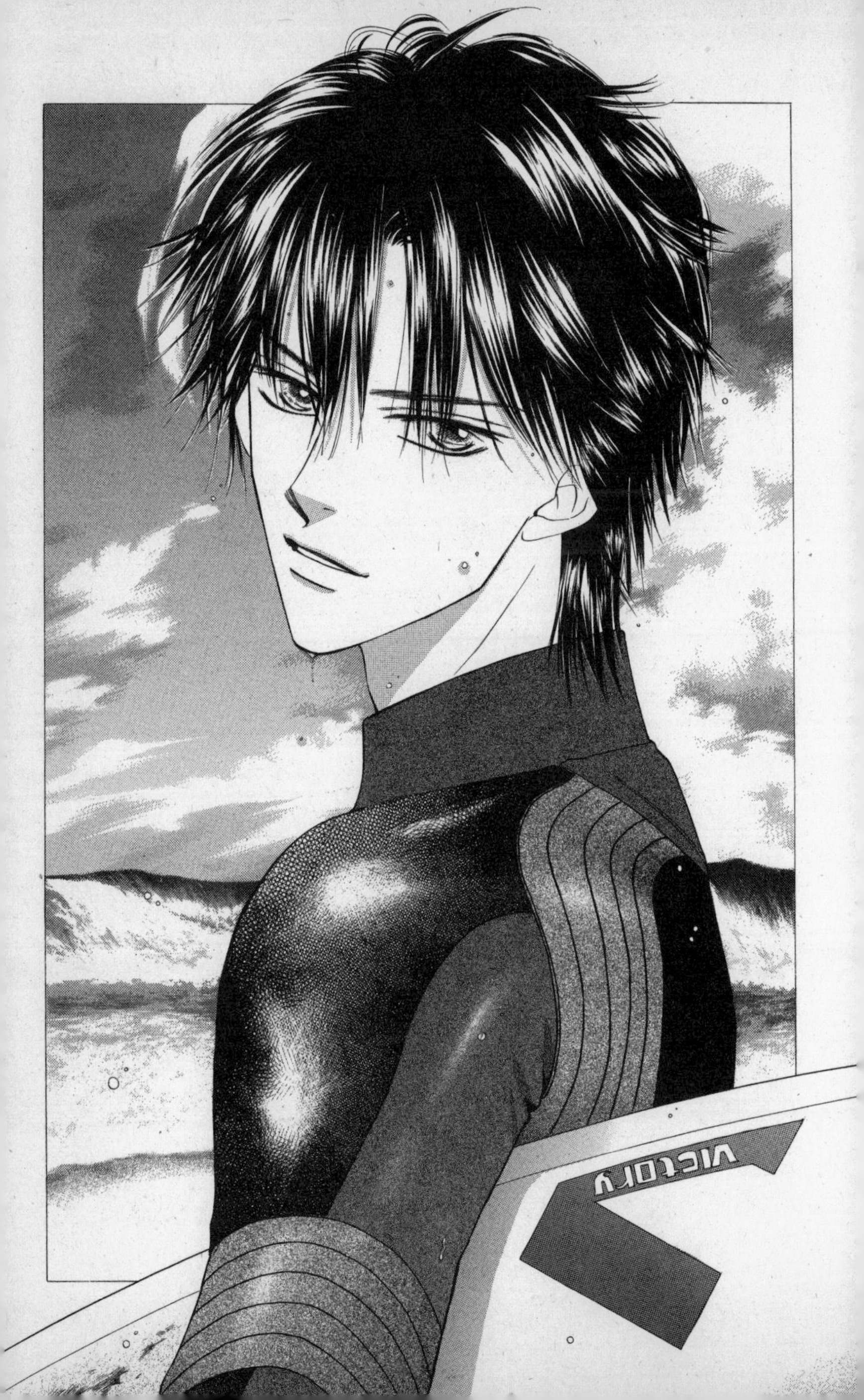
victory

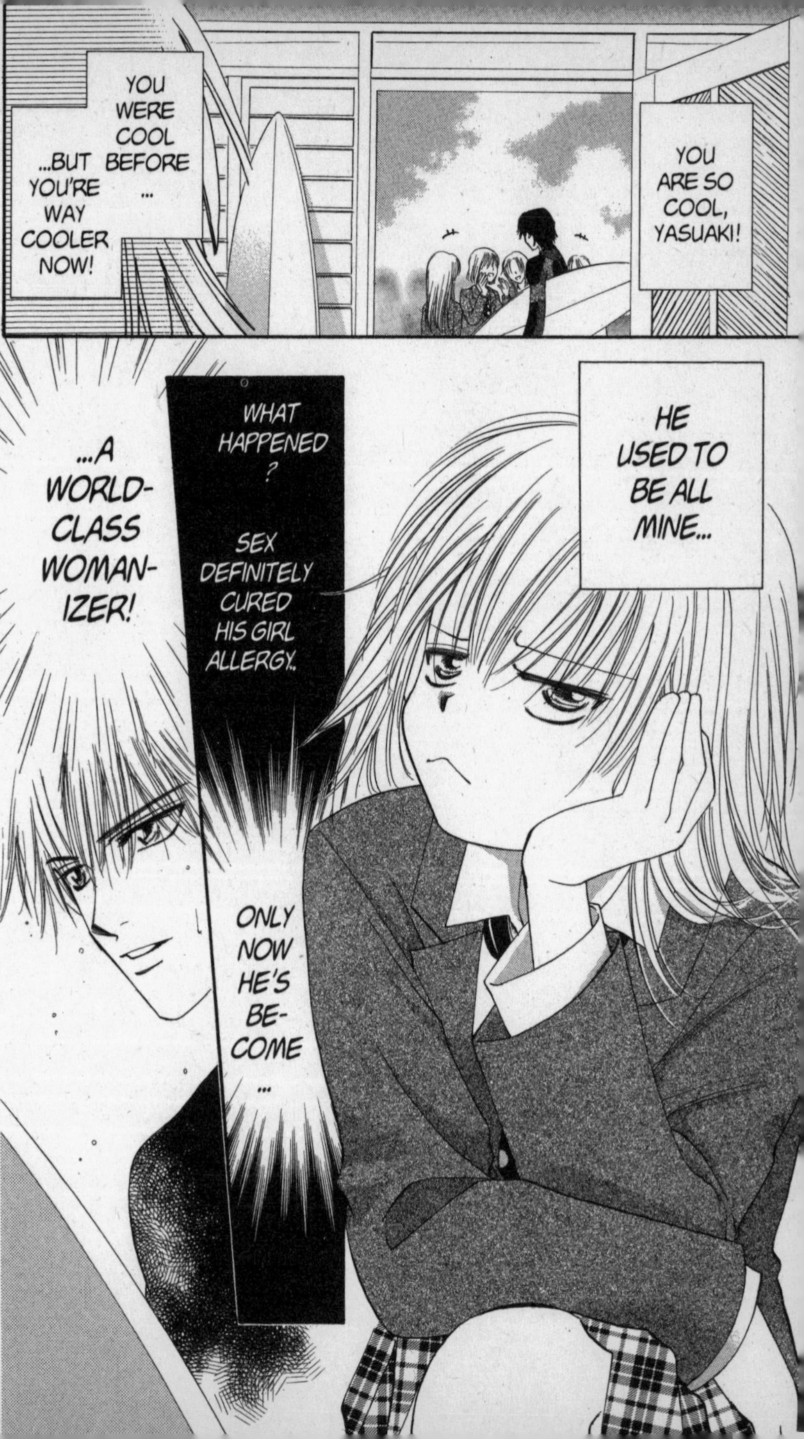
YOU ARE SO COOL, YASUAKI!
YOU WERE COOL BEFORE ...
...BUT YOU'RE WAY COOLER NOW!
HE USED TO BE ALL MINE...
WHAT HAPPENED?
SEX DEFINITELY CURED HIS GIRL ALLERGY..
ONLY NOW HE'S BE-COME ...
...A WORLD-CLASS WOMAN-IZER!

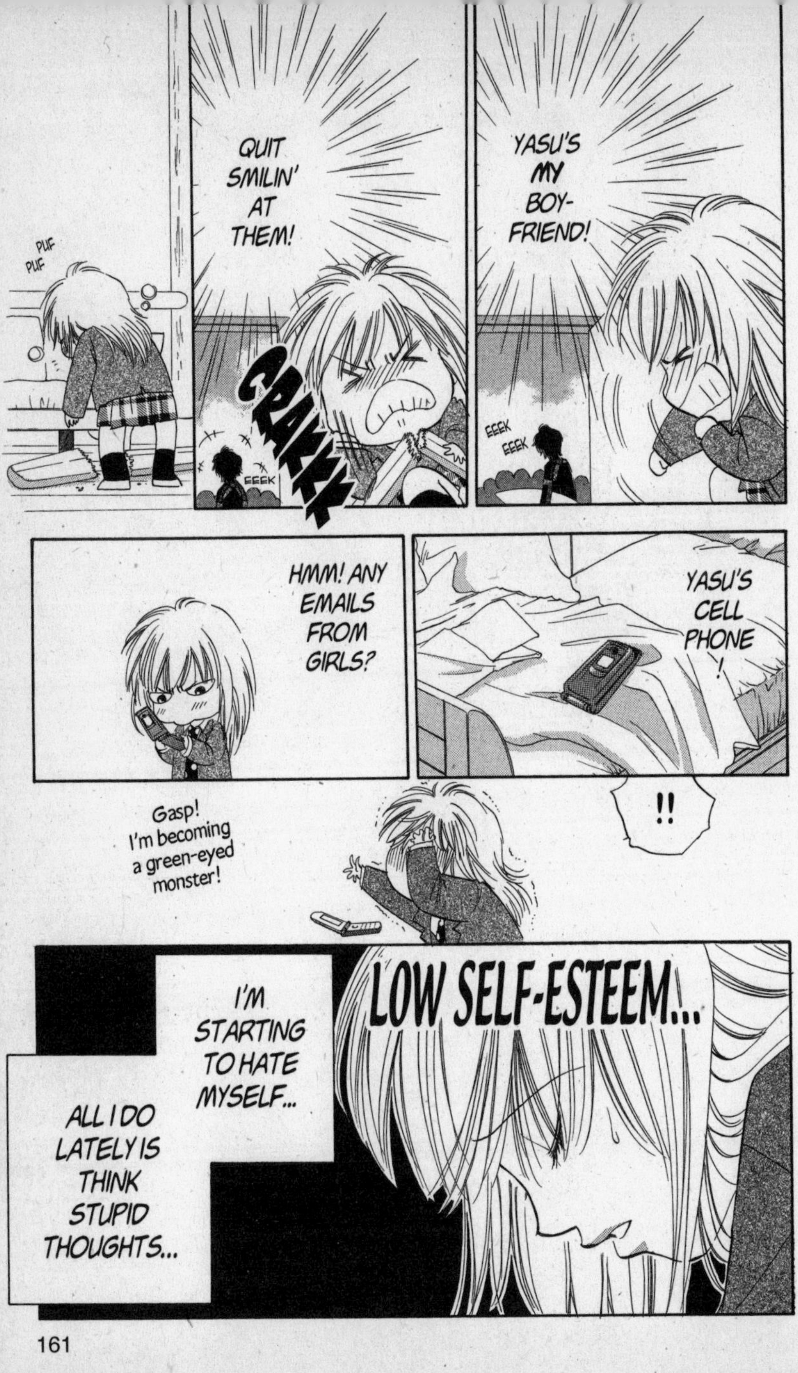
YASU'S MY BOY-FRIEND!
EEEK EEEK
QUIT SMILIN' AT THEM!
CRAKKK
EEEK
PUF PUF
YASU'S CELL PHONE!
HMM! ANY EMAILS FROM GIRLS?
!!
Gasp! I'm becoming a green-eyed monster!
LOW SELF-ESTEEM...
I'M STARTING TO HATE MYSELF...
ALL I DO LATELY IS THINK STUPID THOUGHTS...

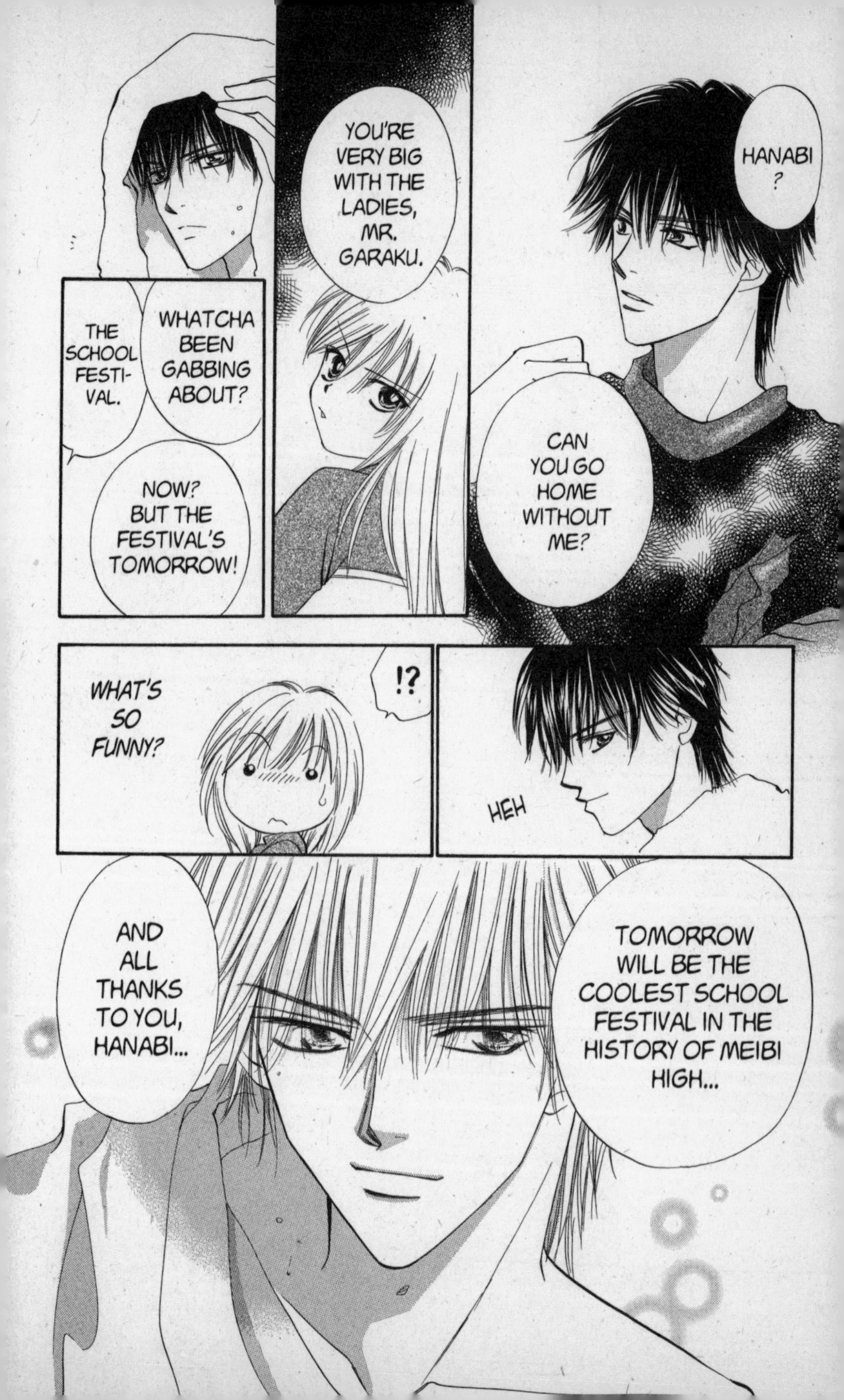
HANABI?
CAN YOU GO HOME WITHOUT ME?
YOU'RE VERY BIG WITH THE LADIES, MR. GARAKU.
WHATCHA BEEN GABBING ABOUT?
THE SCHOOL FESTIVAL.
NOW? BUT THE FESTIVAL'S TOMORROW!
HEH
!?
WHAT'S SO FUNNY?
TOMORROW WILL BE THE COOLEST SCHOOL FESTIVAL IN THE HISTORY OF MEIBI HIGH...
AND ALL THANKS TO YOU, HANABI...

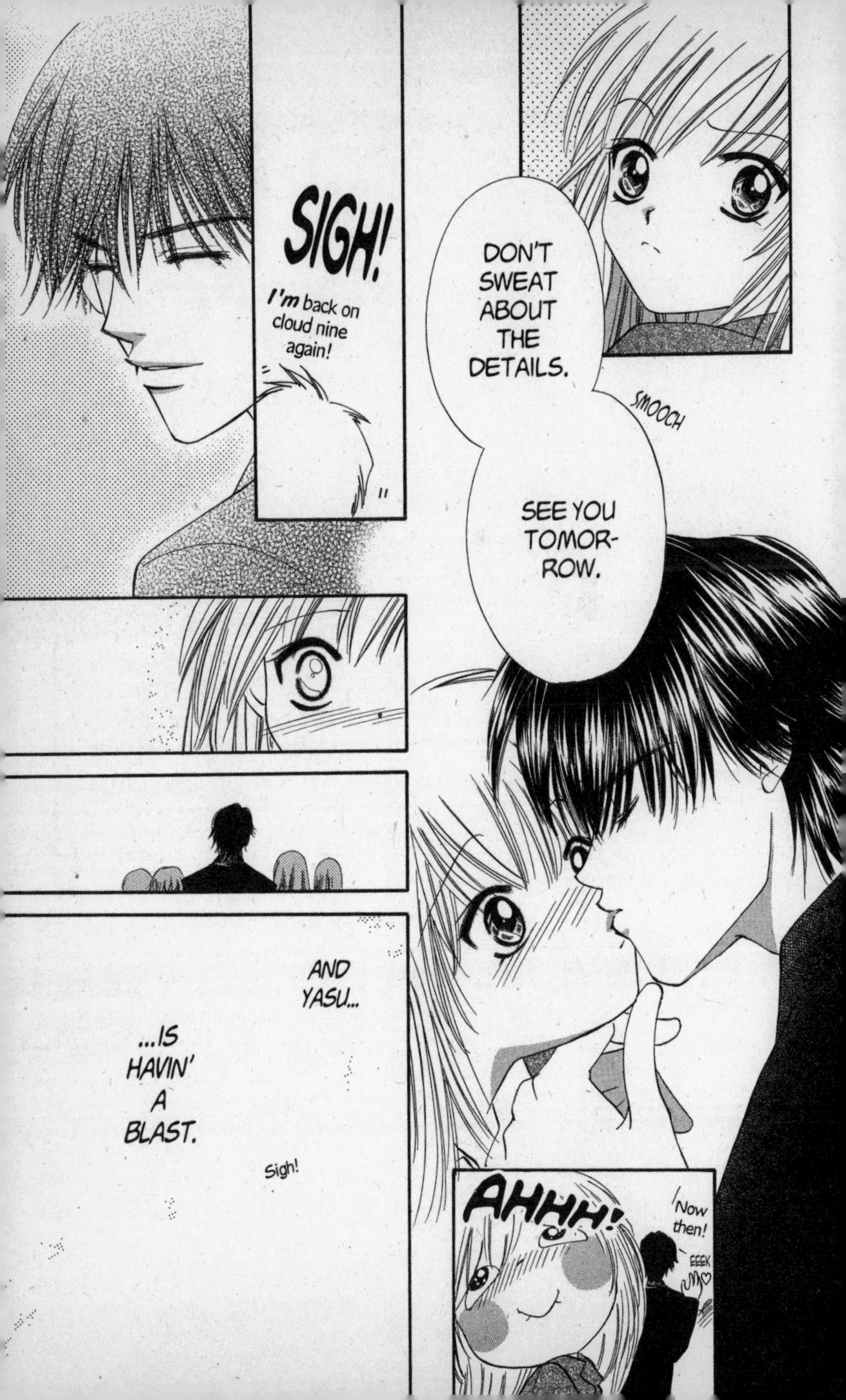
DON'T SWEAT ABOUT THE DETAILS.
SMOOCH
SEE YOU TOMOR-ROW.
SIGH!
I'm back on cloud nine again!
AHHH!
Now then!
EEEK
AND YASU...
...IS HAVIN' A BLAST.
Sigh!

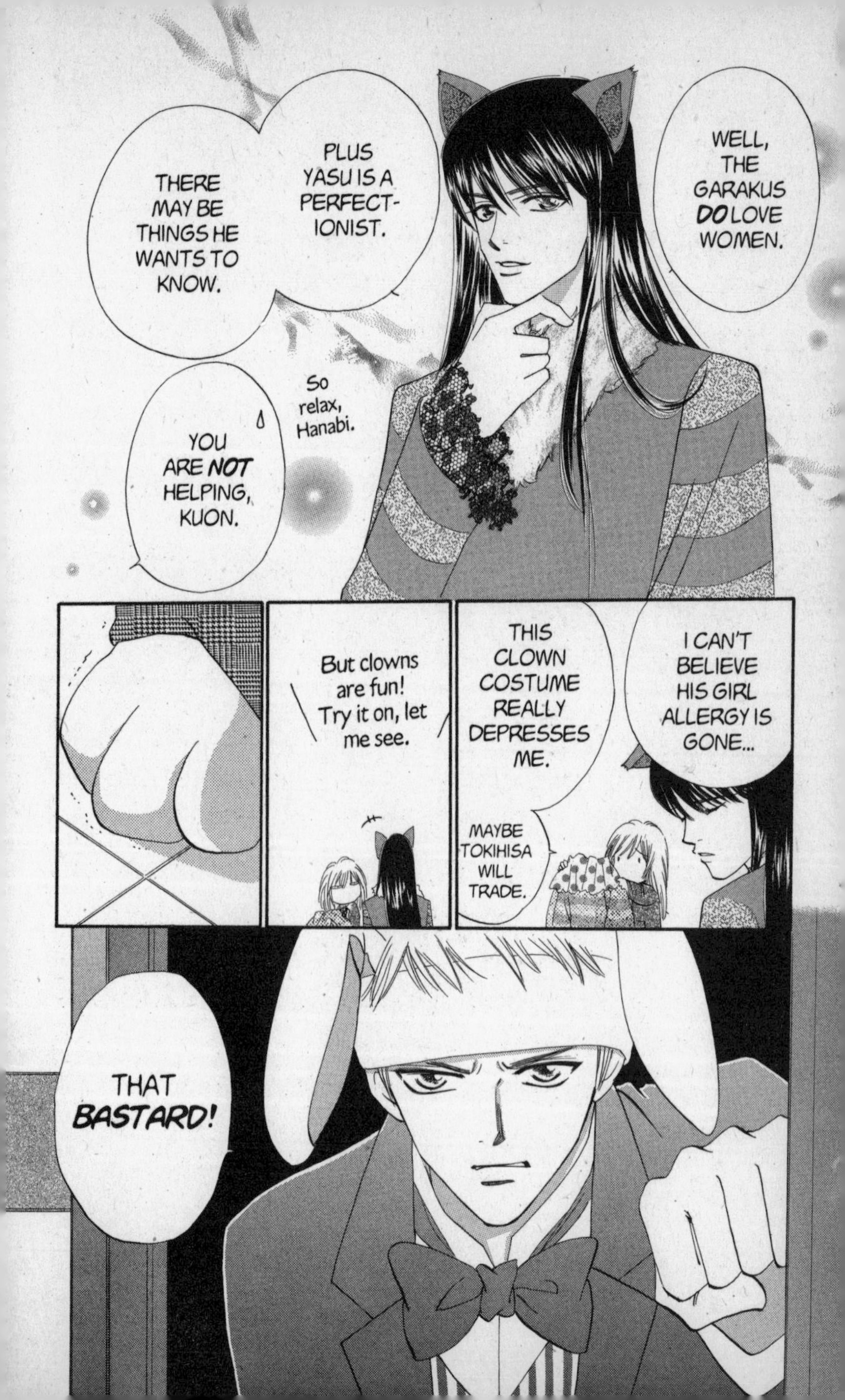
WELL, THE GARAKUS **DO** LOVE WOMEN.
PLUS YASU IS A PERFECT-IONIST.
THERE MAY BE THINGS HE WANTS TO KNOW.
So relax, Hanabi.
YOU ARE **NOT** HELPING, KUON.
I CAN'T BELIEVE HIS GIRL ALLERGY IS GONE...
THIS CLOWN COSTUME REALLY DEPRESSES ME.
MAYBE TOKIHISA WILL TRADE.
But clowns are fun! Try it on, let me see.
THAT **BASTARD!**

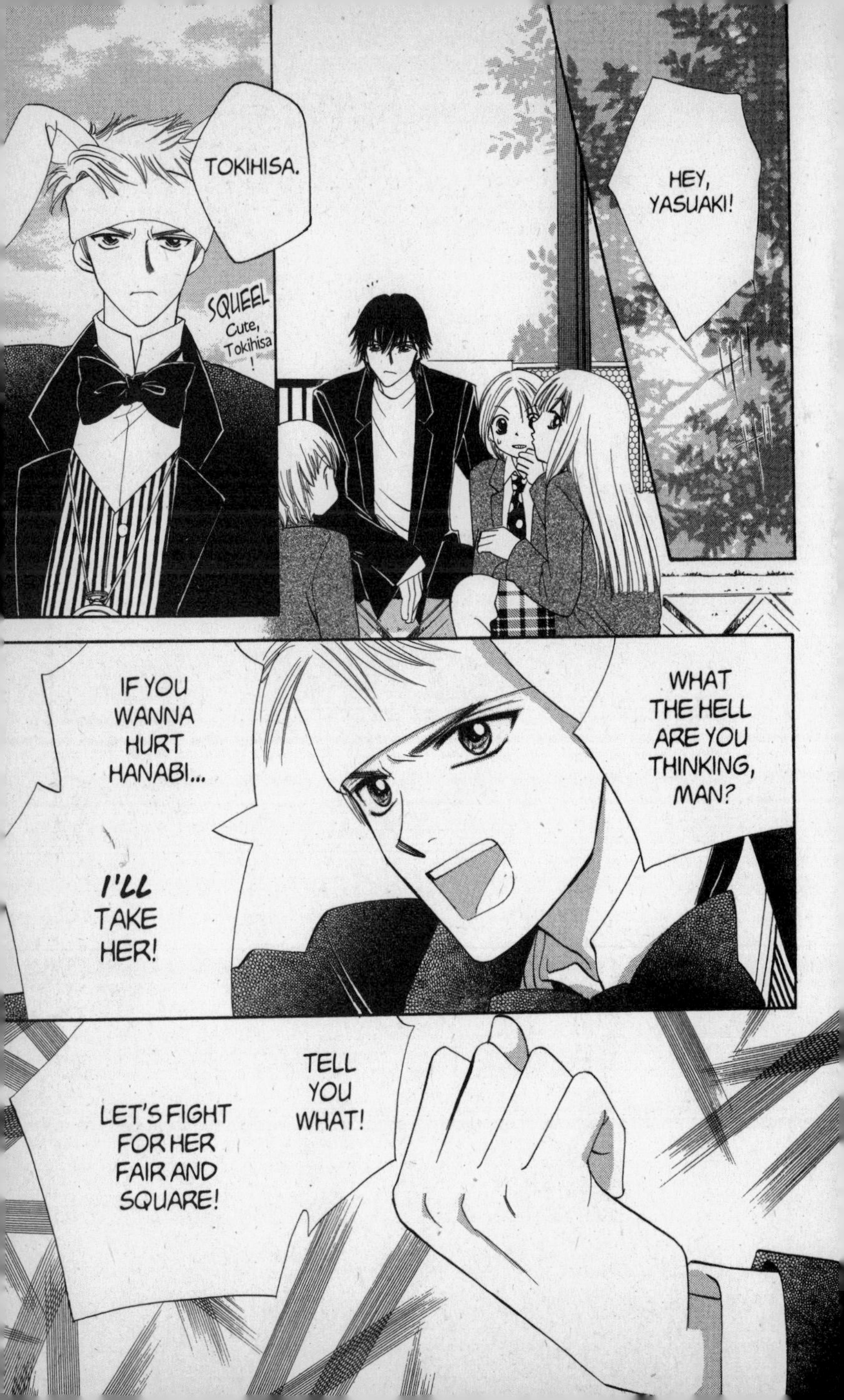
HEY, YASUAKI!
...
TOKIHISA.
SQUEEL
Cute, Tokihisa!
WHAT THE HELL ARE YOU THINKING, MAN?
IF YOU WANNA HURT HANABI...
I'LL TAKE HER!
TELL YOU WHAT!
LET'S FIGHT FOR HER FAIR AND SQUARE!

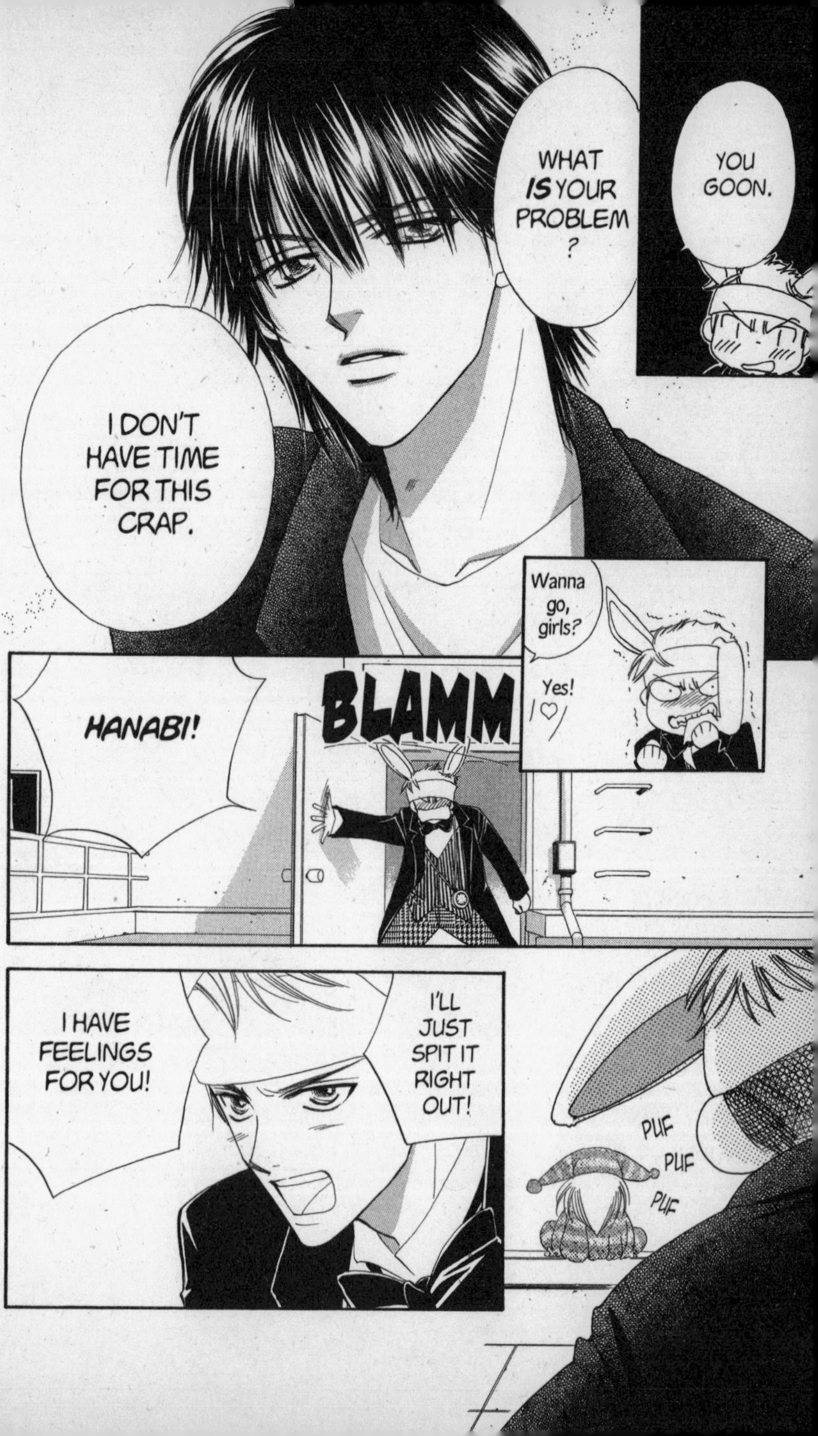
YOU GOON.
Wanna go, girls?
Yes! ♡
WHAT *IS* YOUR PROBLEM?
I DON'T HAVE TIME FOR THIS CRAP.
BLAMM
HANABI!
PUF
PUF
PUF
I'LL JUST SPIT IT RIGHT OUT!
I HAVE FEELINGS FOR YOU!

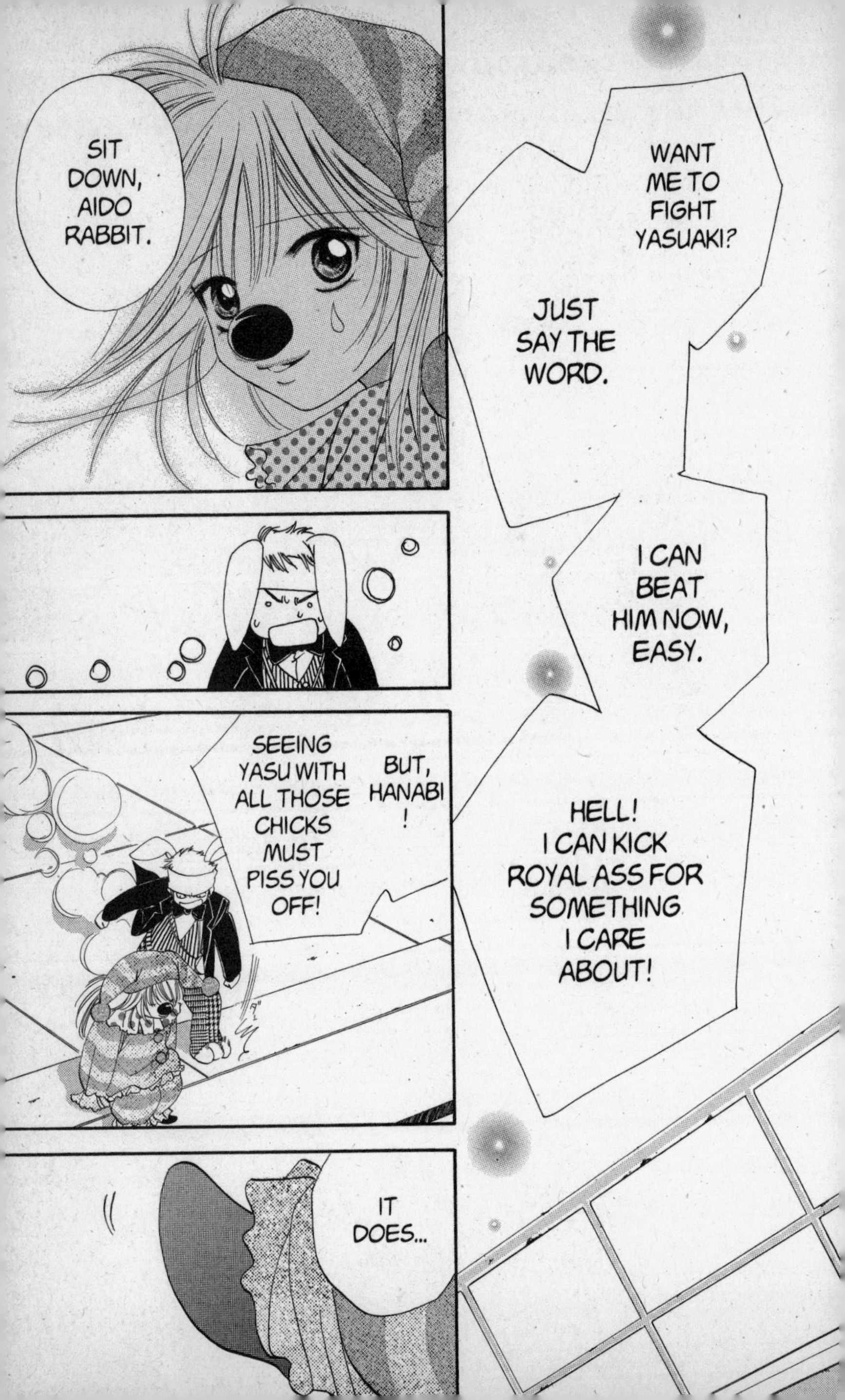
WANT ME TO FIGHT YASUAKI?
JUST SAY THE WORD.
I CAN BEAT HIM NOW, EASY.
HELL! I CAN KICK ROYAL ASS FOR SOMETHING I CARE ABOUT!
SIT DOWN, AIDO RABBIT.
BUT, HANABI!
SEEING YASU WITH ALL THOSE CHICKS MUST PISS YOU OFF!
IT DOES...

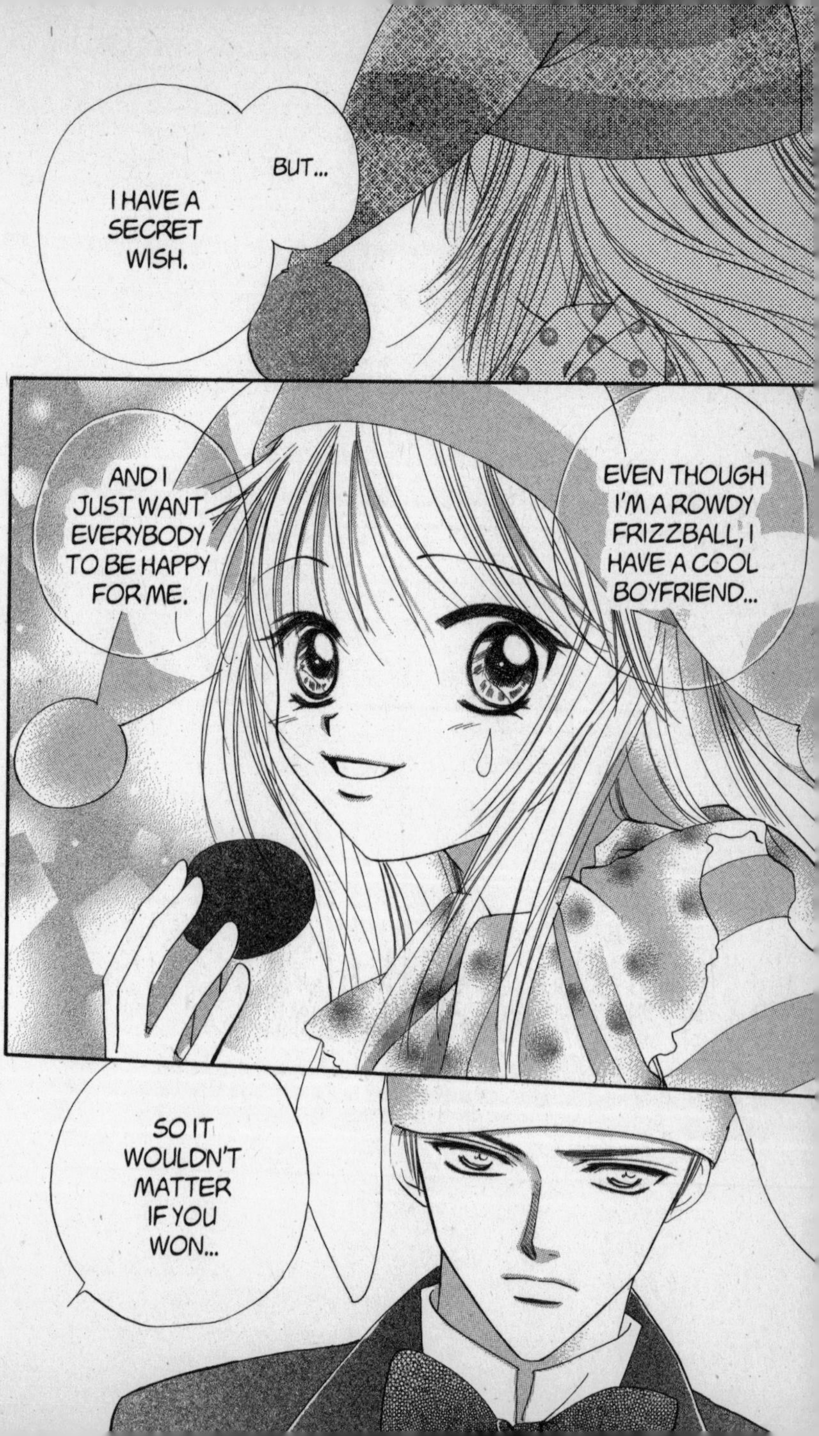
BUT...
I HAVE A SECRET WISH.
EVEN THOUGH I'M A ROWDY FRIZZBALL, I HAVE A COOL BOYFRIEND...
AND I JUST WANT EVERYBODY TO BE HAPPY FOR ME.
SO IT WOULDN'T MATTER IF YOU WON...

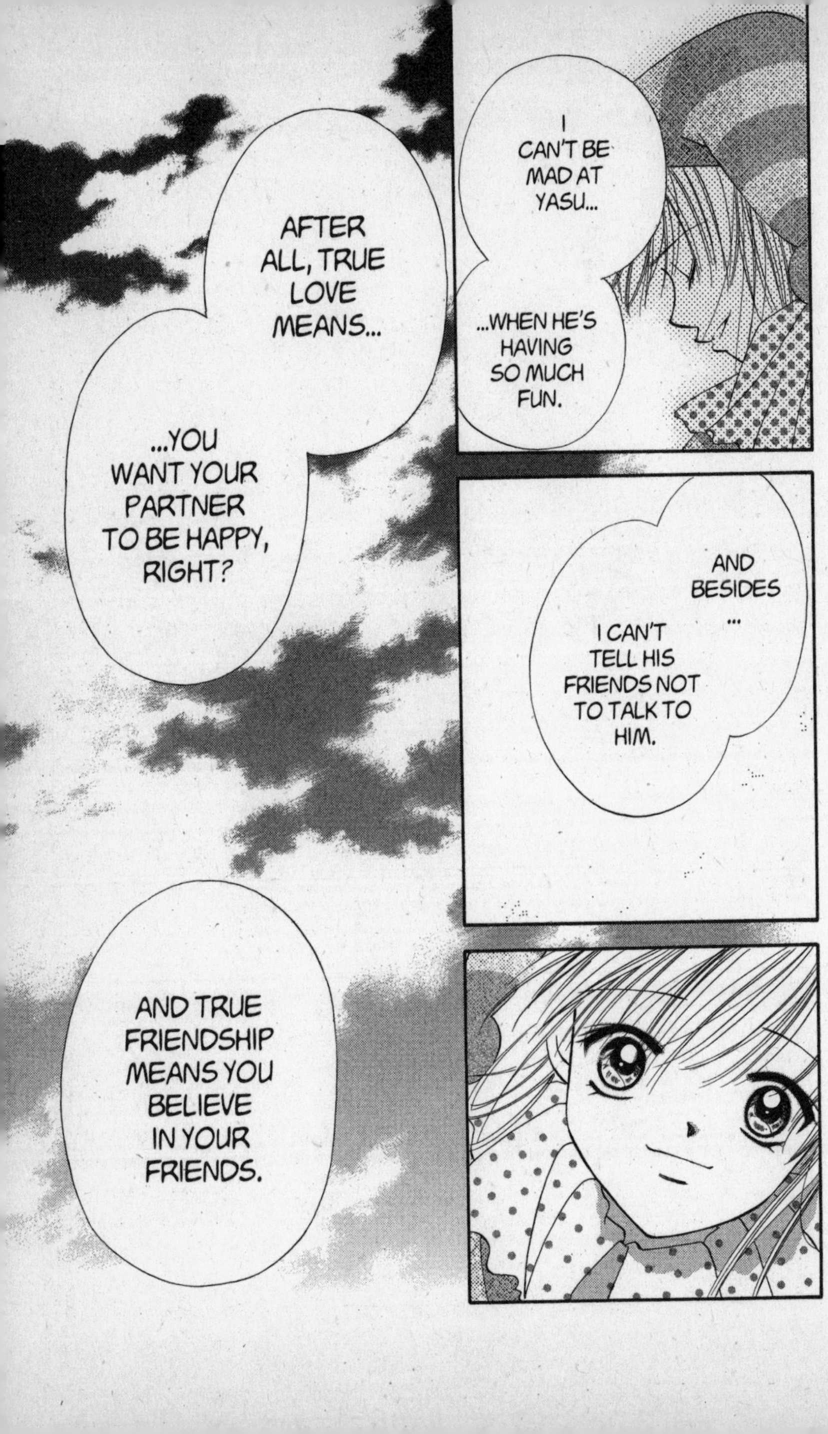

I CAN'T BE MAD AT YASU...
...WHEN HE'S HAVING SO MUCH FUN.
AFTER ALL, TRUE LOVE MEANS...
...YOU WANT YOUR PARTNER TO BE HAPPY, RIGHT?
AND BESIDES...
I CAN'T TELL HIS FRIENDS NOT TO TALK TO HIM.
AND TRUE FRIENDSHIP MEANS YOU BELIEVE IN YOUR FRIENDS.

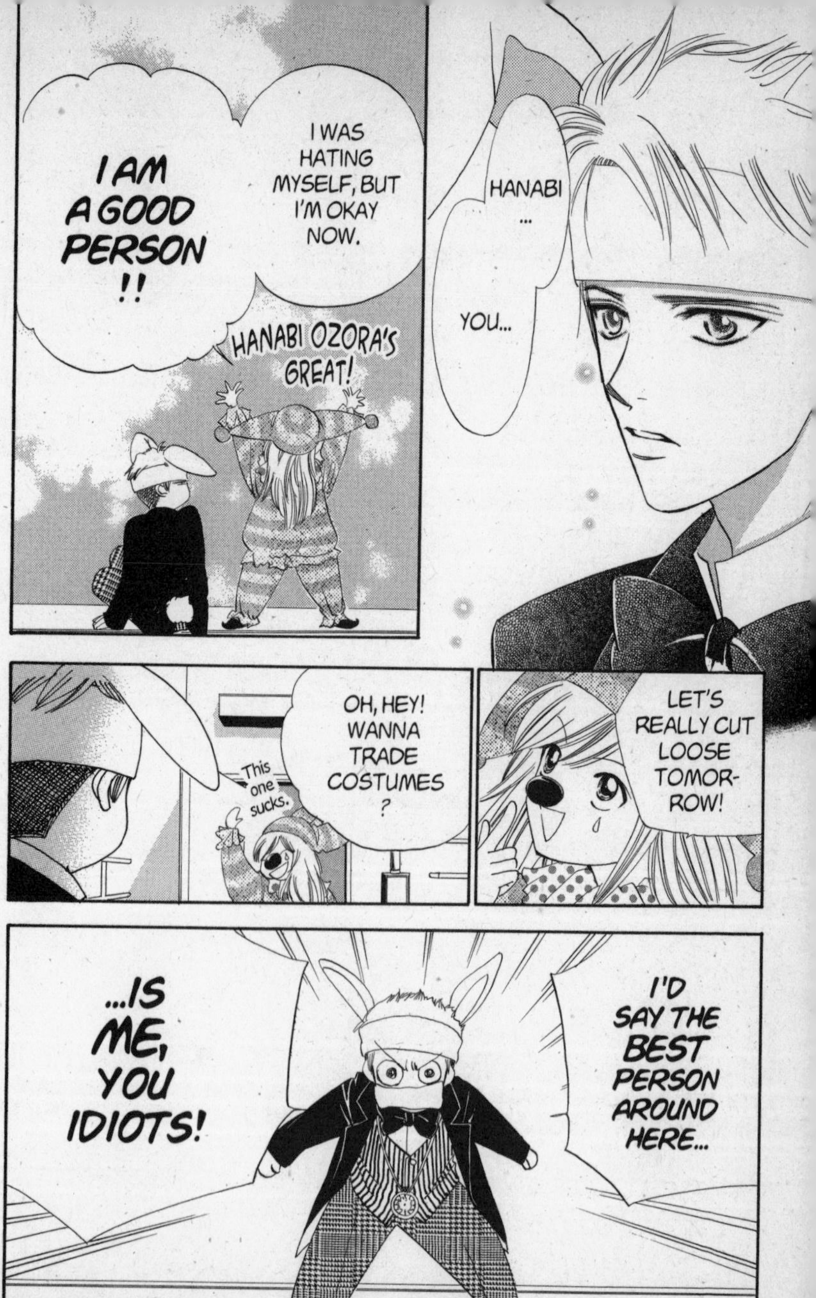
HANABI... YOU...
I WAS HATING MYSELF, BUT I'M OKAY NOW.
I AM A GOOD PERSON!!
HANABI OZORA'S GREAT!
LET'S REALLY CUT LOOSE TOMORROW!
OH, HEY! WANNA TRADE COSTUMES?
This one sucks.
I'D SAY THE BEST PERSON AROUND HERE...
...IS ME, YOU IDIOTS!

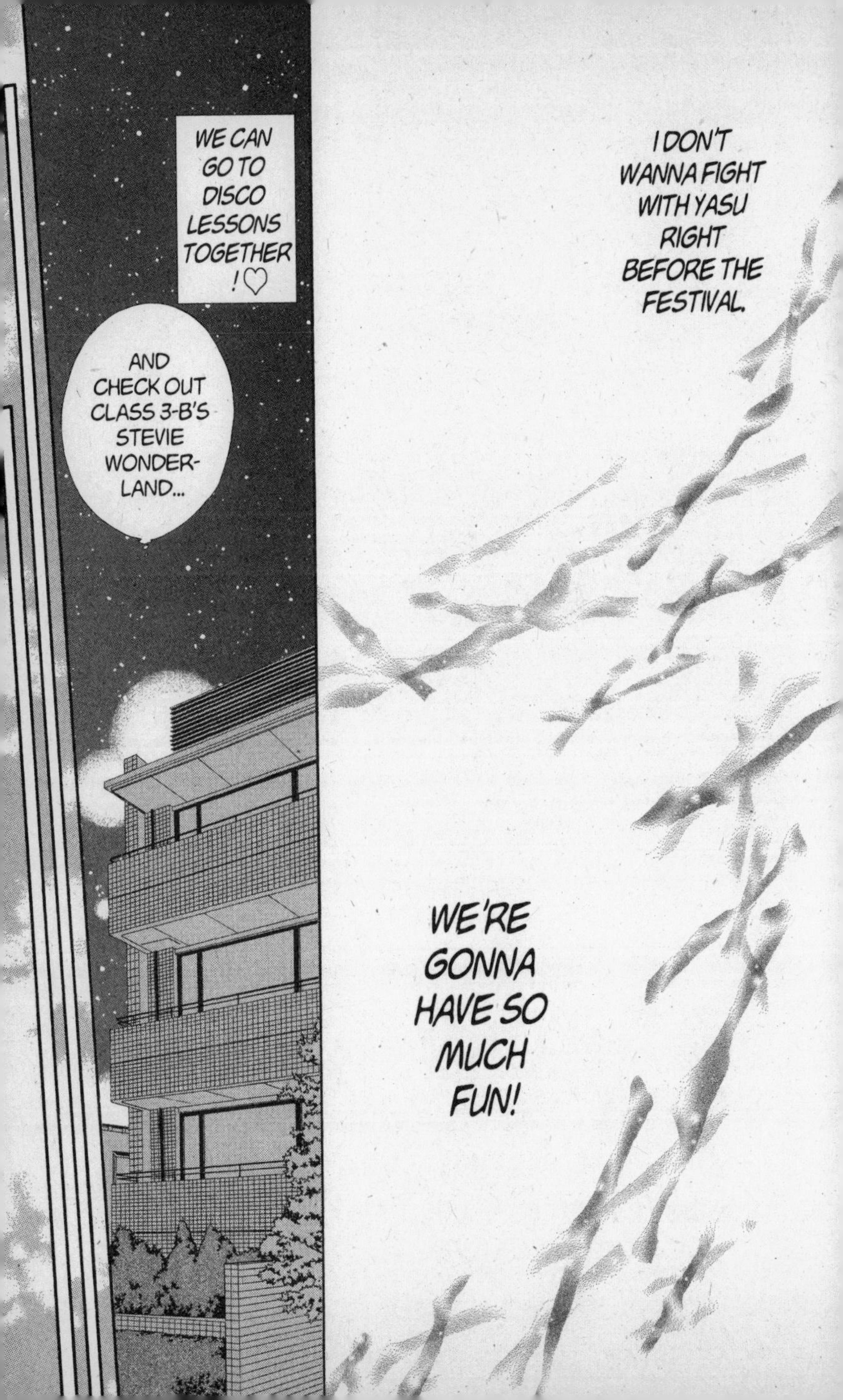
I DON'T WANNA FIGHT WITH YASU RIGHT BEFORE THE FESTIVAL.
WE'RE GONNA HAVE SO MUCH FUN!
WE CAN GO TO DISCO LESSONS TOGETHER!♡
AND CHECK OUT CLASS 3-B'S STEVIE WONDER-LAND...

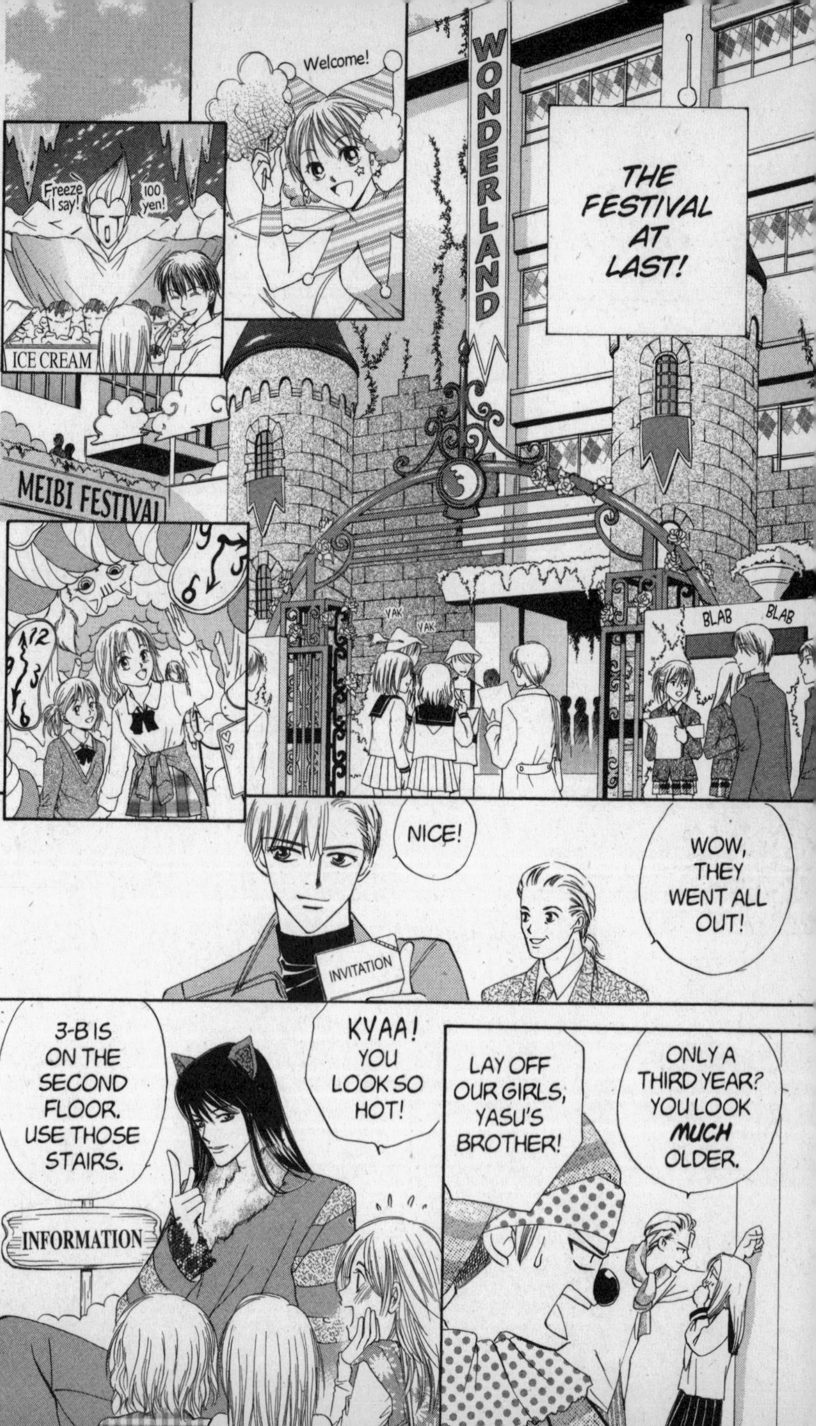
WONDERLAND
THE FESTIVAL AT LAST!
BLAB BLAB
YAK YAK
Welcome!
100 yen!
Freeze I say!
ICE CREAM
MEIBI FESTIVAL
WOW, THEY WENT ALL OUT!
NICE!
INVITATION
ONLY A THIRD YEAR? YOU LOOK *MUCH* OLDER.
LAY OFF OUR GIRLS, YASU'S BROTHER!
KYAA! YOU LOOK SO HOT!
3-B IS ON THE SECOND FLOOR. USE THOSE STAIRS.
INFORMATION

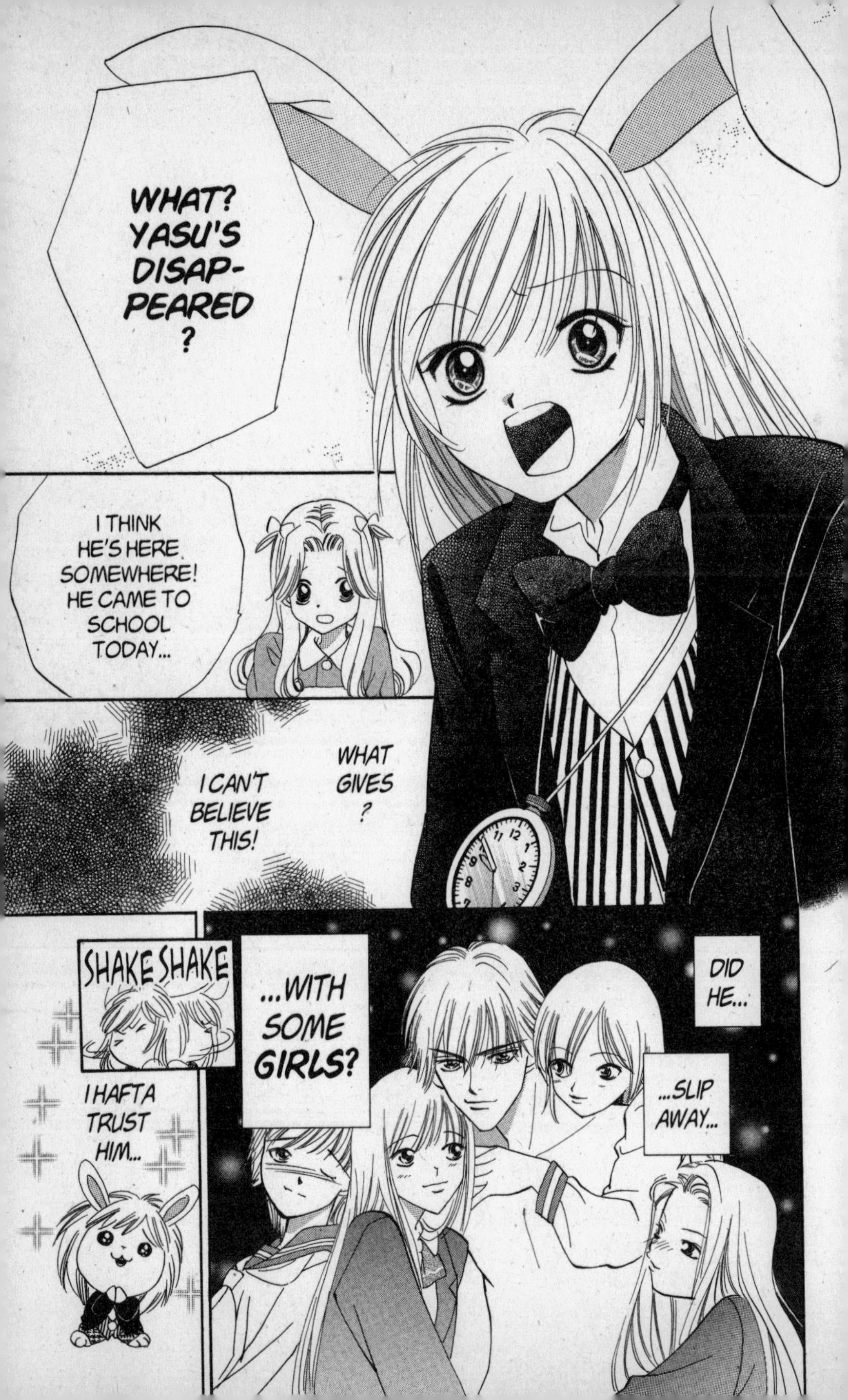
WHAT? YASU'S DISAP-PEARED?
I THINK HE'S HERE SOMEWHERE! HE CAME TO SCHOOL TODAY...
WHAT GIVES?
I CAN'T BELIEVE THIS!
DID HE...
...SLIP AWAY...
...WITH SOME GIRLS?
SHAKE SHAKE
I HAFTA TRUST HIM...

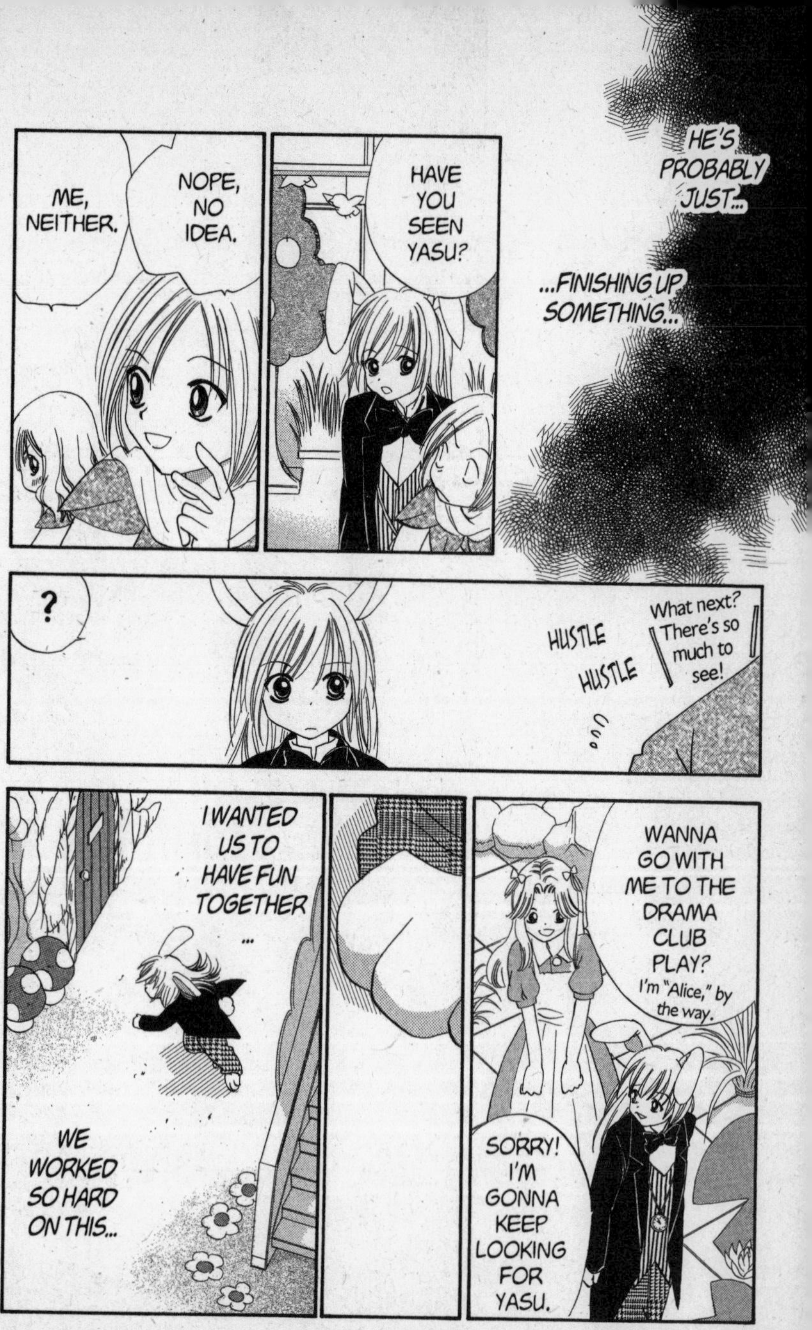
HE'S PROBABLY JUST...
...FINISHING UP SOMETHING...
HAVE YOU SEEN YASU?
NOPE, NO IDEA.
ME, NEITHER.
What next? There's so much to see!
HUSTLE
HUSTLE
?
WANNA GO WITH ME TO THE DRAMA CLUB PLAY?
I'm "Alice," by the way.
SORRY! I'M GONNA KEEP LOOKING FOR YASU.
I WANTED US TO HAVE FUN TOGETHER...
WE WORKED SO HARD ON THIS...

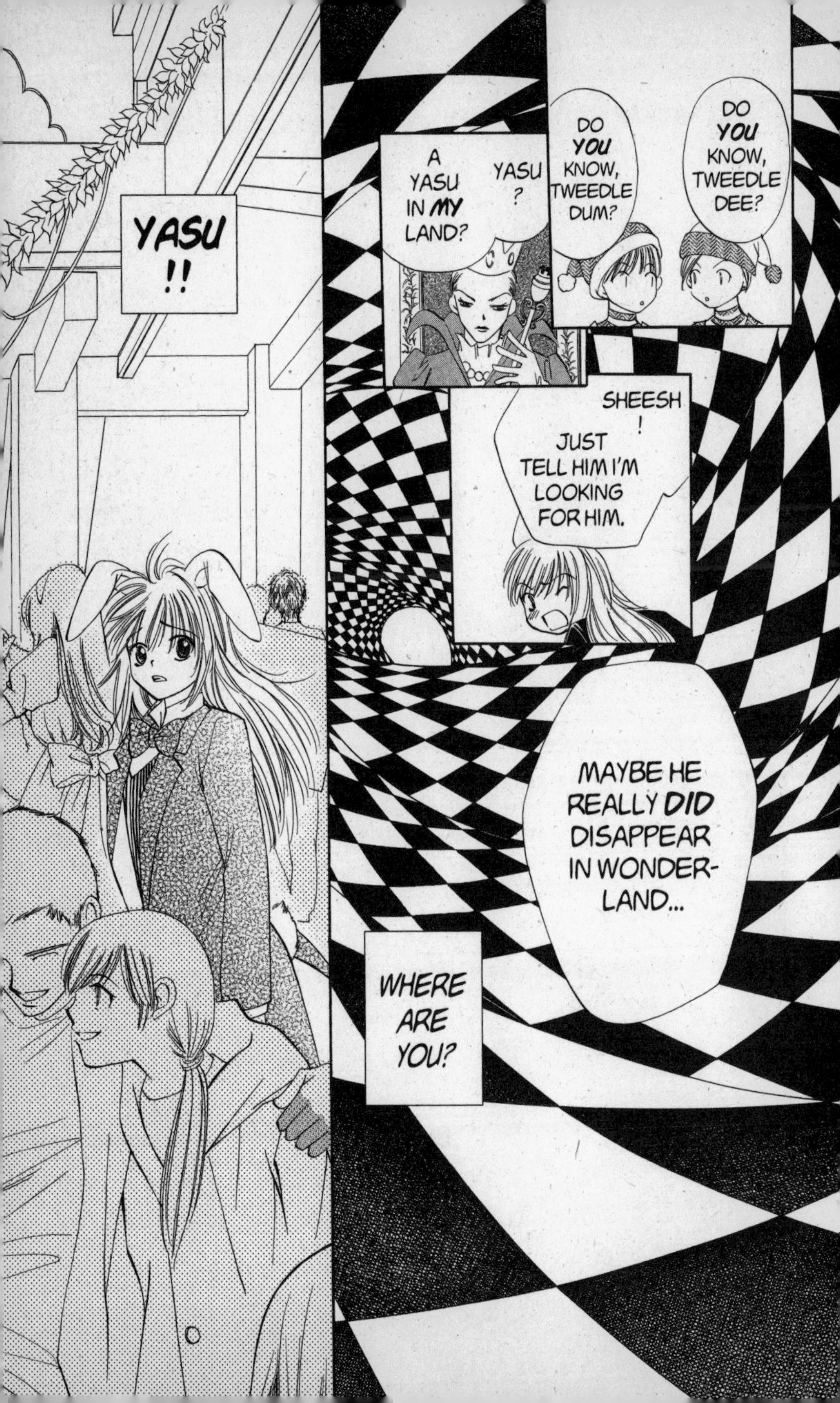
DO YOU KNOW, TWEEDLE DEE?
DO YOU KNOW, TWEEDLE DUM?
YASU?
A YASU IN MY LAND?
SHEESH!
JUST TELL HIM I'M LOOKING FOR HIM.
MAYBE HE REALLY DID DISAPPEAR IN WONDER-LAND...
WHERE ARE YOU?
YASU!!

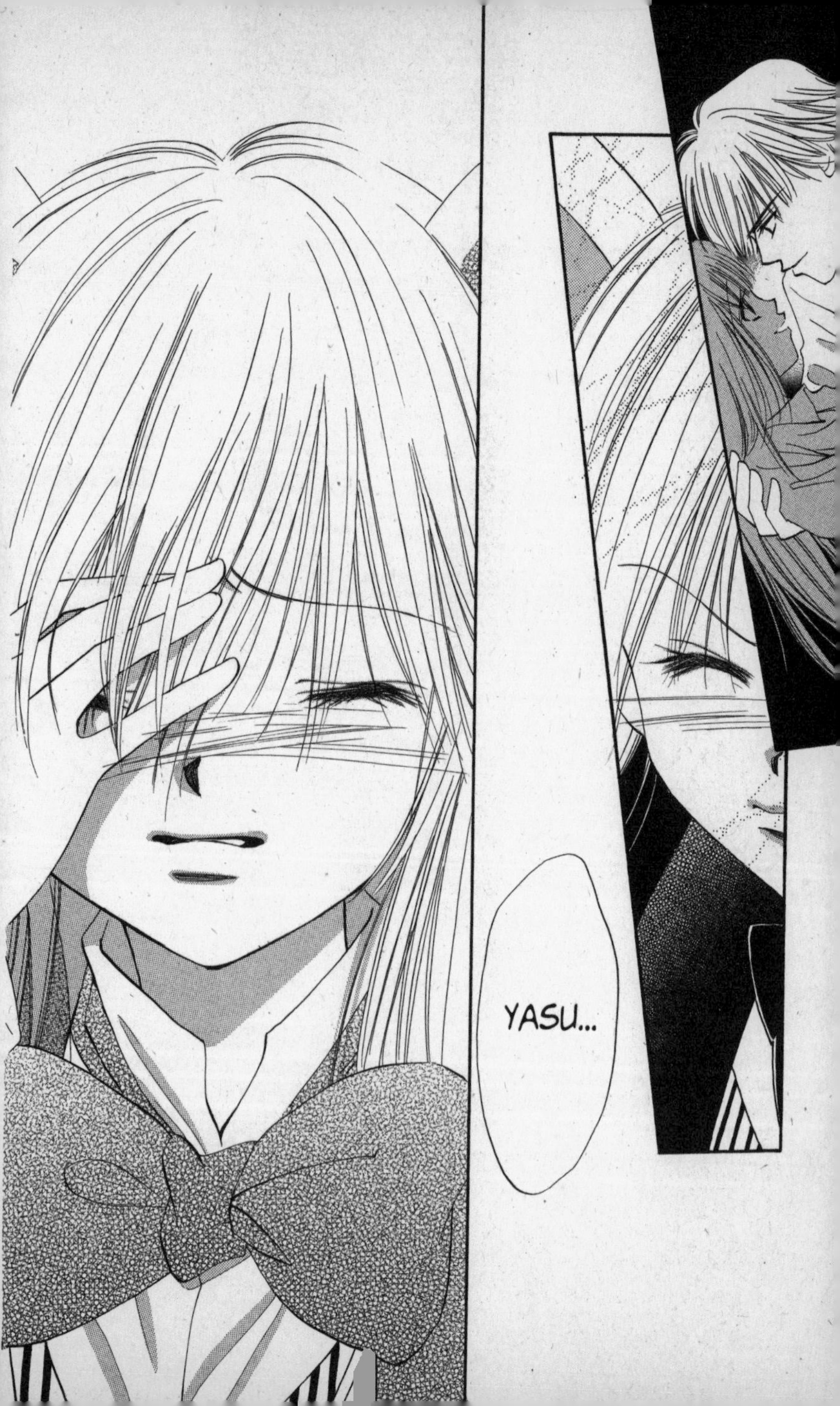
YASU...

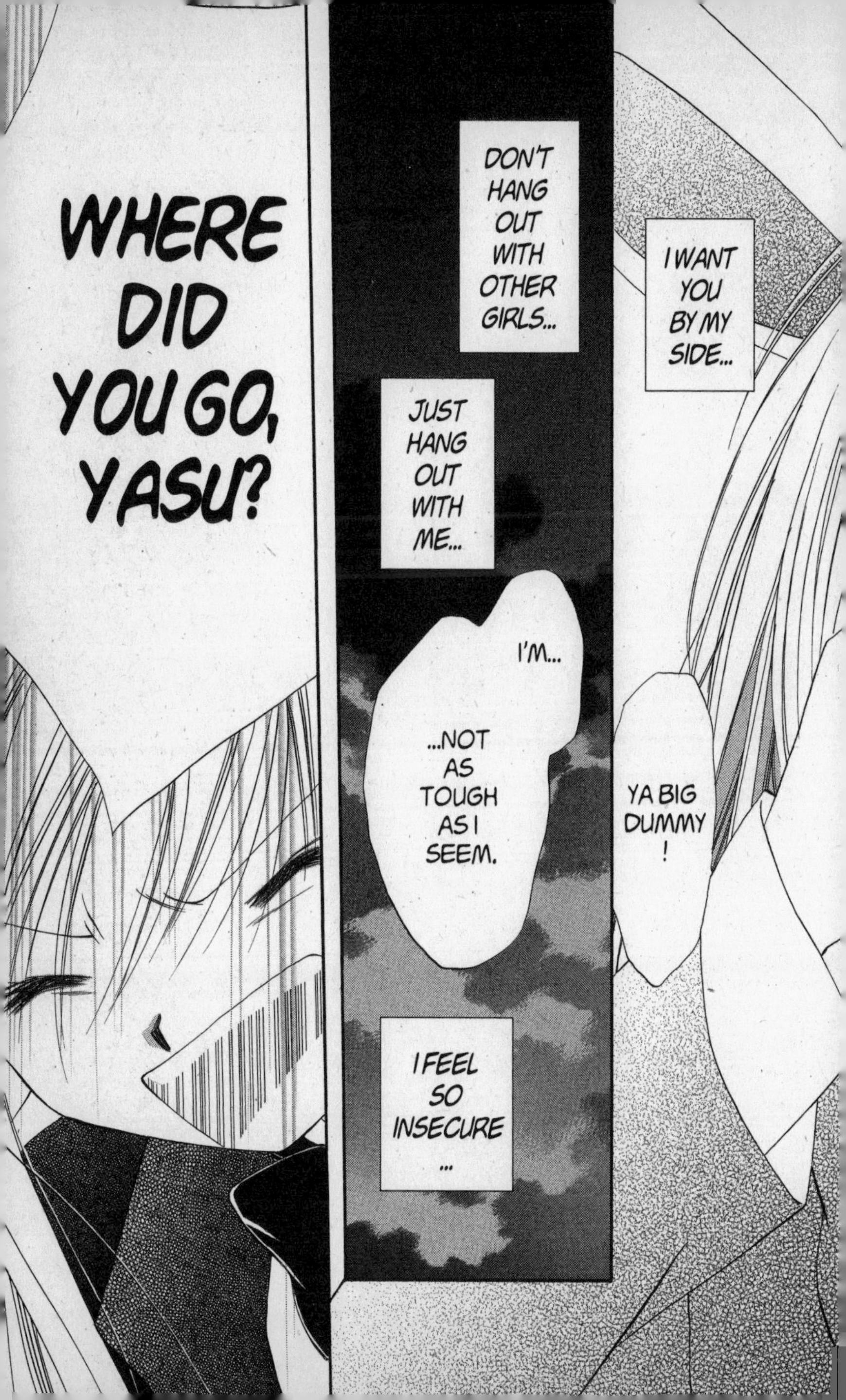
I WANT YOU BY MY SIDE...
YA BIG DUMMY!
DON'T HANG OUT WITH OTHER GIRLS...
JUST HANG OUT WITH ME...
I'M...
...NOT AS TOUGH AS I SEEM.
I FEEL SO INSECURE...
WHERE DID YOU GO, YASU?

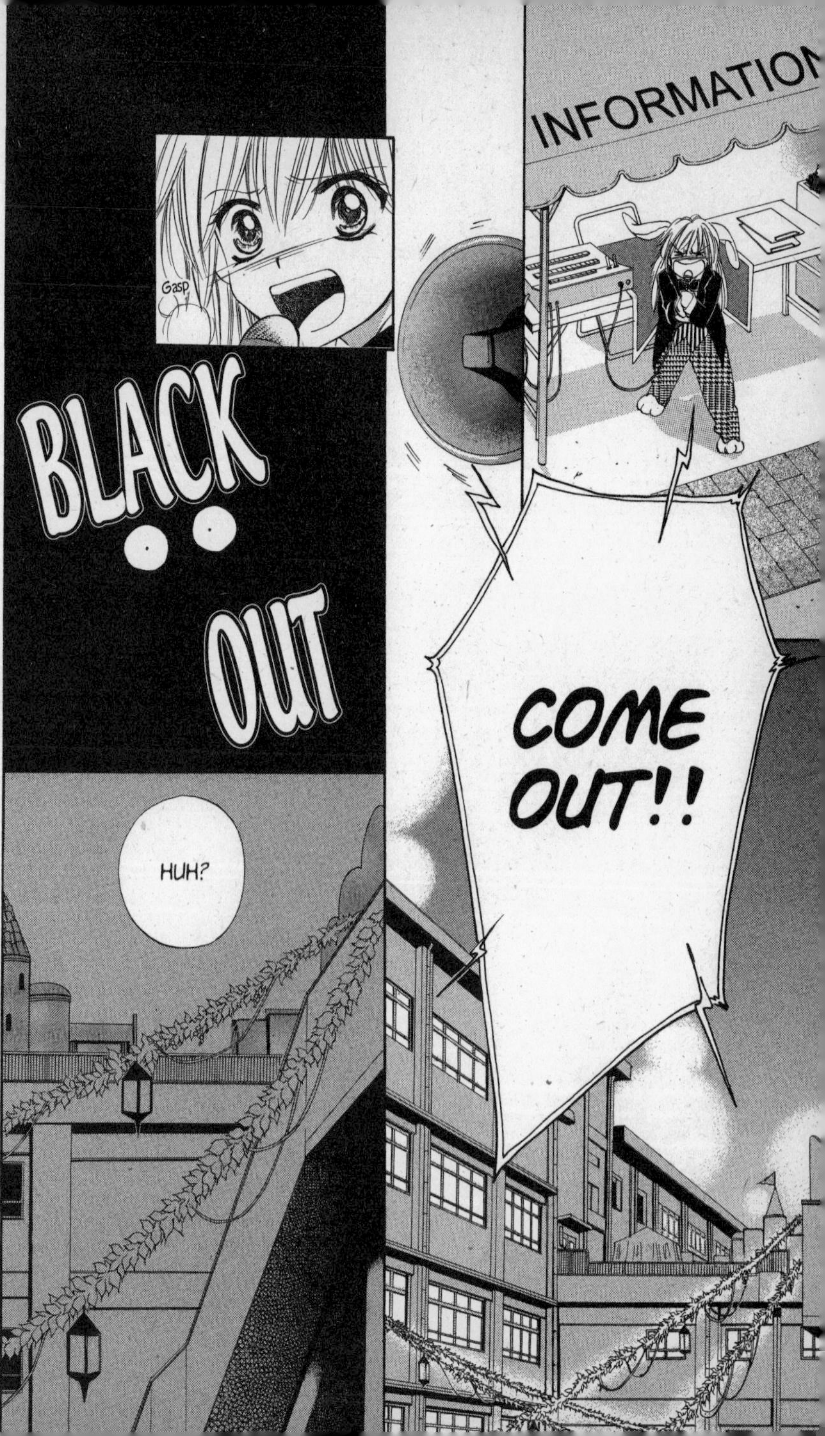
INFORMATION
COME OUT!!
Gasp
BLACK OUT
HUH?

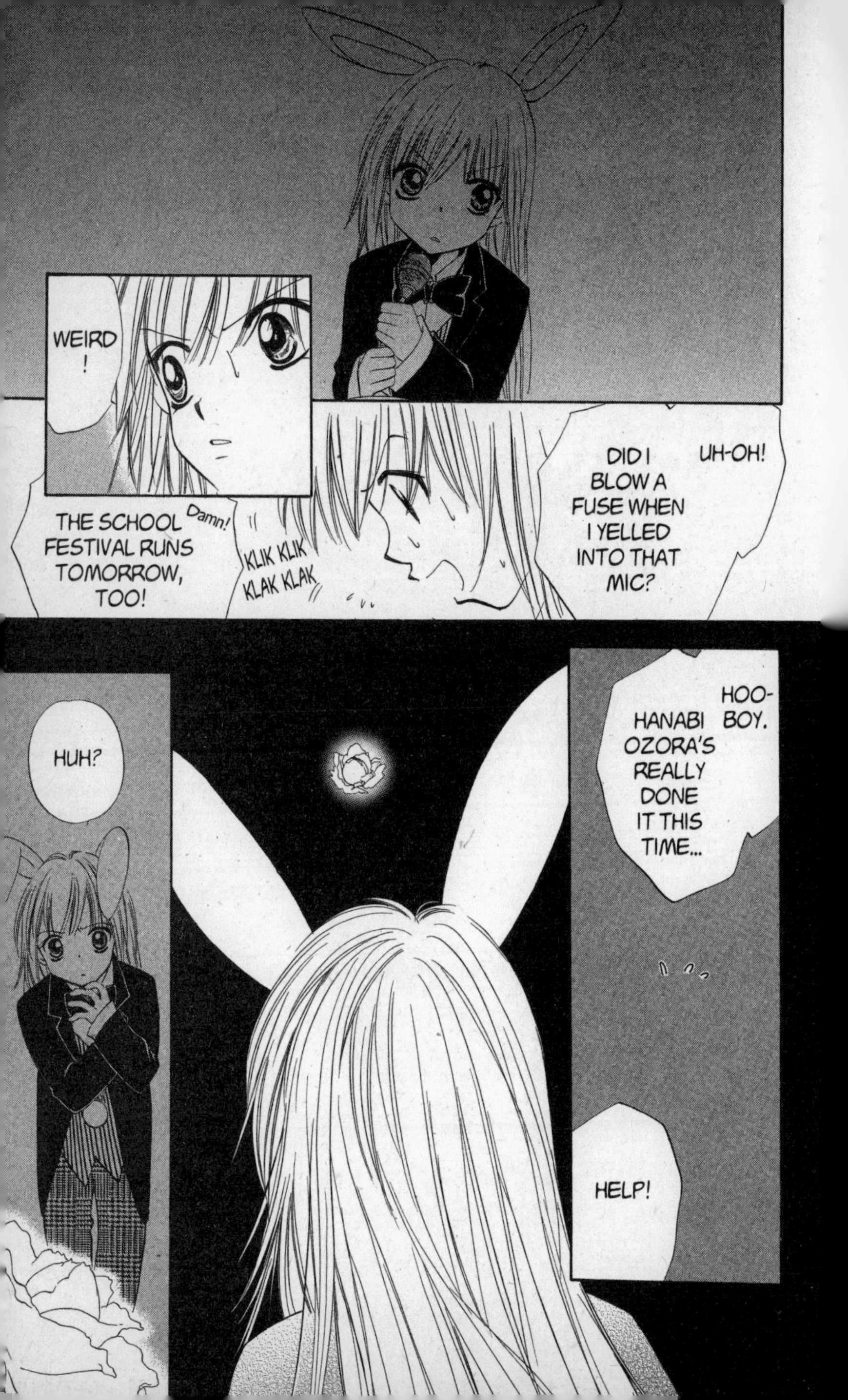
WEIRD!
UH-OH!
DID I BLOW A FUSE WHEN I YELLED INTO THAT MIC?
Damn!
KLIK KLIK KLAK KLAK
THE SCHOOL FESTIVAL RUNS TOMORROW, TOO!
HOO-BOY.
HANABI OZORA'S REALLY DONE IT THIS TIME...
HELP!
HUH?

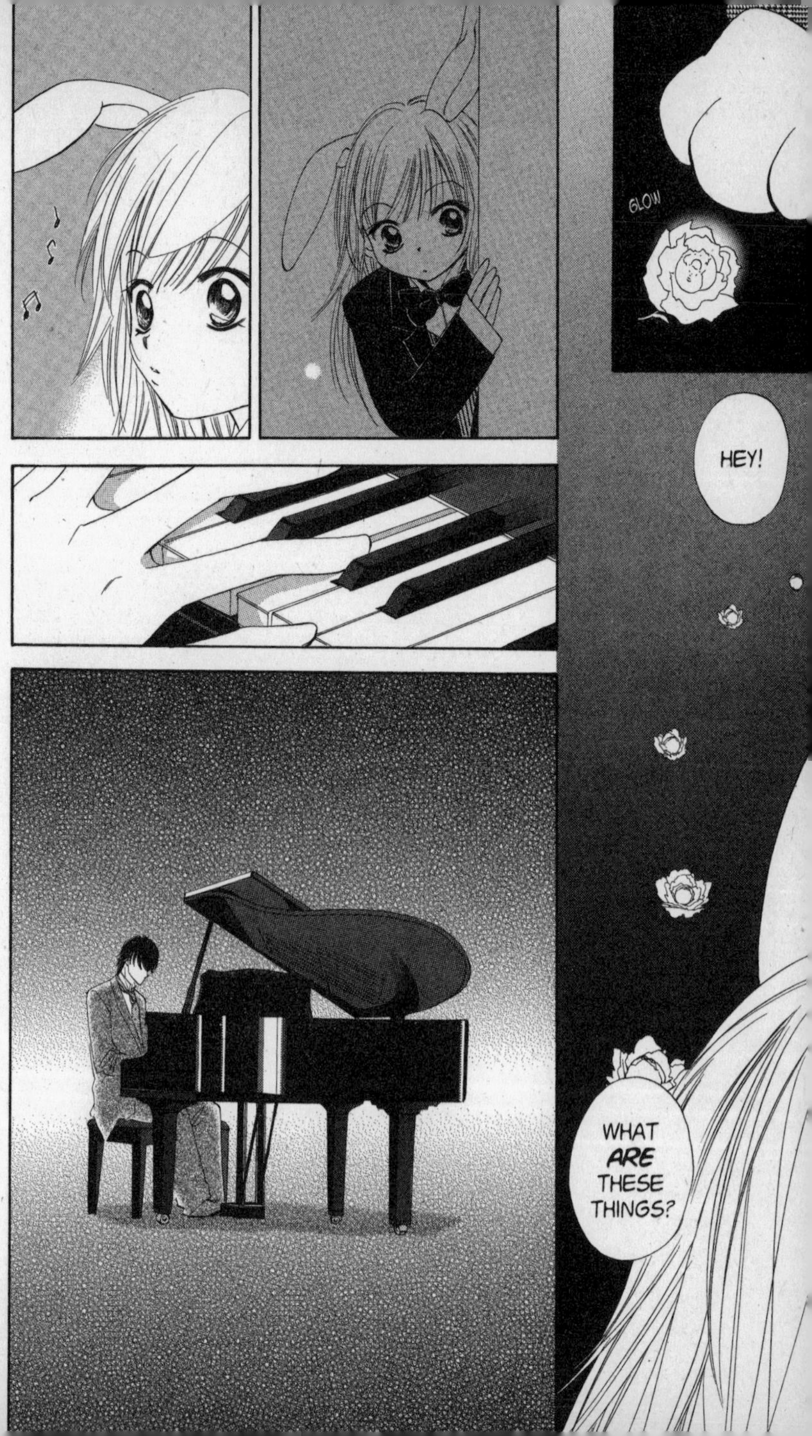
GLOW
HEY!
WHAT ARE THESE THINGS?

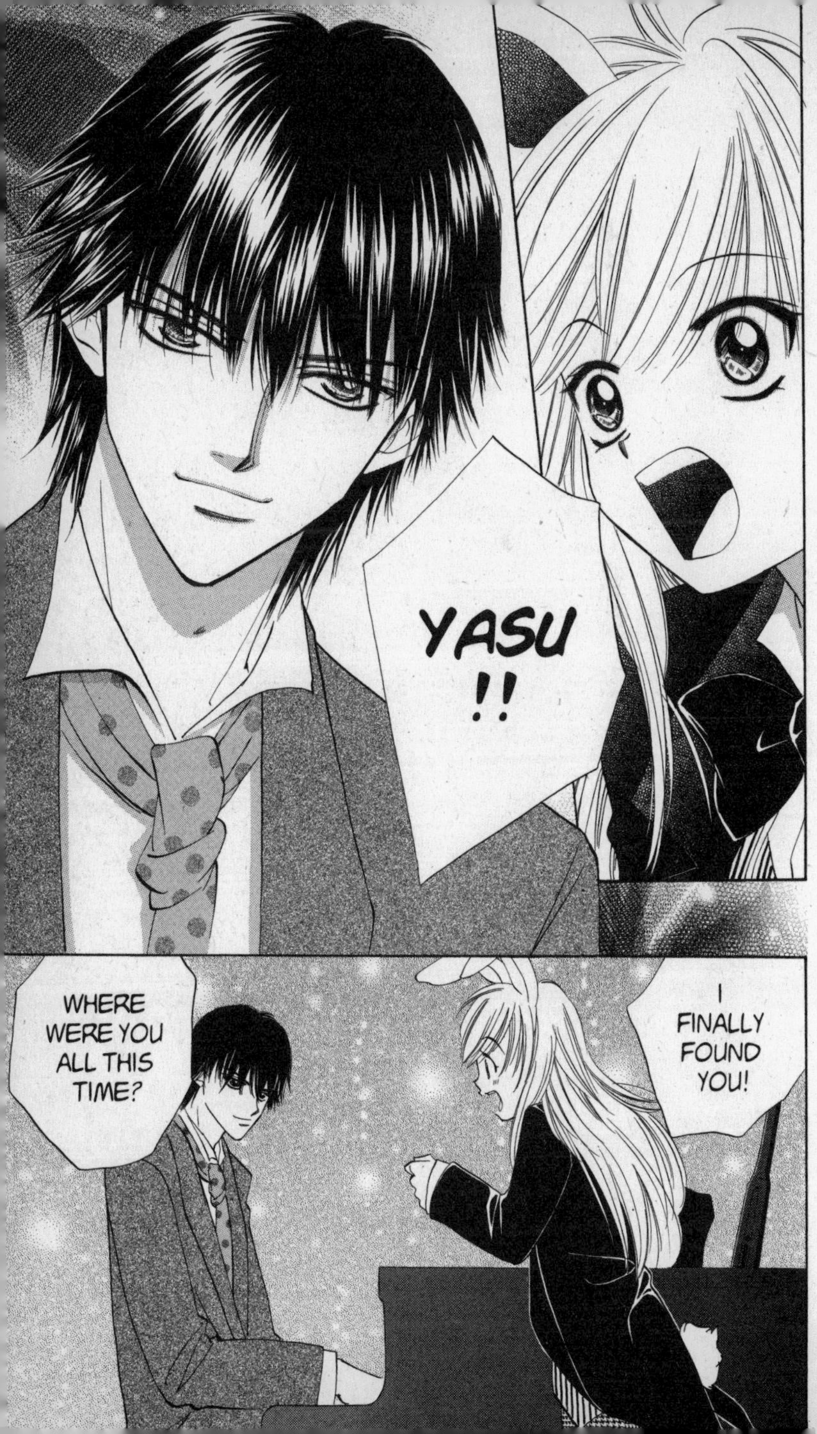
YASU !!
I FINALLY FOUND YOU!
WHERE WERE YOU ALL THIS TIME?

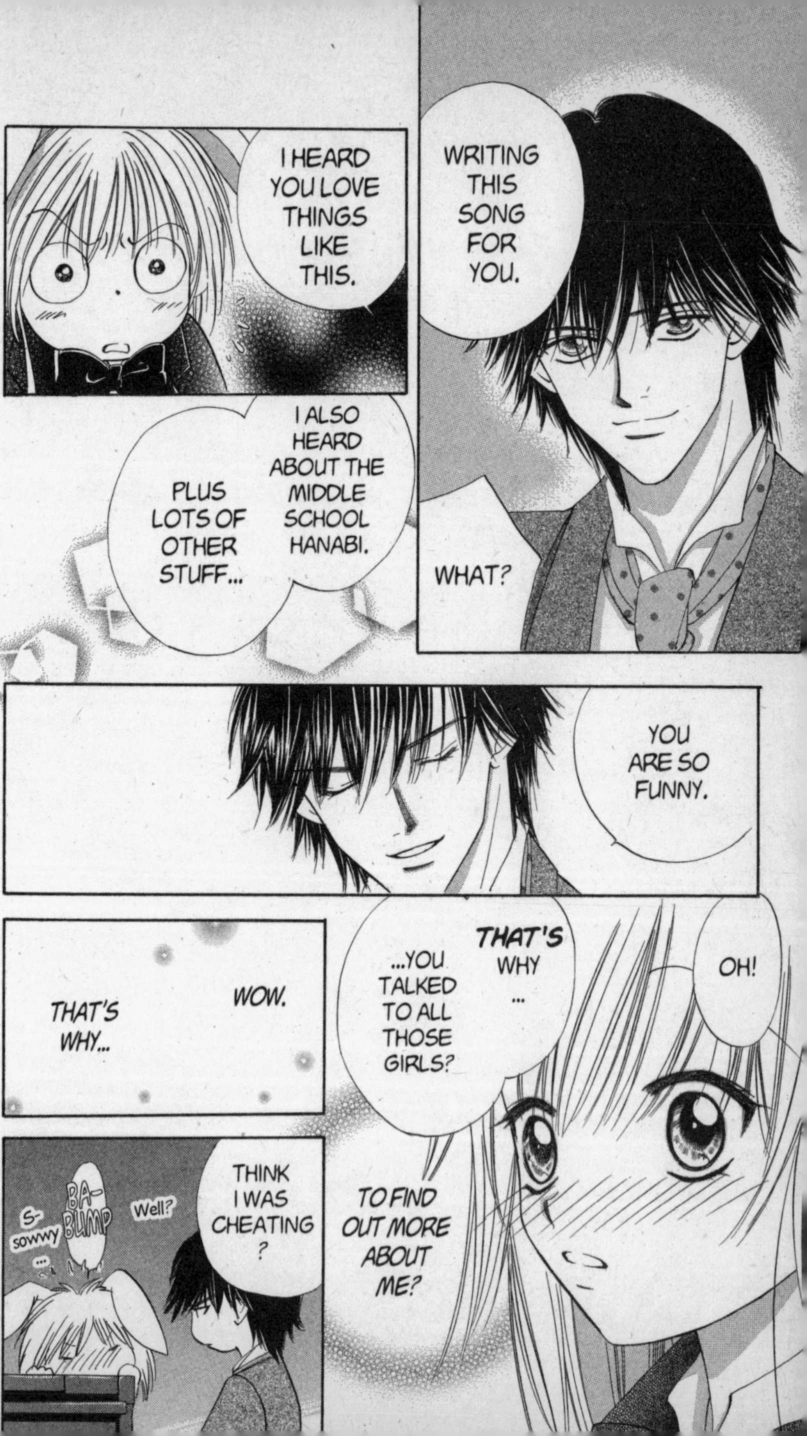
WRITING THIS SONG FOR YOU.
WHAT?
I HEARD YOU LOVE THINGS LIKE THIS.
I ALSO HEARD ABOUT THE MIDDLE SCHOOL HANABI.
PLUS LOTS OF OTHER STUFF...
YOU ARE SO FUNNY.
OH!
THAT'S WHY ...
...YOU TALKED TO ALL THOSE GIRLS?
TO FIND OUT MORE ABOUT ME?
WOW.
THAT'S WHY...
THINK I WAS CHEATING?
Well?
BA-BUMP
S-sowwy ...

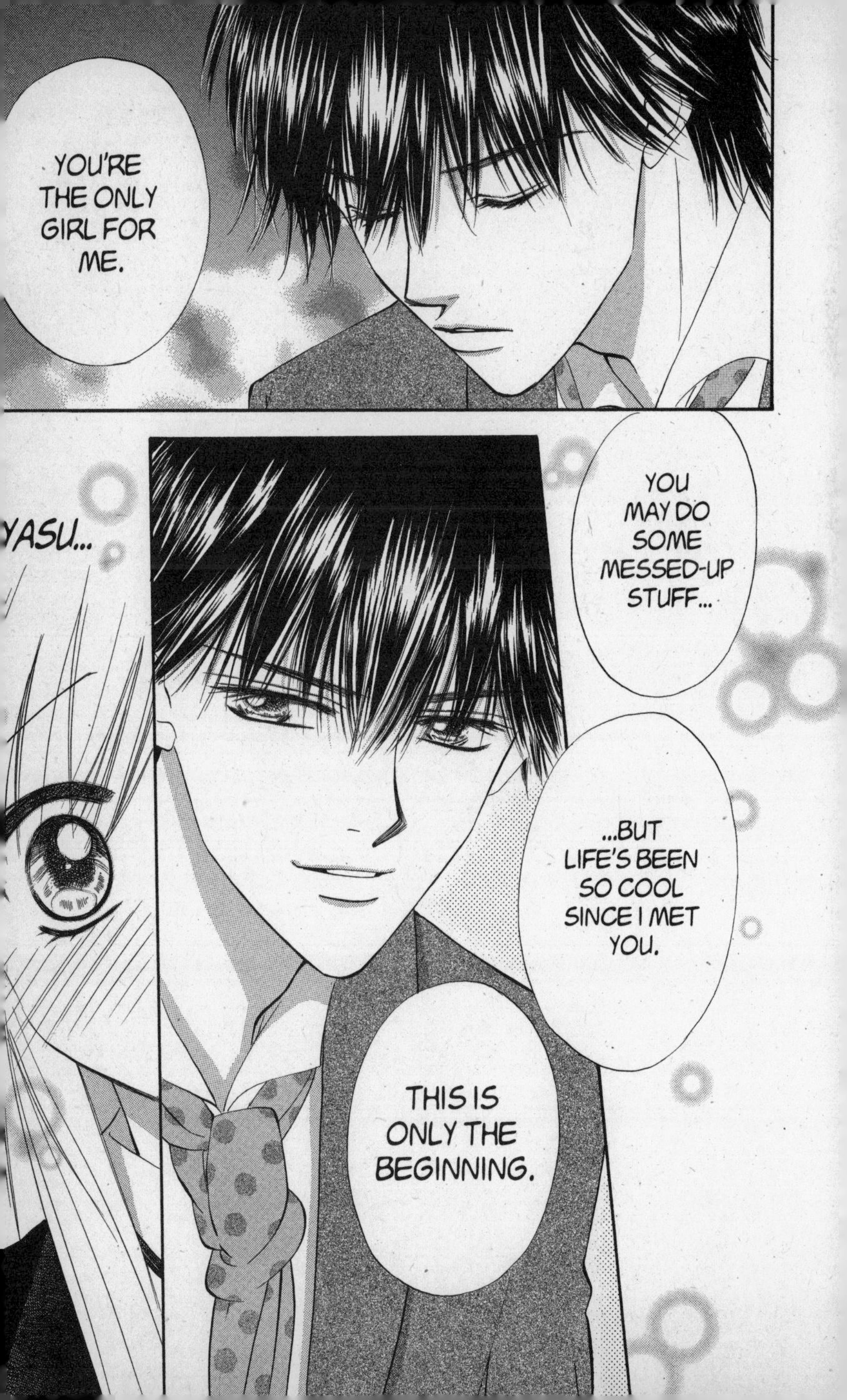
YOU'RE THE ONLY GIRL FOR ME.
YOU MAY DO SOME MESSED-UP STUFF...
...BUT LIFE'S BEEN SO COOL SINCE I MET YOU.
THIS IS ONLY THE BEGINNING.
YASU...

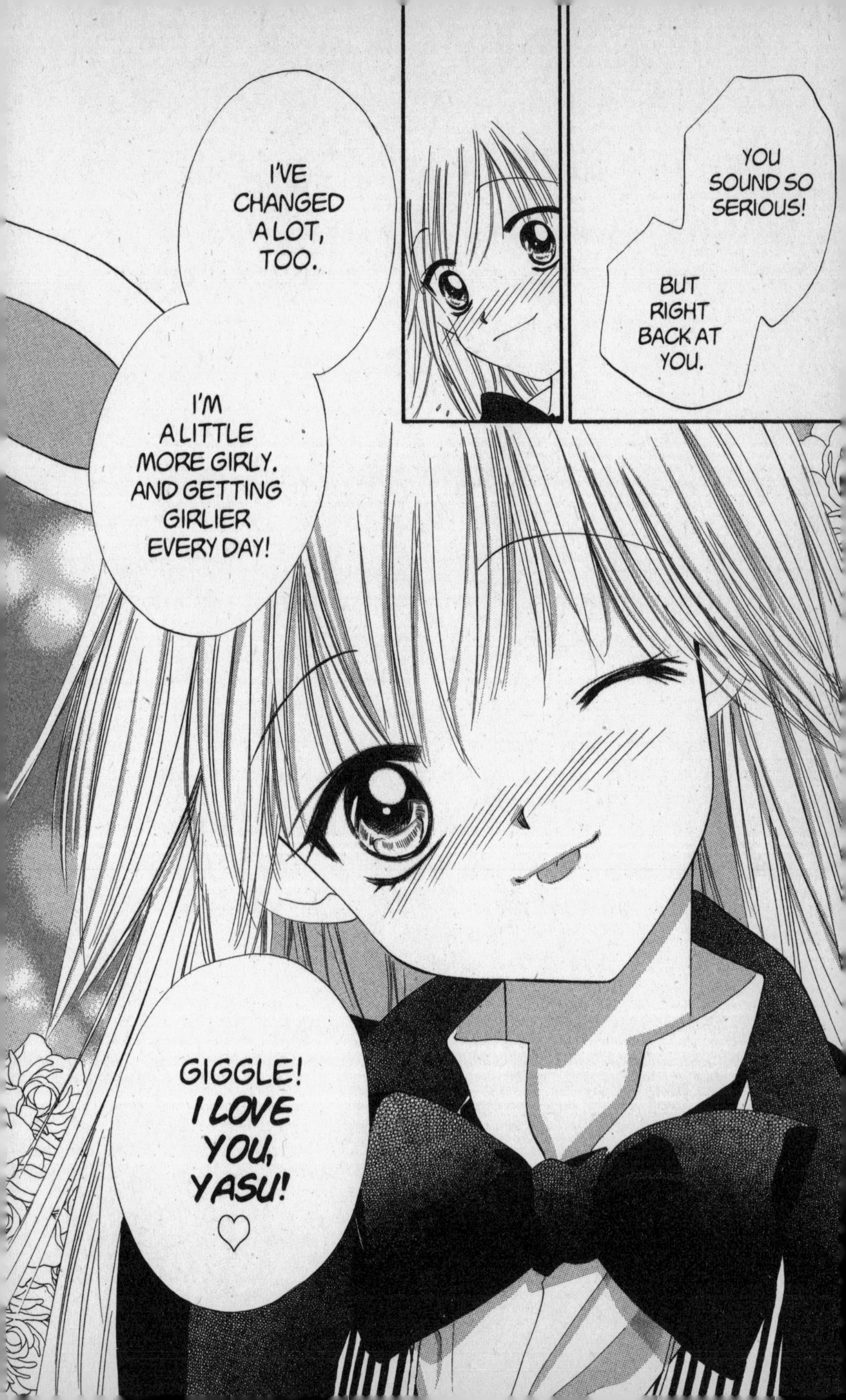
YOU SOUND SO SERIOUS!
BUT RIGHT BACK AT YOU.
I'VE CHANGED A LOT, TOO.
I'M A LITTLE MORE GIRLY. AND GETTING GIRLIER EVERY DAY!
GIGGLE! **I LOVE YOU, YASU!** ♡

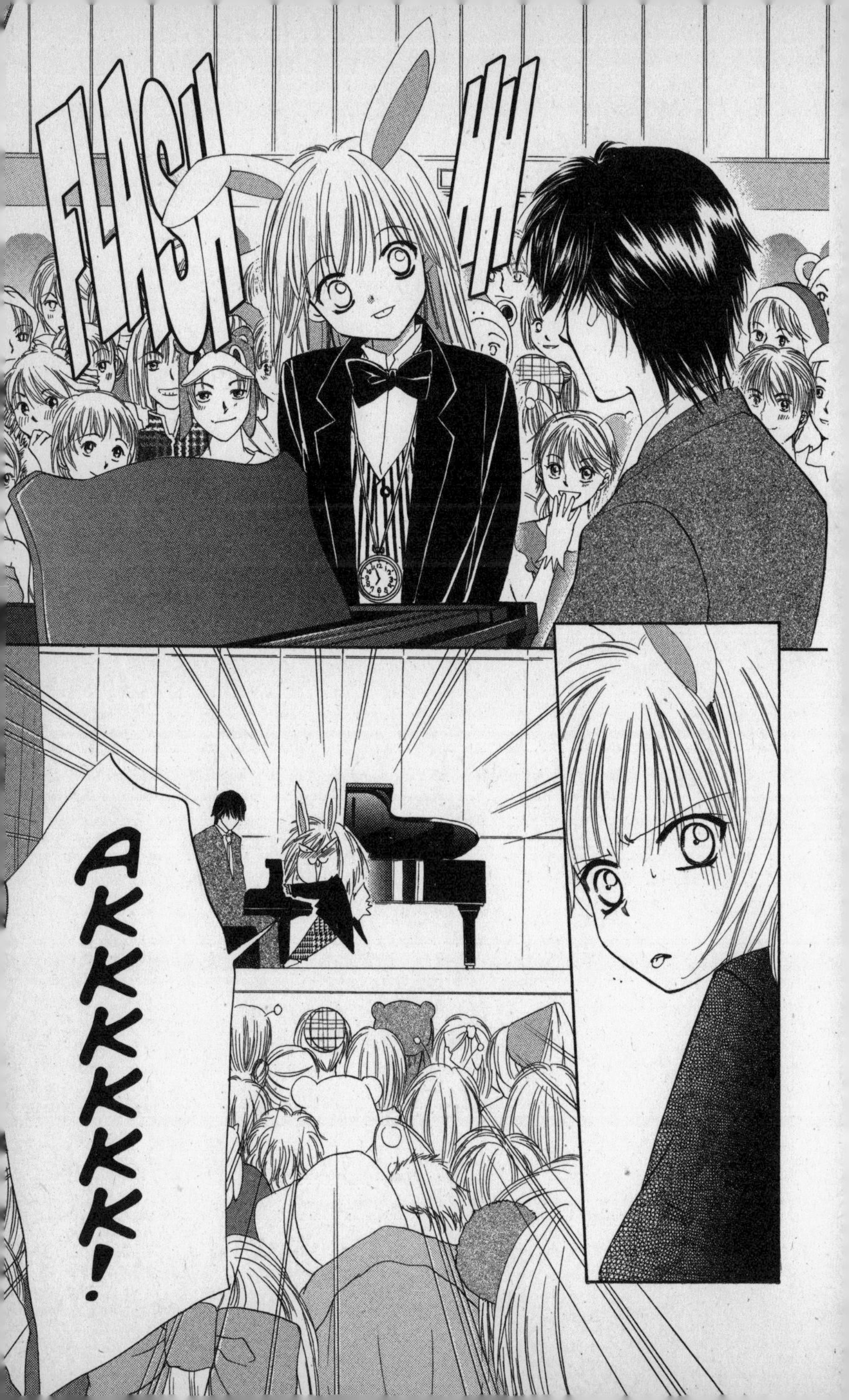
FLASHHH
AKKKKKK!

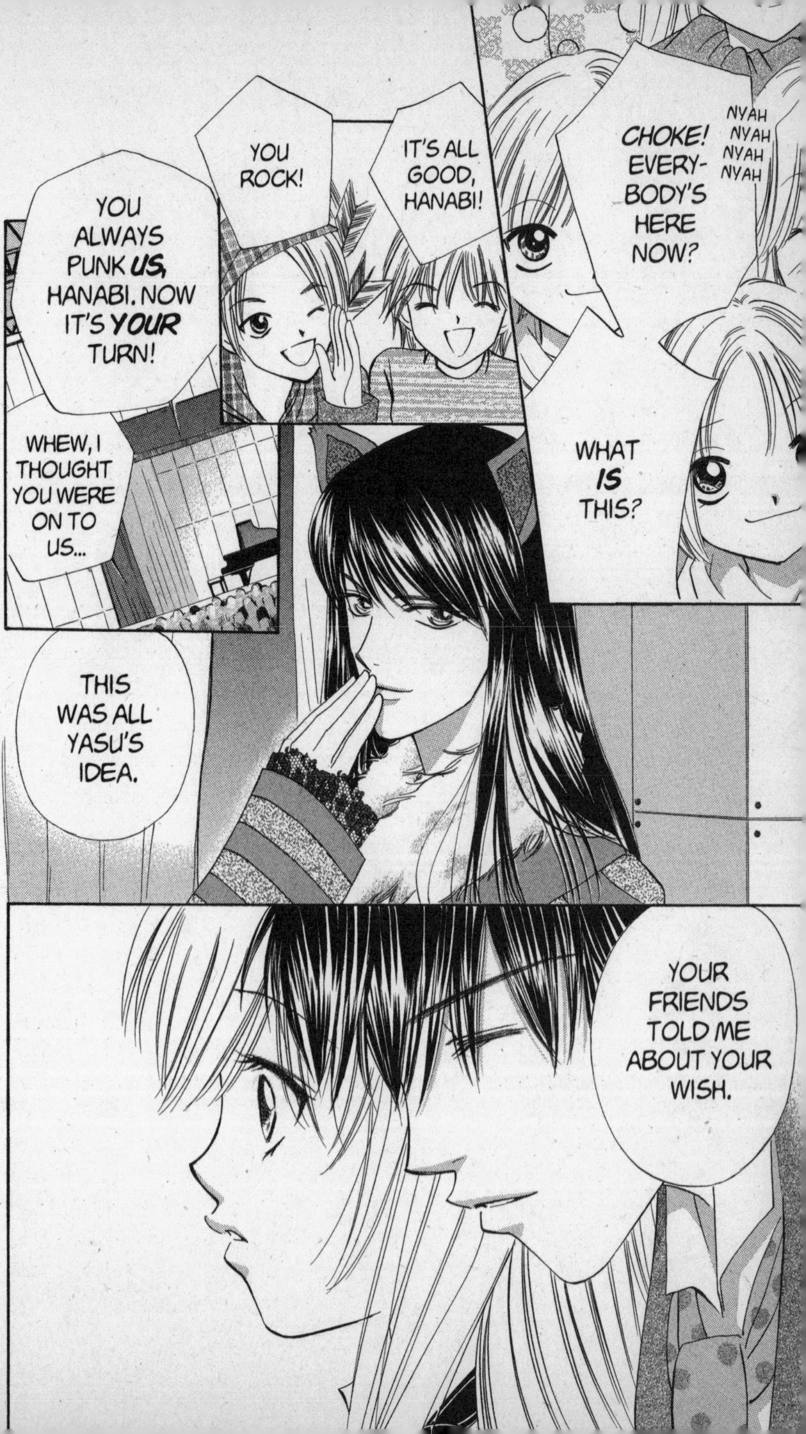
NYAH NYAH NYAH NYAH
CHOKE! EVERYBODY'S HERE NOW?
WHAT IS THIS?
IT'S ALL GOOD, HANABI!
YOU ROCK!
YOU ALWAYS PUNK US, HANABI. NOW IT'S YOUR TURN!
WHEW, I THOUGHT YOU WERE ON TO US...
THIS WAS ALL YASU'S IDEA.
YOUR FRIENDS TOLD ME ABOUT YOUR WISH.

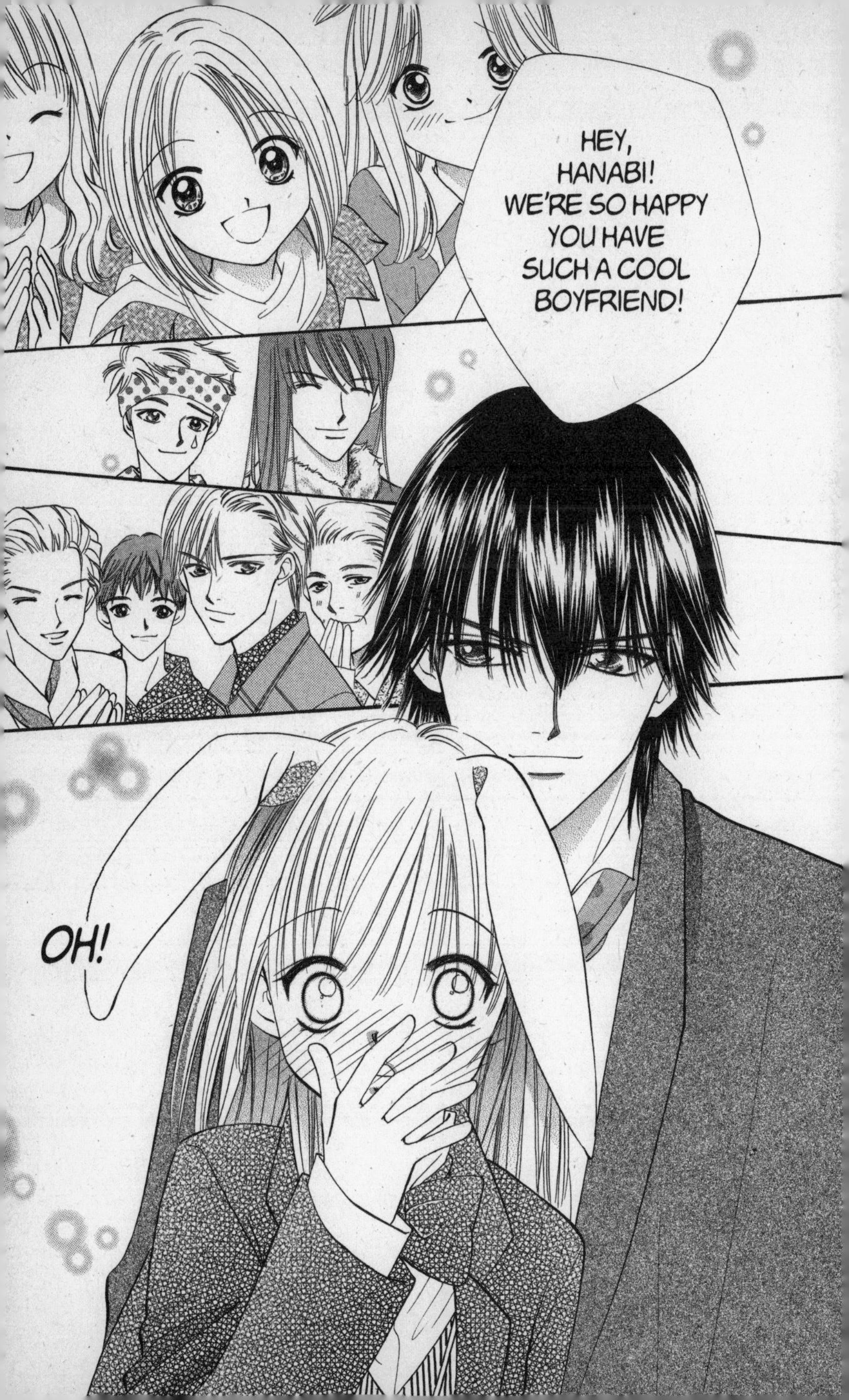
HEY, HANABI! WE'RE SO HAPPY YOU HAVE SUCH A COOL BOYFRIEND!
OH!

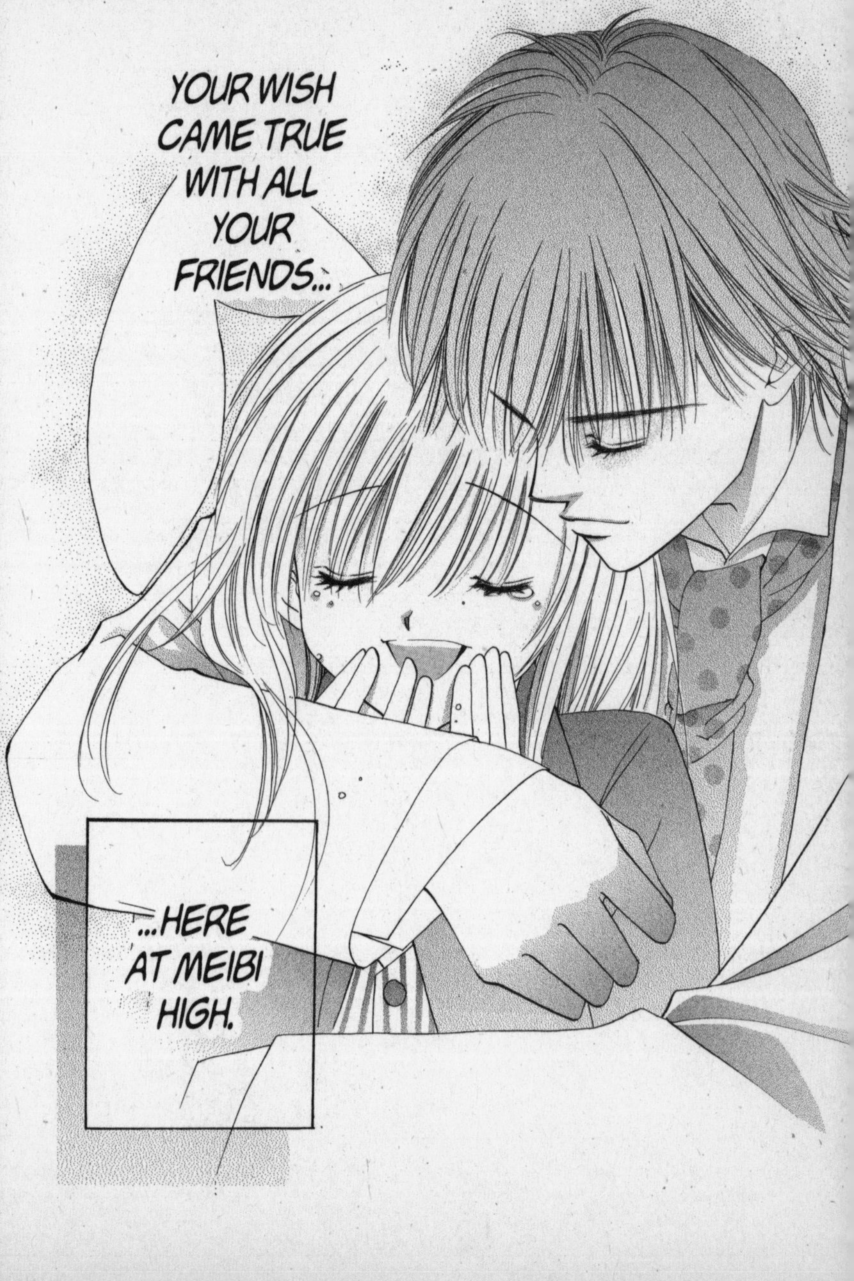
YOUR WISH CAME TRUE WITH ALL YOUR FRIENDS...
...HERE AT MEIBI HIGH.

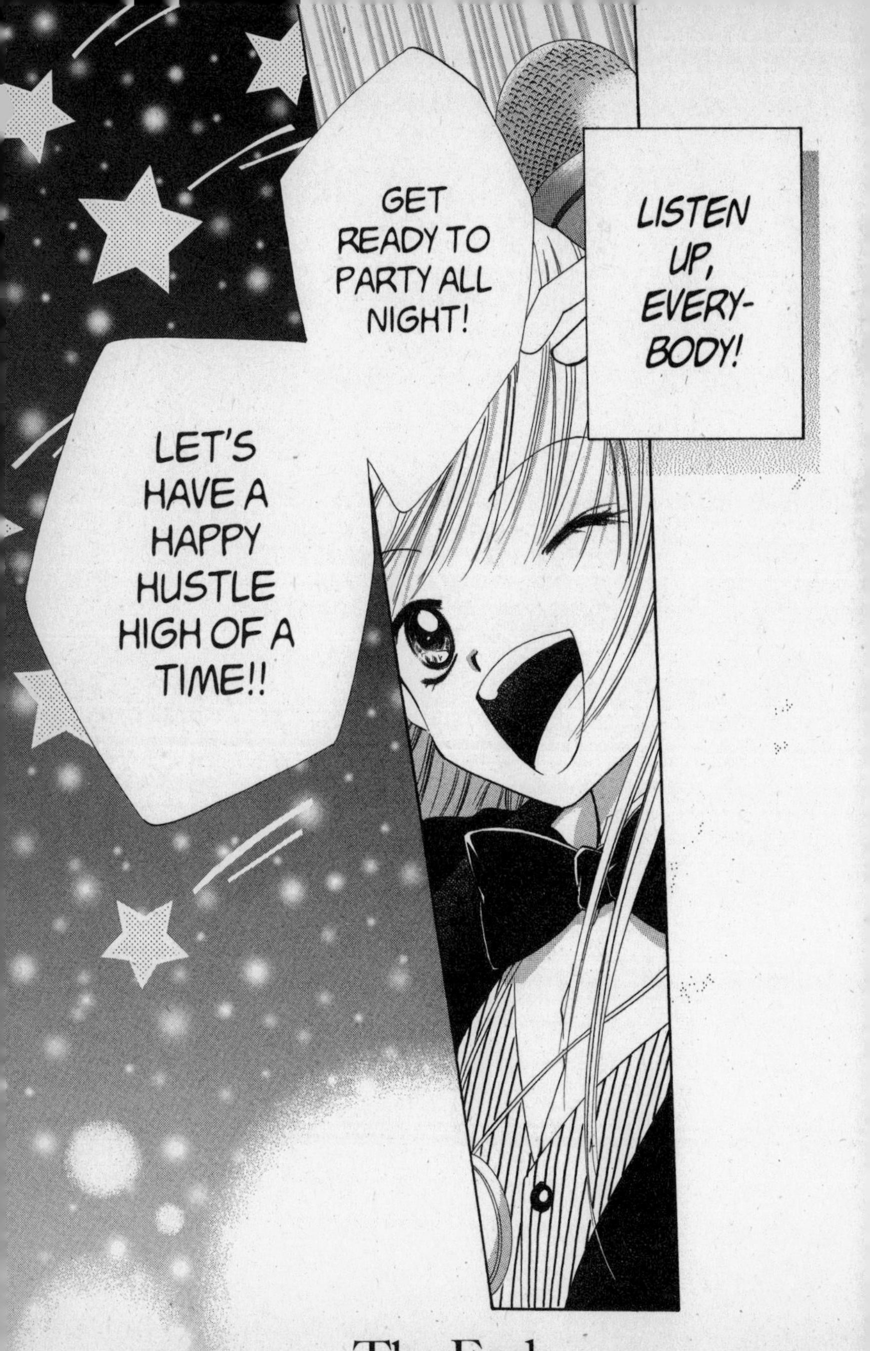
LISTEN UP, EVERY-BODY!
GET READY TO PARTY ALL NIGHT!
LET'S HAVE A HAPPY HUSTLE HIGH OF A TIME!!

The End

HAPPY HUSTLE HIGH
Vol. 5

Story and Art by Rie Takada

Translation/June Honma
Touch-up Art & Lettering/Rina Mapa
Design/Izumi Evers
Editor/Janet Gilbert

Supervising Editor/Kit Fox
Managing Editor/Annette Roman
Director of Production/Noboru Watanabe
Vice President of Publishing/Alvin Lu
Sr. Director of Acquisitions/Rika Inouye
Vice President of Sales & Marketing/Liza Coppola
Publisher/Hyoe Narita

Printed in the U.S.A.

Published by VIZ Media, LLC
P.O. Box 77010
San Francisco, CA 94107

10 9 8 7 6 5 4 3 2 1
First printing, March 2006

www.viz.com
store.viz.com

RATED T+ FOR OLDER TEEN

PARENTAL ADVISORY
HAPPY HUSTLE HIGH is rated T+ for Older Teen and is recommended for ages 16 and up. This volume contains strong language and sexual themes.

EDITOR'S RECOMMENDATIONS

If you enjoyed this volume of

HAPPY HUSTLE HIGH™

then here's some more manga you might be
interested in.

© 2004 Novala TAKEMOTO, Yukio
KANESADA/Shogakukan Inc.

Kamikaze Girls by Novala Takemoto: Meet Momoko,
a gussied-up "Lolita" who never saw a ruffle she
didn't love. Then one day she meets Ichigo, a rowdy,
trash-talking biker chick. Soon Momoko's placid, lace-
encrusted life goes completely blooey! The only thing
these two terrors have in common is living in
Podunk, Japan (aka Ibaraki). Can a princess and a
punk actually become (choke!) friends? Based on the
cult-classic novel that inspired the cult-classic film.

FULL MOON WO SAGASHITE ©
2001 by Arina
Tanemura/SHUEISHA Inc.

Full Moon by Arina Tanemura: Imagine you only had
a year to live. Would you give up on your dreams?
Mitsuki Koyama still desperately wants to sing,
despite a malignant tumor in her throat and a mean,
music-hating grandma. Her future looks grim indeed
until she suddenly gets help from two goofy Grim
Reapers...and a little bit o' magic. One of Japan's
most popular shojo manga.

© 1984 Rumiko
TAKAHASHI/Shogakukan Inc.

Maison Ikkoku by Rumiko Takahashi: True love ain't
easy, but is it worth all the pain, embarrassment and
heavy heavy heart thumping? College student Yusaku
and young widow Kyoko aim to find out in this
classic romantic comedy from manga superstar
Rumiko Takahashi. You'll want to read this touching
tale over and over again.

No One Said Love Was Easy

What do you do when the boy flirting with you is the object of your friend's desire? Between friendship and love, what will Karin choose?

Experience the roller coaster ride of a girl's first love and first kiss. But this is high school, and living happily ever after isn't on the curriculum!

KARE First Love

Only $9.95!

Start your graphic novel collection today!

www.viz.com
store.viz.com

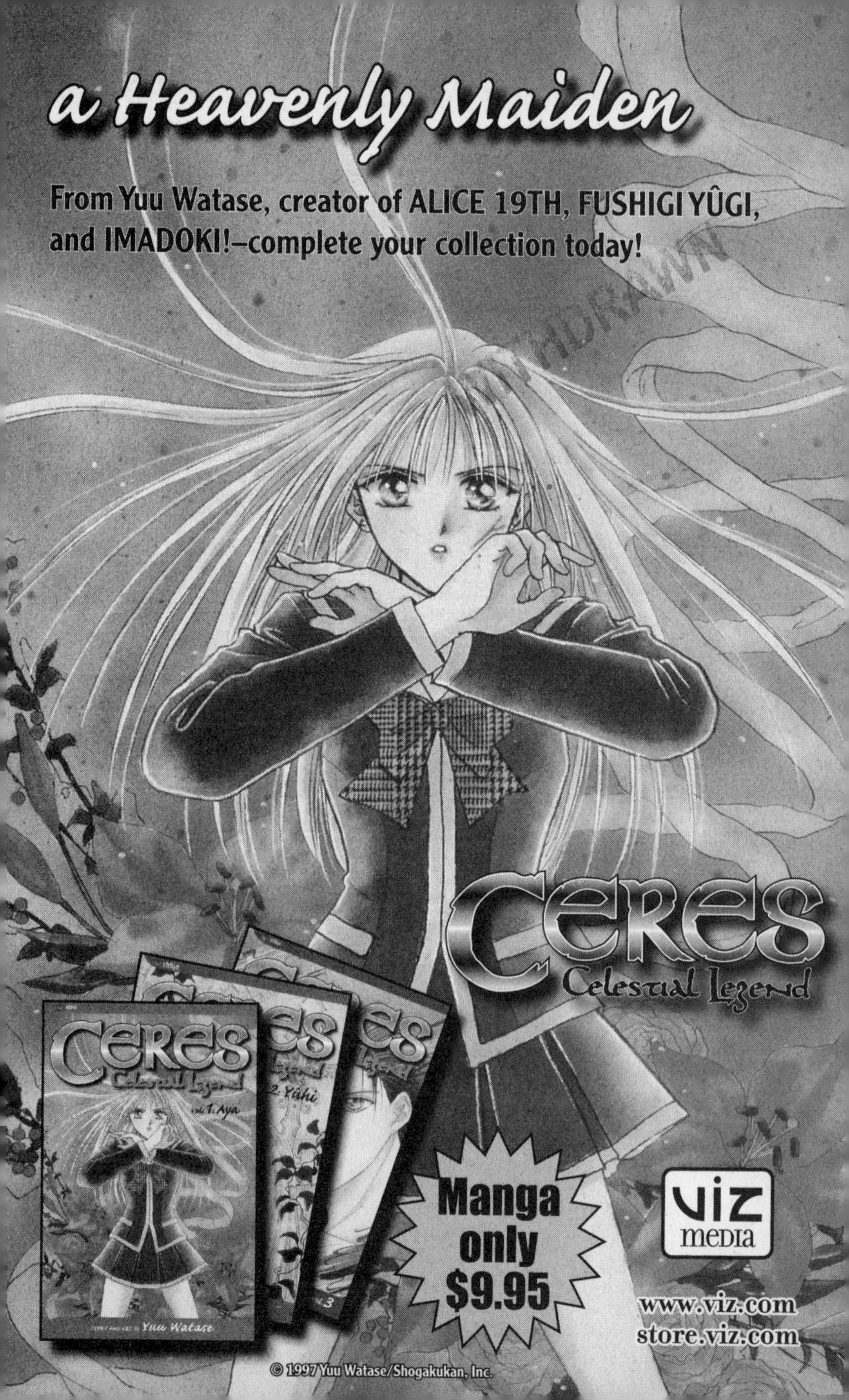
a Heavenly Maiden
From Yuu Watase, creator of ALICE 19TH, FUSHIGI YÛGI, and IMADOKI!–complete your collection today!
CERES
Celestial Legend
Ceres
Celestial Legend
vol. 1: Aya
2: Yûhi
Yuu Watase
Manga only $9.95
VIZ media
www.viz.com
store.viz.com
© 1997 Yuu Watase/Shogakukan, Inc.

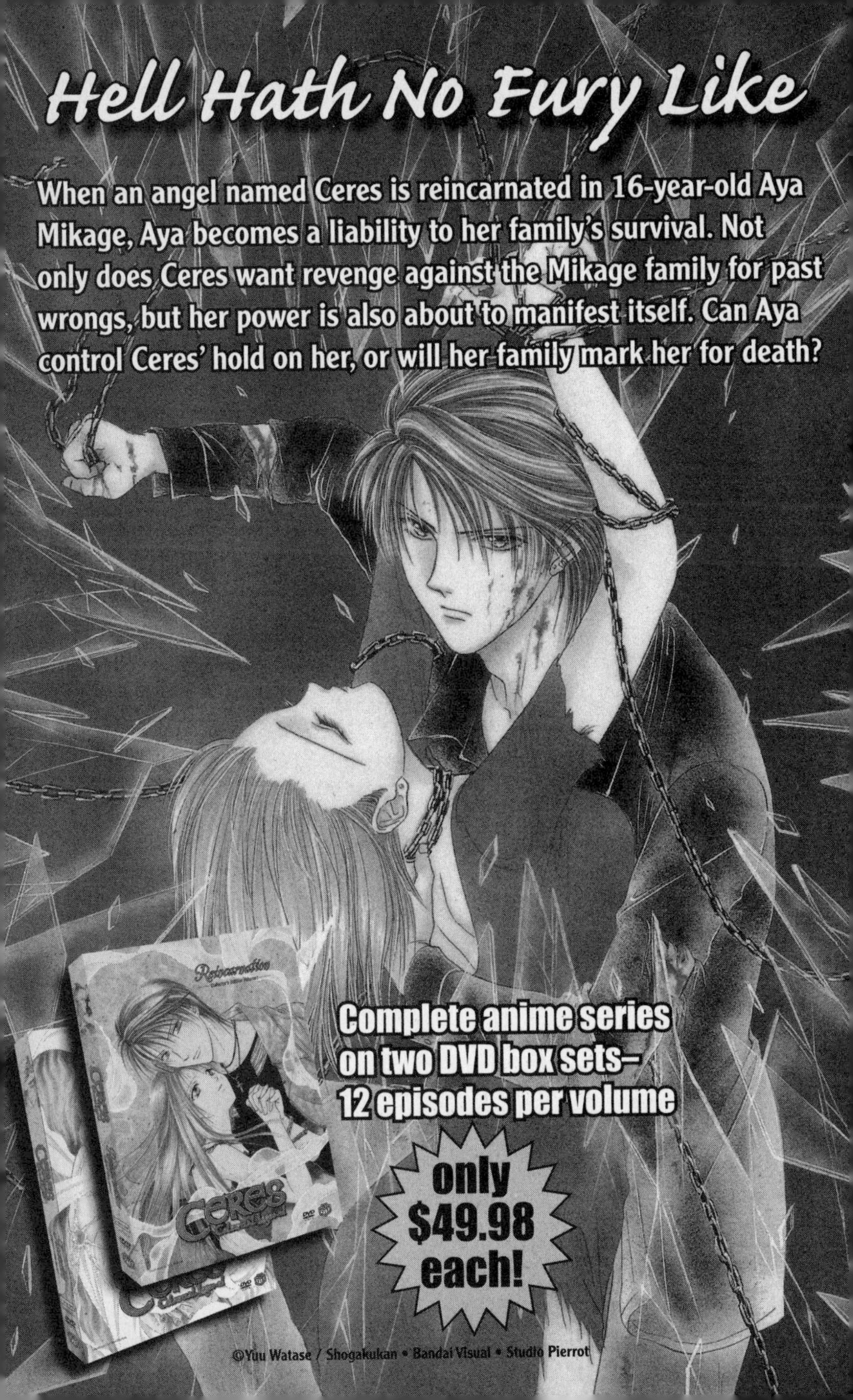
Hell Hath No Fury Like
When an angel named Ceres is reincarnated in 16-year-old Aya Mikage, Aya becomes a liability to her family's survival. Not only does Ceres want revenge against the Mikage family for past wrongs, but her power is also about to manifest itself. Can Aya control Ceres' hold on her, or will her family mark her for death?
Complete anime series on two DVD box sets– 12 episodes per volume
only $49.98 each!
©Yuu Watase / Shogakukan • Bandai Visual • Studio Pierrot

LOVE SHOJO? LET US KNOW!

☐ Please do NOT send me information about VIZ Media products, news and events, special offers, or other information.

☐ Please do NOT send me information from VIZ' trusted business partners.

Name: ______________________________

Address: ______________________________

City: ____________ **State:** ________ **Zip:** ____________

E-mail: ______________________________

☐ **Male** ☐ **Female** **Date of Birth (mm/dd/yyyy):** ___/___/______ (**Under 13? Parental consent required**)

What race/ethnicity do you consider yourself? (check all that apply)

☐ White/Caucasian
☐ Black/African American
☐ Hispanic/Latino
☐ Asian/Pacific Islander
☐ Native American/Alaskan Native
☐ Other: ____________

What VIZ shojo title(s) did you purchase? (indicate title(s) purchased)

____

What other shojo titles from other publishers do you own? ______________________________

____

Reason for purchase: (check all that apply)

☐ Special offer
☐ Favorite title / author / artist / genre
☐ Gift
☐ Recommendation
☐ Collection
☐ Read excerpt in VIZ manga sampler
☐ Other ____________

Where did you make your purchase? (please check one)

☐ Comic store
☐ Bookstore
☐ Mass/Grocery Store
☐ Newsstand
☐ Video/Video Game Store
☐ Online (site:____________)
☐ Other ____________